Victimology

A Canadian Perspective

HANNAH SCOTT

OXFORD

UNIVERSITY PRESS

OXFORD

UNIVERSITY PRESS

8 Sampson Mews, Suite 204, Don Mills, Ontario M3C 0H5
www.oupcanada.com

Oxford University Press is a department of the University of Oxford.
It furthers the University's objective of excellence in research, scholarship,
and education by publishing worldwide in

Oxford   New York

Auckland Cape Town Dar es Salaam Hong Kong Karachi
Kuala Lumpur Madrid Melbourne Mexico City Nairobi
New Delhi Shanghai Taipei Toronto

With offices in

Argentina Austria Brazil Chile Czech Republic France Greece
Guatemala Hungary Italy Japan Poland Portugal Singapore
South Korea Switzerland Thailand Turkey Ukraine Vietnam

Oxford is a trade mark of Oxford University Press
in the UK and in certain other countries

Published in Canada
by Oxford University Press

Library and Archives Canada Cataloguing in Publication

Scott, Hannah, 1966–
Victimology : Canadians in context / Hannah Scott.

Includes bibliographical references and index.

ISBN 978-0-19-542762-2

1. Victims of crime—Canada—Textbooks. I. Title.

HV6250.3.C3S36 2010   362.880971   C2010-903820-7

Cover image: Imageworks/Getty Images

Oxford University Press is committed to our environment. This book is printed on Forest Stewardship Council certified paper,
harvested from a responsibly managed forest.

Mixed Sources
Product group from well-managed
forests and other controlled sources
www.fsc.org Cert no. SW-COC-000952
© 1996 Forest Stewardship Council

FSC

Printed and bound in Canada

1 2 3 4 — 14 13 12 11

This text is dedicated to all those who have been victimized. It is your stories, strength, and courage which inspire this text.

Contents

Acknowledgements

There are many people who made this text possible. I would like to thank the following for their aid in the preparation of this text:

Oxford University Press provided an excellent team. I would like to thank Lisa Meschino and Nancy Reilly, acquisition editors, who helped to get the project up and running; Andrea Kennedy and Dina Theleritis, development editors, for moving the project forward; and Janna Green, copyeditor extraordinaire. I would also like to thank the anonymous reviewers of the early draft of this book. Your thoughtful comments made this text better. I am sure that there were others on this team working hard to make this project successful. For all your efforts, I am appreciative.

I would also like to thank Jennifer Foden, research assistant, who helped with some of the little things and gave me the time to write. Additionally, I would like to thank Juliet Szabo and Amit Rajput, who served as early research assistants gathering information which helped to lay the foundation for this project. I would also like to thank all the students who have ever taken my class and asked those important questions that inspired this book. The enthusiasm and interest in this subject guided many of its chapters.

I would also like to acknowledge my mentors along the way, who took a chance and guided me through the disciplines of sociology and criminology and eventually into the area of victimology: Dr Richard Brymer, Dr Ronald Hinch, Dr Susan McDaniel, and Dr Leslie W. Kennedy. I am forever grateful.

Last, but always first in my books, I want to thank my friends and family, and especially my husband, James, for being ever present and supportive.

Preface

Can you remember a time when someone took something from you without your permission? Have you ever loaned something to someone who never returned it? Have you ever witnessed someone hitting, punching, choking, or otherwise injuring another person in a way that you knew was illegal? Have you ever been hurt in such a way? Although these questions are limited, to some degree, to only those types of victimizations that may involve the criminal justice system, when considered carefully (and truthfully!), almost all of us can answer 'yes' to at least one of them. The idea of victimization most often conjures images of victims of violent acts associated with the criminal justice system. Yet many of us have a limited definition of what being a victim truly means. If we broaden our horizons to embrace a definition of victimization that includes situations such as being diagnosed with a disease or suffering an injury in a car accident, we would be hard pressed to find someone who has not been touched by some form of victimization. Quite simply, none of us are alone in our experience as a victim.

Victimization, however, it is not a subject that people like to talk about. Being victimized often raises powerful emotions, including anger, fear, and humiliation. One common emotional side effect of victimization is feeling alone or abandoned. Despite the fact that victimization is common, many victims believe that no one can understand what they are going through.

Although victimization, and our experiences of it, is seldom discussed outside of our immediate social circles, there is one place where it is often reported: in the media. For example, if you look at a newspaper, television, or the Internet on any given day, you will see a series of stories associated with crime. These reports tend to focus on the criminal, but they also include the story of the victim. Box I.1 lists the victim-related stories that appeared in the front sections of *The Globe and Mail* and the *National Post* on a single day: 7 March 2009. Note that not all of the stories I have chosen are crime- related. As an exercise in preparation for this course, choose a news medium and identify stories where someone has been victimized. Analyze the stories to assess what the victim experienced. In other words, try to gain the victim perspective from what you have collected.

While most people acknowledge that studying offenders is extremely important for our understanding of crime, it is only very recently that we have sought to understand the other half of the equation: the victim. In fact, it is the victim who is often the hero of the story. In the area of crime and criminal justice, it is the victim who is the most valuable source of evidence and who, therefore, often holds the key to any investigation. To treat a victim poorly, or without dignity and respect, reduces the likelihood that he or she will co-operate in bringing the offender to justice.

Box I.1 One-Day Snapshot: Crime Stories in *The Globe and Mail* and the *National Post*, 7 March 2009

The Globe and Mail

- Mark MacKinnon (2009) recounts the story of Tashi, a young Tibetan monk who walked into the town centre of Aba, Sichuan province, and lit himself on fire. This personal protest came just hours after 1,000 monks were prevented from entering a prayer hall during another protest and many of the monks were shot at by police. One report states that the monk was shot at several times by Chinese police before being taken alive to an undisclosed location. The Chinese government states that the monks were celebrating and that no such violent incident occurred.
- Paul Waldie (2009) writes on job losses that have resulted from the recession, as well as the non-profit organizations assisting unemployed individuals by offering free services such as seminars and job searches. He notes that, as the recession deepens, white-collar workers are among the hardest hit.
- Christie Blatchford (2009a) writes of her interview with the families of Warrant Officer Dennis Brown, Corporal Dany Fortin, and Corporal Chad O'Quinn, three Canadian soldiers who were killed in a roadside bomb in Afghanistan. During the blast, two others were injured. The article poses the question: 'Is it worth it?'
- Patrick White (2009) discusses the health care system's shortcomings in treating people with schizophrenia. He illustrates his arguments with the murder of Tim McLean, who was decapitated by Vince Li on a Greyhound bus in July 2008. Li, an individual who had clearly fallen through the cracks in the mental health system and did not get the treatment he needed, killed McLean when he thought he heard the voice of God telling him to do so.
- Caroline Alphonso (2009) details the story of Desiderio Fortunato, a resident of Coquitlam, BC. When Fortunato asked a US border guard for a bit of courtesy and respect, he was pepper-sprayed, pinned down by border guards, and questioned for three hours.
- Dawn Walton (2009) writes on two separate cases of missing teenagers in Alberta. In one, a 16-year-old girl from Red Deer, AB, had vanished earlier in the week. The missing teen finally called home from a local mall 46 hours later. In the second, a 56-year-old man reversed his plea in a case involving a 16-year-old girl who was allegedly kidnapped and raped by an attacker posing as a police officer.
- An Alberta toddler who suffered life-threatening injuries while in foster care will be taken off life-support. The boy and his younger sister had been temporarily removed from their mother's home in June 2008. RCMP is investigating the case (Boy hurt in foster care . . ., 2009).
- Josh Wingrove (2009) reports that Marlon Joseph Cooper, who turned himself in, faces four charges in relation to the February 2009 shooting of a man on a public bus in Toronto. The victim was sent to the hospital with non-life-threatening injuries following the incident.
- Tenille Bonoguore (2009) writes of a group of 30 mattress makers who have not been paid in six weeks and are seeking assurance. Their employer blames the credit-crunch-wary banking system, as the company switched banks.

National Post

- Kevin Libin (2009) recounts that in January 2008, Kaydance Pauchay, age 3, and her sister Santana, age 15 months, froze to death outside their home in the northern Saskatchewan community of Yellow Quill Reserve. Their father, Christopher Pauchay—who was extremely intoxicated—decided to walk the girls to his sister's home. On the way, he lost consciousness; he was later found and taken to a facility to be treated for exposure. When he asked where his children were, the residents of Yellow Quill launched a search. The girls' bodies were found, frozen and wearing only minimal clothing. Christopher Pauchay was sentenced to three years in prison, after pleading guilty to one count of criminal negligence. The judge in the case, Justice Morgan, denied the recommendation of a restorative justice alternative sentence, stating that a more 'old fashioned' sentence was required as Pauchay exhibited a 'wanton' disregard for human life.

- Police in India arrested Vancouver truck driver Manjit Singh Badyal on suspicion of hiring contract killers to murder his wife. On 5 March 2009, Kuldeep Kaur Badyal died instantly after being shot at point-blank range outside her Sikh temple in India, where she had been living with her husband since early January of that year. Her brother told the press that her two children will have to grow up not knowing their mother and that her family has been left in 'distress' (Husband arrested after . . ., 2009).

- A man covered in blood and bound with duct tape was found running down a highway in Richmond, BC. After investigating, police determined that he had been a victim of abduction and charged Mark Anthony Bie with unlawful confinement (Man charged after bloodied . . ., 2009).

- Megan O'Toole (2009) writes that after more than four decades police have identified the remains of a second young man murdered near Coboconk, ON, in 1967. Police had revived the cold case by using facial reconstruction techniques to illicit the public in helping to identify him even though decades had past since the murder. Two days after the initial report and facial reconstruction were released to the media, the victim was identified as Eric Jones of Noelville, ON. The story also remarks that another homicide victim, Richard Hovey, was found outside the town of Schomberg, murdered under similar circumstances around the same time period. Both men were found naked and their hands tied behind them. Police state that these two cold case murders may be related.

- Michael McKiernan (2009) reports that a tractor trailer containing 12,000 kilograms of pre-packaged skinless boneless chicken breasts were stolen earlier in the week near Paris, ON. The truck was found by police, with 7,000 kilograms (an estimated value of $80,000) missing.

- British Business Minister Peter Mandelson had custard thrown in his face by a protester. The protester was demonstrating her opposition of a new runway built at London's Heathrow Airport (Protester throws custard . . ., 2009).

- A baby who died suddenly at three months of age was thought to have been euthanized by a doctor from a Swedish children's hospital, who denied the allegations. The infant was born premature with irreversible brain damage (Doctor accused of . . ., 2009).

- Oscar Kamau King'ara and John Paul Oulu, two Kenyan campaigners and Mungiki gang members who were demonstrating against illegal police killings, were suspected of being murdered by police. These killings sparked further protests that culminated in police firing tear gas at student demonstrators denouncing the killing of 1,721 young people and the disappearance of 6,542 others after they were suspected of being Mungiki gang members or sympathizers (Murder of Kenyan activists . . ., 2009).

- Four hundred cases of potential food poisoning were linked to three-star British restaurant, The Fat Duck, owned by celebrity chef Heston Blumenthal. British health officials are investigating leads in the case (400 potential cases of . . ., 2009).

- In a full-page article, Adam Entous (2009) examines the major issues confronting the citizens of Israel and Palestine, including the depletion of resources and rocket attacks. Although Entous does not mention specific victims, the reasons for peace are implicit: the mounting deaths of victims in this region due to continuous fighting.

- Robert Fulford (2009) discusses how Muslim countries are affected by the recession perpetuating poverty, noting that the poor suffer the most in hard times.

- Columnist David Horovitz (2009) discusses the terrorist attack which attempted to murder the entire Sri Lankan cricket team that was touring in Pakistan earlier in the year. Horovitz suggests that the attack is not evidence of clashing of two religions or civilizations but of two opposing cultures or eras—mentalities that belonged to the Middle Ages and those of the twenty-first century.

Both

- Brian Hutchinson *(National Post*, 2009) discusses several recent victimization incidents in British Columbia where RCMP officers were identified as the perpetrators. Hutchinson writes that these cases have all been overshadowed by the death of Polish traveller Robert Dziekanski, who died in October 2007 after being repeatedly Tasered by RCMP officers, who later justified their actions by stating that Dziekanski was resisting arrest. After Dziekanski's death, it was uncovered that RCMP officers did overreact to this situation and had planned to Taser the upset traveller if he resisted. They also attempted to cover up other evidence in the incident. The article questions the amount of public confidence in the police, with specific focus on the death of Dziekanski. Gary Mason, reporting for *The Globe and Mail* (2009) notes that citizens were outraged that no charges would be pressed in the death of Dziekanski. The reasoning put forth by the Crown was that the reports and verbal statements by the officers were consistent and therefore reliable. Mason also reports that it is now known that the witness statements were not accurate depictions of what really happened.
- Shannon Kari for the *National Post* (2009) and a second article by Christie Blatchford in *The Globe and Mail* (2009b) summarized the day's previous events in the case of homicide victim Stefanie Rengel. Rengel was a 14-year-old girl who was stabbed to death on New Year's Eve, 2008, and left to die in a snowbank outside her home. She had never met M.T., the person who coerced her boyfriend, D.B., to kill her. M.T. and Rengel had only talked on the phone once before her death. M.T. stated that she wanted Rengel dead because she had been allegedly spreading rumours about her. Both D.B. and M.T. were minors at the time of the incident and therefore their identities were withheld from the public. As of this writing, both were sentenced as adults and their names revealed.
- *The Globe and Mail*'s Timothy Appleby and Peter Cheney (2009) report the details of the first appearance of the men who killed Glen Davis, a wealthy philanthropist. Cassandra Jowett (2009) of the *National Post* reports that Davis was shot several times in the torso in a parking garage near his work on 17 May 2007. Police state that his killer had waited for him. Davis had also been brutally assaulted with a baseball bat two years earlier. Appleby and Cheney reveal that police had concluded that the dispute erupted as a result of undocumented loans from Davis to a construction company with underworld ties. Marshall Ross, Davis's nephew and one of three men charged with the murder, was said to have 'expedited' the loans.
- Mike Pflanz and Matthew Moore *(National Post*, 2009) and Angus Shaw *(The Globe and Mail*, 2009) report that Zimbabwe Prime Minister Morgan Tsvangirai was injured and his wife killed in a car crash. The incident is not perceived to be an accident by the Movement for Democratic Change. The story relays distrust of Robert Mugabe, the country's president, as many who opposed him were allegedly 'bumped off' in this way.

In most cases the feeling of singularity, the sense of 'aloneness' that often accompanies victimization, has had ramifications that extend far beyond the individual and can often lead to self-imposed isolation or a retreat from society. However, in the best scenarios, the victim survives the hardship and goes on to raise a family, socialize, work, and generally live his or her life. In some rare cases, a victim will bring awareness to his or her story, or other, similar stories. There have also been extraordinary examples of a victim seeking to change something about his or her world, sometimes going so far as to pursue a change in legislation in order to spare others from going through the same ordeal.

Analysis of the victim is even more practical to the question of criminality. Without a victim or a witness to victimization willing to involve the authorities, the crime itself cannot be reported and the system fails to be initiated. This text is, to some degree, an attempt to bring a heightened sense of awareness to the victim. In fact, the victim is often the only witness to his or her own victimization. He or she is, after all, in need of the greatest protection and support; for without victim/witness co-operation the criminal justice system often grinds to a halt, even if it has been initiated by a courageous person.

In order to fully explore the victim and victimization in a coherent manner, this book covers four main themes. The first two chapters provide background to the subject and explain the terminology as well as some of the issues involved in the study of victims. Chapters 3 and 4 address the second theme: the categorization of victims within the victim–victimizer interaction. In these chapters, we will review historical ideas of victimization, and consider how they have affected current explanations. Chapters 5 to 10 turn to the third theme, an exploration of specific groups of victims and the challenges posed by their unique circumstances. Finally, chapters 11 to 13 discuss the aftermath of victimization. In particular, these three chapters examine the effects of victimization, the criminal justice responses available to victims, and new innovations that address how we administer justice for victims.

Although determining who the victim is in many crime stories is often easy, the real work in victimology comes when we pull back the layers of circumstance and examine in greater detail the totality of the incident. In effect, encouraging and facilitating a deeper study and a 'pulling back of layers' is what this book is all about. As you begin to build a vocabulary and background on this field of study, you will be encouraged, through the chapter material and the critical thinking questions, to broaden your understanding of what it means to be a victim, to explore how society classifies and treats its victims, and to question where victimology is heading as a discipline.

Who Is a Victim?

The study of victims is well established. For centuries, different groups of people with varying interests have examined those who have been victims of harm. It is only in the last 20 to 30 years that we have given this study a name: victimology. In fact, as of the writing of this text, the word 'victimology' is so new to our vernacular that is it not recognized in many word processing packages. If one thinks of all the possible kinds of harm that can be inflicted onto people, one can imagine the many kinds of victims that could be included in this discipline. For example, there are victims of cancer, HIV/AIDS, or other diseases. There are victims of genocide, such as Holocaust victims and the victims of **ethnic cleansing** in Rwanda. There are victims of accidents or of natural disasters, such as the victims of Hurricane Katrina which devastated Louisiana and, to a lesser extent, its neighbouring states. This area, more recently, has been re-victimized by a massive oil spill. There are also victims of crimes or of injustices, such as those who have been wrongly convicted of a crime. All of these examples show that people can become victims by being physically, financially, or emotionally harmed. Victims can also be courageous; they can tell their stories, seek justice, heal their bodies, resume their lives, and seek counselling. One can be a willing victim, a victim of circumstance, of practical jokes, and/or of mean pranks. In some cases, victims can be seen as contributing to their own victimization; in others they can be perceived as innocent of any wrongdoing.

Clearly, being a victim is not an uncommon or limited experience. All of us have been a victim of some form of harm at some point in our lives. While victimology considers various types of victims, it does not include the study of animals—although animals can also be victims, they cannot communicate their experiences as effectively. Therefore, the focus of this book will be on human victims, particularly those of crime, because it is in the area of criminology that we find the most information and discussion about the victim's role.

Definitions of Victim

Given the multitude of ideas about what victimization is and who can be victimized, it is difficult to establish an exact definition of the word 'victim'. Shedding some light on the history of the subject may help. The word comes from the Latin *victimia*, referring to a consecrated animal, or a living sacrifice, offered to a deity. The Online Etymology Dictionary (n.d.) asserts that it was used as early as 1497 to refer to a living creature that was killed and offered as a sacrifice to a deity or supernatural power; the first recorded use of the word referring to a person was *circa* 1690 and indicated someone who was tortured, hurt, or killed by another. By 1718, the term was also used to describe a person who was oppressed or taken advantage of by some power or situation. To **victimize** someone was a term coined *circa* 1830. Currently, 'victim' means any living animal that experiences injury, loss, or hardship due to any cause:

- A person who is killed, injured, or otherwise harmed by another: *a victim of a criminal act.*
- A live animal offered in religious sacrifice: *a lamb became a sacrificial victim.*
- A person who is made to suffer from an act, situation, condition, or circumstance: *a victim of oppression, tyranny, or war.*
- A person who suffers harm as a result of a voluntary undertaking: *a victim of drug addiction.*
- A person who is taken advantage of, as in being tricked or defrauded: *a victim of a practical joke.*

Legal Definitions of Victim

The Criminal Code of Canada (2007 [CCC]) identifies a victim as including any victim of alleged offence (CCC, s. 2, 'victim'). If we were to extrapolate from this basic definition, a victim under the CCC is any person who has been subjected to the acts of an alleged offender, who has presumably violated the law as dictated by the same code. A person is officially an offender only when he or she 'has been determined by a court to be guilty of an offence, whether on acceptance of a plea of guilty or on a finding of guilt' (CCC, s. 2, 'offender').

The Corrections and Conditional Release Act (1992, [CCRA]) more clearly defines the term:

> *victim*
> (a) means a person to whom harm was done or who suffered physical or emotional damage as a result of the commission of an offence, and

(b) where the person is dead, ill or otherwise incapacitated, the person's spouse, an individual who is cohabiting, or was cohabiting at the time of the person's death, with the person in a conjugal relationship, having so cohabited for a period of at least one year, any relative or dependant of the person, or anyone who has in law or fact custody or is responsible for the care or support of the person. (CCRA, s. 2 'victim', 2007)

Note that this definition includes not only the direct victim of an offence but also other victims when he or she has been rendered incapacitated in some way. These victims are most often members of the direct victim's immediate family as defined in the CCRA. However, it is possible that another representative of the incapacitated victim can also be a victim, as the former cannot defend him- or herself. In this case a victim can be defined as a legal representative of someone who has been incapacitated. This person may or may not be a member of the immediate family.

As we can see from these two definitions, the CCRA has a much more inclusive description of the term than the CCC. As with all law, the CCC is very restrictive but depends on its interpretation. These examples also show that definitions depend on the source explaining the term. The definition of 'victim' varies depending on how a person who has suffered harm interacts with the system he or she is engaging and on the politics of that system. For the purposes of this text, **victim** is defined by a more traditional sense of the word: one who is killed, injured, or otherwise harmed by another.

Definitions of Victimology

The discipline of victimology is wide in scope, depending on how one defines the concepts of victim and harm. Such definitions are crucial to victimology, as they determine what and who is studied. Traditionally, victimology has been overshadowed by the study of trends and patterns among crime victims; however, as mentioned above, the field incorporates other types. Victimology also examines the factors that affect victims, recognizing that they do not exist in a social vacuum but are situationally tied to their respective offenders. For the purposes of this text, **victimology** is defined as the study of victims and the social context in which they exist.

Although victimology emerged from **criminology**, the study of crime, the two are different fields. Traditionally offender focused, criminology offers many theories of crime that describe and explain trends in offender's actions and theories of crime prevention that focus on reducing his or her potential for committing criminal acts. In essence, victimology is the study of the other side of the criminal event. Victimologists also study crime but do so specifically from the victim's perspective, providing insight to the challenges facing victims and potential victims.

Summary

At a most basic level, victims are those people to whom harm has been done. In this case, anyone who has experienced harm can claim victim status, whether that harm is in the form of a disease, a natural disaster, or a prank. Perhaps the most identifiable type of victim is a crime victim. We hear or read about criminal events on a daily basis in news reports, in crime novels, or in television shows such as *Law & Order* or *Flashpoint*. Although this text focuses on this type of victim, it is important to keep in mind all forms of victimization as you read the following chapters.

When encountering reports or dramatizations of crime, most of us are conditioned to think about the offender before the victim. Stories of victimization are often stories of the offender. We usually know the name of the offender but not that of the victim. We hear what the offender has done but understand less about what the victim has experienced. Victimology takes the opposite approach. Therefore, in this text we will consider the victim first. We will examine victims of various types of crime in Canada, especially homicide, sexual assault, and fraud, and the victimization of particular groups, such as Aboriginal peoples, homeless people, and prisoners. In later chapters, we will discuss the aftermath of victimization and recovery methods, demonstrating the extraordinary and heroic actions that many victims take—often without the public support that is afforded the offender—in order to reclaim their lives, even if this isn't always easy and they don't always succeed. By addressing these topics, this text places the study of crime within the context of the victim and seeks to humanize the victim in ways that are often overlooked.

Glossary

criminology The study of crime and criminals in context.

ethnic cleansing The process whereby a group of people are identified as different based on ascribed characteristics and are systematically targeted and removed, usually by death, from a population.

victim One who is killed, injured, or otherwise harmed by another.

victimia A consecrated animal.

victimize The act of offending against someone and making him or her a victim.

victimologist A researcher who studies both victims and the context in which victims exist.

victimology The study of victims and the social context in which victims exist.

Critical Thinking Questions

1. How does the definition of 'victim' impact the way we view the issue of victimization?
2. Why do you think we are more concerned with the offender than with the victim when we look at criminal events?
3. Can you be both an offender and a victim in the same situation? Give three examples where this might occur.
4. How might you be victimized by witnessing the victimization of another person?
5. Are first responders (e.g., police, firefighters, ambulance workers, hospital staff) victimized when they respond to situations where people are hurt? Why or why not?

CHAPTER 1

Understanding Victimology

Learning Objectives

After reading this chapter, you will be able to

- situate our current understanding of victims in a historical context;
- understand that victimization is a relatively common occurrence;
- recognize basic trends of victimization in Canada; and
- identify some of the hidden costs of victimization.

Introduction

This chapter will discuss how we have come to adopt certain concepts about victims in our various historical and legal institutions. Although victims have been defined in legal terms, such terms have been shaped by historical events. The way we understand victims of crime informs our definitions of victimization, and this understanding shapes current trends in the subject. Most recently we have seen a renewed interest in the role of the victim, particularly in fields that focus on criminal justice systems.

A Historic View of the Role of the Victim

The modern criminal justice system is a relatively recent entity. The system of common law—so named because it is based on a system of laws applied to all people—originated during the reign of King Henry II, in England's Middle Ages. Prior to the emergence of this formalized system of dealing with offenders, there existed only a set of informal rules regarding conduct between people. Serious crimes were identified as *mala in se*, or offences that are in and of themselves wrong or said to go against nature. A victim was not only expected to state that he or she had been harmed if it was not obvious to onlookers but was also expected to be part of the process of exacting justice on the offender. Justice, or **retribution**, where one exacts punishment in retaliation for harm that has been done to someone, was the responsibility of the victim and his or her friends and family.

Anthropological studies offer excellent examples of this system. Box 1.1 outlines an event in the Dobe !Kung tribe as it was told to Canadian anthropologist Richard B. Lee (1979). The case of Hxome and Gau illustrates how a dispute led to a series of events resulting in death and how early informal justice systems may have worked. The dispute remained unresolved after Hxome was killed. One family had lost a family member, while the other

Box 1.1 The Case of Debe (Dobe !Kung)

From 1963 to 1969, Canadian anthropologist Richard B. Lee (1979) documented the activities of the Dobe !Kung, a hunting and gathering people of the !Kung San of the Kalahari Desert in Africa. According to Lee, the !Kung were a people without a state; all disputes had to be resolved 'from the hearts of the people themselves' (p. 87). While Lee was present, they lived in relative peace. However, discussions with the tribe members revealed that 22 homicides and 15 serious injuries had occurred between 1920 and 1955. Lee also found that feuds accounted for 15 of the homicides and that one killing was usually followed by another in retaliation. When there were a string of such homicides, the surviving !Kung would discuss the case by comparing their situation to others that were similar to it as relayed in oral tradition. Several !Kung informants recalled the killings of Hxome and Gau.

This incident began when Debe asked Bo for his sister-in-law Tisa's hand in marriage and Bo refused because he wanted to make Tisa his second wife. An argument ensued, in which Bo tried to kill Debe's younger sister by shooting an arrow at her, which barely missed, and then tried to kill Debe. Debe's father, Hxome, came to his son's defence, while another man, Samkau, came to Bo's aid by shooting an arrow at Debe. When Hxome retaliated by spearing Samkau in the chest, Gau, Samkau's father, joined the struggle. Fighting between the men continued, resulting in the death of Hxome.

Sometime after the murder, Debe's namesake complained to Debe that it was wrong for Samkau to have a father while Debe did not. The elder Debe agreed and decided to kill Bo because he had started the fight. After further consideration, he decided to kill Gau instead. Both Hxome and Gau were landowners and senior men; killing Gau would result in a dead landowner on both sides. Debe walked into Gau's camp and shot him three times with arrows. Gau's people did not protect him from this attack but did disarm Debe when he tried to stab Gau. The landowner died shortly thereafter. Fearing another retaliatory homicide, the two !Kung families brought in a healer to mediate the dispute.

family had not. Wanting retribution for the loss of his father, Debe reasoned that Gau's life was equal to Hxome's and that for balance to be restored Gau was the appropriate target, even though he had been defending his son. Gau's people did not protect Gau when Debe came for him because they understood that his death would restore some balance. To ensure that this balance was maintained, they later brought in a mediator.

If retribution was deemed necessary in early common law, the community could agree on the appropriate sentence. In other cases, the offender might be asked to pay restitution in an amount

that would make the victim whole again. In law, this concept of re-establishing balance is referred to as *lex talonis*, from the Latin *lex*, meaning law, and *talonus*, meaning retaliation; it is more popularly known by the Old Testament phrase 'an eye for an eye', which indicates that an offender's punishment should be the same as the violation. The underlying philosophy of such a system is victim centred. Victims participated in reaching judgment against their offenders, carried out the punishments, and received the rewards of retribution.

Punishments were guided by the principle of **deterrence**, which aims to exact justice and to dissuade the offender from doing harm again. This concept assumes that witnesses to the punishment would also be deterred from ever committing the harm. In this way, deterrence acts as a form of prevention. To achieve these objectives, the punishment had to be strong enough to help restore the balance of the community and those offended and had to remove any potential gain achieved by the offender in committing the harmful act. Finally, it also had to serve as a preventative measure for other members of the community.

As we moved from smaller communities to larger, more agrarian ones, we also moved from a feudal to a more formalized justice system. The introduction of common laws is a good example of this change. Serious crimes moved from the concept of *mala in se* to *mala prohibita*, or acts that were against laws. Using these laws to their advantage, feudal barons began laying claim to any compensation made to victims (Schafer, 1968). These members of the nobility successfully argued that serfs who had received retribution for being harmed ignored the damage that was ultimately done to the landowner, given that he had lost income, workers, and/or labour. They redefined harm against victims as harm against the state. As 'heads of state', the barons received compensation for the victim's losses and had the option of giving a portion of the payment to the victim. Consequently, victims were recast into the role of 'witness' to the harm that was done to them.

Society's increased urbanization caused many of its systems to become less self-sufficient and more interdependent. In 1887, German sociologist Ferdinand Tönnies described this relationship as moving from *Gemeinschaft* to *Gesellschaft*. The former refers to the state of social existence found in small, tightly knit communities where traditional family and kinship values predominate. For the community to survive, it must work together as a single unit to grow food, make clothes, and provide for all of the community's other needs. Failure to do so can affect the whole community. These societies function autonomously, and self-reliance is paramount for their survival. The latter term refers to a more rational and less personable relationship based on interdependence between the parts of society. These societies are characterized by more diverse groups in which individuals pursue their own self-interest over collective goals. This transition was also found in the justice system, which became a *criminal* justice system that moved further away from the victim and focused more on the actions of the offender. The aim of such a system was to protect people from crime.

The current system has not strayed far from this model. We have a criminal-centred system of common laws that, with the aid of the victim as witness, are aimed at deterring and punishing criminals. Crimes continue to be considered against the state or, in Canada, the Crown. This relationship is reflected in the identification of law cases, where the 'R' in the title (e.g., *R. v. Lavalee*) refers to the British monarch—'Regina' for a queen and 'Rex' for a king, depending on who wears the crown at the time of the case. This legal infrastructure reflects the interests in protecting the state, which a victim must call upon to act on his or her behalf. The state, in turn, recognizes that it cannot expect a solitary citizen to fight its huge social machinery and stands in for the victim, theoretically to bring its power to bear on the victim's plight.

The Victims' Movement in Canada

The study of victims initially emerged out of investigating the treatment of prisoners in both world wars. In particular, the horrors inflicted by the Nazis on prisoners in Germany and throughout Europe became the impetus for the recognition of victims. During and after these wars, we also saw efforts to compensate soldiers for the suffering they endured.

By the 1960s, state welfare systems in the United States began to compensate victims of crime for some offences. By the latter part of the decade, the first compensation programs in Canada indemnified police officers injured during the commission of their duties and had expanded to include other groups. Limited provincial monies were made available to selected victims of crime who were deemed eligible for compensation. Eventually, the federal government followed suit, granting funds to all provinces and territories to encourage the development of criminal injuries compensation programs and financing legal aid programs designed to help those who could not afford legal representation. By the early 1980s, criminal injuries compensation programs existed in all provinces and territories, established by provincial/territorial statute. The victims who were eligible for this service and the dollar amounts awarded, however, remained limited.

Also gaining prominence at this time were the efforts of the Women's and the Civil Rights movements in both Canada and the United States. In addition to increasing awareness of issues such as the effects of racism and discrimination was the idea of the 'glass ceiling', where women were not promoted beyond certain levels in various organizations or were not paid the same as men for doing the same work. The Women's Movement also pointed to the unfair treatment of women who were victims of intimate partner violence or sexual assault and who were blamed for their own victimization, not believed when recounting their victimization, or blatantly ignored by the criminal justice system. This focus sparked awareness of all victims who used the Canadian criminal justice system. Calls for more sensitivity toward victims, more victim participation in the judicial process, and access to more information regarding offenders emerged out of these initial advocacy movements. By 1972, the first Canadian transition houses for women in crisis were operating, in Alberta and British Columbia. The country's first sexual assault centres opened in Vancouver, BC, two years later.

From the mid-1980s to the 1990s these programs grew across Canada. It soon became clear that crime victims needed more than financial resources to help them recover. They required information, social and/or other types of services, and in some cases counselling and other forms of support. Eventually, a director of Victim Services was appointed in all jurisdictions and/or a Victim Services Division was established. Victim services based in courts, police services, and the community were newly developed or adjusted for the needs of crime victims.

Several federal legislative reforms of the 1990s changed how the Canadian criminal justice system interacted with victims, particularly people who had reported sexual assault. Sexual assault laws were amended in 1983 to bring them more in line with standard assault laws (C-127, 1983). In the latter half of the 1990s several bills were introduced, including one that recognized the special cases of child sex-trade workers (C-27, 1997). The new millennium saw Canada's first Victims' Bill of Rights, in Manitoba (2001). In 2003, the federal government also increased funding for victim compensation. Table 1.1 provides a list of these and other significant dates and events in the Victims' Movement. Several of these events will be covered throughout this text.

Table 1.1: Significant Dates in the Victims' Movement, 1963–2005

1963	New Zealand enacts first victim compensation program
1967	Saskatchewan enacts victim compensation program
	Ontario passes Law Enforcement Compensation Act
1968	Newfoundland enacts victim compensation program
1969	Alberta enacts victim compensation program
	Ontario amends compensation act to include victims of a violent crime
1971	Ontario passes Compensation for Victims of Crime Act (replacing Law Enforcement Compensation Act)
	Manitoba and New Brunswick enact victim compensation programs
1972	Quebec and British Columbia enact victim compensation programs
	First transition houses in British Columbia and Alberta
1973	Federal government begins contributing to provincial compensation plans
	First International Symposium on Victimology
1974	Law Reform Commission of Canada expresses support for restitution
	First victim-offender reconciliation takes place in Kitchener, ON
	First sexual assault centres open in Vancouver
1976	Criminal Code amended to limit questions about complainant's past sexual history
1977	Federal contributions to provinces for compensation plans enhanced
1979	Ontario Corrections Minister raises issue of victims at the inaugural meeting of the provincial ministers of justice
	Edmonton Police Victim Service Unit founded; Brampton Victim Witness Program established
1980	Throne Speech references violence against women as an issue
	MADD (Mothers Against Drunk Driving) established in the United States
	R. v. Pappajohn (Supreme Court decision regarding honest, but mistaken belief)
	In the United States, Wisconsin becomes first state to enact a Victims' Bill of Rights
	National Workshop of Services to Crime Victims (Quebec does not participate)

Table 1.1	*continued*
1981	Formation of Federal Provincial Task Force on Justice for Victims of Crime
	In the United States, President Reagan announces first National Victims' Rights Week
	In the United States, President's Task Force on Victims is formed
	Federal government forms Committee on Sexual Offences Against Children and Youth
	Citizens United for Safety and Justice formed in British Columbia
1982	Solicitor General Robert Kaplan encourages police forces to regularly lay charges in domestic violence cases
	National Victim Resource Centre established in Ottawa
	Victims of Violence formed in Ontario
	Bill C-127 (husband could be convicted of raping his wife; rape changed to three levels of sexual assault; questions about complainant's background)
	First General Social Survey (GSS) on Victimization in Canada
1983	Release of Federal Provincial Task Force on Justice for Victims of Crime report
	London Police Force first in Canada to issue mandatory charge policy regarding domestic violence cases
	Federal government issues guidelines re: spousal assault to prosecutors in Territories
1984	Badgley Committee Report makes 52 recommendations
	Federal Provincial Working Group on Victims of Crime established
1985	First National Conference on Victims of Crime in Toronto
	Federal government creates Victim Assistance Fund—2 year funding payments to provinces for victim services and programs
	National Parole Board publishes handbook for victims with assistance from David Nairn, father of a murder victim
	United Nations adopts the Declaration of Basic Principles of Justice for Victims of Crime and Abuse of Power
1986	Manitoba enacts Justice for Victims of Crime Act
1987	US Supreme Court rules Victim Impact Statements not admissible in death penalty cases
	Federal government negotiates interim enhanced cost sharing agreement on compensation
	New Brunswick passes Victim Services Act
1988	Prince Edward Island enacts victim compensation program
	Bill C-15 (screens, videotape statements, publication bans, exclusion of public)
	Newfoundland passes Victims of Crime Services Act
	Northwest Territories passes Victims of Crime Act

Table 1.1   *continued*

1988 *(cont.)*	Prince Edward Island passes Victims of Crime Act
	Quebec passes An Act Respecting Assistance to Victims of Crime
	National Victim Resource Centre transferred from Solicitor General to Department of Justice
	Federal, provincial, and territorial governments adopt the Statement of Basic Principles of Justice for Victims of Crime (amended in 2003)
1989	Bill C-89 (victim impact statements, restitution [never proclaimed in force], victim fine surcharges)
	Nova Scotia passes Victims Rights and Services Act
	National Parole Board releases discussion paper, *Victims and the National Parole Board*
1990	*R. v. Lavalee* (Supreme Court upholds battered women's defence)
1991	*R. v. Seaboyer* (Supreme Court strikes down rape shield laws)
	Canadian Sentencing Commission recommends judges be required to consider restitution; be allowed to impose jail sentence where accused willfully defaults
	US Supreme Court overturns previous decision and allows victim impact statements in death penalty cases
1992	Bill C-49 (rape shield, no means no)
	Bill C-36 (Corrections and Conditional Release Act)
	Federal government ceases contributions for provincial compensation plans
	Newfoundland repeals compensation plan
1993	Yukon repeals compensation plan and then passes Victim Services Act
	Bill C-126 (protection for child witnesses, sex offences)
	Canadian Police Association announces creation of Canadian Resource Centre for Victims of Crime
1994	*R. v. Daviault* (Supreme Court rules extreme drunkenness a defence to rape)
1995	Saskatchewan passes Domestic Violence Act and Victims of Crime Act
	R. v. O'Connor (Supreme Court allows defence access to sex assault complainants' private records)
	Bill C-37 (amends the Young Offenders Act to allow victim impact statements)
	National Victims' Resource Centre closes
	Ontario passes Victims Bill of Rights
1996	Northwest Territories repeals compensation plan
	Bill C-41 (sentencing principles, victim impact statements, restitution, hate crime)
	British Columbia passes Victims of Crime Act
	Alberta passes Victims of Crime Act
	R. v. Swietlinski (Supreme Court rules victim impact statements not relevant to judicial review hearings)

Table 1.1   *continued*

1996 *(cont.)*	Reform Party motion in House of Commons for creation of a National Victims' Bill of Rights BC Victim Advisory Committee formed (NPB/CSC)
1997	Bill C-27 (child sex-trade workers) Bill C-45 (section 745) Bill C-46 (private records of sex assault complainants) British Columbia allows victims to give oral impact statements at provincial parole hearings
1998	Release of *Victims' Rights: A Voice, Not a Veto*, Standing Committee on Justice and Human Rights Ontario government creates the Office for Victims of Crime
1999	*Vanscoy* decision confirms Ontario victims of crime legislation does not give victims any rights Bill C-79 (victim impact statements, victim fine surcharge, bail, etc.)
2000	Department of Justice Policy Centre for Victim Issues opens
2001	Manitoba passes new Victims Bill of Rights Victims permitted to provide oral impact statements at federal parole hearings
2002	New crime victim compensation legislation comes into effect in British Columbia; no longer compensates for pain and suffering Manitoba Minister of Justice Gord Mackintosh calls for amendment to Charter to support victim's rights
2003	BC government eliminates all Crown-based victim services BC government repeals no-drop policy in domestic violence cases Federal-provincial-territorial governments adopt new Basic Statement of Principles for Victims of Crime Policy Centre for Victim Issues commissions research papers on feasibility of amendment to the Charter supporting victims' rights Department of Justice victim conference
2004	Canadian Association for Victim Assistance forms and holds its first conference Canadian Centre for Justice Statistics releases report on Victims Services in Canada
2005	Bill C-10 (victim impact statements at mental health review board hearings) Bill C-2 (expansion of protection for vulnerable witnesses) Creation of fund to assist victims in attending federal parole hearings Creation of National Office for Victims of Crime (CSC/NPB)

SOURCE: Victims' Rights in Canada (2006). Canadian Resource Centre for Victims of Crime. Retrieved from www.crcvc.ca/docs/vicrights.pdf. Reprinted with permission.

Canadian Trends in Victimization

When we compare official crime rates (i.e., crimes reported to police) between Canada and the United States, Canada ranks lower in all violent crimes but has some higher rates of property crimes (Gannon, 2001). In 2000, Canada had a homicide rate of 1.8 per 100,000 persons while the United States had a rate of 5.5. Roughly one-third of Canadian homicides that year involved a victim who was shot, compared to two-thirds of American homicides. Similarly, Canadians were less likely to be victims of what Americans refer to as 'aggravated assault', known in Canada as assault levels II and III, or 'assault causing bodily harm' and 'assault with a weapon', respectively (Canada: 143/100,000; United States: 324/100,000).

More recent Canadian data provides a detailed picture of victimization in this country. The 2004 General Social Survey (GSS) polled Canadians aged 15 and older about their victimization experiences; some of the results can be found in figures 1.1 and 1.2. According to Gannon and Mihorean (2005), just over one-quarter (28 per cent) of those polled stated that they had experienced some form of victimization in the 12 months preceding the survey. Of these, approximately 40 per cent stated that they had been victimized more than once in the previous 12 months. The majority of victimizations consisted of break-and-enter type crimes (34 per cent), while violent victimizations followed closely at 29 per cent. Twenty-five per cent of the victimization experiences were the result of some form of theft.

Figure 1.1   **Rates of Comparable Violent Crimes, Canada and the United States, 2000**

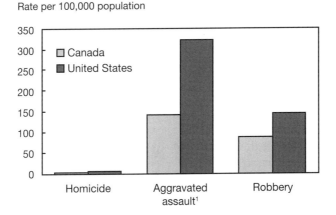

1 For comparison purposes, the Canadian category includes attempted murder, assault with a weapon, and aggravated assault.

SOURCE: Uniform Crime Reporting program, CCJS: uniform Crime Reporting program, FBI; Gannon, M. (2001). Crime comparisons between Canada and the United States. *Juristat, 21(11)*. Statistics Canada: Canadian Centre for Justice Statistics, Minister of Industry, p. 4.

Figure 1.2   Rates of Comparable Property Crimes, Canada and the United States, 2000

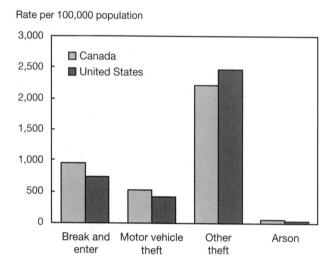

Rate per 100,000 population

SOURCE: Gannon, M. (2001). Crime comparisons between Canada and the United States. *Juristat, 21(11).* Statistics Canada: Canadian Centre for Justice Statistics, Minister of Industry, p. 4.

Although the highest rates of violent victimization in 2004 were in Nova Scotia (160 incidents per 1,000 population) and Alberta (157 incidents per 1,000 population), the rates for violent victimization overall were higher in the western provinces. Quebec, with a rate of 59 incidents per 1,000 population, had the lowest rates of violent victimization in the country. A similar pattern exists with household victimization (i.e., break and enter), with the western provinces recording the highest rates (Saskatchewan: 406/1,000; Manitoba: 403/1,000) and the lowest occurring in Quebec (147/1,000) and Newfoundland and Labrador (127/1,000). These figures also show that while violent victimization rates have not changed significantly since the previous GSS (1999), the rates

of household/break-and-enter crimes and thefts have risen.

Gannon and Mihorean (2005) further note that the GSS shows that those most at risk for violent victimization were between the ages of 15 and 24 (226/1,000). Members of this age category were 1.5 to 19 times more likely to be the victim of a violent crime than the other age groups polled. Rates of victimization in Canada were lowest among the elderly. The survey also found that despite the fact that women were less likely than men to engage in acts of violence, they were almost equally likely to be a victim of violence (women: 102/1,000; men: 111/1,000). Women were five times more likely to be sexually assaulted (women: 35/1,000; men: 7/1,000), while men were more likely to be physically assaulted (women: 59/1,000; men: 91/1,000) and to be victims of robbery (women: 8/1,000; men: 13/1,000). Those who were single were more likely to be victims of violence (203/1,000) than those in common-law relationships (131/1,000) or those who were married (52/1,000).

Turning to the victimization rates of minorities, those who identified themselves as Aboriginal on the survey were more than three times more likely to be victimized than non-Aboriginals (319/1,000 and 111/1,000 respectively). Immigrants who had migrated to Canada prior to 1999 were more than four times less likely (71/1,000) to report violent victimization than the Aboriginal respondents. Those who had immigrated to Canada between 1999 and 2004 were least likely to report violent victimization (53/1,000).

The Costs of Victimization

The costs associated with victimization are extensive. Perhaps the most obvious cost to the victim and his or her family is the loss of productivity, which often results in loss of income. Just over 30 per cent of the 2004 GSS respondents reported that their daily activities had been disrupted for one day, while 27 per cent had experienced a disruption of two or three days and 18 per cent a disruption of more than two weeks. Along with this loss, there could be the added expense of new home-security features, which 30 per cent of the survey respondents who reported victimization had installed. This figure compares with 10 per cent of the non-victimized population. Victims of violence may also need medical care for both their physical and

psychological injuries. The GSS reported that 32 per cent of victims said that they had problems sleeping, compared with 17 per cent of non-victims (AuCoin & Beauchamp, 2007).

If the crime is reported to the police, we must also add the cost of the investigation, any necessary court costs, and the costs of imprisonment or other forms of punishment. However, even if the victim does not file a report, he or she may need to use other public services, such as crisis centres, shelters, social workers, and so on. No matter how one examines the issue, it is clear that the cost of aiding crime victims is prohibitive. The best defence is to reduce the likelihood that people will be victimized. In other words, preventing victimization can be truly cost-effective.

Summary

As society became more urban and the justice system more offender focused, the role of the victim moved from one of full participant to one of witness. The issues addressed by the Women's and the Civil Rights movements of the 1960s helped society to 'rediscover' the victim. While this recognition has not necessarily been compassionate, victims have been given more of a partnership-type status. The criminal justice system has recently begun to engage the victim as an ally in the identification and apprehension of offenders.

This chapter has provided some historical information about the justice system and the role of the victim, as well as trends in Canadian victimization. Keep these details in mind as you turn a critical eye to the study of victims and the processes in which they engage.

Glossary

deterrence A concept aimed at exacting justice and dissuading the offender from doing harm again. Deterrence assumes that witnesses to the punishment will also be discouraged from ever committing the harm.

Gemeinschaft A state of social existence in small, tightly knit communities where traditional family and kinship values predominate.

Gesellschaft A more rational and less personable form of relationship based on interdependence between the parts of society.

lex talonis Legal retaliation, more popularly known by the Old Testament phrase 'an eye for an eye'.

mala in se Offences that are in and of themselves wrong or said to go against nature.

mala prohibita Acts that are against laws.

retribution The process by which a person, either the victim or the victim's representative, exacts punishment in retaliation for harm that has been done to a victim.

Critical Thinking Questions

1. In this chapter we have discussed how the Women's Movement has improved the response of the criminal justice system for women. How has the Civil Rights Movement done the same for minority groups?
2. Which of the following age groups is most at risk of being victimized? What characteristics of this group might put it at particular risk?
    Teenagers and young adults
    People in mid-career
    Elderly people
3. What factors might cause violent crime rates to be higher in western Canada than in other parts of the country?
4. Think about some of the costs that you would incur as a crime victim. What are the public costs that you pay for through your tax dollars? What additional costs would you have to pay for out of your own pocket?

Measuring Victimization

Introduction

Understanding victimization is achieved through extensive study. Researchers carefully examine a particular subject or subject group, using various methods to pinpoint issues affecting it. We learned in the previous chapter that the ability to define the concept of victim, which is more difficult than one might think, is key to the study of victims because it allows victimologists to include or exclude various group members. However, a good definition is only one facet of the issue of measuring this complex subject.

This chapter is concerned with measurement issues beyond the definition of terms, including types of victims, data availability, and the challenges in studying victims. Think about how you would begin to research a victim group. The best way to understand the complications in studying this group is to imagine that you are part of it and to ask yourself the following questions: How would you want to be studied? Would you want to be studied at all?

Types of Victims

Although the focus of this text is crime victims, we cannot forget that there are other types who fall under the umbrella term of 'victim'. For example, if we consider the 2008 vehicle crash in Bathurst, New Brunswick (see Box 2.1), we can see that this tragedy includes several types of victims.

The most obvious victims of the Bathurst crash are the dead and the survivors. However, there are also parents, partners, siblings, friends, and classmates who were all emotionally devastated by the accident. Would they be considered victims? What about people who attended the viewing or the funerals or watched the public funeral on television? At the heart of this issue is the idea of harm and how and when a person experiences harm. Is it enough to be affected by something in a negative way to be a victim? These are difficult questions, and the answers are not often clear. In many ways, we can think of an event like the Bathurst crash as a pebble

Box 2.1 The Bathurst Crash

In the early hours of 12 January 2008, members of the Bathurst High School basketball team, along with their coach, Wayne Lord, his wife, Beth, and their daughter, were returning from a game in Moncton, New Brunswick. Just 5 to 10 minutes away from the McDonalds where their families were waiting to meet them, their vehicle spun out of control on the icy roads and was hit by a transport truck. One survivor recalled how the van felt like it had been pushed suddenly. Bradd Arseneau, a team member, had fallen asleep in the van but awoke when he heard his friend, Tim Daley, say 'Oh my God!' Arseneau recalled reaching over and grabbing Daley's hand and saying, 'I love you.' He also recalled that Daley was praying. Both boys were thrown from the vehicle but survived the crash.

Following the crash, police officers were instructed to contact the families of the victims and tell them to go to the hospital. While the families waited, ambulances transporting Coach Lord, his daughter, Daley, and Arseneau arrived. Emily Cleland, who lost her brother in the accident, recalled 'that the ambulances had stopped coming because the other ones had died on impact'. The accident claimed the lives of Beth Lord and seven of the players: Javier Acevedo, 17; Cody Branch, 17; Nathan Cleland, 17; Justin Cormier, 17; Daniel Haines, 17; Nickolas Quinn, who turned 16 the day of the crash; and Nick Kelly, 15. The four others in the van and the driver of the transport truck were the only survivors. Jordan Frenette, the captain of the team, had been ill and had missed the trip in order to rest for the next day's game. He told reporters: 'There's a relief that I wasn't there; I'm obviously happy about that. But being one of the leaders of the team, in a way I should have been there.'

The victims' families requested a public viewing and funeral, in consideration of the number of people who had been touched by the tragedy and who had expressed concern. On 15 January over 1,000 mourners filed into the town's hockey arena to pay their respects. The funeral for the basketball players was held the next day, to overflow crowds. Much of this town of 12,700 closed its doors to attend the service. Beth Lord was honoured in a smaller ceremony on 17 January. Media from across the country covered the event. Many Bathurst residents stated in media reports that they were hopeful that the small town would recover from this tragedy but knew that it would take a long time.

SOURCES: Moore, O. (2008, 14 January). Deaths darken N.B. community: City faces grim task of organizing mass funeral, while tragedy raises questions on school-trip safety standards. *The Globe and Mail*. Retrieved from www.theglobeandmail.com/servlet/story/RTGAM.20080114.wbathurst14/BNStory/; Moore, O. (2008, 15 January). Tears flow as students try to cope with loss: Memorials for basketball players arrive from around the province as grief counsellors help teenagers begin recovering. *The Globe and Mail*. Retrieved from www.theglobeandmail.com/servlet/story/RTGAM.20080115.wschool15/BNStory/N; Moore, O. (2008, 16 January). Survivor recalls van crash that killed 7 friends: A fellow student was praying, he said: 'I just called his name, reached over my hand and told him I loved him.' *The Globe and Mail*. Retrieved from www.theglobeandmail.com/servlet/story/RTGAM.20080116.wbus16/BNStory/Natio.

dropped into the ocean of everyday life. Figure 2.1 illustrates how different types of victims fit into this model.

Proximity to the event plays a significant role in reaching consensus about victim status. For example, most people would agree that those who died in the crash and those who survived it are clearly victims in this tragedy, due to their being directly involved in and physically and

Figure 2.1 Rippling Effects of Victimization

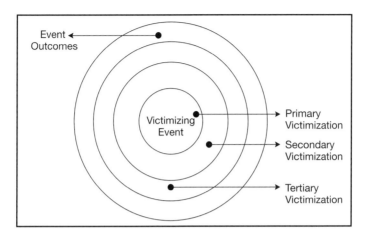

emotionally harmed by the accident. These people are the most likely to recognize that they have been victims, and others are most likely to identify them as such. Victimologists refer to these obvious victims as **primary victims**.

Many would also agree that the immediate friends and families of those directly involved in the crash are victims too, but not in the same way. In victimological terms, they are known as **secondary victims**. This type of victim is emotionally close to the primary victim, is often the first to be with him or her after the event, and is often helpful with his or her recovery. The closer the emotional ties, the more a secondary victim is said to 'share the pain' of the primary victim. Although not physically harmed by the event, the former's social proximity to the latter allows him or her to be hurt in other ways. Such victims are less likely to be identified as victims, by themselves or others, but they do acknowledge the hardship that has been placed on them because of their relationship to the primary victim and the event.

There are also those victims who are not in close social proximity to the primary victim, but who are harmed in some way by the accident. These are **tertiary victims** of the event. In the case of the Bathurst tragedy, this type would include the town residents who were saddened by the crash, who knew the families of the victims, and who mourned with them and/or helped in a less intense way. Tertiary victims in this case may also experience some psychological effects, such as refusing to drive in bad weather even though they had done so in the past. Although they may not know the primary victims, and may or may not know any of the secondary victims, they are nonetheless affected by the event in a negative way.

Finally, there are those who are least likely to know either the primary or secondary victims and may or may not be acquainted with the tertiary victims but are moved by the events in some way. These people do not identify as victims and are not recognized as such; they represent **event outcomes** of the victimizing incident. Although the people in this group had nothing to do with the event, their actions are affected because of their knowledge of it. The outcomes are boundless and can be either negative or positive. In the Bathurst crash, positive event outcomes could range from parents hugging their children more to school boards increasing safety precautions on school outings. Negative outcomes include parents being more anxious when their children go on school outings or refusing to let them go.

As Figure 2.1 illustrates, the farther one moves temporally and spatially from the victimizing event, the more diffuse the effects and the larger the category of victim. In other words, even though the event may have involved only a few people, the number of secondary victims will be much larger and the number of tertiary victims larger still. Another feature of this model is that as the distance from the event increases, the boundaries between victim types may also become blurry. For example, how would one classify the teachers at Bathurst High School who taught the members of the basketball team? Recall that Bathurst is a small community. The teachers may also have been relatives or familial and/ or personal friends. What about immediate family members of the victims who reside outside of the town or even the province? These distinctions, which consider social and physical proximity, make it more difficult to classify victims.

Measuring Victimization

The idea of measuring something may seem simple enough, but it can actually be quite complex. There are several factors that come into play when we think about measuring victimization. First and foremost, individuals may be uncomfortable talking about their experiences. As stated in the introduction to this chapter, researchers must place themselves in the subject's position. For example, what would be your initial reaction if someone asked you about the last time you were victimized? It is likely that you would respond with some form of resistance. Would you answer the question? Chances are you would not. Under what conditions would you be more inclined to answer? What would you want to know about the researcher? Do you think you would be more or less likely to answer if you had been the victim of a theft? What if you had been sexually assaulted? If you had been victimized twice in the last year, would you want to share your experiences of just one incident or both? What other factors would affect whether and how you answered?

These are all very important questions to ask before entering into any victimization study. Your answers can not only help you to understand your subject's point of view, but they can also help to determine which research method is most appropriate. Some methods are more obtrusive than others; the following sections discuss some popular techniques and highlight their advantages and disadvantages.

Obtrusive Methods

Obtrusive methods are those research practices where the researcher inserts him- or herself into the victim's personal space, effectively studying the victim at close range. The discussion below is by no means an exhaustive list of the possible methods that one can use to study victims but is merely meant to illustrate some more commonly used research techniques and to highlight issues with measurement and this vulnerable population.

Researchers perform obtrusive studies in several ways. To understand this concept, let us use the example of studying car accident victims. One method that a researcher might consider is attempting to talk with victims of car accidents at the scene; however, doing so would be a challenge. First, it would be highly unlikely that a researcher would be in the proximity of enough car accidents to collect a relatively acceptable sample of participants. Second, it would be inappropriate for a researcher to conduct a study while someone is clearly trying to deal with his or her victimization. Researchers are ethically bound to minimize the amount of harm that may occur in any study they conduct. It is this ethical code of conduct that can limit what a researcher can study. Therefore, the researcher in our example would have to find another way to find subjects for the study.

Another way to gather subjects is to use the 'snowball' sampling method. The technique is named because, like a snowball, it starts off small but grows as subjects are encouraged to participate. In this method, a researcher finds an initial participant by chance and, if he or she agrees to be involved, asks if the research subject knows anyone else who would qualify for and be willing to take part in the study. The researcher asks each participant, in turn, to refer others to the study. Although this sampling process is useful, it also has methodological problems. The quality of the sample is largely influenced by the initial contact and the people that

he or she recommends. For example, if the researcher's first contact was a college student who lived in residence, any referrals the researcher would get would be within that person's social network. Such referrals may include other students who live in residence or other friends, acquaintances, and family members. Then again, the participants may not recommend a family member because they may not want them to know about the accident. As a result, the sample will probably not be representative of all car accident victims. In methodological terms, this sample is considered to be **biased**, or containing an estimated form of error. This error is either known or unknown and is created by flaws in study design, such as in the development of the measurement instruments, sample selection, study implementation, or study questions.

Snowball samples are appropriate for some research topics, especially in cases where the kind of victimization is severe, the number of people who may have had this experience is very small, and/or there is a reluctance to talk with a researcher because of the sensitive nature of the victimization. Additionally, when the topic is particularly sensitive, such as incest survival, the researcher must work harder to earn the trust of one participant and get him or her to not only talk about the experience but also to refer others who might participate. Although using this approach to study incest victims may yield biased results, the very nature of the victimization limits the choice of methods. For example, we could not pass out a questionnaire or conduct a telephone survey on this subject. Many studies done with this group have used snowball samples or other, less obtrusive methods, such as the study of documents generated from reported cases.

Asking questions directly of a respondent may be intrusive, but it is one of the most effective ways that we can come to understand social phenomena. We can ask questions in a survey, with or without a researcher present. Talking with someone directly often allows the respondent to gauge whether the interviewer can be trusted and to ask questions about the study. Potential subjects are also less likely to decline an offer of participating in a study when contacted personally. Often, it is the best way to encourage people to engage with a study. Therefore, it is a very effective method of getting a good response rate. It also allows the researcher to probe answers that are not clear, thereby ensuring that the answers received are of a very high quality. Online and paper surveys are often the most common form of data gathering because they are less obtrusive and give the participant more anonymity in answering the request for data. Because there is no one with them asking the questions, they are also probably more likely to choose not to participate.

Obtrusive methods do require direct contact with the victim and therefore can be enormously beneficial, but the methods include some risks. In-person interviewing can become very time consuming. Talking with a respondent about a victimization experience may also increase the risk of doing harm to the victim for a number of reasons. For example, the interviewer may not be effective. He or she could be intimidating and willingly or unknowingly try to force the respondent to answer a question. Being directly involved with the victim in asking questions is also a very expensive way to conduct a study due to the extensive hours spent in the field, travelling, and so on. Answering a survey, even without the researcher present, may also trigger the victim to relive the victimization experience. For these and other reasons, researchers can opt for less obtrusive methods.

Unobtrusive Methods

Given the researchers' ethical code to minimize the amount of harm in any study, victimologists often take advantage of less obtrusive methods than those described in the previous section. If done appropriately, these measures can often minimize bias and reduce the impact on the victim. **Unobtrusive methods** are research methods whereby the researcher, or observer, has indirect contact with the participant through existing documents, survey data, attitude questionnaires, and so on. Going back to our example of devising a study on car accident victims, a researcher who wanted to use an unobtrusive method could analyze media reports of car accidents, focusing on what the victims told reporters. However, this sample would be a very select group, as the study would include only accidents covered by the media, usually consisting of those causing a great deal of damage, road closures, serious injuries, and/or fatalities. More common accidents, such as fender-benders, would not be reported in the press unless there was something unusual about them. Although the researcher would be able to study the affects of noteworthy car accidents, the study may not increase understanding about the everyday experience of being a car accident victim.

Another approach would be to examine police reports and court records relating to car accidents. In most serious crashes, the police and other required emergency services are called to the scene. If the accident is not serious (i.e., there was minimal damage and no one was hurt), the participants may not call the police and instead file a report at the police station. In either case, victims are asked to recount what happened just before, during, and after the accident, information which can become part of the public record. If the researcher is given access to these documents by the police and agrees that the participants will remain anonymous, this method is minimally intrusive.

Unobtrusive methods are limited only by the creativity of the researcher. There may be several accounts of victimization experiences already existing in public documents. The key to a good study is in understanding how the documents came to be public and how this circumstance might affect the representativeness in the research sample (i.e., how those documents are biased).

Another issue to keep in mind is that the more violent the victimization, the more uncommon it is. In other words, it will be harder to find victims of more serious crimes because there are less of them. On the other hand, the more common the type of victimization, the less interest there seems to be in studying the victims. The example used in this chapter is one such case; hundreds of car accidents occur in this country every day. People tend to want to know about victims of violent crimes, perhaps because they usually have a greater fear of these crimes (Ferraro, 1996; Warr, 1984). Because violent victimization generates such fear, learning about others who have been victims may be a pre-emptive measure to having a similar experience.

One of the most common ways researchers study victimization is by using surveys. Although these studies are somewhat obtrusive, in the sense that they can involve talking to people who may have been victimized, as with other research methods extensive precautions to protect the participant are taken. Furthermore, the data generated from surveys can be used by many others without having to contact a victim repeatedly. That is not to say that absolutely no harm can be done by this type of survey—or the data it generates—but that the potential for harm is reduced significantly. Therefore, while conducting a survey can be obtrusive, analyzing data from an existing data set is categorized as unobtrusive.

Surveys Examining Victims of Crime

Surveys that collect data on the victimization experience can be conducted in a variety of ways. They can be carried out by individual researchers working independently or in affiliation with an institution, such as a university or a government office. In Canada, the most widely used data are generated from studies administered by the federal government, often with the help of university researchers. These surveys are very expansive, as the government has the resources to question thousands of people. Government surveys are also more likely to take advantage of the significantly more expensive random sampling methods; therefore, the data they gather are considered relatively representative of the Canadian population.

Victimization surveys have an advantage over police data in that they can include not only crimes reported to police but also those that were not reported. For example, the Violence Against Women Survey reported that one in four women had been victimized by some sort of attempted or completed sexual assault in their lifetime (Johnson, 1996). Although some of these incidents were considered serious, most consisted of unwanted sexual touching or grabbing. Ninety-four per cent of the respondents did not report these incidents to police for a variety of reasons. As this case shows, a carefully designed victimization survey can capture not only reported crimes but also the considerably larger number of unreported offences.

However, even surveys might not give a clear representation of a victim group. Take, for example, a study of reported violent crimes in Canada. Recall that violent crimes are a relatively rare occurrence. In 2006, there were 7,518 Criminal Code violations reported to the police for every 100,000 Canadians (Silver, 2007). This number may seem large, but when we think about studying these victimization experiences, we realize that we would need a very large subject group to achieve effective results. Large Canadian victimization surveys typically poll approximately 10,000–20,000 people. Assuming that a survey polled 10,000 people, when we break down the numbers we find that we would have a chance of capturing approximately 750 crimes reported to police, only 10 per cent of the 2006 total. We would have to contact 50,000 people in order to get information on approximately 3,000 victimizations which classify as Criminal Code violations and were reported to police. What if we were not interested in all reported crimes, but wanted to focus our study on victims of robbery who reported the crime to police? Silver (2007) estimated that there were 94 per 100,000 Canadians who had this experience. If we surveyed 10,000 people, we would potentially reach only 9 or 10 victims meeting this criterion. Can we formulate any valid conclusions based on these limited results? It might be better to use another method to look at this problem.

There are several surveys currently available from Statistics Canada which focus on victims specifically. Although some, such as certain cycles of the General Social Survey, poll people on direct experiences with victimization, other surveys ask questions which seek to understand victimization as part of another social problem, such as homelessness. Below is a list of surveys and data sets that question respondents about victimization and, in some cases, the respondents' reaction to this experience.

General Social Survey (GSS)

The GSS was established in 1985. This program conducts an annual telephone survey of randomly selected Canadians, aged 15 and over, from all 10 provinces (it does not include people living in the territories). The regularity of this survey allows for cross-sectional analysis and for the documentation of trends among issues facing Canadians. The survey can also be adjusted to capture and address new issues. The GSS has two primary objectives:

a) to gather data on social trends in order to monitor changes in the living conditions and well-being of Canadians over time; and

b) to provide immediate information on specific social policy issues of current or emerging interest. (Statistics Canada, 2006b, p. 5)

One of the trends that Canadians are interested in is crime and victimization. The GSS has dedicated portions of five surveys, or cycles, to issues of victimization: Cycle 3 (1988), Cycle 8 (1993), Cycle 13 (1999), Cycle 18 (2004), and Cycle 23 (2009). Although the data has been collected for Cycle 23, the publications summarizing the analysis of the data have not been released as of the writing of this text. Cycle 18 gathered specific data on victimization rates and public perceptions of crime and the justice system; some of the results are discussed in Chapter 1 of this text. This cycle has extensive data on several aspects of victimization and has generated reports on a wide variety of subjects, including hate crime; victimization of seniors, minorities, women, and immigrants; sexual orientation and victimization experience; family violence; and persons with disabilities. Cycle 18 also looked at victimization of Canadian northern peoples, which the survey had not previously done.

Victim Services Survey (VSS)

The first VSS was conducted in 2003 and received responses from 484 victim services agencies that serve primary or secondary victims of crime in all provinces and territories. Although a second VSS was conducted in 2009, publications from this data have not been released as of the writing of this text. This survey collects information on agencies, including the type of agency, types of services offered, populations targeted, client accessibility, and training and support opportunities for staff and volunteers during the 12-month reference period. Another section of the survey provides a one-day snapshot of those individuals seeking victim services, focusing on the number of clients served and the following client characteristics: sex, age, type of victimization, type of services received, incidence of reported crime, and source of agency referral. The VSS also collects information on activities of eight criminal injuries compensation/financial benefit programs during the reference period.

Transition Home Survey (THS)

This biennial survey began in 1992 and was developed out of the federal government's Family Violence Initiative, which strives to reduce incidents of family violence in Canada. The THS is a census of all residential agencies providing services to battered women and their children across Canada (Vaillancourt & Taylor-Butts, 2007). Its objective is to collect data on residential services for abused women and their children during the previous 12 months, including the number of women and children receiving services, the reasons for their admission, the age of residents, the resident–abuser relationship, and the involvement of the criminal justice system. The THS also provides a one-day snapshot of the clientele being served on a specific date. The most recent cycle of this survey looked at services from 2007 to 2008, taking a snapshot of service use on 16 April 2008.

The International Crime Victimization Survey (ICVS)

This survey was initiated by a team of European criminologists as a means of providing comparable international information on the nature and extent of crime. The ICVS has been carried out in five cycles to date—1989, 1992, 1996, 2000, 2004–05—with a sixth planned for 2010. Respondents from countries all over the world supply detailed information on the following crime categories: vehicle-related crimes (e.g., car theft), burglary, attempted burglary, personal property theft, and contact crimes (e.g., robbery, sexual offences, and assault and theft). Questions regarding street level corruption, consumer fraud, drug-related crime, and hate crime are included. Respondents are also asked to give their opinions on public safety, policing, and sentencing. In the latest version of the survey, data was collected from 30 countries and 33 main cities within both the developed and developing word. Canada is one of five industrialized countries to have participated in all cycles of the survey.

Violence Against Women Survey (VAWS)

This one-time survey was conducted in 1993 to assess women's experiences with and responses to violence. In particular, this study asked women aged 18 and over about sexual harassment, sexual violence, physical violence, and threats by strangers, dates/boyfriends, other known men, husbands, and common-law partners. This survey also examined the safety of women both inside and outside the home as well as women's perceptions of fear (Johnson, 1996). Finally, this survey polled respondents about how they handled the experience, including asking questions about whether they reported the victimization to police, with whom they discussed the matter, and whether they

sought out additional support from medical staff.

Pilot Survey on Police-Reported Hate Crimes (PRHS Pilot)

In January 1999, the Canadian Centre for Justice Statistics (CCJS) received a four-year funding commitment from the federal government's Policy Research Initiative (PRI) to conduct a study on hate crime in Canada. Police services from the Royal Canadian Mounted Police (excluding detachments from British Columbia), Montreal, Halton Regional, Ottawa, Sudbury, Toronto, Waterloo, Windsor, Winnipeg, Regina, Calgary, and Edmonton participated in the survey. This pilot project had two goals: to enhance our understanding of hate crime in Canada and to assess the feasibility of collecting national police-reported hate crime statistics.

The Canadian Urban Victimization Survey (CUVS)

This one-time survey conducted with funding from the Solicitor General's Office was designed to provide information for planning and evaluating crime prevention programs. The CUVS was carried out in 1982, using a previous 12-month reference period, and was comprised of a random sample of the adult population (aged 16 and over) from seven cities: St John's, Halifax/Dartmouth, Montreal, Toronto, Winnipeg, Edmonton, and Vancouver. Over 61,000 telephone interviews were conducted in which residents were asked to report on various topics including the extent and distribution of selected crimes, the impact of selected crimes, the risk of criminal victimization, and the functioning of the criminal justice system.

Police Data Surveys

Uniform Crime Reporting Survey (UCR)

Established in 1962, the UCR was designed to measure annually the occurrence and characteristics of crime and traffic incidents that have been reported to the police. Information collected by the survey includes the number of criminal incidents, the clearance status of those incidents, and persons-charged information. Data from the UCR provide key information to federal and provincial policy-makers, the policing community, and public and private researchers for the purposes of crime analysis, resource planning, and program development. The focus of this data set is on the collection of information on the offender, which can inform our understanding of victim experiences. However, some information on the victim is also collected.

The United States also surveys crime and traffic incidents not only through its version of the Uniform Crime Report but also through a National Incident-Based Reporting System (NIBRS). Unlike these reports, the Canadian UCR does not collect data on the race of either the offender or the victim. The reasons for this exclusion are varied and have been addressed in several journal articles. Essentially, although it is agreed that there may be some interest in collecting data on race, concerns over racial profiling and the stereotyping of people based on their racial identity are deemed of greater importance. Those who disagree with this argument claim that to omit race from this research is to deny communities access to appropriate culturally sensitive programming, given that there are no clear numbers indicating whether there is more or less representation of a particular race in criminal or victim populations (Gabor, 1994; Roberts, 1994; Scott, 2003).

Homicide Survey

This annual survey collects detailed data on homicides in Canada. The survey has collected police-reported data on the characteristics of all murder incidents, victims, and accused persons since 1961 and all homicides (including murder, manslaughter, and infanticide) since 1974. Like the UCR, this data collection includes some information on the victim but is offender focused.

Non-Government Surveys

In addition to the large-scale surveys carried out by the government, other surveys can also be done. In some cases, the government may fund this research, thereby making it publicly accountable. Research can be conducted by several groups of people, including university professors, research consultant companies, and researchers who work for non-profit organizations. Although these studies are often carried out on a much smaller scale, they can be invaluable to our knowledge and understanding of victims.

Research can also be conducted through private companies or by research organizations that receive private monies. When research is carried out by the private sector, with no connection to government funding, it may or may not be made available to the public. Private organizations are not accountable to the public; therefore, any research that they perform can be released or not released, depending on what best serves their interests. Private research that is released to the public should be read with caution because it may have the most bias and the most suspect results.

Differences in Measurement

Clearly how a researcher asks questions and to whom these questions are posed are important elements in designing and/or understanding surveys. These two factors alone can strongly influence the responses. For example, suppose we were interested in interviewing people about their assault experience. We would probably start by asking if they have been assaulted in the following way:

> Have you been assaulted in the 12 months prior to this study?

In many ways this is a good question. We have clarified what we are interested in and set a time frame for the participant's reference. However, there are also several problems with this question. Are we interested in physical, sexual, or some other kind of assault? We can narrow our focus to physical assault:

> Have you been physically assaulted in the 12 months prior to this study?

We have made our question more specific, but there is still room for improvement. The participant may not know the definition of the term 'physical assault' or may censor him- or herself based on the seriousness of an assault or the nature of his or her relationship with the offender. For example, if the participant had been slapped by a stranger in the last 12 months, he or she would clearly identify this as an assault. Would the same participant be as likely to identify the action as an assault if it was done by a friend? A

spouse? We can account for these possibilities by reforming our question:

> Have you been physically assaulted (slapped, pushed, punched, etc.), by either a stranger or a person known to you, in the 12 months prior to this study?

The data set that a researcher uses can also make a huge difference to the survey results. This point is illustrated in Figure 2.2, which charts results from two data sets looking at the number of sexual assaults in Canada in 1999. While both sets analyze the same topic in the same time period, they show starkly different results. The first column represents the results of the 1999 General Social Survey, which claims that there were approximately half a million assaults. The Uniform Crime Reporting Survey reports a considerably lower number: 23,859 (Kong, Johnson, Beattie, & Cardillo, 2003). The GSS estimates a rate of 21 sexual assaults per 1,000 people, while the UCR estimates a rate of 0.78 per 1,000 people (Kong, Johnson, Beattie, Cardillo, 2003). Given that the results are for the same year, the difference cannot be explained by a change in the country's population. What, then, is causing the discrepancy?

Recall that the GSS is a victimization survey that polls randomly selected people from across the country and asks them whether or not they have had a victimizing experience in the last year. The UCR looks at data that the police have gathered on calls for service. In other words, the victimization survey captures both reported and unreported sexual assault, while the UCR captures only those crimes reported to police. It is important to remember that not all victimization events that occur are reported to police.

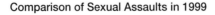

Figure 2.2 Number of Sexual Assaults in Canada, 1999, Comparing the General Social Survey and the Uniform Crime Reporting Survey

Comparison of Sexual Assaults in 1999

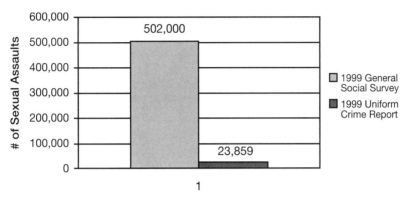

SOURCE: Kong, R., Johnson, H., Beattie, S., & Cardillo, A. (2003). Sexual offences in Canada. *Juristat 23*(6), Statistics Canada: Canadian Centre for Justice Statistics,1–26.

Another reason for the different results in these two surveys is the criteria used to capture the data. While the UCR includes all police reported crime, the GSS uses information gathered from two questions. Respondents answered 'Yes', 'No', or 'Don't know' or refused to respond to the following (Statistics Canada, 2000):

(Excluding incidents already mentioned,) during the past 12 months, has anyone forced you or attempted to force you into any unwanted sexual activity, by threatening you, holding you down or hurting you in some way? This includes acts by family and non-family but excludes acts by current or previous spouses or common-law partners. Remember that all information provided is strictly confidential.

(Apart from what you have told me,) during the past 12 months, has anyone ever touched you against your will in any sexual way? By this I mean anything from unwanted touching or grabbing, to kissing or fondling. Again, please exclude acts by current or previous spouses or common-law partners.

These questions are interesting for a variety of reasons. They do not ask about sexual assault, per se, but instead ask about the behaviour of forced/unwanted sexual activity. By asking the questions in this manner, the survey designer does not allow the respondent to define what a sexual assault is but asks a question that reflects the behaviour of what would be considered a sexual assault under Canadian law. More about the specific victimization of sexual assault, and the laws that govern this crime, are found in Chapter 6. For now, it is enough to note the effect and the power of asking a good question.

Summary

In this chapter we have discussed some of the methods of classifying and studying victims, as well as the major issues concerning these processes. We have given particular attention to the survey, one of the most common means of researching victims. When designing victimization studies, researchers must use the appropriate subject group, ask the right questions, and strive to limit bias as much as possible. The researcher's ability to achieve these objectives will greatly affect the study's results and their value to the discipline. No matter what type of method is used or what type of victim is being studied, it is imperative that researchers also minimize harm in any study that they conduct. Studying victims, especially those of severe crimes, requires not only high ethical standards but also a great deal of compassion. While collecting information that may enhance our understanding of the victim experience and help to prevent further crime, researchers must be constantly aware of the delicacy of examining their subjects.

Glossary

bias   Error that is either known or unknown and created by flaws in study design, such as in the development of the measurement instruments, sample selection, study implementation, or study questions.

event outcomes   Larger social effects of victimization that can be either negative or positive.

obtrusive methods   Research methods whereby the researcher, or observer, has direct contact with the participant.

primary victims   Individuals or institutional entities directly affected by harm.

secondary victims   Individuals or institutional entities indirectly affected by harm done to a primary victim but who are in close social proximity to the primary victim.

snowball sampling   A sampling method by which participants in a research study are asked to refer other members to the study.

tertiary victims   Individuals or institutional entities that have no relationship with the primary victim but who suffer as a result of knowing about the victimization experience.

unobtrusive methods   Research methods whereby the researcher, or observer, has indirect contact with the participant through surveys, attitude questionnaires, and so on.

Critical Thinking Questions

1. Think about the surveys mentioned in this chapter. Which focus on primary victims of crime and which focus on secondary crime victims? Support your answers.

2. If you were conducting a study, when would you purposely use a non-random sample of respondents? What kind of studies work best with a random sample of respondents?

3. What crime victim group do you think would be the hardest to study and why? What obstacles would you face as the researcher and how would you overcome them?
4. Assume you are a researcher who wishes to observe street activity on Saturday nights in a particular part of town. On the fourth night you witness someone being victimized. Would you call the police? What do you think a research ethics board would require you to do?

CHAPTER 3

Typologies of Victim–Victimizer Interaction

Learning Objectives

After reading this chapter, you will be able to

- examine early victimologists' ideas about victim vulnerability;
- understand how those ideas have extended throughout twentieth-century theory;
- understand the concepts of victim precipitation and its assumptions; and
- identify how these concepts continue to shape some of our current thinking about victim vulnerability.

Introduction

Although victims have only recently come into focus as subjects of more intensive research, some philosophers, lawyers, and others interested in criminal events have previously hypothesized about the role of the victim. In particular, these theorists noticed that there seemed to be patterns to victimization. Moreover, some observed that certain groups of people were more vulnerable to victimization than others and would be repeatedly victimized. In this chapter we will look at a number of theorists who have examined the role of the victim and his or her culpability in the victimizing act. We will follow the ideas of some of the earliest writers on the subject, such as Hans von Hentig and Beniamin Mendelsohn, and see how their ideas have progressed into the new millennium.

When we hear about victimization, we tend to want to know why it happened, possibly in an effort to understand the event or even to protect ourselves. We may compare ourselves to the people involved and ask how we would react in the same situation. We may also ask ourselves whether the actions of the victim and offender were reasonable. We often find the latter odious, but in some cases we also find fault with the actions of the former, especially if we are seeking to defend the victimizer's actions. Where we see this type of situation more clearly is in the legal system. On one hand, the Crown argues that its client—the victim—is innocent of any wrongdoing, placing full responsibility for the victimization on the offender. On the other hand, defence lawyers often try to blame the victim, demonstrating that their client is not guilty because his or her actions were somewhat reasonable. Boxes 3.1 and 3.2 illustrate two cases where these tactics have been used. As you read about these cases, think of how the legal system and the media portrayed the victims and how this treatment might have affected both women.

Box 3.1 Blaming the Victim: The Case of Katelyn Faber

In the summer of 2003, 19-year-old Katelyn Faber, an employee of Colorado's The Lodge and Spa at Cordillera, reported to the police that she had been raped by NBA All-Star Kobe Bryant, who was staying at the hotel. Bryant was arrested and charged with sexual assault. What followed was a highly publicized case in which the media, basketball fans, lawyers, and society appeared to be placing the blame on the alleged victim.

Media tabloid headlines read 'Did she really say no?' and claimed that, because Faber willingly flirted with and kissed Bryant, she 'must have' wanted the sex as well. When Bryant returned to the basketball court, he received standing ovations from the crowd.

The Colorado court allowed details of Faber's sex life to be admitted into evidence. Bryant's lawyers also attempted to have her mental history entered. They claimed that Faber had made false accusations to gain attention from a former boyfriend and that she had financial motive.

In September 2004, the criminal case was dropped because Faber was unwilling to testify in court. She did, however, file a civil suit, which was settled out of court. These actions generated more speculation about the case. Wendy Murphy, a professor at a Boston law school, maintains that the prosecution and government had an obligation to pursue the case. 'It's a different way of blaming the victim,' she says. 'It's the government sloughing off onto the victim the failure of the justice system.'

SOURCE: The Associated Press. (2004). Little sympathy for Kobe case prosecutors; Blame for dropping process shifted to victim: legal expert. The Spectator. Retrieved 10 April 2008 from http://proquest.umi.com.uproxy.library.dc-uoit.ca/pqdweb?did=691258961&sid=1&Fmt=3&clientId=72790&RQT=309&VName=PQD.

Box 3.2 Blaming the Victim: The Case of 'A'

In November 2003, 14-year-old 'A'[1] was raped and nearly beaten to death with a rock in a riverside park on Montreal's south shore. After enduring hours of the attack, 'A' escaped by swimming in frigid waters to an island in the St Lawrence River. She then walked two kilometres and, at 5:00 a.m., showed up nude at a stranger's door asking for help. As if this ordeal wasn't painful enough, 'A' has been blamed for the attack.

Lynda Bureau, the defence lawyer in this case, perpetuated the idea—in court and in the media—that 'A' bears some responsibility because she agreed to go to the park and meet the man who attacked her. Bureau argued that 'A' 'wanted to have a good time, she knew these men drank beer . . . she permitted [the accused] to sit next to her'. Closer investigation of the case showed that the attack appeared to be well planned and that the man brought along an accomplice.

[1] Name is protected in original for privacy purposes.

SOURCE: Riga, A. (2005). Lawyer blames victim in rape sentencing case. CanWest News. Retrieved 10 April 2008 from http://proquest.umi.com.uproxy.library.dc-uoit.ca/pqdweb?did=894674821&sid=1&Fmt=3&clientId=72790&RQT=309&VName=PQD.

The first box details a famous American case against basketball star Kobe Bryant. In this case, the lawyers defending Bryant tried to argue that the plaintiff, Katelyn Faber, effectively should have known not to flirt with their client. They told the court of her past sexual experiences and offered that she was only accusing their client because she wanted attention from another man. Eventually Faber reached a deal with Bryant, contending that she was unable to continue dealing with the pressure of being in the public spotlight. Because the contents of the deal remained between the two parties, the public was left to speculate on whether she was in fact just fabricating a story. It is interesting to note that the public may also have seen Faber as less than innocent, given that Bryant received a standing ovation on his return to the basketball court.

In a less well-known but similar case in Canada, the victim, 'A', was attacked in a public park in Montreal. The defence argued that this victim was not totally innocent because she knew that the men she accompanied to the park had been drinking alcohol. They further contended that she should have known that she would be in danger if she continued to socialize with the men who eventually sexually assaulted her. In this chapter, we will review how we have come to think about victims as more or less innocent and how certain theorists have come to shape these ideas over time.

The Early Victimologists

As with early criminology, victimology has spawned several theories about the role of the victim in the victim–offender relationship. Early victimologists wrestled with the idea of this role and intensely debated its nature and extent. We continue to question not only what role the victim plays in this relationship but also the amount of responsibility he or she holds for the victimization.

Hans von Hentig (1887–1974)

Son of business lawyer Otto von Hentig in Berlin in 1887, Hans von Hentig was one of the earliest writers on the subject of the victim. According to Fahrmeir (2010), von Hentig studied in Paris, Munich, and Berlin before receiving his doctorate in 1912. His career changed after he served in World War I. In 1923 he joined the Communist Party and eventually became involved in planning a Communist uprising. In 1925 his participation was discovered, causing him to flee Germany. After brief professorships of criminal law at the universities of Kiel and Bonn, he lectured in several locations in Europe and the United States. Even though his degree was in law, he did not pursue this career avenue in a traditional way but followed a more scientific approach. Throughout his career, his work was heavily influenced by the methodological approaches of science. His work in victimology sought to bridge the gap between law and psychology. As a scientist, he was in favour of medicalizing the language of criminology and the study of victims. Von Hentig died in 1974, not far from his birthplace, in Bad Tölz, Germany.

Von Hentig penned *The Criminal and His Victim* in 1948. He was one of the first to look at the relationship between the offender and the victim, whom he referred to as the 'doer and the sufferer' (p. iii) and the 'subject and the object' (p. 384). He saw both people as being engaged in a relationship, although often brief. He likened the criminal to a predator, arguing that 'it would not be correct nor complete to speak of a carnivorous animal, its habits and characteristics, without looking at the prey on which it lives. . . . To know one we must be acquainted with the other complementary partner' (p. 385). He stressed that victim potential was dictated by a combination of biology, socialization, and chance.

Throughout his writing, von Hentig emphasized the importance of exploring the victim–offender relationship so that effective treatment and prevention programs for both could be developed and administered. He claimed that 'increased attention should be paid to the provocative function of the victim . . . With a thorough knowledge of the interrelations between doer and sufferer new approaches to the detection of crime will be opened' (1948, p. 450). His basic assertion was that the victim can play a determinant role. In other words, the victim can often engage in behaviour that contributes to his or her own victimization. He also argued that examining the outcome can often give a biased interpretation as to the actual roles of victim and offender. As Wolfgang (1958) later observed, the eventual victim may have been the initial aggressor. Von Hentig asserted that often the victim as provocateur had to be examined.

To this end, he developed a typology of victim types, which is shown in Table 3.1, ranging from what he referred to as the weakest in our society (children and youth, women, and the elderly) to those who are weakened by reason of mental defect or disorder and to those who are seen to have an 'artificial handicap' (p. 414), such as race or immigration status, or who are simply inexperienced, uneducated, or poor.

Von Hentig also stressed the importance of the psychological strength of the victim, offering the following scale of 'reciprocal operation' (pp. 420–421):

1. apathetic, lethargic
2. submitting, conniving, passively submitting
3. co-operative, contributory
4. provocative, instigative, soliciting

Those who suffer from ailments such as depression were considered by von Hentig to be the most vulnerable, as he argued that there was a disturbance in the instinct for self-preservation. Those who engaged in lifestyle choices that put them at increased risk were more reciprocal, or more engaged, in their own victimizations. Those who were greedy and those who had many sexual encounters were said to be more active in their victimizations. Still others are bereft and lonely, making them perfect 'suckers' for predators. The most active victims, according to this scale, included those who tormented others, those who were defending themselves in a combative situation, and those who were living 'double lives' and thereby inviting someone to extort their situations.

Last, but certainly not least, von Hentig acknowledged that there were some situations where the victim could actually act out and become an offender. Elements such as age, any predispositions, drug and alcohol use, and lack of self-confidence and/or self-esteem come to bear on the victim as 'activators'. This person is a sufferer but, because of the pain, acts out on others, becoming a 'doer' who inflicts suffering on others.

Table 3.1   Von Hentig's Victim Typology

The General Class

	Classification	Example
1	The Young	children and infants
2	The Female	all women
3	The Old	all elderly persons
4	The Mentally Defective and Other Mentally Deranged	including, but not limited to, idiots, imbeciles, feeble-minded persons, and moral imbeciles; e.g., the insane, drug addicts, alcoholics, bigamists
5	Immigrants	individuals from other countries unfamiliar with the culture
6	Minorities	racially disadvantaged persons
7	Dull Normals	'simple-minded', uneducated, and often poor persons

The Psychological Class

	Classification	Example
8	The Depressed	persons with various psychological disorders and psychoses
9	The Acquisitive	the greedy, those who look for quick gains
10	The Wanton	promiscuous persons
11	The Lonesome and the Heartbroken	widows, widowers, and those in mourning
12	The Tormentor	often found in families: an abusive parent, spouse
13	The Blocked, Exempted, or Fighting	victims of blackmail, extortion, confidence games
14	The Activating Sufferer	the sexually abused who becomes a sexual offender; one who is raised by an alcoholic tormentor, torments their own family and becomes an alcoholic.

SOURCE: von Hentig, H. (1948/1967). *The criminal and his victim: Studies in the sociology of crime.* Hamden, CT: Archon Books. pp. 404–7.

The Criminal and His Victim reflects many of the cultural idioms of its time. The ideas behind von Hentig's typology are still a source of discussion. The basic assumptions about his work is that there is a symbiosis between the victim and the offender. In essence, he argues that it is the nature of this relationship that can affect how the two parties interact. Although von Hentig does acknowledge that many victims are chosen because they are ultimately vulnerable, he also asserts that victims can provoke their attackers to varying degrees. He identifies that both the physical weakness (the general class) and mental weakness (the psychological class) can lead to **victim vulnerability**, which is the risk of victimization attributed to an individual or group. It is possible for victims to have characteristics from both scales, as humans are composed of both the physical body and mental processes.

It is this provocative status of victim that recurs throughout later discussions of victims. A critical flaw in the idea of victim influence is the implication that victims wish, on some level, to be victimized and therefore cause the actions against them. A second fault in this line of thinking is the assumption that the victim has control over the predator's actions; it is the predator who engages the malicious action. It is also erroneous to suggest that the victim plays a part in the predator's ultimate goal. Although the victim may be active, he or she does not share control of the situation. Finally, it is wrong to suppose that a person's engagement in any particular activity somehow warrants his or her victimization.

Beniamin Mendelsohn (1900–1998)

Often thought of as the 'father' of victimology, Beniamin Mendelsohn was born in Bucharest, Romania, in 1900 and died in Jerusalem, Israel, in 1998. He introduced the term 'victimology', meaning the science of the victim, in a lecture to the Romanian Psychiatric Society in 1947. A lawyer by trade, Mendelsohn became interested in not only the offender but the victim as well. While preparing each case, he would survey the offender, the victim, and any witnesses to the event with an extensive questionnaire. The purpose was to garner a complete understanding of the event. One striking finding of this research was that the victim and offender often knew each other.

Mendelsohn's law practice greatly shaped his interest and interpretation of his data. Law is concerned with the culpability of the offender; the more responsible the offender for his or her actions, the less culpable the victim in the interaction. Logically, Mendelsohn sought to understand the role of the victim, recognizing that not all offenders are assumed totally responsible for their actions. In 1956, Mendelsohn published 'The Victimology', a short article describing six classifications of victims that he had identified as a result of his research. A detailed description of his typology is shown in Table 3.2.

Like von Hentig, Mendelsohn was also interested in examining the culpability of the victim. However, his model is somewhat less categorical and assumes more of a continuum that ranges from non-culpable victims to people who are victimized while engaging in criminal acts. Mendelsohn argues that people in this latter group are the most responsible, in many ways, for their own victimizations. He also adds another category of victim: those who, for some reason, misrepresent their status as victims.

Mendelsohn's typology suffers from many of the same criticisms as the works of von Hentig and other victim theorists. By assigning culpability to the victim, the issue of offender motivation, a key component to criminal law, loses consideration. What the victim did in the past or directly prior to being victimized has little bearing on the motivation of the offender to victimize. The law is also based on what *reasonable* individuals would do in any given situation. These are not necessarily the same underlying guiding principles behind typology

Table 3.2   Mendelsohn's Victim Typology

	Classification	Description	Example
1	the completely innocent victim	The victim is free of any contribution to the criminal act.	Small children, those attacked 'out of the blue'.
2	the victim with minor guilt/victims due to ignorance	The victim foolishly did something that put them in harm's way.	A person who is attacked while walking alone late at night in a known high-crime area.
3	the victim as guilty as the offender/voluntary victim	Victims who commit suicide or who receive injury due to the involvement in 'victimless crimes'.	A person who engages in prostitution, and/or drug and alcohol use.
4	the victim is more guilty than the offender	The victim provokes the attack.	A person who starts a fight but ends up losing it.
5	most guilty victim	The victim is injured while engaging in another crime.	A person who is injured while carrying out an illegal drug sale.
6	simulating or imaginary victim	Individuals who are not victims but who lead others to think that they have been victimized.	A person who lost a significant amount of money in a card game but states they were mugged.

SOURCE: Mendelsohn, B. (1956). *The victimology. Etudes Internationale de Psycho-sociologie Criminelle.* July, 23–6.

building. Finding fault with the victim suggests that he or she was not acting reasonably and therefore may be responsible, in whole or in part, for his or her own victimization. However, one could equally make another assumption: that harming another is not reasonable, regardless of victim behaviour.

More significant than his examination of culpability is Mendelsohn's contribution to the discipline of victimology. He argued that there needed to be a complement to criminology and that the study of victims was necessary to understand the crime in a more holistic fashion. Although he was the first to bring the term 'victimology' to the forefront, it had previously appeared in psychiatrist Frederic Wertham's 1949 study of murderers, *The Show of Violence.*

Mendelsohn coined a number of other words to describe components of victimology that were adopted by the discipline. In 1963, he used the term **victimal**, meant as the opposite of the word 'criminal'. As an adjective, it is used to describe the behaviour of a victim (e.g., victimal conduct). **Victimity**, according to Mendelsohn, is the opposite of **criminality** and refers to the quality or state of being a victim or that which constitutes being a victim. He argued that people had the potential for **victimal receptivity**, meaning that there was, to varying degrees, an unconscious propensity in individuals to being victimized. He also adopted the term **penal couple**, initially used by Henri Ellenberger (1955) to refer to the understanding that both the victim and the offender often share many of the same characteristics and enter into an often short relationship, complete with assigned roles, during the act of victimization.

Stephen Schafer (1911–1976)

Stephen Schafer, a Hungarian-born victimologist and criminologist published *The Victim and His Criminal* in 1968, choosing a title that plays on the significant contribution of von Hentig. In this book, Schafer dedicates a chapter to what he terms 'the functional responsibility'. He argues that responsibility is an instrument of social control and touches upon the criminal–victim relationship. He states that where criminals are said to criminally trespass, the victim's responsibility 'is to prevent a choice that will result in criminal trespassing' (p. 144). In essence, he directs attention onto the victim, bringing him or her back into the analysis while not necessarily directing attention away from the criminal. As shown in Table 3.3, Schafer's typology is similar to von Hentig's but is based on the underlying principle of culpability and victim responsibility rather than specific risk factors. Schafer died suddenly in 1976, just days before The Second International Symposium on Victimology, which he had organized and intended to chair, was to begin.

Criticism of Early Victimology Typologies

The typologies of von Hentig, Mendelsohn, and Schafer contain both positive and negative elements. First and foremost, they generated interest in the victim. Recall that before these writings, the victim had largely become invisible to the state, often ignored by the system and therefore not considered in any explanation of crime.

These early theorists acknowledged that when we are trying to understand aspects of social ills such as crime, looking at only one aspect of the problem—in this case the offender—may create a significant amount of bias in our findings or our proposed prevention strategies.

However, these and other theorists (Barnes & Teeters, 1943; Lamborn, 1968) failed to shed light on the power dynamics between the victim and offender. Furthermore, although there was an increased effort to look to the victim for some solutions, the primary focus still remained with the offender, in that the theories did not look at damage inflicted on the victim once the criminal act had ceased. As a result, these early pioneers in the area failed to adequately address victim recovery in their typologies. By the late 1960s their ideas had formed the basis of victim precipitation, whereby it was not only thought that the victim could control aspects of his or her victimization but that it was also his or her duty to do so. Not doing everything culturally prescribed to avoid victimization often led to holding the victim responsible.

Victim Precipitation

Victim precipitation is also sometimes referred to as **victim blaming** or **victim facilitation** and refers to the idea of shared responsibility between the offender and the victim in a victimizing event. Behaviours that can be interpreted as contributing to victim precipitation are those of the victim that bring about, in whole or in part, his or her own victimization. Implicit in this definition is the assumption that the victimization process is an interaction between two or more people that

Table 3.3   Schafer's Victim Precipitation Typology

Victim Culpability	Type	Definition	Example
No responsibility	Unrelated victims	There is no previous relationship between the victim and offender.	Attacks by strangers, sudden outbursts of violence.
	Biologically weak victims	These individuals have physical characteristics that make them vulnerable to victimization.	The young, the elderly, the infirm, etc.
	Socially weak victims	Individuals who are not adequately integrated into society become vulnerable to victimization.	Immigrants, minorities.
	Political victims	Individuals who oppose those in power or are made to be victims to enforce a subservient social position.	Jewish people in Nazi Germany.
Some responsibility	Precipitative victims	Individuals who make themselves vulnerable to victimization.	People who put themselves in dangerous situations, say the wrong words, dress inappropriately, etc.
Responsibility equal to offender	Provocative victims	Individuals who engage the offender, forcing the offender to react.	A person who insults another in a bar in an effort to start an altercation.
Total responsibility	Self-victimizing victims	These are individuals who victimize themselves.	Those who engage in drug use, prostitution, gambling, etc.

SOURCE: Adapted from Schafer, S. (1968). *The victim and his criminal: A study in functional responsibility*. New York, NY: Random House.

results in victimization. The criminal event is therefore a *social* event, in that it involves interfacing, in some fashion, with another person or people. The event is not a positive experience for the victim; therefore it is a negative social event.

Historically, there was a tendency to place responsibility for victimization on the victim. During this time, there was still a strong emphasis on finding biological, rather than social, causes of criminal activity. Von Hentig (1948) asserted that there were 'born' victims just as there were 'born criminals' (Lombroso, 1899/1911). In describing victim precipitants von Hentig stated that 'these people were self destructive individuals who solicited the actions of their "predators".' (1948, p. 303). According to him, women and children were born victims, suggesting that there was something inherently weak about these population groups that 'naturally' made them victims.

Key to victim precipitation is assigning the victim an active rather than a passive role. Most other theories of criminality assign this role to the offender. Also implicit in this concept is the idea that the victim and the offender enter into their interaction as equals, both with the power to control the situation. Herein lies a paradox: victims are both 'prey' (i.e., powerless) and equal (i.e., powerful). Victim precipitation is evident in Marvin Wolfgang's study of homicides and in Menachem Amir's research on rape.

Marvin Wolfgang (1924–1998)

In 1994, Marvin Wolfgang was identified by *The British Journal of Criminology* as 'the most influential criminologist in the English-speaking world' (Adler, Mueller, & Laufer, 1998). His contribution to victimology is considered so significant that he was awarded the Hans von Hentig Award by the World Society of Victimology in 1988. Wolfgang was a prolific writer, and one of his seminal works, *Patterns in Criminal Homicide* (1958), looked at 588 homicides in Philadelphia that occurred between 1948 and 1952. One of the most interesting findings of this rigorous and extensive study was that in 26 per cent (N=150) of the sample the ultimate victim was sometimes

> the first in the homicide drama to use physical force directed against his subsequent slayer. The victim-precipitated are those in which the victim was the first to show and use a deadly weapon, to strike a blow in an altercation—in short, the first to commence

the interplay of resorting to physical violence. (1958, p. 252)

In other words the victim was also the initial aggressor, but because they were killed in the altercation they were defined as the victim. He came to call this phenomenon 'victim-precipitated homicide'. His study found that in this type of homicide the victim and the offender knew each other prior to the encounter and, in several cases, had had prior altercations. The killing was often the result of a small disagreement that evolved into something much more serious. The majority of the sub-sample were male-to-male confrontations; women murdered in reaction to suffering violence from a male (1958).

When compared to the non-victim-precipitated homicides in the study, victims of victim-precipitated homicides were more likely to have a previous arrest record (62 per cent versus 42 per cent) and to have used alcohol (69 per cent versus 47 per cent). Alcohol was thought to contribute to the altercation by reducing the inhibitions of the eventual victim so that he or she would be more likely to use aggression and/or by reducing the ability of the victim to defend him- or herself. The idea that a victim could somehow contribute to his or her own homicide became very attractive to other theorists. The most well-known criminologist to adapt Wolfgang's ideas was Menachem Amir.

Menachem Amir (b. 1930)

A student of Wolfgang, Israeli criminologist Menachem Amir extended the idea of victim precipitation to other crimes, particularly in his book *Patterns in Forcible Rape* (1971), which analyzed rape cases reported to the Philadelphia Police Department between 1958 and 1960. He defined victim-precipitated rapes as

> those rape situations in which the victim actually, or so it was deemed, agreed to sexual relations but retracted before the act or did not react strongly enough when the suggestion was made by the offender(s). The term applies also to cases in risky situations marred with sexuality, especially when she uses what could be interpreted as indecency in language and gestures, or constitutes what could be taken as an invitation to sexual relations. (1971, p. 266)

Only 19 per cent of the rapes documented in the study qualified under this broad definition of victim-precipitated rape. Most of the victims were relatively young, Caucasian females. When compared to the non-victim-precipitated rape cases they were more likely to have met their assailant in a bar or at a party.

Amir's definition acknowledges the importance of the offender's interpretation of events. In essence, he aligned his definition with legal terms that examined victim culpability. In other words, the actions and reactions of the offender take precedent over those of the victim. Amir argued that the emphasis of the offence was placed on whether the offender perceived precipitative behaviours of the victim, including provocative or seductive actions, and whether the offender was aware that the victim had a 'bad reputation' and/or engaged in 'risky behaviour'.

Although Wolfgang's initial work on victim precipitation was relatively well received, Amir's application of these ideas to victims of sexual assault was heavily criticized. Researchers have had little success in replicating his study using his definition of victim-precipitated rape (Silverman, 1973). The definition is so broad that inclusion or exclusion from the victim-precipitation group is highly subjective depending on who is using the definition. Robert A. Silverman even went so far as to conclude that the definition of victim precipitation does not really explain the victim–offender interaction outside the specific crime of homicide.

Weis and Borges (1973) assert that too much emphasis in Amir's work is placed on the interpretation of behaviour. They argue that it is often the case that a woman changes her mind about having sexual relations. We also know that some offenders have been told that a woman is 'easy' and that when she says 'No', she really means 'Yes'. Under these circumstances, 'the only ingredient necessary for constituting a victim precipitated rape is the offender's imagination' (p. 80).

One of the most vocal critics of Amir's work has been Laura J. Moriarty (2003). She claims that Wolfgang referred to a victim who precipitates his or her own homicide as being the one who initiates the violence or who uses violence in a volatile situation. The implication is that this person attempted to murder or assault an individual and was killed as a result of the attempt to do harm. This scenario is not found in Amir's study; the victim was not trying to rape someone before he or she was raped. Moriarty asserts that Amir misused the term and generalized it beyond its initial meaning. According to Amir, 'in a way, the victim is always the cause of crime' (1971, p.258). Moriarty states that even in his own work, using his definition of victim precipitation, Amir encapsulated less than one-fifth of the raped population. His generalizations greatly exceeded his available data.

Five Problems with Victim Precipitation

Helen Eigenberg (2003) has examined the issues surrounding victim precipitation to a considerable extent. By examining the work of von Hentig, Wolfgang, and others, she has become one of the foremost authorities on the subject. Eigenberg identifies five major problems with the concept of victim precipitation, or what she refers to as 'victim blaming'.

The first of these problems is that the victim's behaviour is never compared to that of non-victims. Therefore, the concept suffers from circular or tautological reasoning. Victim precipitation is identified only in light of victimization, but without victimization there is no precipitation. In other words, research has not revealed any other common precipitative factors other than being victimized and, as a result, victims are indistinguishable from non-victims. For example, most people are told never to get into a vehicle with a stranger, as doing so is a risk factor for victimization. However, people do it all the time. A case in point is a professor on a job interview who is met at a hotel or airport by a chaperone. The professor allows this person to escort him or her to various parts of the interview, to meals, back to the hotel, and so on. Despite the fact that the chaperone is a stranger, the professor simply trusts that he or she will not be harmed. If this is the case, the experience is considered normal. However, if the professor is harmed, then getting into the vehicle

was considered 'precipitative'. Another case involves dating. People meet potential mates throughout their daily activities. At some point one or the other of a potential couple asks the other on a date. If the date is completed without a negative event, it is considered a normal part of everyday life. If, on the other hand, one of the pair hurts the other, the date suddenly becomes 'precipitative', suggesting that somehow this date created a dangerous situation and that the victim should have known better. Hence, the argument is tautological.

Second, Eigenberg agrees with Karmen (1980) that the concept implies a form of continuum like the one in Figure 3.1. On one side we have the victim who is devoid of responsibility and on the other side the victim who is completely accountable for his or her own victimization. The idea of a 'totally innocent' victim, however, is problematic because most people—either looking at their own victimizations or that of others—can identify things that might have prevented the crime. The continuum also assumes that victims know how to prevent victimization but simply choose not to and that all potential victims can tell those who will commit crimes from those who will not.

Eigenberg also identifies a flaw on the other side of the continuum. Again, she concurs with Karmen (2007) that a truly innocent victim can exist only when there is no offender. As a result, victims become offenders who are posing as victims for some reason. This situation changes the dynamics of the continuum to one of blame. As illustrated in Figure 3.2, the focus is now on the offender and his or her responsibility in the victimizing process.

Figure 3.1   The Victim Precipitation Continuum

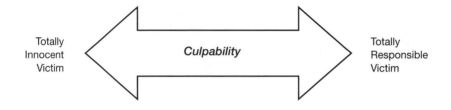

Totally
Innocent
Victim

Culpability

Totally
Responsible
Victim

Figure 3.2   The Blame Continuum

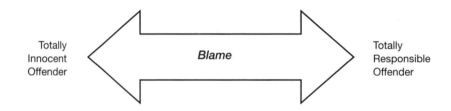

Totally
Innocent
Offender

Blame

Totally
Responsible
Offender

Eigenberg argues that those who seek to explain victimization and to categorize victim behaviour by building typologies are actually creating a model for assigning undue responsibility to the victim, her third criticism of the concept. If victims actually precipitate their own victimizations, then there is the implication that they can also control the victimization experience. However, the only true method of control that a potential victim can exercise is to lock him- or herself in a fortress and hide from all potential threats. Because we cannot possibly identify every person who might harm us, living in this way is not a reasonable means of control.

Fourth, if we set aside the other problems with victim precipitation and accept the idea that there are victims who can be blamed, we create culturally legitimate victims. Eigenberg uses arguments put forth by Ryan (1971), who asserts that victims must be different from non-victims in some physical or mental way that makes them more likely to be victimized. Therefore, to avoid victimization one must conform to the non-victim group. If one does not conform, one distinguishes oneself from the crowd and risks being targeted as a victim. If one chooses not to conform and is victimized, he or she is to blame. The victim becomes 'deserving' in some way.

There are several implications involved in legitimizing the victim. One is that those with more money and power tend to use fewer public resources. Using public resources can put those with less access to power and private resources at higher risk, as it is more difficult to get what they need at various stages of the victimization process. Looking at victim recovery, those who have more money and power are less likely to use public resources in the aftermath of their victimization. In other words, one group of people (those living closer to the poverty line) is more likely to be at higher risk for victimization because of the daily routines that can accompany a life with fewer resources. Because those with less power have less resources (e.g., money for lawyers, psychologists, personal protection, and so on) from which they can draw, one option that can be exercised is simply not to report victimization to the police, thereby bypassing many of the associated costs (emotional, financial, etc.) with this course of action.

For example, let's consider the risks involved in a resident of a public housing project with a high crime rate reporting a victimizing experience. This resident is well aware that the offender may be able to figure out who reported the crime. He or she also knows that a police officer will come to follow up on the report. All the resident's neighbours will probably notice that he or she is being visited by the police. Reporting the crime may lead to the resident being considered different (i.e., not conforming) from the rest of the community, drawing attention to him- or herself. Increased awareness of the resident's involvement with the police in such a neighbourhood may anger others (including the original offender) and may cause increased victimization in the form of retribution. The irony is that while reporting the crime could cause the resident to be fearful about being re-victimized as a form of retribution, not reporting it could also cause these feelings because the offender might consider him or her an easy target.

Lastly, Eigenberg posits that the concept of victim precipitation excuses the offender's behaviour. Common law supposes that if the victim is responsible for any part of his or her victimization, the offender should receive a reduced sentence. This assumption provides a cultural framework in which offenders can justify their victimizing behaviour. Statements by offenders that the victim 'had it coming' or assertions that they were obligated to act because the victim 'deserved it' are concerning because the language hints to a justification of harming another person.

In her study of how rapists rationalized their behaviours, Diana Scully (1990) found that the rapist often constructed culturally acceptable stereotypes about women to blame them for their own victimizations. This practice is evident in the following excerpts:

> A gang rapist: 'I am against hurting women. She should have resisted. None of us were the type of person that would use force on a woman. . . . I loved her—like all women.' (p. 129)

> A man who abducted a woman at knifepoint: 'To be honest, we [his family] knew she was a damn whore and whether she screwed 1 or 50 guys it did not matter.' (p. 180)

> A sexual sadist who reported that his victims physically 'enjoyed the sex [rape]. Once they got involved, it would be difficult to resist. I was always kind and gentle until I started to kill them.' (p.130)

The effects of these rationalizations are far-reaching and can go beyond the individual. They can be more collective and be created and accepted by courts, judges, and juries. As a result, prosecutors may not take cases where victims are vulnerable. Vulnerable victims, in turn, become systemically discriminated against by not being protected by the law in the same way as less vulnerable victims.

Considering that victim precipitation is so widely challenged by theorists, why do we continue to see situations where the victim is accused of having contributed to his or her own victimization? There is evidence that society is receptive to its basic assumptions. Victim precipitation strangely empowers us by asserting that we can control our environment and avoid victimization. If we accept the theory we do not have to answer difficult questions about offender motivation. With its focus on the individual, victim precipitation allows us to ignore the larger questions about the structural causes of inequality.

Victim Provocation, Victim Facilitation, and Victim Participation and/or Co-operation

In an effort to clarify some of the issues regarding victim precipitation, later victimologists have attempted to examine and apply specific parts of the concept. Drawing our attention to the crime of car theft, Andrew Karmen (1980) states that victims have a range of responsibility and involvement from total innocence to complete guilt. Victims in the former group take special precautions to prevent their cars from being stolen, while those in the latter make arrangements with criminals to have their cars stolen.

Between these two extremes are varying degrees of victim responsibility. These victims are negligent or careless, make mistakes, and exercise poor judgment. Those who carry a greater burden of responsibility actually wish their car to be stolen or conspire with others to have it taken. Karmen also makes the distinction between victims and those who are actually criminals engaging in fraudulent enterprises and only claiming to be victims in order to profit from insurance claims. Table 3.4 provides more detail regarding Karmen's typology of auto-theft victims.

What is interesting about this theory is that, despite the fact that his victim typology focuses on the individual offender and victim, Karmen notes that most of the auto thefts in his analysis were the result of organized crime. He openly acknowledges that fraudulent victims are peripheral to the typology. In many ways, this factor highlights a critique of continuum-based typologies. Continuums imply not only that that there is a wide range of behaviours but also that these behaviours are somewhat evenly distributed over the spectrum of behavioural possibility. Table 3.4 demonstrates that Karmen feels that the majority of victims (55 per cent) are totally innocent. Perhaps, then, it is the continuum's distribution of behaviours that creates the difficulty in interpreting these typologies.

More recently, there has been an effort to separate ways that victims may interact with their victimizers and to understand patterns within these relationships. Karmen (2007), in looking at different kinds of victims of auto theft, argues that there has been a concerted effort by automakers, insurance companies, and

Table 3.4   Karmen's Types of Auto-Theft Victims

Type of victim	Totally innocent	Largely innocent	Partly innocent	Substantially responsible	Largely responsible	Fully responsible
Actions of victim	Conscientious	Cautious	Careless	Initiator	Conspirator	Simulator
	Takes special precautions	Takes conventional measures	Facilitates theft through negligence	Precipitates theft by leaving car exposed and vulnerable	Provokes theft by arrangement with criminals	Fabricates theft of non-existent car
Motivations of victim	Seeks to minimize risks	Concerned about risks	Indifferent to risks	Wants car to be stolen	Determined to have car stolen	Seeks to make it look like car was stolen
Financial outcome after theft	Loses money	Loses money	Loses money	Gains money from victimization	Gains money from victimization	Makes large profit form alleged victimization
Approx. proportion of all victims	←——— 55% ———→		←— 20% —→		←——— 20% ———→	
Legal status	←——————— Actual victims ———————→				←— Criminals posing as victims, in order to commit insurance fraud —→	
Degree of attention	←— Overlooked —→		Object of public education campaigns, sometimes scapegoated		←— Object of investigations and new legislation —→	
Typical victimizer	Professional	Professional	Amateur	Amateur	Professional	None

SOURCE: Karmen, A. (1980). Auto theft: Beyond victim blaming. *Victimology: An International Journal, 5*, 161–74.

law enforcement agencies to find fault with the victims. These lobby groups are quite powerful and have a definite advantage in finding the auto-theft victim at least partially responsible for the victimization. If a victim is found to have participated in the theft, either willingly or through neglect, the automakers do not have to spend as much money to enhance theft prevention devices in their automobiles. Likewise, insurance companies have to make fewer payouts to victims and offenders can argue for lighter sentences.

Rather than consider all types of victim involvement as precipitation, Karmen establishes other forms of victim participation. He argues that a victim can contribute to his or her own victimization by creating a situation that is more likely to lead to a successful victimizing event; Karmen refers to this type of participation as **victim facilitation**. The potential victim can facilitate his or her victimization by being careless, negligent, or unaware, as well as by doing something by mistake or by accident. Again using the example of auto theft, Karmen (2007) illustrates several scenarios where the victim's actions may facilitate his or her victimization. For example, if a car owner leaves his or her keys somewhere (such as on his or her kitchen table) where they can be easily taken by someone (such as friends of his or her children) to use the car for a 'joy ride', the car owner could be said to have facilitated the crime by not putting the keys in a safer place. Although Karmen advises that facilitation is not a cause of crime, he does state that it certainly acts as a catalyst to opportunistic thieves who are looking for an easy way to carry out their crimes.

In Karmen's typology, victims can precipitate their own victimizations if they were thought to significantly contribute to the actions carried out against them. If they used poor judgment or acted in what could be interpreted as an excessively risky or self-destructive manner, they are said to have precipitated the victimizations. The underlying assumption here, as with other theories regarding victim precipitation, is that victims seem to either consciously or unconsciously want to receive harm and act in ways that will bring this about.

According to Karmen (2007), victims can also provoke their attackers. **Victim provocation** occurs when a victim either instigates or incites the violence committed against him or her by acting in confrontational ways. Examples of provocative behaviour are name-calling, taunting, instigating physical violence against another person, and so on. The theory behind this type is that these acts encourage an otherwise non-victimizer to break the law and lash out against the victim.

Additionally, there are those victims who actually co-operate with the offender. Traditionally, when we think of the term **victim co-operation**, we think of how willing the victim is to work with the authorities to identify and prosecute the offender. However, in victimology terms, this type is in many ways a co-conspirator with the offender. This victim works with the victimizer to bring about a mutual reward. An example of such a victim is an individual who agrees to be in a car accident in order to collect the insurance money, which he or she shares with the other party. In this case the person is an accident victim, but he or she also aids in designing the victimization event as part of a larger criminal enterprise. Therefore, many would argue that this person is not, in fact, a victim but a victimizer and that it is the insurance company that has been victimized.

Another form of victim participation is **victim compliance**. This type of victim complies with the demands of the victimizer in order to protect him- or herself or another who has been threatened. For example, if a carjacker demands that a person leave his or her vehicle and hand over his or her keys, this victim is urged to comply with those demands to reduce the potential for further victimization. A similar response may occur if the carjacker demands the victim's car and threatens to hurt the victim or another person. The victim may act out of compassion, even though he or she might not be threatened with personal harm. Although this victim is abiding by the offender's demands, he or she is also operating to reduce further damage and is therefore not considered responsible for the victimization.

Criticisms of the New Terms

Karmen (2007) notes that as we move from victim facilitator to victim provocateur the application of these terms seems to change. Although there is no prescribed way in which these types should be assigned, they create an interesting pattern. For example, facilitation tends to be used with relatively minor crimes, such as car theft, while provocation is often used to describe those who use force against the victim, such as in cases of robbery, physical assault, sexual assault, and homicide. The fact that the types are not applied equally to all categories suggests that there is bias in their application to various groups.

It can be difficult to see how these new terms address Eigenberg's (2003) criticism of the original concept. The terms continue to suffer from circular reasoning, in that the only distinguishing feature between victims and non-victims is the experience of victimization. In the case of victim facilitation, it is unreasonable to expect people to take every single precaution in every aspect of their lives. Although we may acknowledge that it is important to keep car keys in a safe location, most people assume that their houses are secure and that they do not have to be vigilant when at home. The idea that people should be aware of any potential for criminal behaviour in their environments at all times and should conform to official and/or unofficial modes of behaviour is problematic, as is the notion all people can control what happens to them by simply engaging in self-protective behaviours. People are not machines. Are we ready to say that people who are distracted, tired, and so on 'deserve' what is coming to them and should know better? Suggesting that victims are somehow to blame is a dangerous precedent to pursue. This type of thinking can lead to legitimizing victims and to downplaying the role of the victimizer as a motivated offender.

The various forms of victim participation also do not rectify the problems concerning the idea of the fully responsible victim. Is it possible to provoke someone to the point where he or she has no responsibility for their actions? This scenario is understandable in cases of justifiable homicide, where the victim was originally an offender threatening the lives of others and was killed after all other alternatives were exhausted. But what about other offences? Can a sexual assault victim provoke his or her attacker to the point of justifiable rape? Most individuals would say no. As a result, the conceptual issues persist.

Summary

As the discussion in this chapter shows, the concepts developed to explain the role of the victim in criminal acts are complex. The typologies of early theorists such as von Hentig and Mendelsohn drew attention to the victim, but they also led to the idea of victim precipitation, which assigns a degree of responsibility to the victim for his or her own victimization. Later victimologists have attempted to apply the theory in more practical ways; however, the underlying problems remain.

Although we understand that the offender does not exist in a social vacuum, we must be careful about the kinds of assumptions we make about how the victim operates and the connections we make between his or her actions and his or her culpability. Common law states that we must consider what is reasonable behaviour on the part of both the offender and the victim. Is it reasonable to expect people to be all-knowing about crime prevention techniques or to view all others as potential offenders? Assigning blame to a victim also ignores the broader social issues that need to be addressed in order to understand the victim–offender relationship and to prevent further crime. Victim precipitation does not ask why the victim is being victimized, why the offender is being excused for his or her actions, or why a particular behaviour is considered dangerous or non-conforming.

In the next chapter, we will move beyond typologies to theoretical explanations of victim behaviour. These theories, most of which originated in criminology, serve to examine the cause of victimization rather than to simply categorize victims.

Glossary

compliant victim A victim who complies with the demands of the victimizer in order to protect him- or herself or another who has been threatened. This type of victim is assumed innocent.

criminal One who commits a crime.

criminality Behaviours associated with law violation.

penal couple The relationship between the victim and the offender.

victimal Coined in 1963 by Beniamin Mendelsohn, a term that means the opposite of the word 'criminal'. As an adjective it is used to describe the behaviour of a victim (e.g., victimal conduct).

victimal receptivity An individual's unconscious propensity to being victimized, which exists in varying degrees.

victim blaming The process of assigning some level of responsibility to the victim for his or her own victimization.

victim facilitation The concept whereby a victim is said to create circumstances, through neglect or carelessness, that increase his or her potential for victimization.

victimity According to Beniamin Mendelsohn, the opposite of criminality. Victimity refers to the quality or state of being a victim or that which constitutes being a victim.

victim precipitation Also sometimes referred to as victim blaming or victim facilitation, the idea of shared responsibility in victimization between the offender and the victim. Behaviours that can be interpreted as contributing to victim precipitation are those actions that bring about, in whole or in part, a person's victimization.

victim provocation The notion that the victim has incited or instigated his or her own victimization.

victim responsibility The idea that there is a level of shared participation and culpability between the victim and the offender in the victimizing event.

victim vulnerability The risk of victimization that is attributed to an individual or group.

Critical Thinking Questions

1. What are some of the advantages to creating a victim typology? What are some of the disadvantages?
2. If an individual is assaulted while jogging at night, should he or she be held somewhat responsible for the crime? Should the offender be granted leniency by the courts? Give reasons for your answers.
3. In the context of the victim role, what is the difference between facilitation, precipitation, and provocation?
4. Do you think the argument that some people have a propensity to victimization is valid? Why or why not?

Criminological Theories and the Victim

Introduction

In the previous chapter we looked at some of the early thinking regarding the role of victims, particularly how it developed into typologies of victims and the victim–offender relationship. Although typologies serve to categorize behaviour, they are not considered fully developed theories of victim behaviour. These typologies have affected some more recent ideas about the role of the victim, which we will examine in this chapter through various theoretical lenses originating in the discipline of criminology. We will focus on the predominant theories of the last half of the twentieth century, beginning with the criminal event perspective and moving to the following groups of theories, which contain the strongest statements about victim behaviour: rational choice theories, feminist perspectives, critical perspectives, and labelling/social reaction theories. Many of these concepts assume that the criminal and, by default, the victim are rational

people who make choices that may affect their chances of being involved in a victimizing event. Others, such as feminist, critical, and labelling theories, see victims as more passive and more strongly influenced by larger social actions than by those in their individual day-to-day lives.

The Criminal Event Perspective

Unlike a theory, the **criminal event perspective** shapes the outlook of individuals seeking to explain criminal behaviour. It is not an explanation, per se, but a way of looking at crime and victimization that helps us to understand how theories interplay. Vince Sacco at Queen's University and Leslie Kennedy while working at the University of Alberta (1998) put forth the criminal event perspective in order to encourage people to look at crime in a larger social context. They noticed that there was little in the way of an organizing framework in which to place theories. In essence, theories are like looking at a problem through various lenses or windows. Although some theories seek to understand the act of crime by the offender, there are others that look at wider social contexts, such as the influence of gender on criminal offending and victimization. Still others are interested in what happened to the offender before the criminal act, as a means of examining preventative measures, and some examine the victims of crime. Each view gives a different formulation of the situation. The criminal event perspective seeks to rectify this problem by asserting that a criminal event is like any other event, albeit with a criminal outcome. By using this event framework, we can place theories in accordance to what phenomenon they are trying to explain in time and what players are involved.

According to this perspective, participants in the criminal event include the offender, the victim, and any public reaction that may occur either directly through witnessing the event or indirectly through other means. The criminal event can be broken into three stages. **Criminal precursors** include all factors that lead up to the event for all participants. The **criminal transaction**, or the actual victimizing activity, is relatively short in comparison to the other stages of the event, often lasting less than five minutes. The **aftermath of crime** includes all events that happen to the participants after the victimization has taken place.

Criminal Event Perspective: Underlying Assumptions about the Victim

In the criminal event perspective, the victim is a rational being and an active participant in the criminal event, as are the offender and any witnesses. This viewpoint considers the transaction to be dynamic, where all participants are influenced by their previous experiences. Likewise, all participants will deal with the aftermath of the event in different ways, depending on what resources have been and are provided to them. This perspective acknowledges that most efforts to explain crime have focused on the criminal, with less attention paid to the victim and even less on any public reaction to criminal events. However, it still maintains this offender focus while placing the act of victimization in context. Note that the perspective is called 'the criminal event' and not 'the victimizing event'.

By considering the victim to be rational and active, the criminal event perspective assumes victim responsibility, thereby creating the risk of victim blaming. Those who study crime are often interested in the person before he or she was a criminal or a victim. They want to know the precursory variables, what happened to the parties before the criminal event. In this perspective, precursory factors to any victimizing event may protect or promote victimization. This theory, then, encourages protective acts such as target hardening for victims (see page 55), as well as other security measures. The criminal event perspective works well with rational choice theories in that it shares some of the same assumptions regarding the victim's nature and also fails to offer explanations as to why crime patterns occur in the way that they do.

Rational Choice Theories: The Transaction

Developed in the 1970s, **rational choice theories**, like the criminal event perspective, see the victim as a rational participant in the criminal event and as active in his or her life. These theories—lifestyles, routine activities, deterrence, rational choice perspective, and situated transaction—also predominantly focus on what happens just immediately before and during the criminal event, or transaction, and why these events occur. The basic tenants and assumptions of these five theories are described below.

Lifestyles Theory

Developed by Michael J. Hindelang, Michael R. Gottfredson, and James Garofalo (1978, pp. 251–64), **lifestyles theory** posits that certain behavioural patterns create an opportunistic structure for criminals. The most common examples of victimization risk being affected by lifestyle choices are those surrounding activities in taverns and bars. After analyzing an early victimization survey, the authors came to recognize patterns. For example, people who frequent bars and consume alcohol tend to be at these locations at night. People who choose to engage in any or all of these activities also substantially increase their risk for victimization. After looking at problems of victimization, the authors drew the following eight conclusions about the nature of patterning victimization behaviour:

1. The more time that individuals spend in public places (especially at night), the more likely they are to be victimized.
2. Following certain lifestyles makes individuals more likely to frequent public places.
3. The interactions that individuals maintain tend to be with persons who share their lifestyles.
4. The probability that individuals will be victims increases according to the extent to which victims and offenders belong to the same demographic categories.
5. The proportion of time individuals spend in places where there is a large number of non-family members varies according to lifestyle.
6. The chances of individuals being the victims of a crime (particularly theft) increase in conjunction with the amount of time they spend among non-family members.
7. Differences in lifestyles relate to the ability of individuals to isolate themselves from those with offender characteristics.
8. Variations in lifestyles influence the convenience, desirability, and ease of victimizing individuals.

Lifestyles Theory: Underlying Assumptions for the Victim

Lifestyles theory suggests that patterning our lives to the point of creating regular routines can place us at risk for victimization. Furthermore, in Hindelang, Gottfredson, and Garofalo's study, routines that involve the regular consumption of alcohol increase our chance for victimization. Given that the majority of victimizations are carried out by non-family members, these conclusions suggest that the more we are in large public settings and in contact with non-family members who are in our own age group the greater our risk for victimization.

Likewise, the theory suggests that those who do not engage in these specific lifestyle choices reduce their risk of victimization and that a lifestyle patterned upon staying home and engaging in activities without alcohol is protective. While this idea addresses large and aggregate patterns of how and when people are victimized, it may not be true for all groups of people. It does not explain, for example, why patterns of victimization differ between men and women. Women are more likely than men to be the victims of the most severe forms of spousal assault, as well as spousal homicide, sexual assault, and criminal harassment (e.g., stalking; Johnson, 2006). Therefore, lifestyle theory stands as a better explanation of male victimization patterns.

Routine Activities Theory

Another theory that looks at the role of the victim is **routine activities theory (RAT)**. Developed by Lawrence Cohen and Marcus Felson (1979), RAT posits that three elements must be present in order for a criminal event to occur: a motivated offender, a suitable target, and a lack of capable guardianship. If one or more of these elements are missing, a crime will not occur. While the theory does say that the offender must be motivated to offend, the specific motivation is not important. The theory requires only that motivation be present. Offenders cannot offend without a suitable target such as a location or a potential victim. Where there is a suitable victim but also a form of guardianship serving as a protective force, the potential victim becomes less attractive as a target. Protection from a guardian can take several forms. Essentially, guardianship is any person, thing, or activity—including dogs, security cameras, walking with others, etc.— that serves to make the potential victim less suitable and to reduce the risk posed by a potential offender.

Routine Activities Theory: Underlying Assumptions about the Victim

In this theory, it is assumed that people must engage in a process called **target hardening** to protect against victimization. In this process, a potential victim is educated, or 'hardened', about how offenders operate. He or she is encouraged to take protective measures against victimization by several means, such as those mentioned above or carrying a weapon, dressing in a way that enhances escape from a potential offender (e.g.,, wearing running shoes instead of shoes that may hinder escape), and so on. By being proactive, victims become less suitable targets to offenders.

The expectation of target hardening and the perception of the victim and the offender as being active and rational participants in the criminal event place the onus for the victimization on both parties. Focusing on the victim, he or she can lessen the offender's motivation by being less of a suitable target. A victim who does not educate him- or herself in the methods of becoming less suitable or who chooses not to engage in 'hardening' processes is implied to be partly responsible for his or her own victimization. This claim ignores the power dynamic between a victim and an offender and assumes equality between all three parties: the victim, offender, and guardian. Therefore, we must be careful how we use this theory to explain victimization.

Deterrence Theory

The idea that people can be deterred from crime has been around for a long time. In its most rudimentary form, punishment is assumed to deter crime. A good example of how punishment was meted out during the Dark Ages is found on the first pages of Michel Foucault's *Discipline and Punish* (1977), where he recounts a case of drawing and quartering. A man is being pulled in opposing directions by horses while being burned with hot pokers and having salt rubbed in his wounds. The idea was that a person who had committed a crime should suffer as part of their punishment, even if he or she were sentenced to death. In this way, if the accused lived, it was assumed that he or she would be deterred or disabled from committing another crime. These punishments were also often carried out in public, with the idea that observing the suffering of the criminal would deter others from committing similar acts of violation. The punishment was usually excessive and inflicted upon the lower classes by the nobility, who were often able to avoid such forms of social justice.

The refinement of the use of punishment for deterrence purposes is originally associated with eighteenth-century English philosopher Jeremy Bentham (1789). In addition to being one of the first to advocate for incarceration as a form of punishment, Bentham felt that punishment was a negative tactic that could reverse the effects of deterrence. Therefore, it should be used sparingly and only when other options have been exhausted. When it is used, the pain inflicted should be in direct proportion to the pain that the victimizer caused. In essence, it was paramount that the punishment fit the crime. Bentham eventually made elaborate calculations on the application of punishment. He felt that it was important to be precise with punishment, basing the amount of punishment or pain inflicted to be a specific deterrent on the pleasure that was gained when the victimizer committed the offence.

Deterrence theory claims that while many people have compulsive thoughts of doing harm, the fear of punishment keeps all but a few from acting on these thoughts. Again, this theory considers people as rational beings who are active in controlling their behaviour. Deterrence theory points to two forms of prevention that work upon the conscience of offending individuals as well as others who may witness or hear of the punishment carried out on the guilty. **Specific deterrence** occurs when an individual is directly punished for his or her deviant behaviour. If this form of deterrence is successful, the individual will cease the offending behaviour for fear of further punishment. **General deterrence** occurs when other individuals learn of someone being punished and, as a result, are dissuaded from participating in deviant acts for fear that they may also be punished. These individuals do not directly experience punishment, but they fear the potential of punishment.

This theory also states that there are three components to administering punishment that make it most effective in terms of achieving deterrence. The first element is the speed at which the punishment is administered, or the **celerity of punishment**. The criminal should be punished in close temporal proximity to when the crime was committed, and/or soon after the criminal is apprehended. If delayed significantly, the punishment loses its deterring strength. Second, there should be a **certainty of punishment**. That is, when an act of **deviance**—an act that is considered outside a prescribed set of cultural norms—is committed, punishment should consistently follow; inconsistency may serve as a weak deterrent to committing future deviance. Finally, **severity of punishment** must be appropriate. Too much or too little punishment can weaken the effect on deterring the individual from future deviance.

Deterrence Theory: Underlying Assumptions about the Victim

This theory assumes that deterrence is key to reducing the expression of victimizing activity, specifically in relation to the victimizer. However, acts of deterrence also have a protective effect for potential victims. Victims, under this theory, are active and are acted upon by victimizers. This theory assumes that all people are rational, weighing pain against the idea of pleasure. Therefore, it stands to follow that potential victims can also be deterred from engaging in deviance. We assume that potential victims also make choices. One of these choices could be to conform to social norms, thereby not drawing unwanted attention to themselves, discouraging deviance, and insulating themselves against victimization. Potential victims who make preventative choices are deterred from taking risks that may put them in harm's way. In this scenario, it is the potential victimizer who exacts punishment in the form of criminal victimization, inflicting specific deterrent effects on the future behaviour of the potential victim. Further, other potential victims, having either witnessed or heard about the victimization, may be deterred more generally from engaging in similar risks.

While this theory was not intended to explain victim behaviour, its assumptions make it useful in studying the rational processes and deterrent effects of victimization for both the victim and the offender. At the same time, deterrence theory should be used with caution because, like other rational choice theories, it implies that the victim holds some degree of control over his or her own victimization. Again, it ignores other factors, such as social and physical inequalities that may also affect the outcome of the event. This theory also presents a false sense of security in the idea of conformity as a protective measure against victimization.

Rational Choice Perspective

Widely associated with Derek Cornish and Ronald Clarke (1986), both of the London School of Economics, **rational choice perspective** seeks to explain the victimizer's motivation and decision-making process. This perspective considers the offender to be a rational and active person who makes choices based on the presence or absence of potential gain and the cost of committing the crime. In other words, crime is the result of rational thinking in the offender's mind. This idea, however, does not mean that the offender's choices are completely rational but that victimizing behaviour is the process of successful rationalization based on the offender weighing the pros and cons of committing crime.

Rational Choice Perspective: Underlying Assumptions about the Victim

According to this perspective, victims come along in the form of opportunities to be taken advantage of. Although not explicitly stated, the perspective assumes that all people are rational, not just those who are potential victimizers. Like routine activities theory, rational choice perspective includes a suitability factor, in the sense that victims give off cues that may attract or repel a potential predator. While victims are also rational and make choices in a similar way to offenders, they are assumed to be weighing the risk of victimization in everyday activities rather than focusing on an offence. Victims also weigh the potential gains and losses in engaging in risky behaviour.

For example, a victimizer may wander into a park looking for a potential victim. He or she scans the park for someone who looks like an easy target and who does not pose a threat, perhaps someone who is smaller than him- or herself, someone who is in an isolated part of the park, someone who is elderly, and so on. At the same time, the potential victims (those using the park for legitimate purposes) evaluate the risk of being in a public place and make choices about their behaviour and activities. Again, the decisions of both parties do not have to be fully rational but are the result of this cognitive weighing process.

Situated Transaction Theory

The term 'situated transaction' was originally coined by sociologist Erving Goffman (1963) to refer to a process of interaction between two or more individuals. **Situated transaction theory** was developed by David Luckenbill (1977) and seeks to locate crime in time and place. Luckenbill studied 70 transactions involving 71 homicides (one was a double murder) randomly selected from all homicides occurring in a medium-sized California county between 1963 and 1972. In this study, he noted that 'participants interact in a common physical territory. (1977, p. 196). Because participants interact in close proximity within a common territory, people interact in a variety of ways. In some cases, the outcome may not be a positive experience. In the criminal situated transaction, the roles of the victim and offender are not predetermined. The outcome is determined by action and reaction, in an exchange. The interactions that Luckenbill studied tended to have a specific pattern: in a surprising number of cases the eventual victim was, ironically, the first to initiate action in the altercation. He also noted that the victim and the offender were often known to each other and that the homicide took place in an informal setting.

Before any altercation, according to the theory, both participants have the potential to be either a victim or an offender. The roles are defined by the outcome. Luckenbill identified six stages of the situated transaction where a homicide was the end result:

1. The eventual victim insults the honour of the eventual offender. This affront to 'face' is usually in the form of an unprovoked verbal communication or a physical gesture.
2. The eventual offender finds the affront offensive. At this point, the offender has two choices: he or she can ignore the offensive behaviour and stop the situated transaction or he or she can react.
3. The eventual offender reacts to 'save face' or protect honour. This reaction can be in the form of verbal or physical threats.
4. The eventual victim responds aggressively suggesting a violent resolution. During this stage, onlookers may verbally or physically promote violence by yelling words of encouragement and/or physically blocking exits. In this way, the offender and the victim can become committed to the altercation by the actions of those surrounding them.
5. The two parties enter a physical interchange and the victim is killed. This stage lasts a very short time and the actions are precise: the eventual victim is stabbed, shot, or otherwise fatally injured.

6. The offender either remains with the victim, is prevented from leaving by witnesses, or flees the scene of the crime.

Situated transaction theory draws heavily on symbolic interactionism, which developed out of the Chicago School and the work of several theorists. According to sociologist Herbert Blumer (1969), major contributors to this school of thought included George Herbert Mead (1934), Clifford Shaw (1930), W.I. Thomas (Thomas & Znaniecki, 1918), and Frederick M. Thrasher (1927). **Symbolic interactionism** asserts that human interaction is based solely on the interpretation of symbols, such as language and behaviour, communicated between individuals. Symbols are not inherently good or deviant but are subject to interpretation, which depends on culturally prescribed norms and the social environment in which the transaction occurs. These symbols can be misunderstood between individuals; both correct and incorrect interpretations can result in conflict. Once we have interpreted the symbols, we react to them in prescribed ways, fulfilling roles that are expected of us in specific situations. For example, one of the most powerful symbol systems humans have is the ability to communicate with language. When we communicate, we use a series of symbols arranged in a particular order and often in a particular intonation which conveys meaning to others. When we hear words we formulate meaning in them and then react with more communication symbols. If we find the language offensive, we respond in kind, leave the situation, or react in another manner.

Situated Transaction Theory: Underlying Assumptions about the Victim

In situated transaction theory, individuals use behaviour and language that is interpreted as threatening. Interestingly, Luckenbill noted that it is the victim who often initiates the disagreement and that it is the eventual offender's understanding of those actions which leads to the initiator's eventual downfall. Once the situation has been interpreted, both the offender and the victim engage in socially prescribed ways to resolve the altercation, with the offender eventually using lethal violence. The fact that many of these altercations have such similar event structures, adhering to these six stages of interaction, is evidence for these role expectations in the situation transaction. The participants' interpretation of the actions, along with expectations about specific ways in which to respond to these actions, suggests that there are powerful common ideas about how one is to respond to certain types of interaction.

A product of its time, this theory addresses male-to-male violence, ignoring other types. Again, male victims are often victimized by an acquaintance in a public location, usually as the result of a disagreement. However, incidents of **uxoricide** (a man's killing of his wife) often do not follow these patterns. Trends in spousal abuse suggest that before the victim is killed, there is a long history of abuse, often lasting for hours at a time. In essence, there is a series of situated transactions that do not result in homicide but which eventually escalate and culminate in the wife's death. This term is often confused with **mariticide**, which is the killing of either spouse by the other. Therefore, although this theory may explain the patterns of lethal violence between males, it does little to clarify other forms of victimization.

Criticisms of Rational Choice Theories

This set of theories is reminiscent of the 'hunter and the hunted' model of thinking. Victimizers are the predators to be dissuaded, while non-victimizers serve, to varying degrees, as potential prey. These concepts assume the main principle of social Darwinism, a term first coined by Herbert Spencer (1864/1900). **Social Darwinism**, like Charles Darwin's theory of evolution, suggests that the dominating assumption about social interaction is that of 'survival of the fittest'. In other words, it is believed that society consists of those who are stronger and therefore will survive and those who are weaker and therefore will be preyed upon by the strong. If we extrapolate this idea to victimization, social Darwinism assumes that preying on those who are weak is justified because it is necessary to 'cull the herd', to weed out the weak so that society can continue to grow and become stronger.

Although rational choice theories are popular with criminal justice and law enforcement officials, they are considered to be very conservative and should be applied with extreme caution. These theories serve to maintain the status quo and do not question why certain groups of people are more likely than others to be victimized in a particular way. By assigning responsibility to the victim for his or her actions in a criminal event, those who use these theories run the risk of blaming the victim and ignoring the power dynamic between the victim and the victimizer. More critical

approaches, such as feminist theories, address these concerns.

Feminist/Critical Criminology

Both feminist and critical criminologists argue that any discussion of victimization (i.e., criminal behaviour) is not complete without considering the effects of power dynamics. At the risk of oversimplifying these very complex theoretical frameworks, both seek to reinsert the role of power dynamics into the victim–victimizer interaction. For feminist criminologists, this power is rooted in patriarchal (male-dominated), hegemonic (ideological) structures. Males, particularly Caucasians, have traditionally been privileged within society; white, male, heterosexual, middle- and upper-class ideologies permeate our economic, social, and legal systems. These systems, in turn, seek to undermine women and minorities, giving them unequal disadvantage in the interactions with those systems. In terms of victimology, **feminist perspectives** attempt to reveal the gendered patterns of crime and victimization, as well as the lack of explanations of these experiences in traditional male-dominated criminological thinking.

Critical criminologists also acknowledge the role of power but assert that it can come from many sources. Although they include in their theories the effects of patriarchy on women, they argue that such consequences extend beyond gender and involve many different minority groups. Critical criminologists note that there are different patterns of victimization depending on the victim's class, race, or gender. The existence of these various patterns within a patriarchal system suggests that there is bias in this system. Those who do not favour the values established and promoted by the elite, which reinforce the status quo, become subordinated in such a system. Minorities become targeted as victims of 'hate crimes', where they are selected because of their gender, sexual, and/or racial difference and are victimized because of this difference. When applied to victimology, **critical perspectives** investigate the role of power in its various forms and its influence on crime patterns, differential experiences of crime and victimization, as well as the social responses to victimization and victimological thinking.

In both feminist and critical theories, crimes against women and minorities are the result of the reinforcement of power and dominance over these groups. For example, women are sexually assaulted to reinforce the dominance of men over women, making women fearful and thereby reducing their participation in the public, male-dominated world. Both perspectives regard theories that do not address power and its manifestations in the form of victimization as ideas that reinforce the status quo and the privileges of those in power.

Rational choice theories acknowledge the role of the victim and see the criminal act as a social interaction. All five theories, however—whether accidentally or intentionally—seek to blame the victim. Where it is acknowledged that there is a role for the victim to play, responsibility of that role also seems to be highlighted. This situation becomes especially clear when we look at victimization patterns within minority groups, such as women, Aboriginal peoples, and others.

For example, Leonard (1982) acknowledged that gender, albeit one of the strongest influences on crime patterning, largely remains unexplored in traditional criminological theories. Women are significantly less likely to be offenders but significantly more likely to be victims of crime. They are the majority of victims in spousal homicides, and they are more likely to be victims of intimate partner violence. Rational choice theories imply that, as victims, these women made rational choices that lead to their victimization. These theories ignore the social context in which minorities, such as women, live. By excluding such elements, they run the risk of blaming victims for something that they can do nothing about. A woman might be able to avoid certain situations that increase her chances of being victimized; however, she cannot change the fact that members of her gender are more likely to be victims of certain crimes.

In particular, feminist and critical criminologists (Klein, 1973) have taken issue with the victim-blaming nature of many of the neo-classical traditions in criminological theory. They assert that these theories do not include the role of power in their construction. They also point out that no one questions the ontological assumptions put forth by victim blaming. These more traditional theories expect women and others at increased risk of victimization to be vigilant about keeping out of harm's way and, if they cannot do this, to be able to defend themselves from potential attackers. To be less than constantly alert and prepared is to be blameworthy. However, as feminist and critical criminologists state, this expectation places an unequal form of restriction and monitoring on the more powerless groups in society. By monitoring the powerless (i.e., potential victims) and granting freedom to those with power (i.e., victimizers), the latter group continues to assume dominance. Status quo is maintained and the powerless are subjected to the tyranny of the powerful majority.

A good example of how these ideas can be used to hurt minority groups is Menachem Amir's work on rape, discussed in Chapter 3. The idea that a woman could participate in her own sexual assault has been used at countless trials to suggest that the victim brought about her own victimization by dressing scantily, by acting provocatively, etc. In other words, the woman's choices and actions led to her rape. However, such a claim does not recognize that men are also perfectly capable of making choices. Instead, it suggests that men are both the leaders of nations and slaves to their uncontrollable bodies. Ultimately, positing men as simultaneously powerful and powerless is flawed logic. Either men can choose to control their behaviour or they cannot.

Feminist/Critical Criminology: Underlying Assumptions about the Victim

Feminist and critical theories generally see the victim as more of a product of social forces than that of his or her individual decision-making. In this sense, they take the opposite stance of rational choice theories and assign victims a more passive role. This theoretical group also questions the assumption that people are equal and instead contends that those in power seek to maintain an imbalance by continuing to disempower others. Feminist theories argue that this imbalance is predominantly based on gender. Women have less power than men and, as

such, are more likely to be victimized by men than men are to be by women. The victimization of women by men serves to perpetuate the disparity and is echoed in the male-dominated criminal justice system, which has only recently passed legislation regarding spousal violence. Critical criminologists extend this imbalance to include other characteristics, such as race and socioeconomic status. For example, minorities and poor people are subject to particular types of victimization. This victimization, and the lack of understanding by the criminal justice system, serves to enable inequality between races, classes, and other social groups.

Social Reaction Theories: The Aftermath

Of increasing interest to victimologists are **social reaction theories**, which examine a victim's behaviour in response to his or her environment. Initially these theories were developed to explain deviance, but they have since been used to explain a variety of reactions to a person being identified as part of a particular group, including that of victim. This practice is not intended to identify victims as deviant but rather to acknowledge that being a victim is considered outside the norm, even though statistics show that most of us have experienced at least one form of victimization in our lifetime. When applied to victimology, this concept attempts to explain how people come to accept or reject being identified as a victim.

Symbolic Interactionist Theory

Starting at the turn of the twentieth century, early theorists eventually identified as symbolic interactionists began writing about the importance of perception of oneself and others in the development of the self. As discussed on page 59, symbolic interactionists understand human interaction and socialization as the result of meanings that society attaches to certain symbols, behaviours, gestures, and so on. One of the concepts that emerged from symbolic interactionism was **social interactionist theory**, founded by the Chicago School's Charles Horton Cooley and George Herbert Mead in the early part of the twentieth century. Cooley (1902) asserted that individuals possess a 'looking glass self' whereby they create judgments of themselves based on others' observations. In other words, people create an identity in relation to how others perceive them. Although the reactions of others directly affect us when we are young, we internalize these 'others' in our minds as we get older, anticipating how people might respond if we were to behave in certain ways. In doing so, we eventually come to monitor and regulate our own behaviour in anticipation of how others will view us.

During the 1920s, Mead (1913, 1934) elaborated and reflected on Cooley's ideas, developing a theory of what he called the 'socialized self', which was comprised of the unrestrained and spontaneous self ('I') and the more restrained self ('me') which was concerned with the outward appearance of the self. The 'me' part of the self serves to store the rules of social interactions and experiences of past interactions. It is the part of the self that provides social guidance of what is considered to be socially appropriate behaviour. The 'I', however, is less predictable and acts solely on behalf of the self. It allows the self to be active but not solely determined by the rules and norms of social interaction. The 'me' absorbs cultural norms and values and becomes the social self, while the 'I' reacts to these interactions with the world. One never knows how the 'I' will interact with the world until after it has done so.

In 1938, Frank Tannenbaum was one of the first theorists in this school to introduce the idea that people could be 'tagged' by others as members of a group. Although he was specifically looking to explain the identification and subsequent behaviour of delinquents by mainstream society, his ideas can explain a variety of reactions to various group members. He argued that being tagged as a delinquent often led to further delinquency. This is not to say that being labelled a victim would lead to further voluntary victimization but that being identified as a victim carries with it certain assumptions and **stigma**—characteristics that can lead to disgrace, embarrassment, and/or reproach—that can alter how one is viewed by others. Statistics show that one of the best predictors of becoming a victim of a crime is previous victimization. Therefore, according to this theory, victims may be 'tagged' in some way that possibly leads to a social reaction that changes the way they interact within their social environment.

Labelling Theory

In 1951, Edwin Lemert penned what many acknowledge as the first version of **labelling theory**. In essence, Lemert was interested in how the deviant identity is formed out of the reaction of others to the actor. The first to write about the process of becoming deviant, Lemert noted that simply participating in a deviant act did not necessarily force an individual into a deviant identity. This initial participation in an act considered 'outside the norm' and identified by an authority figure as such was called **primary deviance**. This label remains primary as long as the individual identified can manage the identity but does not accept the label. Once the label of deviance or 'otherness' has been accepted and the actor engages in the social world as a deviant, he or she is engaging in **secondary deviance**. Although this theory was initially meant to explain how criminals are labelled and how they react as a result, the process can be used to understand any labelling process. In victimology, some individuals who have been victimized may reject the label as victim for a number of reasons. They may rationalize the victimizing event as a bad experience but refuse to accept any victim role. Others, however, may willingly or unwillingly adopt and even embrace the victim identity, proceeding to engage in the social world with this supplemented identity. For example, a person may adopt the role of victim in order to gain sympathy from friends, family, and officers of the court as he or she goes through the criminal justice system.

Most commonly associated with the ideas of labelling is sociologist Howard Becker (1963). In his classic book, *Outsiders*, Becker argues that those who are labelled deviant or 'other' by those in power can eventually come to see themselves as different from mainstream society. Labelled actors come to see themselves as outsiders, feeling marginalized from the rest of society. In particular Becker emphasizes that it is the process of becoming an outsider, characterized by a drift from primary to secondary deviance, which is crucial to understanding the labelled identity.

Although the first transgression of norms may be accidental or deliberate, Becker argues that it is the labelling of the actor that is most important in primary deviance. How the label is accommodated and the power of the labeller are key in understanding how people engage in secondary deviance.

For example, let us look at the hypothetical case of 'Steve', who is out at a pub with his girlfriend and a number of other friends. As the night progresses, some of the women start talking about their experiences of men touching them inappropriately in various situations. One woman states that she hates being on the dance floor in a club because men sometimes touch her inappropriately just because she is dancing. One of Steve's male friends says women have done that to him, but he likes it most of the time. Steve's best friend, a law student, states that this is 'technically' sexual assault because they were touched in a sexual manner without their consent.

While listening to this exchange, Steve recalls an incident from when he was 14 years old; he was on an airplane, and the man in the seat next to him grabbed his genital area. He remembers everything about the incident, including that he was able to get the flight attendant to find him another seat. He never told anyone about this incident, including his family, because he felt embarrassed. At the end of the night, he leaves the pub with his girlfriend, but he is quiet. Eventually he discloses this memory to her, commenting that after listening to the law student he now understands what happened on the plane. He openly admits that he does not feel comfortable with this realization, but he is old enough now to understand that he was a victim of sexual assault.

Although he shared many of the same symptoms reported by sexual assault victims—having vivid memories of the incident, feelings of embarrassment, keeping the incident secret for a long time—Steve never considered himself a victim of a crime until that night out with his friends. In essence, he had been an unwilling participant in primary deviance. After the conversation in the pub, Steve clearly identified himself as a victim of sexual assault, adopting the label assigned by his best friend. Despite his unease with this label, Steve has begun to engage in the social world with this supplemented identity and to absorb it into his perceptions of himself.

Before Steve's realization, the actions of his assailant were primary deviance. Once Steve accepted that he was a victim of sexual assault, he engaged in secondary deviance. Remember that using the term 'deviance' here does not imply that Steve's actions were wrong or inappropriate. In this sense, the word means only that the actions were out of the ordinary; Steve's experience was not that of a typical airplane passenger.

Labelling Theory: Underlying Assumptions about the Victim

Adherents of labelling theory assume, like critical and feminist theorists, that the victim is passive to some degree. Although the victim engages in his or her world, it is the reactions of others that shape his or her experiences. Moreover, it is the power of the labeller that is important in labelling the victim. For example, the criminal justice system has tremendous power in labelling individuals it deems as having violated the law. A person who is identified as a law breaker becomes labelled a 'criminal'. This label is a powerful one, often influencing how the labelled person is perceived by society and reducing a person's chances for gainful employment, ability to travel, and so on. Being identified as a victim of a criminal act can also have serious social, emotional, and economic consequences. Both labels carry with them stigmatizing effects, many of which will be discussed in future chapters.

Summary

This chapter has looked at a few of the theories that consider the victim's role in the criminal transaction and its aftermath. While victimology borrows these traditional ideas from criminology in order to examine victim behaviour before, during, and after the criminal event, it is important to view them with a critical eye. For the most part, traditional theories of crime have not sought to explain the actions of victims but have been more concerned with the actions of the offender immediately before or during the event. Furthermore, these theories stem from a patriarchal system and therefore tend to look at crime in terms of maintaining the status quo. In doing so, these concepts fail to consider the difference in crime patterns between particular groups (such as women and men) and the function of dominance within the criminal transaction, something that is always held by the offender. Where victims are addressed, they are often assigned an active role in the victimization, which creates the risk of victim blaming. Overall, what is clear from evaluating these theories is that victimology, as a relatively young discipline, needs to develop its own theories of victimization.

Glossary

aftermath of crime The third and final stage in the criminal event perspective. This particular stage spans a considerably long period of time and looks at the offender's, victim's, and public's reaction to the criminal transaction.

celerity of punishment In deterrence theory, one of the three components of effective punishment. This part claims that the punishment for a crime should be measured and specific to the offence and that the offender and the public must perceive it to be appropriate.

certainty of punishment In deterrence theory, one of the three components of effective punishment. This part states that the offender and the public must perceive that the chance for being punished for a particular deviant act is high, thereby deterring the act from being committed again.

criminal event perspective The idea that criminal activity has three phases: criminal precursors, criminal transaction, and the aftermath of crime.

criminal precursors The first stage in the criminal event perspective. This stage includes the experiences, demographics, etc. that occur before the crime and influence its transaction and aftermath.

criminal transaction The second stage in the criminal event perspective. In this stage, the offender engages in a criminal event, which usually lasts only a few minutes.

critical perspectives A set of theories that seeks to explain the biases occurring in social systems. When applied to victimology, these theories investigate the role of power in its various forms and its influence on crime patterns, differential experiences of crime and victimization, as well as the social responses to victimization and victimological thinking.

deterrence theory The theory that criminal acts are prevented by appropriate sanction. According to this theory, there are two forms of deterrence (specific and general) and three components of punishment (celerity, certainty, and severity).

deviance The study of any action, group, and/or members of that group that are considered to be outside a prescribed set of cultural norms.

feminist perspectives A gendered set of theories used to explain women's experiences. When applied to victimology, these theories attempt to reveal the gendered patterns of crime and victimization, as well as the lack of explanations of these experiences in traditional male-dominated criminological thinking.

general deterrence A form of deterrence in which the public is indirectly deterred from criminal activity as a result of seeing sanction against an offender.

labelling theory Credited to Edwin Lemert, a social reaction theory that examines how the deviant identity is formed out of the reaction of others to the actor.

lifestyles theory A rational choice theory claiming that certain behavioural patterns create an opportunistic structure for criminals.

Mariticide A type of homicide in which a person kills his or her spouse.

primary deviance Coined by Edwin Lemert, the initial participation in a deviant act. In victimology, primary deviance occurs during a victimizing event.

rational choice perspective Widely associated with Derek Cornish and Ronald Clarke, a rational choice theory that seeks to explain the victimizer's motivation and decision-making process. This perspective claims that victimizing behaviour is the process of successful rationalization based on the offender weighing the pros and cons of committing crime.

rational choice theories A set of theories, including lifestyles, routine activities, deterrence, rational choice perspective, and situated transaction, in which the offender is assumed to be a rational and active person who makes choices based on the presence or absence of potential gain and the cost of committing the crime.

routine activities theory (RAT) A rational choice theory that posits that three elements must be present in order for a criminal event to occur: a motivated offender, a suitable target, and a lack of capable guardianship. If one or more of these elements are missing, a crime will not occur.

secondary deviance Coined by Edwin Lemert, describes an individual's acceptance of the label of deviance or 'otherness' and his or her subsequent engagement in the social world as a deviant. In victimology, secondary deviance occurs when an individual accepts the label of victim.

severity of punishment In deterrence theory, one of three components of effective punishment. In this part, the offender and the public should perceive that the punishment is neither too lenient nor too harsh, in order to maximize the benefit of deterring criminal activity.

situated transaction theory Developed by David Luckenbill to explain homicide, a theory that seeks to locate crime in time and place. In this theory, the offender and victim often go through six stages of engagement before the criminal activity is completed.

social Darwinism Developed by Herbert Spencer, the idea that social dynamics are governed by evolutionary principles. This theory is also encapsulated by the phrase 'survival of the fittest'.

social interactionist theory Developed by sociologists Charles Horton Cooley and George Herbert Mead, the idea that people base their individual identities on how others perceive them.

social reaction theories Initially developed to explain deviance, a set of theories that examine the various reactions to a person being identified as belonging to a particular group. In victimology, the concept is used to examine how a person comes to accept or reject being labelled as a victim.

specific deterrence A form of deterrence in which the offender is directly deterred from criminal activity as a result of experiencing sanction for an offence.

stigma From the Greek, meaning a physical mark or spot on the body that can lead to disgrace, embarrassment, and/or reproach. In sociology, the term refers to any characteristic that causes these effects.

symbolic interactionism A theory asserting that human interaction is based solely on the interpretation of symbols, such as language and behaviour, communicated between individuals.

target hardening The process by which a potential victim is educated, or 'hardened', about the way offenders operate and is encouraged to take protective measures against victimization.

uxoricide A type of homicide in which a man kills his wife.

Critical Thinking Questions

1. What are some of the benefits of taking precautions while walking alone at night in your neighbourhood? How might these precautions differ between the following groups of people? Who in these groups do you think is least fearful when walking alone at night and why?
   a. Children and adults

    b. Women and men

    c. Elderly people and young adults

2. Are there different patterns of victimization when comparing men and women? What are they and why do you think these patterns occur?

3. Choose any two sets of theories mentioned in this chapter and try to explain the occurrence of crime patterns.

4. If a person is identified as a victim, are they truly deviant? Why or why not?

5. Are certain theories better able to explain certain crime patterns than others? Give specific examples to support your answer.

CHAPTER 5

Special Topic: Homicide

Learning Objectives

After reading this chapter, you will be able to

- understand how homicides that receive the most media attention are very different from more common forms of this crime;
- understand the role of age, gender, and race in homicide victimization trends; and
- re-examine some theories as they pertain to homicide victimization and their ability (or inability) to explain the differences between genders, races, and ages of victims.

Introduction

Although Canada has a relatively low homicide rate, there are certain cases that remain prominent in our minds. A homicide may be memorable for many reasons. In some instances, it is because of the sheer anomaly of the event. In others it is the number of victims or their innocence. The more innocent a victim, the more tragic and senseless his or her death appears to be. Remembering such cases may also cause us to ask questions about homicidal victimization. This chapter examines some of the trends in the various types of homicide in Canada, particularly those concerning women, Aboriginal peoples, and youth. We will also revisit three of the theories relating to homicide and the victim–offender relationship from previous chapters and apply these concepts to specific cases.

Genevieve Bergeron and the Montreal Massacre

If you asked a group of friends or random individuals to name as many homicide cases as they can recall, which ones do you think they would mention? For many, the Montreal Massacre is one of the first that would come to mind. At École Polytechnique on 6 December 1989, 21-year-old Genevieve Bergeron and 13 other women were murdered and another 14 women and men were wounded by Marc Lépine. According to one CBC news report, Lépine, armed with several guns and rounds of ammunition, walked into the building and up three floors, yelling 'I want women.' He shot at all the women he encountered as he walked through the halls. One male victim stated that he was shot at and faked his own death because he was helping another woman who had been shot. The offender then entered a classroom where 60 students were sitting with a professor.

Witnesses recall that the assailant demanded that the women and the men, including the male professor, stand on opposite sides of the room. When the class did not move, he shot at the ceiling. He threatened the men with a .22-calibre rifle and told them to leave the classroom. The women took cover under the desks, where they could hear the offender jumping from desk to desk and shooting the women as he found them. He called the women 'une gang de féministes' and said 'J'hais les féministes (I hate feminists).' One of the wounded students, Nathalie Provost, told the shooter that they were not feminists, just students taking an engineering class, but he refused to listen (Massacre kills, 1989). He also shot students and staff in the building's cafeteria and in another classroom before killing himself.

The women who were murdered in the Montreal Massacre and those that survived made a lasting impression on this country. Two years after the event, men in London, ON, started wearing a white ribbon around their arms, symbolizing that men should 'give up their arms' and stop perpetrating violence against women (Men wearing white ribbons, 1991). A memorial service is held on most if not all campuses on the anniversary of the massacre, reminding people of this event and remembering the women who had sought their education in this traditionally male-dominated discipline (Victims of Montreal school massacre, 2004). Those who attend these ceremonies may notice an increase in security on this day and the days leading up to the memorial service, indicating that there is still a concern for violence.

Unfortunately, the tragedy of the victims' deaths overshadows their lives. Genevieve Bergeron is not just the first name read on the list of the women who died that day. She is not just a civil engineering scholarship student who was killed because of her gender. She was a loving sister, an amazing student, a talented athlete and musician, and an inspirational woman. She left an impact on those who lost her; they cope with her death by remembering how she lived. Her sister Catherine recalls: 'For me, she was like the sun . . . she was a very happy person and a very sensible person too. I remember her crying easily, a very emotive person.' Catherine and her family hope that Genevieve's legacy won't be about the massacre or the fight for stricter gun laws. Genevieve's death has forever affected her family, but Catherine hopes that Genevieve's life will affect people further, the way it has for her. She 'would like Canadians to remember [Genevieve] and the other 13 women, not to be sad, but to go on in life in a better way' (Victims of Montreal School Massacre, 2004).

Reena Virk, Jane Creba, and Nina de Villiers

Among the other names that people might mention if you asked them which homicide cases they recall are Reena Virk, Jane Creba, Nina de Villiers, and the murdered women who were taken from the Downtown Eastside of Vancouver. We shall profile these cases in the boxes throughout this chapter. While you read the following definitions and statistics, be mindful of how these notable cases differ from the more common forms of homicide victims. Try to remember other homicides and ask yourself why you might remember them more than others.

Definition of Homicide in Canada

Literally meaning 'the killing of man', **homicide** refers to the killing of a person by another. In the Criminal Code of Canada (CCC), there are four types of offences included in the homicide category: first-degree murder, second-degree murder, manslaughter, and infanticide. All of these types are considered culpable homicide (CCC, s. 222.4). According to the CCC (s. 222.1), a person is a **homicide victim** when his or her death is caused by another person, either directly or indirectly, by any means. However, if the offender killed the victim and was found not to be culpable, or not criminally responsible, then the homicide is not considered an offence under the CCC. Although one can be a victim of homicide, the victimization may or may not be the result of a Criminal Code offence (CCC, s. 222.3). For example, if the victim was attacking the offender and the offender killed him or her in self-defence, no offence has technically been committed because the victim used similar force and was killed as a result of the altercation.

To be a victim of homicide, an individual's death must be caused by another. This death can be caused by an unlawful act, as in the result of a lethal assault, or by the negligence of another, as in the failure to provide basic necessities of life. Homicides can also be caused by someone threatening another person and creating a fear of violence or by deceiving a person into doing something that causes his or her death. For example, if someone convinced another person that large sums of money would be paid to a benefactor if he or she were to end his or her own life, it could be argued that this person is the victim of a homicide. One can also be a homicide victim if he or she was deliberately frightened and that fear led to his or her death. For example, if an elderly person was told a lie that caused undue stress on his or her body to the point where that individual experienced heart failure, he or she could be considered a victim of homicide. **Murder** is a culpable homicide (CCC s. 229) in which the victim's death is deliberately caused or was the result of reckless or negligent behaviour. A victim of **first-degree murder** is one who has been killed deliberately, killed while being the victim of another serious crime, or killed as the result of carrying out duties associated with the protection of the state, such as those performed by a police officer, judge, prison warden, or corrections officer. All victims of murder not classified as first-degree are considered **second-degree murder** victims. Murder victims are classified as **manslaughter** victims when they are killed in the heat of passion or when they provoked the offender before they were killed. If the victim was a newborn child and his or her death was caused deliberately or through an act of omission by his or her biological mother, he or she is considered a victim of **infanticide**. It is assumed that this type of victim was killed as the result of mental defect on the part of the offender, caused by either the birth process or the effects of lactation.

Risk of Homicide Victimization in Canada

Cases of homicide tend to dominate newscasts, films, and television dramas. The fear of becoming a victim of homicide

Table 5.1 Types of Lethal Victimization

Androcide	The killing of men.
Deicide	The killing of God or deities.
Ecocide	The killing of the environment.
Ethnocide	The killing of ethnic groups.
Femicide	The killing of females. Some have used this term to refer to the specific killing of women by men.
Feticide	The killing of a fetus by legal or illegal means. Legal means include medical procedure, while illegal means include killing either accidentally or intentionally by way of a criminal act, such as assault on the mother.
Filicide	The killing of one's own daughter or son.
Fratricide	The killing of one's own brother. This term has also been used more generally to refer to the killing of siblings.
Genocide	The systematic killing of a group of people who share common nationality, racial profile, ethnic identity, or religious, and/or political beliefs.
Gynocide	The intentional and systematic killing of women in a population.
Herbicide	The killing of plants.
Homicide	The killing of man. More generally, this term has come to mean the killing of humans.
Infanticide	The killing of infants, often under one year of age.
Insecticide	The killing of insects.
Mariticide	The killing of one's spouse.
Matricide	The killing of one's own mother.
Parricide	The killing of one's own parents. Also referred to as parenticide, this term can also refer to the killing of other patriarchs and matriarchs, such as kings and queens, respectively.
Patricide	The killing of one's own father.
Prolicide	The killing of one's own offspring, either before or shortly after birth.
Pseudocide	The faking of one's own death.
Regicide	The killing of monarchs, either by illegal means, such as assassination, or as the end result of due process of law.
Sororicide	The killing of one's own sister.
Suicide	The killing of oneself.
Tyrannicide	The killing or assassination of a tyrant.
Uxoricide	The killing of one's wife.
Vaticide	The killing of a prophet.
Vivicide	The killing of all life forms in a particular area.
Xenocide	The killing of life outside one's own species. This term is often used in science fiction to describe the killing of alien life forms.

or other severe forms of violence is one shared by many people (Ferraro, 1996). However, homicide victims are, by and large, the smallest proportion of victims when compared to other crimes. In Canada, homicide victims accounted for approximately only 0.02 per cent of all crime reported to police.

As this number shows, Canada experiences a relatively low homicide rate. One has a chance of being a victim of homicide in Canada 1.85 times per 100,000 people. According to Li (2007), although there are several countries that had lower homicide rates in 2006, one had a better chance of being a victim of homicide in the following countries: Turkey (6.23/100,000), United States (5.69/100,000), Germany (2.90/100,000), Switzerland (2.73/100,000), Sweden (2.64/100,000), New Zealand (2.37/100,000), and Finland (2.12/100,000). When looking at the risk of homicide victimization across Canada, one was most likely to be a victim of homicide in the west and in the north. Quebec City continues to be one of the safest cities in North America, with a homicide victimization risk of 0.96/100,000 in 2006 and no reported homicides in 2007 (White, 2007).

In terms of weapons used in homicides, trends show that victims were **less** likely to be shot with a firearm in 2006 than they were in the mid-1970s (Li, 2007), with less than one-third (31 per cent) of deaths reported to be the result of a gunshot wound. Homicide victims were slightly more likely to be stabbed (35 per cent). The remaining 34 per cent of deaths were caused by other methods, such as physical force, strangulation, poisoning, fire, exposure, hypothermia, Shaken Baby Syndrome, vehicular incidents, and so on.

Gender and Homicide Victimization

Gender plays a strong role in the likelihood of being a victim of homicide. According to Li (2007), 86.7 per cent (approximately 8 in 9) of all homicides occurring in 2006 involved a male offender, while males represented 73.2 per cent of all victims. Women were accused of committing approximately 1 in 9 homicides (13.3 per cent) but are twice as likely (26.8 per cent) to be identified as a homicide victim. Women continue to be more likely to be victims of spousal homicide. In 2006, women were 2.6 times more likely to be a victim of this crime (71.8 per cent of all spousal homicide victims) as compared to men, at 28.2 per cent. Looking at all solved homicides between 1997 and 2004, Aboriginal Peoples were more likely to know their attacker (88 per cent) than non-Aboriginals (83 per cent). When we look at the relationship-gender interplay, Aboriginal women were more likely to be attacked by a stranger (15 per cent) as compared to non-Aboriginal women (6 per cent).

Relationship between Victim and Offender

As demonstrated in Figure 5.1, trends in solved homicides indicate that the victim of a homicide is more likely to know his or her attacker. In 2006, 83 per cent of victims knew one or more of their attackers. Almost one-fifth (17.3 per cent) of victims were killed by someone with whom they were engaged in a spousal relationship, either at the time of their death or before (i.e., the victim and offender were married, living in a common-law relationship, separated, or

Table 5.2 Victims of Homicide and Accused Persons, by Sex, Canada, 1996–2006

Year	Victims					Accused				
	Males		Females		Total	Males		Females		Total
	number	percent	number	percent		number	percent	number	percent	
1996[1]	435	68.5	200	31.5	635	520	88.4	68	11.6	588
1997[1]	381	65.0	205	35.0	586	445	85.7	74	14.3	519
1998	381	68.3	177	31.7	558	474	87.9	65	12.1	539
1999[r]	365	67.8	173	32.2	538	446	90.3	48	9.7	494
2000[r,2]	397	72.7	149	27.3	546	423	88.1	57	11.9	480
2001[2]	392	70.9	161	29.1	553	449	87.5	64	12.5	513
2002[r,1]	376	64.6	206	35.4	582	484	89.3	58	10.7	542
2003[r]	391	71.2	158	28.8	549	488	88.7	62	11.3	550
2004[r]	425	68.1	199	31.9	624	532	89.6	62	10.4	594
2005[r]	483	72.9	180	27.1	663	580	90.2	63	9.8	643
2006[3]	442	73.2	162	26.8	604	476	86.7	73	13.3	549
Average 1996 to 2005	403	69.0	181	31.0	583	484	88.6	62	11.4	546

r   revised
1   Total of accused excludes one person whose gender was reported by police as unknown
2   Total of accused excludes two persons whose gender was reported by police as unknown
3   Total of victims excludes one person whose gender was reported by police as unknown

SOURCE: Li, G. (2007). Homicide in Canada, 2006. *Juristat, 27(8)*. Ottawa, ON: Canadian Centre for Justice Statistics, Minister of Industry, p. 18.

Figure 5.1 Most Homicides Committed by Someone Known to Victim[1]

Rate per 100,000 population

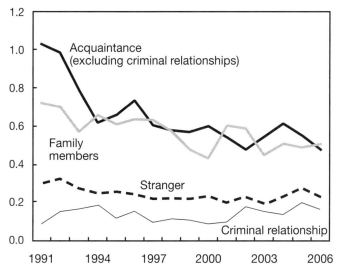

1 Criminal relationship data unavailable prior to 1991.

SOURCES: Li, G. (2007). Homicide in Canada, 2006. *Juristat, 27(8)*. Statistics Canada: Canadian Centre for Justice Statistics, Minister of Industry, p. 6.

Figure 5.2 Spousal[1] Homicides Peaked in mid-1970s

Rate per 100,000 population

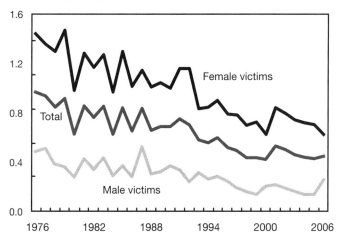

1 Spouses include legally married, common-law, separated, and divorced persons ages 15 years or older. Excludes same-sex spouses due to the unavailability of Census data on same-sex couples prior to 2006.

SOURCES: Li, G. (2007). Homicide in Canada, 2006. *Juristat, 27(8)*. Statistics Canada: Canadian Centre for Justice Statistics, Minister of Industry, p. 7.

divorced). In 2006, 78 homicide victims were killed by their partners.

Another 3.3 per cent of victims were killed by a current or former girl- or boy-friend (Li, 2007). From 1998 to 2004, deaths caused by ex-husbands represented the largest homicidal victimizing group (Johnson, 2006). During this time, deaths caused by ex-boyfriends have come to be the second-largest offending category. Unfortunately, the rate per 100,000 population cannot be calculated for this group because data on this type of relationship are not collected by the Canadian census. Therefore, it is difficult to determine if there were simply more of

this type of relationship during these years or if there has actually been an increase in homicide victimization of this group.

One in five victims was killed by someone who was identified as a non-intimate family member (19.2 per cent). Still another fifth were likely to be killed by a casual acquaintance (20.1 per cent). Just over 1 in 10 (10.7 per cent) of victims were killed by a close friend, a neighbour, someone in authority, or someone who shared a business relationship with the victim, while 11.9 per cent were killed by someone with whom they had engaged in criminal activity. Roughly one in six (16.6 per cent) were killed by a complete

Figure 5.3   Rates of Spousal Homicide, by Sex of Victim and Aboriginal Status[1], 1997–2000

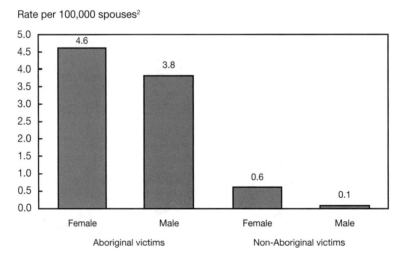

Rate per 100,000 spouses[2]

1   These data exclude those victims where police-reported Aboriginal status was unknown or not collected. In accord-'ance with internal guidelines, some police services (e.g., RCMP and Toronto Police Service) do not report the Aboriginal status of victims and accused persons to the Homicide Survey. This analysis excludes 32 victims whose Aboriginal/non-Aboriginal status was unknown, undisclosed, or not collected between 1997 and 2000. For data prior to 1997, it is not possible to separate 'non-Aboriginal' status form 'not collected'.
2   Rates are caluculated per 100,000 spouses (legally married, separated, divorced, and common law men and women 15 years of age and over) of self-identified Aboriginal origin (North American Indian, Métis, or Inuit). Population estimates were derived from 2001 post-censal estimates and 1996 Census counts, provided at July 1st by Statistics Canada, Census and Demographic Statistics, Demography Division.

SOURCES: Johnson, H. (2006). Measuring violence against women: Statistical trends 2006. Statistics Canada: Canadian Centre for Justice Statistics, Minister of Industry, p. 67.

stranger. In just over one in four cases, much of the information about the offender is unknown because the cases remained unsolved as of the end of 2006.

Homicide among Youth

Among those highest at risk for homicide victimization are youth. Although the homicide rate has generally been declining since the early 1970s, homicides committed by youth are on the increase and actually peaked in 2006 (Li, 2007). In that year, 15 per cent of all homicides in Canada were committed by youth between the ages of 12 and 17. Like adult homicide trends, youth homicide risk is higher in the western regions of the country than in the central or eastern parts. Although the number of victims has remained relatively stable since 2005, there has been a greater trend of multiple assailants. Just over half of the homicide victims killed by youth were attacked by more than one lethal victimizer. Box 5.1 provides an example of such a case. Other trends are evident when comparing youth homicides with adult homicides. Youths

Box 5.1 Reena Virk

On 14 November 1997, 14-year-old Reena Virk was approached by a group of teenagers— mostly girls— and was attacked and beaten under a bridge on Vancouver Island. As Reena attempted to make it towards a bus stop to escape her attackers and get home, two members of the group grabbed her and beat her to death in Victoria's Gorge waterway. The shocking brutality of her murder was evident when the police found her body eight days later. During the investigation, witnesses claimed that one of the accused bragged to others that she had put her foot on Virk's head and smoked a cigarette while Virk suffered and died in the water.

According to many reports, Virk's murder was blamed on the fact that she was identified as overweight and non-white and was therefore socially isolated. Her untimely death resulted in a lot of media discussion regarding racism, sexism, female-to-female violence, and acceptance of social norms, such as being white and thin. This attention, along with the subsequent, often lengthy, trials, continued to remind Virk's family of their loss.

Virk's grandfather Mukand Virk spoke openly about the pain of outliving his grandchild and missing out on all the things that life had to offer her, such as graduation, her career aspirations of becoming a nurse, getting married, and having children. Nightmares followed, and his wife wept in order to cope.

Virk's mother, Suman Virk, maintained that one of the most difficult things was 'not to be able to hold [her] child'. When she went to view the body she was not allowed to touch Virk, as her body was needed for evidence purposes. The pain of this experience, among others, will forever affect the life of this mother. She understands that the ache will always be there: 'I think that the name Reena Virk will always bring back the horrors of November 14, no matter when and where it's mentioned.'

SOURCES: Crown wants Ellard sentenced to maximum for killing Reena Virk (2005, 7 July). *CBC News Online.* Retrieved 19 January 2008, from www.cbc.ca/canada/story/2005/07/06/virk050706.html; Jiwani, Y. (1997). Reena Virk: The erasure of race. *The FREDA Centre for Research on Violence against Women and Children.* Retrieved 19 January 2008, from www.harbour.sfu.ca/freda/articles/virk.htm; The murder of Reena Virk: A timeline (2005, 13 April). *CBC News Online.* Retrieved 19 January 2008 from www.cbc.ca/news/background/virk/.

are more likely to kill strangers (30 per cent) than their adult counterparts (16 per cent) and are much more likely to kill other youths (58 per cent) than to kill adults (22 per cent). Victims who were killed by youth are also slightly less likely to have been shot (17 per cent) than homicide victims of adults (22 per cent).

Aboriginal Peoples as Homicide Victims

Before we can talk about victimization of Aboriginal peoples, we first have to discuss how 'Aboriginalness' is measured. Statistics Canada establishes the ethnic identity of Aboriginal peoples by asking a series of questions about Aboriginal identity and status. If respondents report that they self-identify with an Aboriginal group (North American Indian, Métis, or Inuit), that they are either a Registered or Treaty Indian, or that they hold First Nation or Band membership, Statistics Canada identifies them as having Aboriginal identity. If we look to data collected prior to the 1996 Census, only a single question on ethnic origin (i.e., ancestry) was used to establish this identity (Siggner, 2003).

From 1997 to 2004 there were 2,468 victims of homicide in Canada. Of these, 19 per cent (470) were identified as Aboriginal (Johnson, 2006). Because the Aboriginal population represents approximately 3 per cent of the population (Kong & Beattie, 2005), this figure suggests that Aboriginal peoples are strongly overrepresented in these statistics by more than six times their representative population. Of the 470 Aboriginal deaths recorded, 70 per cent involved male victims.

The majority (53 per cent) of male Aboriginal victims were killed by an acquaintance, with 19 per cent killed by a non-intimate family member. Women were also more likely to be killed by a non-intimate family member (35 per cent) or by an intimate family member (27 per cent). Looking at strictly family versus other types of victimizers with respect to Aboriginal victims of homicide, women were far more likely than men to be killed by a family member (56 per cent and 34 per cent, respectively). This pattern is more pronounced in the non-Aboriginal part of the population (76 per cent for women and 22 per cent for men), which has a lower overall chance of homicide victimization.

Johnson also reports that Aboriginal peoples were more likely to know their attackers (88 per cent) when compared to non-Aboriginals (83 per cent). When we look at the relationship–gender interplay, this figure is largely attributed to Aboriginal male victims. Aboriginal women were more likely to be attacked by a stranger (15 per cent) as compared to non-Aboriginal women (6 per cent), whereas Aboriginal men were less likely to be attacked by a stranger than their counterparts (Aboriginal: 13 per cent; non-Aboriginal: 23 per cent).

Three Theories of Homicide

Most homicides occur between men who are an acquaintance of each other. Many of these homicides are unplanned and occur as the result of an argument that accelerates to lethal violence. Recall from chapters 3 and 4 that two theories of crime were specifically developed to explain what happens in a typical homicide. The first of these is Marvin Wolfgang's (1958) victim precipitation. The second is David Luckenbill's (1977) theory of the situated transaction. Both theorists recognized that in some cases there was a pattern to homicide victimization. A third set of theories, critical and feminist theories, looks beyond the interaction of the typical homicide and seeks to explain the larger trends in homicide victimization. The statistics presented above illustrate some of these patterns, particularly the previous relationship between the victim and the offender. Many homicides occur between people who are known to each other and are often the result of a disagreement. Before we consider these theories, let us look at a few newspaper reports of homicides that reflect these common patterns:

- Jeff Shuckburgh, age 29, was the owner of Shuckaluck's Pub in Calgary. On 7 January 2004, Adrian Walle was at the pub and was escorted out after becoming unruly. He returned, only to continue his behaviour and to be thrown out again. The third time, he was escorted out of the pub by Shuckburgh and two other bartenders. In the parking lot of the establishment, Shuckburgh was shot and killed by Walle with a sawed-off .22-calibre shotgun concealed in his clothing (Slade, 2008).
- Ronald Boucher, Arnold Peter Cardinal, and Leonard Bellam were arguing on 5 June 2005, in Rosie's Bar and Grill in Edmonton. During the argument Ronald was dragged out into the parking lot, where he was beaten and fatally stabbed in the chest by one of the other men (Man pleads guilty, 2008).
- In September 2005 James McNabb, age 36, was a new resident of the Neeginan Emergency Shelter in Winnipeg, where he was also working as a temporary labourer with fellow resident Virlin Bird. Bird was fired after being accused

of stealing someone's cigarettes. Bird blamed McNabb for the theft and attacked him outside the shelter a few days later. McNabb was stabbed eight times then repeatedly kicked after he had fallen; he succumbed to his injuries. Bird removed his bloody ball cap and shirt in a nearby alley and then went to a Chinese restaurant, where he was arrested a short time later (Winnipegger who killed, 2008).

- In August 2006 four teens in the remote northern community of Pauingassi, MB, were drinking 'bean juice' (a homemade liquor concoction) out of a pail when they decided to attack 30-year-old Jeremy Wesley Crow, father of four. Crow was beaten with a baseball bat, a pool cue, a hockey stick, and an axe over an extended period of time, while a nine-year-old girl watched. At one point he was hit repeatedly with the axe by each of the young men. He was heard to say 'All right, that is enough now,' shortly before he was dragged through the house and left outside to die. During the trial, one of Crow's brothers said in his victim impact statement that the killing caused him to resume 'sniffing gas', while another brother said that he had become more angry since the attack and had increased his alcohol consumption. Two teens, who could not be named because of the Youth Criminal Justice Act, pleaded guilty and were sentenced to time served in custody and two years supervised probation (McIntyre, 2008).
- On 17 November 2006, Marco Duric and his friends Ryan Milner, age 22, and Kyle Hicks left Grimsby, ON, to attend a hip-hop show at a Hamilton nightclub. Milner became an 'overzealous fan' and the three were kicked out of the club after getting too close to the band's lead singer. Outside the club they became involved in a shouting match with

George Gallo, age 25, and Gallo's friend. The fight became physical; Duric was stabbed in both arms and lost a significant amount of blood. He would later testify in court that, as a result of these injuries, he had nerve damage in both arms and did not have full use of his hands. Milner was also stabbed and was pronounced dead at the scene when police arrived. Gallo turned himself in one month after the attack and pleaded guilty to reduced charges of manslaughter and aggravated assault in March 2008 (Hamilton man admits, 2008).

• At the end of August 2007, Gerald Walker, age 49, of Windsor, ON, met and befriended a drifter named Donald Miller, age 46, who had only recently stepped off a bus in the city. Walker agreed to let Miller stay in his apartment. In the early hours of 2 September, after a night of drinking and smoking marijuana, Miller lost his temper and fatally struck Walker on the left side of the head; he died beside his bed in his basement apartment (Williamson, 2008).

Homicide and Victim Precipitation

As we discussed in Chapter 3, Marvin Wolfgang's homicide study revealed that, in 26 per cent of the cases, the eventual victim was the instigator in the victimizing event. Wolfgang coined the term 'victim precipitation' to describe these offences; the victim would precipitate his or her own death by being the first to resort to violence. Wolfgang also noted that the victim and the offender often knew each other prior to the encounter and had often had prior disputes. The argument that led to the homicide was often the product of a small disagreement that evolved into something much more serious. The victim and the offender were almost always male, and the victim was

more likely than the offender to have been drinking alcohol.

The cases listed above illustrate these points. Many of the cases involve the consumption of alcohol and/or other substances by the victim and/or the offender or took place in an establishment that served alcohol. The victims and the offenders are all men who participated in a series of events that led to homicide. Looking back at these reports, it is often difficult to establish exactly what the victim was doing because the stories are principally concerned with the actions of the offender. We can often glean what the victim experienced but only through this offender-focused lens. Unless the victim's actions in such cases are extraordinary, they are often not reported.

The cases also feature what Wolfgang would call victim precipitation. In one case the eventual victim became loud and obnoxious as an 'overzealous fan'. In another, the victim was thought to have committed the theft that cost the offender his job. In the other cases, however, it is unclear who started the series of events that eventually lead to the act of lethal victimization. In the case of the stabbing at Shuckaluck's Pub, it is assumed that the offender gave reason to be removed from the pub three times and that he had the opportunity to leave the premises after each incident. However, it is unclear who started the argument between the three men at Rosie's. Likewise, it is not known why Jeremy Crow and the four young offenders were in close proximity to one another or why the teenagers felt that resorting to lethal victimization was an option. It is not clear why Donald Miller lost his temper and killed his host. Our bias remains with the offender in these cases.

Included in the theory of victim precipitation is the importance of interpretation. The concept presumes that the eventual victim carries out some sort of act that someone finds offensive. Also outlined in this theory is the idea that if the eventual offender had not found the act offensive, or had taken evasive manoeuvres to avoid further escalation, the homicide may not have taken place. Because it is often only the offender who can provide the details of the event, there is the possibility of bias. This situation can be summed up by the old adage 'History is defined by the victors.'

In other words, without the victim's contribution to the interpretation of events, it is more likely that the offender would claim that he or she interpreted the actions of the victim as offensive.

The majority of homicides—even those in Wolfgang's study—do not fit the pattern of victim precipitation. Therefore, this theory fails to provide an adequate explanation of homicide victimization. Boxes 5.2 and 5.3 highlight two homicides that were not victim precipitated. Neither Jane Creba nor Nina de Villiers knew their murderers. They also did not instigate the events that caused their

Box 5.2 Jane Creba

For Virginia and Bruce Creba, their 'bright light tragically scattered into darkness on Boxing Day 2005' when their 15-year-old daughter, Jane, was killed during a gang shootout on Toronto's Yonge Street. Jane Creba was shopping with her 18-year-old sister, Alison, who did not realize that Jane had crossed the street, been gunned down outside of the Eaton Centre, and taken to the hospital. After a frenzied search, Alison Creba called her mother, asking if her sister had returned home. When Virginia Creba realized that her daughter was not home she raced downtown and joined the search. Jane Creba died hours later in emergency surgery.

The reaction to Jane Creba's death was evident in the days and months that followed. A memorial of flowers, candles, and stuffed animals was set up on a stretch of sidewalk beginning at Yonge and Dundas streets and continuing several blocks north of the Eaton Centre. Her death was widely publicized, highlighting the fact that Toronto had dealt with many shooting-related homicides in 2005 or, as it became known in the city, the 'year of the gun'. During this time, many people shared with the media their memories of the impact Jane Creba had had in her short 15 years. One classmate wrote that she was 'the funniest, prettiest and all around nicest person'. Another friend said, 'I can't think of a single person who didn't like her and everyone loved laughing and joking with her. She had the nicest fun-loving attitude toward everything and I know everyone will miss her.' Her family commented: 'Her life has been transformed into a shooting star that will be forever a light for her devoted parents, uncles, aunts, cousins and close friends.'

SOURCES: Blatchford, C., Friesen, J., & Appleby, T. (2005, 29 December). Slain teenager veered blithely into crossfire: Dead victim in Yonge Street shootings has been identified as Jane Creba. *The Globe and Mail*. Retrieved 19 January 2008, from www.theglobeandmail.com/servlet/story/RTGAM.20051228.wcreba1228a/ BNStory/National/; Classmates of slain teenager share their loss (2005, 30 December). *CBC News Online*. Retrieved 19 January 2008, from www.ctv.ca/servlet/ArticleNews/story/CTVNews/20051230/grieving_ students_051230?s_name=election2006&no_ads=CTV; Family of slain Toronto teen remembers their 'bright light' (2005, 29 December). *CBC News Online*. Retrieved 19 January 2008, from www.cbc.ca/canada/ story/2005/12/29/newshooting-Toronto051229.html.

Box 5.3 Nina de Villiers

On 9 August 1991, Nina de Villiers, a 19-year-old biochemistry student at McMaster University, was abducted and murdered while jogging in Burlington, near the shore of Lake Ontario. The apparent randomness of this act instilled fear in her community and resonated with Canadians across the country as well as deeply impacting her family and friends. 'You are left so helpless,' her mother, Priscilla, recalls, 'You lose your ego, your whole sense of having control over your life.' While trying to cope with their grief, de Villiers's family and friends learned that her murderer, Jonathan Yeo, had been released on bail and had a long history of physically and sexually assaulting women.

The impression that de Villiers made on others can be seen in the way they paid tribute to her after her death. Her family created a petition encouraging the Canadian criminal justice system to be more responsive to the needs of Canadians; the initial submission of this petition included 2.5 million signatures. At Yeo's trial, the jury returned with 137 recommendations to ensure that victimizers like Yeo did not continue to fall through the cracks of the criminal and mental health systems.

In addition, a sexual assault and domestic violence crisis centre was named Nina's Place, in memory of de Villiers. At McMaster University the Nina de Villiers Garden was dedicated in front of University Hall in 1993; almost 1,000 people attended the ceremony to see the garden and remember de Villiers. The garden combined two things that she loved: music and flowers. Her mother recalled that her daughter 'saw gardening as a way of finding peace. She would dig, plant, prune and compost and come back refreshed . . . a garden would have been Nina's best birthday present.'

SOURCES: CAVEAT. (2000). Background. Retrieved 6 April 2008, from www.caveat.org/history; CAVEAT. (1993). Lasting Living Tribute to Nina d Villiers. Retrieved 8 April 2008, from www.caveat.org/publications/sw/cav_1993_nov.html; *MacLean's*. (1995). de Villers, Priscilla: Maclean's 1995 Honour Roll. Retrieved 6 April 2008, from www.thecanadianencyclopedia.com/index.cfm?PgNm=TCE&Params=M1ARTM0010547; Nina's Place. (2008). Retrieved 6 April 2008, from www.ninasplace.ca.

deaths but were unfortunate victims of seemingly random violence. Therefore, at the very least, this theory falls short of explaining the lethal victimization carried out by strangers and by those who routinely abuse others to the point of death.

Homicide and the Situated Transaction

In his study of 71 California homicides, David Luckenbill (1977) noted that congregating in a common physical space causes people to act in ways conducive to their spatial limitations. He identified six stages to the situated transaction where a homicide was the end result, beginning with an affront to 'face' and ending with the eventual offender either remaining at the scene or fleeing from it. These stages are discussed in greater detail in Chapter 4.

Like Wolfgang, Luckenbill noted that not all homicides followed the situated transaction but that the theory explained an observed pattern in one of the most common forms of homicide. This theory also relies heavily on interpretation, leaving question as to the final version of events. Because the eventual victim is dead, the eventual offender is often the key witness in describing the events and is therefore more likely to define the former's actions as initially offensive. This theory also fails to explain other common forms of homicide, such as spousal homicide, stranger homicide, and so on.

Feminist/Critical Explanations of Homicide

Unlike victim precipitation and situated transaction theory, feminist and/or critical concepts include different groups of victims and offenders in their explanations of homicide victimization. Recall that critical criminologists see disputes as one possible outcome of power dynamics. For example, the theories above do not consider why homicides are predominantly committed by men or why men and women have very different homicidal victimization patterns. Victim precipitation suggests that victims of spousal homicide somehow provoked their attackers repeatedly and therefore had control over the violence they were being exposed to. Situated transaction theory poses a similar explanation as to why women are more likely to die at the hands of an intimate or another family member while men are more likely to be killed by another man who is not a relative.

Feminist/critical theories argue that social values have predominantly been shaped by and for men. Therefore, male violence against women is considered one manifestation of males exerting and reinforcing this dominance. As a natural extension of this patriarchal form of thinking, the theories of victim precipitation and situation transaction may offer suitable explanations of male-to-male violence but fall flat when we apply them to matters of homicide involving minorities, such as uxoricide and crimes identified as **hate crimes**, where a particular person or group is targeted for victimization because of minority status, such as racial or ethnic identity and/or sexual orientation.

Finally, feminist/critical explanations of victimization and criminal behaviour may explain why we identify the patterns of lethal victimization the way that we do. For example, when someone is killed because he or she is adheres to a particular religious doctrine or because he or she is homosexual, we are quick to label these crimes hate crimes. However, we are slower to identify crimes against women as hate crime. We started this chapter by looking at the Montreal Massacre. The victims in this tragedy were systematically sought out and gunned down because they were women. The offender made several statements, both during the victimization period and in letters to be read after his death, about his profound hatred for women; he had even created a list of other women whom he had identified as 'feminists'. Yet a close examination of the coverage of this case reveals that few identify this crime as a hate crime.

Multiple Homicide Victims

Although the risk of being the victim of serial homicide is extremely rare (Scott, 2005), television and film stories about these events seem to capture people's imaginations and fuel their fears. The patterns that have been identified above for more common forms of homicide are very different from those that explore serial homicides. Homicide experts have divided the phenomenon of multiple murder into three categories: mass murder, spree murder, and serial murder. Although the types appear distinct, there is considerable overlap in their construction, largely due to the fact that they are defined by the presence or absence of certain characteristics, including body count, time interval between killings, number of murderous events, and, to a lesser degree, intent of the murderer(s).

Mass murder is the act of killing many people in a single murderous event with very little time between murders. A mass murderer is a killer who murders his or her victims all at one time (Egger, 2002, 1990, 1984; Hickey, 2002; Levin & Fox, 1985; Leyton, 1986; Lunde, 1979). This type of killer chooses a location and a set of targets, then attempts to kill as many as possible in one sudden outburst. The victims of the Montreal Massacre were victims of mass murder. They were all shot in a very short time period, culminating with the killer shooting himself.

A **spree murder** shares some of the characteristics of mass murders, in that each killing event usually involves more than one victim. Unlike mass murderers, however, the offender stops killing only temporarily. He or she does not kill themselves or surrender but moves on to kill again at another time. This pattern has only recently been identified, and there are few examples to illustrate this type of killer. One of the most famous cases took place at the University of Texas at Austin in 1966. Charles Whitman, a student at the university, killed both his mother and his wife before heading to the observation deck on the 32-storey administrative building on campus. From there he shot and killed 14 people and wounded 31

Box 5.4 Sereena Abotsway

Sereena Abotsway, born with Fetal Alcohol Syndrome, had an infectious laugh and passion for helping others. Even though one of her boyfriends turned her to a lifestyle of drugs, prostitution, and abusive relationships, she continued to have a 'bubbly' attitude. Abotsway never made it home to celebrate her thirtieth birthday on 20 August 2001 with her adoptive mother, Anna Draayers, whom she had known since the age of four. The Draayers knew something was wrong when Abotsway didn't come home: 'She was our girl, and we loved her a lot. She phoned daily for 13 years since she left our home at age 17.' The Friday following Abotsway's birthday, the police informed the Draayers that their daughter was dead. She was the forty-eighth of fifty women to disappear from downtown Vancouver since 1983.

In 2007, pig farmer Robert Pickton was found guilty of her murder and of the murders of five other women. Ironically, Abotsway had participated in several community marches asking for deeper investigations into the disappearances of the Vancouver women. She wrote a poem about them, saying 'when you went missing each and every year, we all fought so hard to find you.'

The stories shared by Abotsway's friends display their sense of loss over their friend, who was a beam of hope and happiness in the dark life of prostitution and drugs. Cheryl Bear Barnetson said 'we did definitely see the bright side of Sereena . . . It was great to know her in that short period of time. She always had a smile for everybody. A big hello . . . It was really tragic when we saw her picture on the missing women's list.'

SOURCES: Fournier, S., Fraser, K. & Jiwa, S. (2002, 26 February). Daughter phoned daily for 13 years. *The Province*. Retrieved 19 January 2008, from www.missingpeople.net/cgi-bin/2002/sereen_abotsway-2002.htm; Meissner, D. (2007, 19 January). Sereena Abotsway: Life was always about hope. *Canadian Press*. Retrieved 19 January 2008, from www.ctv.ca/servlet/ArticleNews/story/CTVNews/20070117/missing_abotsway_071117/20070119/.

others. He was eventually shot and killed by an Austin police officer.

Serial murders differ from both of these groups. Victims of serial murder are often killed one at a time, with long 'cooling-off' periods between homicide events. There are further differences within this category, depending on whether the murderer is male or female. On the one hand, male serial murderers tend to choose their victims from a social group that holds less social power (Egger, 1990), such as women, children, homosexuals, homeless people, and prostitutes. Sereena Abotsway, the victim of a serial murderer in British Columbia (see Box 5.4), was in many ways a typical victim of serial killers. She was a drug addict and was engaged in a risky lifestyle (prostitution) in order to support her addiction. On the other hand, female serial murderers are more likely to lethally victimize males whom they are intimate with, their own children, or other adults and children in their care (Scott, 2005).

In Keeney and Heide's (1994) study of serial murderers, the authors compared victim experiences based on the gender of the offender. They reported that victims of male serial murderers suffered more damage to their bodies, while still alive or after death, than victims of female serial murderers. Both Scott (2005) and Keeney and Heide (1994) found that women who committed serial murder were less likely to use torture, resulting in less physical damage. Female serial murderers were more likely to use some form of poison rather than more aggressive methods of killing and were more likely to lure their victims rather than stalk them. The reasons for killing also differed markedly between male and female serial killers; the latter

group killed largely for instrumental reasons, such as monetary gain, or for affective reasons, achieving some sort of emotional satisfaction from the killings. Sexual fantasy, while a motivating force for male serial murderers, was not a factor for female killers.

In many ways traditional theories of homicide fail to explain these patterns in serial homicide. This type of victimization is not the result of fights or interactions. Male serial killers choose victims who are not known to them, while female serial killers seek out victims who are traditionally powerful in society. Female killers also establish a sense of trust between themselves and their victims (similar to how pedophiles groom their victims and build trust) in order to make their victims more vulnerable. Overall, there is a paucity of explanations for both victim experience and offender behaviour in this category of multiple homicide.

Summary

This chapter has defined the various types of homicide in Canadian law and explored trends in homicidal victimization. While traditional theories of homicide, such as those put forth by Wolfgang (1958) and Luckenbill (1977), have contributed to our understanding of male-to-male homicides, they are less able to explain incidents that involve victims of minority status; examples of these cases have been profiled in the chapter. There is also little known about victims of multiple homicide, as the offender has been the focus of most studies in this area.

Because homicide is considered one of the most severe offences a person can commit against another, victims of homicide are the type of victim most likely to be discovered and/or reported to the authorities, when compared to other types of crime victims. However, even here we do not have an adequate understanding of the victim, his or her experiences, or how his or her loved ones recover from their loss. The fear generated by this type of victimization and the recovery process of those left behind will be discussed in later chapters. First, though, we will look at victimization in another specific crime: sexual assault.

Glossary

first-degree murder A type of homicide where the victim has been killed deliberately, killed while being the victim of another serious crime, or killed as the result of carrying out duties associated with the protection of the state, such as those performed by a police officer, judge, prison warden, or corrections officer.

hate crime A crime where a particular person or group is targeted for victimization because of minority status, such as racial or ethnic identity and/or sexual orientation.

homicide Literally, 'the killing of man', refers to the killing of a person by another.

homicide victim According to the Canadian Criminal Code (s. 222.1), a person whose death is caused by another person, either directly or indirectly, by any means.

infanticide Literally, the killing of infants or very small children. In legal terms, infanticide is a form of manslaughter in which a newborn child is killed, either deliberately or through an act of omission, by his or her biological mother. It is assumed that the mother suffers from a mental defect caused by childbirth.

manslaughter A type of homicide where the offender is found to have killed the victim in the heat of passion or when the victim is found to have provoked the offender before he or she was killed.

mass murder The act of killing many people in a single murderous event with very little time between murders.

murder A culpable homicide in which the victim's death is deliberately caused or was the result of reckless or negligent behaviour.

second-degree murder Any type of murder not classified as first-degree.

serial murder The act of killing people individually and sequentially, with long 'cooling-off' periods between homicide events.

spree murder The act of killing one of more individuals in multiple locations, over relatively short periods of time. Spree killers share characteristics of mass murderers, in that multiple people may be targeted in one location, but there is a short cooling-off period while the killer moves to another location with another set of targets.

Critical Thinking Questions

1. Review the case of the Montreal Massacre. List the primary, secondary, and tertiary victims of this tragic event.

2. Using the figures and tables presented in this chapter, identify at least three patterns that show differences between male and female homicide victims.

3. Aboriginal Peoples in Canada face particular issues. What are these issues and how do they contribute to the higher homicide rate among this population?

Special Topic: Sexual Assault

Introduction

In this chapter we will examine the crime of sexual assault, paying particular attention to the Criminal Code of Canada's definition of the crime, trends within sexual assault research, and the issues regarding collecting this data. One of these issues is that many victims, including males, homosexuals, and women in intimate relationships, do not report the crime because of the significant social stigma attached to it. For example, historically the law deemed that only women who were not married to their victimizers could be raped. Victims of sexual assault were also more likely to be blamed for bringing about their assaults, often accused of wearing sexually suggestive clothing or being out late at night and therefore putting themselves in unnecessary danger. Changes to legislation have tried to overcome these problems by comparing sexual assault to acts of physical assault, acknowledging the former as an act of violence, power, and control, rather than one of sex. Such changes, combined with public cases like the ones below, have encouraged more victims to come forward. These examples and the others in the chapter illustrate the various forms of this crime and the courage of those victims who have reported their experiences to the authorities.

Victims of Sexual Harassment in the Workplace

In June 2008, Louie Rosella of *The Mississauga News* reported that women who had worked as personal assistants or secretaries in a Mississauga Re/Max office testified in court that their employer, Akbar Zareh, repeatedly touched them in an inappropriate sexual manner and consistently made sexual jokes and innuendos from February 2001 to April 2005. One former employee testified that Zareh would touch her in a sexual way on her shoulders and that she was coerced into sitting on his lap. She stated that she often felt that she had to 'laugh it off' because she did not want to cause trouble or lose her job. Counsel for Zareh argued that the women never let their attitudes about his behaviour known and that the 'sexual joking and banter' was widely accepted in the office by all employees. Zareh was found guilty of one of the 11 charges brought against him. The jury were hung on four of the others and found him not guilty of the remaining six.

Victim of Sexual Assault in a Park

In June 2008, a 39-year-old man told Winnipeg police that he had been physically and sexually assaulted by a man in a public park. The victim stated that he was walking alone in the park when he was approached by his assailant. The police commended the man for coming forward, recognizing that males and females often do not report incidents of sexual assault for a variety of reasons. The police then went on to ask people not to walk alone in the park at night (Winnipeg police looking for suspect, 2008).

Victims of Unprotected Sexual Intercourse with an HIV+ Man

In early 2007, two women testified in a Saskatchewan provincial court that they had had sexual relations with CFL player Trevis Smith and that he had not disclosed his HIV status. Smith found out about his HIV infection in November 2003 (Former CFLer guilty, 2007). One of the women, who lived in British Columbia, testified that she and Smith had been in a long-distance relationship from 2001 to 2005 and that, although they did use protection during the first year, they had decided that it was no longer necessary. The witness also stated that Smith failed to divulge the fact that he was married and had two children at the time of the relationship. In August 2004, she found a 'Living With HIV' pamphlet in his luggage and immediately went to be tested; her status was negative. When the victim confronted Smith regarding the pamphlet and some changes in his behaviour that she had noticed, he told her that he was acting strange because a woman had accused him of giving her HIV. She eventually learned about Smith's HIV status through a phone conversation with another woman, the second witness at the trial. When this woman confronted Smith in 2005, she stated he said he did not tell her because he was scared and worried that she would go to the police (2nd woman says, 2007). Smith was found guilty of two counts of aggravated sexual assault in February 2007 (Former CFLer guilty, 2007).

These cases are only a few examples of the variety and form that sexual assaults can take. However, they do highlight some interesting issues. Sexual assault is one of the most difficult crimes to estimate, largely because many incidents are not reported to police (Johnson, 1996) for a whole host of reasons.

A Brief History of Rape and Sexual Assault

While the term 'sexual assault' is how we currently refer to various forms of sex crimes, historically we have referred to a more limited set of crimes by the term 'rape'. The word *rape*—originally used in law to mean the forced (by physical threat or coercion) sexual intercourse upon a woman by a man—comes from the Latin derivative of *rapare*, which literally means to 'take by force'. In her landmark book, *Against Our Will*, Susan Brownmiller (1975) argues that historical ideas regarding the act of rape, and specifically the rape of women, differ depending on several factors. For example, in acts of war, victors rape the women of their enemies not only to demoralize the defeated but also to impregnate them and thus contaminate their genetic lineage.

In the Bible, the rape of women is considered a moral sin, and the rape of a virgin punishable by death. However, the rape of a married woman could lead to the execution of both the victimizer and the victim. Unless the woman's husband intervened in the assault, it was assumed that the woman had consented to sexual activity or had done something to cause the victimizing behaviour of her attacker. Under biblical law, men were forbidden on punishment of death to 'lay' with other men, but rape of men was never addressed.

Brownmiller (1975) notes that during the medieval era a man of low social class could abduct and rape an unmarried woman from a wealthy family in order to obligate her to marry him and thereby increase his social power. As feudalism developed, the rape of women was limited to the upper classes. Poor women forced into sexual activity had no recourse against their victimizers. During times of slavery and segregation in the United States, an African-American male had only to be accused of raping a Caucasian woman to be put to death, often without trial. Throughout these historical periods, rape was viewed specifically as a male-to-female attack. While the law considered that men could be victims of other forms of sex crime, such as sodomy, they could not technically be raped.

In the 1960s and 1970s, the Women's Movement highlighted the plight of raped women, and their experiences with the criminal justice system became a pre-eminent example of the 'battle of the sexes' and the inequality of women.

England, Canada, and the United States were among the first countries to redefine rape as a form of violence rather than one of sexual activity. Old ideas that women somehow brought about their rape were dismissed in favour of interpretations of sexual assault as an act of violence. Rape was no longer considered an act of 'passion' or 'lust' but a violent act that served to inflict deep personal injury onto the victim. Within this viewpoint, victimizers were seen as operating out of choice rather than uncontrollable sexual desire. The paradox of males being socialized to be leaders but somehow not in control of their own bodies became highlighted. During this time, men who had been sexually assaulted could also have their victimizers charged.

Despite these advances, there are still those today who adhere to more traditional ideas of gendered expectations and responsibilities when evaluating cases of sexual assault. We continue to see these values conveyed in news reports and other media. In many instances, victims of sexual assault continue to be blamed—by both attackers and defence counsel—for provoking assaults. Many offenders continue to assert that the victim, by engaging in behaviour that was misinterpreted, is to blame for the attack. Chapter 3 highlights two cases in which these arguments were made (see page 33). When Katelyn Faber accused basketball superstar Kobe Bryant of sexually assaulting her, she was vilified by the media, Bryant's fans, and many members of the public. Bryant's defence counsel argued that because Bryant had invited Faber to his hotel room, she should have expected to have sex with him. When she said that she did not want to, he misinterpreted this as being insincere. Similarly, the defence counsel in the case of 14-year-old 'A' claimed that because she willingly met her attacker in a park at night there was a reasonable expectation that she would come to harm; therefore, she was partially responsible for her own attack. In both cases, the defence relied on the assumption that victims can control the actions of potential offenders, regardless of their intentions or amount of pre-planning. It would be interesting to know if the defence would have made the same argument if the assault had been physical and not sexual.

Legal Definitions of Sexual Assault

There are several definitions of sexual assault available, depending on the source. For the purposes of this chapter, we will focus on the current definition found in the Criminal Code of Canada (CCC). Canadian law prior to 1983 stated that only women who were not married to their assailants could be raped; the law did not recognize cases involving male victims or cases involving sexual assault within a marriage (Hinch, 1985). While men who were sexually assaulted could press other types of charges, they were not able to press rape charges. Women who were sexually assaulted by their husbands had no legal claim. Both groups, then, were denied the opportunity to have their assailants charged appropriately, if charged at all. The implication of separate charges for similar crimes against different genders reinforced inequality in sentencing. The charge of 'rape' had a stronger sentence than many of the other sex crimes listed in the legislation. Not being able to charge an offender with rape may have translated into lesser sentences against those who victimized males and/or were the same sex as the victim or their intimate partners. In a pamphlet announcing the new legislation, the Department of Justice stated that 'the old views about the role of women and the position of men are no longer applicable' and that 'men and women have a right to equal treatment' (as cited in Hinch, 1985, p. 33).

Amendments to the CCC were made in 1983, replacing the crimes of rape and indecent assault with a definition of sexual assault that was more in line with physical assault. According to the Department of Justice (1985), the intention was to remove the sexual nature of the crime, lessen discrimination against gender or marital status, and ensure that victims understood that the law conceptualized sexual assault as an act of violence rather than sexuality. It was hoped that these changes would encourage victims to report these crimes to police. The new laws created the following three classifications of sexual assault, also referred to as *sexual assault I*, *sexual assault II*, and *sexual assault III*, respectively:

Sexual assault

271.(1) Every one who commits a sexual assault is guilty of

(a) an indictable offence and is liable to imprisonment for a term not exceeding ten years; or (b) an offence punishable on summary conviction and liable to imprisonment for a term not exceeding eighteen months.

Sexual assault with a weapon, threats to a third party or causing bodily harm

272. (1) Every person commits an offence who, in committing a sexual assault,

(a) carries, uses or threatens to use a weapon or an imitation of a weapon;
(b) threatens to cause bodily harm to a person other than the complainant;
(c) causes bodily harm to the complainant; or
(d) is a party to the offence with any other person.

Aggravated sexual assault

273. (1) Every one commits an aggravated sexual assault who, in committing a sexual assault, wounds, maims, disfigures or endangers the life of the complainant.

These classifications recognize that an individual cannot only be physically harmed during an assault but that he or she can also be forced or coerced into sexual activity by threats to him- or herself or to another person. Section 271 is considered the least harmful form of sexual assault because there is no occurrence of serious injury or coercion. Under the old laws, this category would be considered simple sexual assault. In addition to the above offences, there is another set of crimes commonly referred to as 'other sexual offences', which are primarily geared to sexual offences against children and animals. These crimes include bestiality (s. 160), anal intercourse (s. 159), incest (s. 155), sexual exploitation (s. 153), invitation to sexual touching (s. 152), and sexual interference (s. 151).

While these definitions are more inclusive, they can also create difficulty when trying to assign the appropriate classification to an incident of sexual assault. For example, how would you classify a case where someone is touched in the genital area at a bus stop by someone passing by on a bicycle?

What if the victim falls as a result of the attack or is run over by one of the tires of the bike? What if other people witness this action and the victim must manage these observances? What if the victim finds it difficult to ride the bus after this incident?

A key component to discussing any case of sexual assault is that of consent. This issue is important because sexual assault is one of the few crimes in the CCC that implicitly requires that consent must be obtained freely in order for the act not to be considered illegal. In other crimes, such as assault, aggravated assault, homicide, robbery, and so on, consent does not need to be proven because it is assumed that these acts are not desired. If one is punched, it is assumed that he or she did not give consent. If one is touched in a sexually specific area, the law implicitly assumes that consent may have been given. Therefore, extra effort has to be made to assess whether the act was consensual. In this way, the law is still somewhat accommodating to victimizers, as the act of consent often becomes critical in many defence arguments. Victims bear the added responsibility of proving that they did not consent to the act, which is akin to victims having to prove that they are innocent of contributing to their own victimizations.

Sexual Assault Victimization Reported in the Canadian General Social Survey (GSS)

Recall from Chapter 2 that crimes reported to police are recorded in the Uniform Crime Reports (UCR). The cases mentioned at the beginning of this chapter were not only reported to police but are even more unusual in that they were also covered by the media. In addition to crimes reported to police, the Canadian government also collects data on victimization but does so in rather large sample surveys of randomly selected households. These other kinds of surveys, or victimization surveys, can often have drastically different results when trying to understand the similar forms of victimization. Victimization surveys are important because they not only estimate crimes reported to the police, but they also ask about crimes that were not reported. This is not to say that all crimes asked about will be reported in these surveys, but they do contain more criminal activity as reported by the victims of those crimes.

The General Social Survey (GSS) is a series of surveys that run in 'cycles' or themes (see also Chapter 2). These cycles can vary in length, but their purpose is to revisit issues and study how they change and fluctuate over the long term. Methodologically we say that these surveys provide *longitudinal data* on various subjects. One of these subjects is victimization, which is on a five-year rotation. As of this writing, the GSS has completed five cycles examining various forms of victimization: Cycle 3 (1989), Cycle 8 (1994), Cycle 13 (1999), Cycle 18 (2004), and Cycle 23 (2009). In addition to asking about experiences with various types of property crime, the survey also asks respondents whether they have had experiences with violent crime, including sexual assault. In the latest GSS for which data has been analyzed (Cycle 18), each respondent was asked the following questions regarding their experiences with unwanted sexual activity:

(Excluding incidents already mentioned,) during the past 12 months, has anyone forced you or attempted to force you into any unwanted sexual activity, by threatening you, holding you down or hurting you in some way? This includes acts by family and non-family but excludes acts by current or previous spouses or common-law partners. Remember that all information provided is strictly confidential.

(Apart from what you have told me,) during the past 12 months, has anyone ever touched you against your will in any sexual way? By this I mean anything from unwanted touching or grabbing, to kissing or fondling. Again, please exclude acts by current or previous spouses or common-law partners.

During the past 5 years, has your current or previous spouse or common-law partner forced you into any unwanted sexual activity, by threatening you, holding you down, or hurting you in some way?

The questions in this survey, and others like it, specifically ask about unwanted sexual activity. In this way, the questions reflect the changes made to the CCC in 1983. The phrasing of the questions is important, as it requires little interpretation on behalf of the respondent. The first question attempts to illicit responses about aggravated sexual assault and coercive sexual assault (sexual assaults II and III), while the second attempts to learn about the prevalence of more common forms of assaults, or simple sexual assaults (sexual assault I). The final question asks about these acts committed by partners.

Trends in Sexual Assault According to the General Social Survey

Cycle 18 of the GSS asked a random sample of Canadians about victimization experienced during the 12-months prior to the survey. Data collected estimate that sexual assault rates remained relatively stable at the rate of 21 persons per 1,000 population in both 1999 and 2004 (Gannon & Mihorean, 2005). The report also states that 7 per cent of women and 6 per cent of men who responded to the survey stated that they had experienced some physical or sexual violence from their current or previous spouse or common-law partner in the last five years.

Table 6.1 illustrates some rather interesting correlates of violent victimization, including sexual assault. According to Gannon and Mihorean (2005), who looked at trends in violent victimization in Canada in 2004, there were certain patterns that increased the risk for violent victimization: being younger (ages 15–24), being single, living in an urban area, and having an income below $15,000 per year. The authors also found trends regarding the reporting of sexual victimization. Women over the age of 15 years were five times more likely to report sexual victimization (35/1,000 population) than men (7/1,000 population), who were more likely to report robberies and physical assaults. What is interesting to note about the information presented in this table is that women are only slightly less likely to report violent victimization (102/1,000 population) as compared to males (111/1,000 population). Those who were most likely to report sexual assault in the victimization survey were single and between the ages

of 15 and 24, followed by people who were divorced or separated, lived in an urban environment, and reported being a student or unemployed as their primary activity during the day. Although Statistics Canada advises that the results illustrated in Table 6.1 should be used with caution for methodological reasons, the data suggest that people with lower household incomes were also more likely to report sexual victimization than those in households with higher incomes.

Gannon and Mihorean (2005) report that 94 per cent of incidents of sexual assault reported in the survey were committed by a single offender. In 91 per cent of these cases, the victim was sexually assaulted by a male. In just over half, the perpetrator was estimated to be between the ages of 18 and 34. This percentage is slightly lower than for robbery (57 per cent) but higher than for physical assault (47 per cent). On average, however, the authors note that the age of the perpetrator of sexual assault was slightly older than that of the perpetrator of robbery or physical assault. Almost all of the sexual assaults reported in the GSS, Cycle 18, did not involve a weapon (91 per cent).

In order to assess the extent to which alcohol or drugs were involved in sexual assault, respondents were asked whether they believed the incident was related to the perpetrator's alcohol or drug use. In just under half (48 per cent) of the sexual assault cases reported in the victimization survey, the victim believed that the accused's alcohol or drug use played a role. Those who reported participating in 30 or more evening activities in a given month also reported the highest rates of violent victimization (174/1,000 population), including sexual assault at

Table 6.1 Number and Rate of Violent Victimization by Victim Characteristics, 2004[1]

	Number of incidents				Rate per 1,000 population		
	Total violent	Sexual assault	Robbery	Physical assault	Total violent	Sexual assault	Robbery
Victim characteristics							
Total	2,752	547	274	1931	106	21	11
Sex							
Females	1,339	460	104[E]	775	102	35	8[E]
Males	1,412	86[E]	170	1,156	111	7[E]	13
Age (years)							
15 to 24	967	243	142	581	226	57	33
25 to 34	692	133	46[E]	513	157	30	10[E]
35 to 44	595	102	44[E]	449	115	20	8[E]
45 to 54	296	37[E]	31[E]	229	62	8[E]	6[E]
55 to 64	153	25[E]	F	120[E]	45	7[E]	F
65 and over	48[E]	F	F	39[E]	12[E]	F	F
Marital status							
Married	689	87	45	558	52	7	3[E]
Common law	352	44	22	286	131	16	8[E]
Single	1,386	339	182	866	203	50	27
Widow or widower	F	F	F	F	F	F	F
Separated or divorced	285	70[E]	23[E]	192	159	39[E]	13[E]
Don't know/not stated	F	0	F	F			
Main Activity							
Working at a job	1,701	267	158	1,276	114	18	11
Looking for work	86[E]	9	17	60[E]	207[E]	F	F
A student	586	178	70[E]	338	183	56	22[E]
Household work[2]	154	31[E]	F	118	78	15[E]	F
Retired	80[E]	F	F	56[E]	18[E]	F	F
Other[3]	101[E]	33[E]	13[E]	55[E]	167[E]	55[E]	21[E]
Don't know/not stated	43[E]	F	F	27			
Evening Activities (# per month)							
Less than 10	277	52[E]	F	209	44	8[E]	F
10 to 19	459	81[E]	28[E]	350	77	14[E]	5[E]
20 to 29	525	105	57[E]	363	104	21	11[E]
30 and more	1,491	309	174	1,009	174	36	20
Don't know/not stated	0	0	0	0			
Household income ($)							
0 to 14,999	177	43[E]	19[E]	115	156	38[E]	17[E]
15,000 to 29,999	277	64[E]	32[E]	180	104	24[E]	12[E]
30,000 to 39,999	236	42[E]	F	174	105	19[E]	F
40,000 to 59,999	418	95	30[E]	293	94	21	7[E]
60,000 and over	997	155	82[E]	759	106	16	9[E]
Don't know/not stated	647	147[E]	92[E]	409			
Location of home							
Urban	2,307	469	32	1,596	112	23	12
Rural		445	78[E]	242[E]	335	84	15[E]

Note: Figures may not add to total due to rounding.
0   true zero or a value rounded to zero.
[E]   use with caution
[F]   too unreliable to be published
1   Includes all incidents of spousal sexual and physical assault.
2   Includes taking care of children and maternity/paternity leave.
3   Includes long-term illness and volunteering.

SOURCES: Gannon, M., & Mihorean, K. (2005). Sexual offences in Canada, 2004. *Juristat, 25(7)*. General Social Survey, 2004. Statistics Canada: Centre for Canadian Justice Statistics, Minister of Industry, p. 23.

a rate of 36/1,000 population. In fact, the rate of violent and sexual assault victimization increased with the number of reported evening activities reported per month. Thirty-nine per cent of sexual assaults were most likely to occur in a commercial establishment, with 20 per cent occurring in a bar or restaurant and 19 per cent in an office, factory, store, or shopping mall.

In 35 per cent of cases, respondents reported that they were sexually assaulted in the workplace. One-quarter of these victims reported that, after they were assaulted, they had difficulty carrying out their main activities. Finally, Cycle 18 found that, while victims of sexual assault were more likely to seek help from a formal help agency (such as police, rape crises centres, and so on), they were less likely than victims of robbery or physical assault to turn to informal support, including that available from friends, family, or co-workers. Gannon and Mihorean (2005) report that it is estimated that less than 1 in 12 (8 per cent) sexual assault incidents were reported to police in 2004. This number is considerably lower than the number of robberies (46 per cent) and physical assaults (39 per cent) that were reported in that same year.

While the GSS provides valuable information on incidents of sexual assault, it is important to remember that it is not designed to contact every citizen. The GSS surveys only a random sampling of individuals 15 years of age and over regarding their experiences of victimization. Children below the age of 15, individuals who are homeless or living in institutions, and others who do not have phones are not included. Often this excluded population is most vulnerable to victimization. Therefore, we can only assume that the numbers regarding sexual assaults are much higher than those estimated above.

Trends in Sexual Assault Victimization Reported to Police

According to Kong, Johnson, Beattie, and Cardillo (2003), there were 27,094 reported incidents of sexual assault in Canada in 2002. The vast majority of these were categorized as level I sexual assaults. Ten per cent of sexual offences were level II assaults, while the remaining two per cent were the most severe, or level III assaults. Sexual assaults made up 8 per cent of all violent crime reported in 2002, while other sexual offences comprised 1 per cent. Overall, the rate of sexual offences per 100,000 population was 86. From 1992 to 2002 the proportion of sexual offences in all reported crime remained constant at 1 per cent. The authors also note that, since the legislative changes in 1983, incidents of sexual assault level I peaked in 1993 at a rate of 136/100,000 and then declined, while sexual assault levels II and III have both declined since the change was implemented. The rates in 2002 remain 47 per cent higher than they were in 1983. However, as figures 6.1 and 6.2 illustrate, rates of sexual assault reported to police can vary between cities and between provinces/territories.

There has been much discussion as to why these police reported crime rates are falling but still remain higher than in 1983. After the definition of who could be sexually assaulted became more inclusive, it was expected that these rates would rise to reflect the more inclusive

Figure 6.1   Rates of Police-Reported Sexual Offences among CMAs, 2002

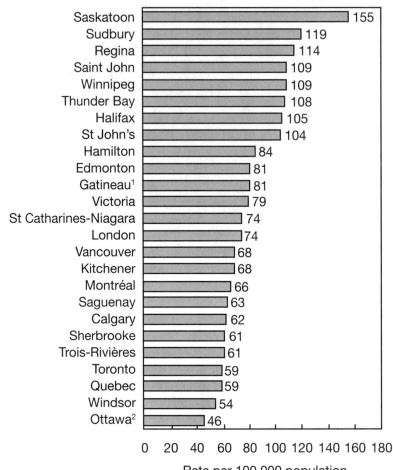

1 Includes Gatineau portion of the Ottawa–Gatineau CMA.
2 Includes the Ottawa portion of the Ottawa–Gatineau CMA.

SOURCE: Kong, R., Johnson, H., Beattie, S., & Cardillo, A. (2003). Sexual offences in Canada. *Juristat, 23(6)*. Statistics Canada: Canadian Centre for Justice Statistics, 1–26.

population of all potential sexual assault victims, including married women, males, and those assaulted by same-sex partners. The rates did increase but only for the most minor assaults. Although the changes in legislation were supposed to encourage reporting, is it possible that they were not effective for victims of more serious forms of sexual victimization?

Roberts and Gebotys (1992) and Roberts and Grossman (1994) state that social change, as reflected in the changes in legislation, is a more likely explanation. Over the last 30 years, the advent of the Victims' Movement (see Chapter 1) brought about a series of social, political, and economic changes of attitudes towards both the equality of women and

Figure 6.2   Provincial and Territorial Rates of Police-Reported Sexual
Offences, 2002

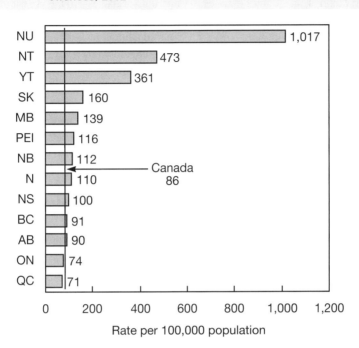

Rate per 100,000 population

SOURCE: Kong, R., Johnson, H., Beattie, S., & Cardillo, A. (2003). Sexual offences in Canada. *Juristat 23(6)*. Statistics Canada: Canadian Centre for Justice Statistics, 1–26.

acceptability of violence. Additionally, in recent years we have seen a decline in the number of younger persons as a proportion of the entire population. Given that younger people are more at risk for both victimization and criminality, the lower proportion of individuals below the age of 34 results in a decrease in these events.

Comparing the GSS and the UCR on Sexual Assault Data

One of the factors to keep in mind when learning about and diagnosing trends in this particular crime is the large discrepancy between those crimes reported to police and those that victims will admit to on a victimization survey. Both the UCR and the GSS report similar data identifying those most at risk for this crime among adults as young females (ages 15–24) who are single, divorced, or separated; who are students; and/or who admitted to more than 30 activities outside the home per month (Kong, Johnson, Beattie, & Cardillo, 2003). Although the GSS can only estimate victimization for those who are 15 years of age and over, the UCR reports all crime reported to police, including crimes against children. Among children, females are most at risk for sexual assault, with the highest risk group being between the ages of 11 and

19. According to the UCR, females age 13 were most at risk for sexual assault victimization. For boys, those ages 3 to 14 were most at risk (Kong, Johnson, Beattie, & Cardillo, 2003).

While the UCR focuses on reported crimes, the GSS is used to estimate the number of crimes that are not reported to police for certain categories of crimes. Figure 6.3 illustrates the very different numbers for sexual assault generated by both surveys. Recall that these surveys use different ways of counting information. The GSS requires that the respondent in the telephone interview be truthful to the best of his or her ability. The crime that occurred does not have to have been reported to any authority, and the victim is assured anonymity in the interview process. A set of questions—designed to approximate the behaviour of what would be considered criminal activity under the CCC—is asked to have the respondent self-identify whether he or she has been the victim of a crime. In this way, the determination of criminal victimization is carried out by the respondent. The ability to capture this information is only as good as the person or team who designed the survey. For example, many people would answer the question 'Have you ever been raped?' differently than the question 'Have you ever been forced into sexual activity against your will using physical force or threat of physical force?' The first question requires the victim to make more of a value decision and admit that he or she was the victim of a very specific crime, whereas the second question requires that the victim only identify whether he or she has had a specific behavioural experience.

On the other hand, data in the UCR is coded after a report is made and filed with the police. The victim relays information to the officer on the scene, who eventually decides on whether a charge is warranted, or whether no identifiable criminal activity took place. If the officer determines that a charge is required, he or she chooses from a variety of available options, depending on the determined severity of the offence. The categories of offence are determined by the CCC.

Looking at Figure 6.3, it is easily determined that there is huge discrepancy between what is reported in the GSS and what is reported to police. In the graph showing results for 1999, the survey discrepancies estimate that only 4.75 per cent of those who were sexually assaulted filed a police report. In 2004, both surveys reported an increase in the number of sexual assaults; there also appears to have been a slight increase in the percentage of reported cases (5.03 per cent).

Reasons for Not Reporting Sexual Assault

Sexual assault, like other crimes, does not always get reported to police. However, unlike other crimes, certain reasons for not reporting the crime seem to predominate. According to Kong, Johnson, Beattie, and Cardillo (2003) both sexual assault victims (61 per cent) and physical assault victims (57 per cent) stated that they dealt with the crimes in another way. Both victim types agreed with the statement that the crime was 'not important enough' to warrant calling police (sexual assault: 50 per cent; physical assault: 52 per cent). Among respondents reporting being sexually assaulted, 50 per cent stated that they did not report to police because it was a 'personal matter and did not concern police', as compared with a

Figure 6.3   Comparison of Sexual Assaults in 1999 and 2004 Using the General Social Survey and the Uniform Crime Reports

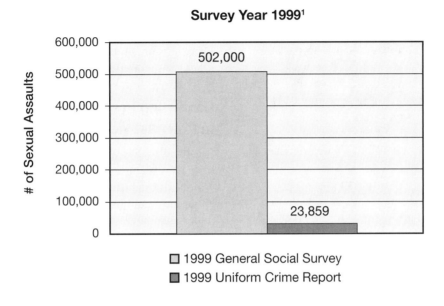

Survey Year 1999[1]

Survey Year 2004[2,3]

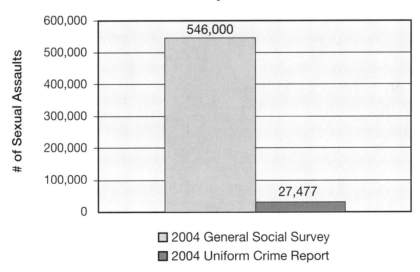

SOURCES: 1. Kong, R., Johnson, H., Beattie, S., & Cardillo, A. (2003). Sexual offences in Canada. *Juristat 23*(6). Statistics Canada: Canadian Centre for Justice Statistics, 1–26. 2. Gannon, M., & Mihorean, K. (2004). Criminal victimization in Canada. *Juristat, 25*(7). Statistics Canada: Canadian Centre for Justice Statistics, 1–27. 3. Sauve, J. (2004). Crime statistics in Canada. *Juristat 25*(5). Statistics Canada: Canadian Centre for Justice Statistics, 1–23.

much lower agreement rate for physical assault victims (30 per cent).

This same report also documents that more sexual assault victims stated that they did not want to get involved with the police (sexual assault: 47 per cent; physical assault: 36 per cent). An equal proportion of both victim types agreed with the statement that the 'police couldn't do anything about [it]' if they had reported (sexual assault: 33 per cent; physical assault: 32 per cent). More sexual assault victims were concerned about fear of revenge (sexual assault: 19 per cent; physical assault: 10 per cent) and feared publicity (sexual assault: 14 per cent; physical assault: 4 per cent). About equal proportions stated that they felt that the police would not help (sexual assault: 18 per cent; physical assault: 17 per cent) and/or had other reasons for not reporting (sexual assault: 9 per cent; physical assault: 8 per cent). Sexual assault victims were also much less likely to report that they discussed the matter with a family member, friend, neighbour, co-worker, doctor, nurse, or lawyer.

Responses by the Criminal Justice System

According to Kong, Johnson, Beattie, and Cardillo (2003), 16 per cent of all sexual assault cases reported to police were determined to be unfounded, to have insufficient evidence to warrant a charge. This rate has remained relatively stable since the early 1990s. Additionally, the clearance rate (i.e., cases that were cleared by having a charge laid or cleared by another process) has been steadily decreasing since the early 1990s. Research done by Scott and Beaman (2004) suggest that charges are more

likely to be laid if the sexual assault was not completed. In cases that do go to court, the offender was more likely to get a conviction if he or she was charged with sexual assault level I and more likely to receive a prison sentence over other forms of punishments as compared to other violent offences.

Conflicting Prevention Advice to Potential Victims

Because women fear sexual assault more than men (Ferarro, 1996; Warr 1985), women have probably thought more about the possibility of being raped, and in particular what they should do in case of an attack. The traditional advice given when faced with any crime is to comply with the attacker to avoid injury. For example, in the case of a carjacking, potential victims are encouraged to hand over the car keys rather than risk being hurt or killed. Likewise, in a robbery situation, most employees are encouraged to protect themselves and to comply with the offender by handing over any available cash or merchandise. People are reminded that cars and money are only possessions and that they are not worth being hurt or killed over. This advice is similar for most crimes: comply with your attacker or you will get hurt. It is important that you not risk injury to yourself.

In the early 1970s, this advice was also given to potential sexual assault victims (Ullman, 1998). Women were encouraged to not resist their attacker for fear that it would escalate the violence. These ideas were fuelled by the fear that rapists were also sexual sadists, possibly prone to homicide. As a result, women were told to simply submit to their attackers to avoid serious injury or a sexually sadistic death. As Ullman (1998) and Scott and Beaman (2004) point out, this advice has probably done more harm than good. First, it presents potential victims with conflicting information. If they do fight, they have a better chance of thwarting the attack and getting an arrest (Scott & Beaman, 2004). Combative victims also run the risk of injury. If they do not physically resist their attackers, their chances of experiencing a completed sexual assault increase and their chances of seeing an arrest of their offender decrease due to lack of physical evidence. Also causing possible confusion is the advice to comply with the offender's demands to avoid injury and the expectations placed on victims to prove that they were forced into sexual activity. If a victim obeys the attacker's commands in order to prevent injury, there is only his or her word that the sex was not consensual. There is a common misperception that someone who truly does not want to have sex will fight to protect his or her honour. In reality, victims of sexual assault operate in their own best interests of self-preservation, dealing with their perceptions of situations as they arise and making choices that will operate in their best protective interests without risking their health. Victims may choose to comply or not comply, depending on their individual risk assessments of the circumstances at the moment that they become aware of being in danger.

Canadian Case Law Protecting the Victim: *R. v. Seaboyer* and *R. v. Gayme*

In addition to the changes to the sexual assault laws in the CCC, there have also been recent developments with respect to protection for the sexual assault victim. Both Canada and the United States have implemented 'rape shield' laws to protect the victim from prejudicial practices of the court. In particular, rape shield laws protect the victim from being cross-examined about his or her prior sexual practices. The landmark cases of *R. v. Seaboyer* and *R. v. Gayme* (see Box 6.1) served to uphold decisions to protect the Crown from unlawful evidence gathering beyond the incident in question.

In *R. v. Seaboyer* (1991) the court struck down existing legislation that served to protect the victim from not being cross-examined as to his or her version of events. In essence, this important case stated that not being able to cross-examine the victim/witness violated the constitutional rights of the offender. This finding was later tested by *R. v. Gayme* and upheld. In 1992, new legislation was crafted that effectively made a new 'rape shield law' that addressed what evidence could be brought before the court regarding the victim, including the inadmissibility of medical and counselling records. In 1995, the new legislation was tested when Bishop Hubert Patrick O'Connor (*R. v. O'Connor, 1995*), charged with sexual assault, asked for counselling and medical records of his accuser to be admitted as evidence. The court upheld that limitations on this type of evidence should be maintained and ruled that this evidence can be considered under only two conditions:

1. the applicant must establish, without seeing the actual records, that the documents are likely to be relevant to the case.
2. the judge must review the records and decide whether to disclose them

based on balancing the right to an appropriate and suitable defence and the right to privacy.

Crisis Centres

One unique service offered to women who are sexually assaulted is the crisis

---

Box 6.1 Rape Shield Legislation: *R. v. Seaboyer* and *R. v. Gayme*

Steven Seaboyer	*Appellant*
v.	
Her Majesty The Queen	*Respondent*
and	
The Attorney General of Canada, the Attorney General of Quebec, the Attorney General for Saskatchewan, the Canadian Civil Liberties Association and Women's Legal Education and Action Fund et al	*Interveners*
and between	
Nigel Gayme	*Appellant*
v.	
Her Majesty The Queen	*Respondent*
and	
The Attorney General of Canada, the Attorney General of Quebec, the Attorney General for Saskatchewan, the Canadian Civil Liberties Association and Women's Legal Education and Action Fund et al.	*Interveners*

At issue here was whether the *Criminal Code*'s 'rape shield' provisions (R.S.C., 1985, c. C-46, ss. 276 and 277) infringe on the principles of fundamental justice or the right to a fair trial as found in ss. 7 and 11(*d*) of the *Canadian Charter of Rights and Freedoms*. The 'rape shield' provisions restrict the right of the defence on a trial for a sexual offence to cross-examine and lead evidence of a complainant's sexual conduct on other occasions.

Seaboyer was charged with sexual assault of a woman with whom he had been drinking in a bar. The judge at the preliminary inquiry refused to allow the accused to cross-examine the complainant on her sexual conduct on other occasions. The appellant contended that he should have been permitted to cross-examine as to other acts of sexual intercourse which may have caused bruises and other aspects of the complainant's condition which the Crown had put into evidence. Such evidence might arguably be relevant to consent since it might provide other explanations for the physical evidence tendered by the Crown in support of the use of force against the complainant.

The *Gayme* case arose in different circumstances. The complainant was 15, the appellant 18. They were friends. The Crown alleged that the appellant sexually assaulted the complainant at his school. The defence, relying on the defences of consent and honest belief in consent, contended that there was no assault and that the complainant was the sexual aggressor. In pursuance of this defence, the appellant at the preliminary inquiry sought to cross-examine and present evidence on prior and subsequent sexual conduct of the complainant. Accordingly, he brought a motion that ss. 276 and 277 of the *Code* were unconstitutional. The judge rejected the motion, on the ground that he lacked jurisdiction to hear it, and committed the appellant for trial.

Both Seaboyer and Gayme applied to the Supreme Court of Ontario for an order quashing the committal for trial on the ground that the judge below had exceeded his jurisdiction and deprived the appellant of his right to make full answer and defence by enforcing the provisions of s. 276 of the *Criminal Code*. The orders were granted on the ground that ss. 276 and 277 violate the *Charter*, and the cases were remitted to the preliminary inquiry judges for a ruling on the evidentiary issues unhampered by the statutory provisions. An appeal to the Ontario Court of Appeal was allowed on the ground that the preliminary inquiry judges lacked the jurisdiction to determine the constitutional validity of the sections in question. They accordingly had not erred in applying the sections and the orders quashing the committal therefore had to be set aside. The Court went on, however, to consider the constitutionality of ss. 276 and 277 of the *Criminal Code* and found that the sections were capable of contravening an accused's rights under the *Charter* in some circumstances. It held that while the provisions had a constitutionally valid purpose, they were not saved by s. 1. The court nevertheless found that the provisions would be operative except in those limited and rare circumstances where they would have an unconstitutional effect.

The constitutional questions stated in this Court queried whether ss. 276 and 277 infringed ss. 7 and 11(*d*) of the *Charter* and, if so, whether they were saved by s. 1. Also queried was whether the constitutional exemptions doctrine applied and, if the legislation was invalid, what was the law. With respect to the jurisdiction of the preliminary inquiry judge, the evidence sought to be tendered in the two cases was not at issue. In neither case did the preliminary inquiry judge consider whether the evidence would have been relevant or admissible in the absence of ss. 276 or 277 of the *Criminal Code*.

Held (L'Heureux-Dubé and Gonthier JJ. dissenting in part): The appeals should be dismissed; however, s. 276 of the *Criminal Code* is inconsistent with ss. 7 and 11(*d*) of the *Charter* and that inconsistency is not justified under s. 1 of the *Charter*. Section 277 is not inconsistent with the *Charter*.

SOURCE: *R. v. Seaboyer* and *R. v. Gayme*, [1991] 2 S.C.R. 577 Retrieved 8 January 2010, from http://csc. lexum.umontreal.ca/en/1991/1991scr2-577/1991scr2-577.html.

centre. The first crisis centres in Canada were opened in Vancouver in 1974. These centres emerged as the result of the recognition that women who experienced sexual assault had specific needs because of their victimization and were designed to expand on the services provided by police and hospital staff. For example, they offered more long-term aid, as compared to the emergency responses provided by the other services. The centres were also active in promoting safety among women, becoming the locus of many of the anti-sexual assault movements in Canada and the United States.

Services provided by such crisis centres reflect the varying needs of sexual assault victims. Most crisis centres offer 24-hour telephone counselling service to those in crisis. These counsellors deal with the immediate concerns of women who have just been assaulted and need to talk as well as those who continue to experience trauma years after the event. Many centres have caseworkers and/or volunteers who will meet victims of sexual assault at the crime scene and/or the hospital, offering support, clothing, and so on, as victims deal with the police and hospital personnel. Crisis centres may also offer peer counselling or group counselling sessions as well as act as a hub for many other community services that can help a woman get the services she needs. For example, crisis personnel can help a woman find a temporary place to stay if she is afraid to go home, temporary childcare, someone to discuss the crime with, a social worker if long-term services are required, and other resources to help her cope with the sexual assault. Finally, these centres serve as an educational centre, often disseminating information that counters common myths or false perceptions about sexual assault, its victims, and its victimizers.

Sexual Assault of Males

Sexual assault crisis centres, because they were designed as a haven for women, given their underprivileged status in society and in the criminal justice system, rarely deal with male clients. Therefore, men who have experienced sexual assault tend to have fewer options for dealing with this crime.

Prior to changes in the legislation, Canadian law did not consider that men could be raped. Not allowing men to be acknowledged in this victim class denied them certain opportunities for apprehension of the victimizer and recovery from the crime; victimizers who were apprehended for this crime were charged under other statutes. However, the inclusion of male sexual assault victims in the law has not eliminated all of the difficulties of men reporting such crimes. First, men who are sexually assaulted may be doubly stigmatized, because of society's traditional view that males are supposed to be strong and therefore less prone to this kind of victimization. This gendered response to sexual victimization strongly discourages males from reporting sexual assault. Second, once they have experienced this victimization, men are discouraged from communicating the event to others, for fear of social reprisal.

Boxes 6.2 and 6.3 discuss two well-known cases involving sexual assault of males. The first details the abuse scandal that played out in Toronto and in the national newspapers in the late 1990s. After Martin Kruze reported his

Box 6.2 Sex Scandal at Maple Leaf Gardens

Martin Kruze played hockey at Toronto's Maple Leaf Gardens for most of his teenage and early adult years. In early 1997, Kruze went public with charges that from 1975 to 1982 (when he was between the ages of 13 to 20), he was regularly sexually assaulted by two staff members: equipment manager George Hannah and maintenance person Gordon Stuckless. Kruze told police that the majority of the abuse took place in utility rooms and offices at the Gardens. Kruze had previously sued the Gardens for $1.75 million dollars in 1993 but settled out of court for a suspected $60,000. Conditions of the deal stated that he was not allowed to talk about the details of the settlement.

Within one week of Kruze's story going public, more than 60 people from all over Canada and the United States reported that they too had been abused. These reports of abuse spanned approximately 30 years, from the 1960s to the final report in 1991. Detective Dave Tredrea of the Metropolitan Toronto Police led the investigation into these claims. He noted that more than one child in a family was abused in some cases and that there was no evidence that the men worked or assaulted victims together, rejecting speculation of a pedophile ring.

In February 1997, Stuckless was charged with two counts of gross indecency and indecent assault. An usher who had worked at the Gardens for 26 years, Paul Roby, was charged with 11 counts. Tredrea stated that they were also to be charged with additional counts when they appeared in court the following week. Hannah was not charged because he had died of heart failure in 1984.

Although the court agreed not to publish the names of the alleged victims in this case, two additional men have come forward asking that their names be made public: John McCarthy and Darryl Bingham. Along with Kruze, these men have stated that they would like their names to be used in hopes that it might encourage other victims to come forward. In addition to the 60 victims identified, police spoke to another 100 callers since the story broke.

Roby was eventually convicted in 1999 of multiple counts of criminal assault involving the sexual abuse of young boys while he worked at Maple Leaf Gardens. He was declared a dangerous offender in 2000 and died of a heart attack in 2001. Stuckless received a sentence of 2 years less a day, which was later commuted to 5 years, after pleading guilty in 1997 to 24 counts of sexual and indecent assault. He served two-thirds of his sentence and was paroled in February 2001.

SOURCE: Brazao, D., & Mascoll, P. (1997, 26 February). Sex scandal at Gardens 'snowballs', *The Toronto Star*, Final Ed. p. A1. Retrieved 8 January 2010, from Lexis Nexis; Brazao, D. (2007, 5 May). Maple Leafs owners to face new round of sex-abuse claims: Man seeks $4M for alleged molesting by usher in '70s; lawyer says 5 more on way. Retrieved 27 May 2010, from www.thestar.com/news/article/210749.

Box 6.3 The Mount Cashel Orphanage

Mount Cashel Orphanage, a home for boys in St John's, NL, was run by the Christian Brothers of Ireland in Canada (CBIC), a branch of the Roman Catholic order founded in Ireland, for nearly 100 years. For many years, the CBIC opened schools in several countries, and the priests and church clergy were highly respected for their good work in the communities. Between the mid-1970s and late 1980s, however, allegations of sexual and physical abuse at the orphanage—involving children as young as five and dating as far back as the 1950s—were made by more than 300 former residents. The government, police, and Catholic Church attempted to cover up the scandal. However, media coverage in 1989 resulted in the case being re-opened. Within six months, the last remaining resident was placed in alternative accommodation, and Mount Cashel Orphanage was closed. Many individuals were eventually charged and the CBIC was ordered to compensate the victims. Christian Brothers in Rome transferred ownership of some of their assets out of Canada to prevent millions of their dollars from being liquidated. Barry Stagg, a Newfoundland lawyer representing one of the Mount Cashel Orphanage victims, knew that if money was recovered there would be 'hell to pay in St. John's'.

The money eventually came—years after the orphanage closed—from the liquidation of the CBIC's assets, including the sale of the orphanage property and two schools in Vancouver. 'The government has a responsibility, liability for what went wrong,' says J.J. Byrne, a former resident of the orphanage and spokesperson for the victims. Byrne described the pain of the past when local businesses in St John's posted advertisements around a Mount Cashel Orphanage monument. 'It's meant solely for the purpose of commemorating what we, as victims of Mount Cashel, went through while we lived at Mount Cashel—the physical, sexual abuse, the emotional and psychological abuse.' The abuse and scandal may be over at Mount Cashel (even the court settlements are over), but the pain surrounding this scandal will always be in the lives of the victims and in Canada's history.

SOURCES: CBCnews.ca. (2000, 13 April). Former Mount Cashel victim rips down signs. Retrieved 19 February 2009, from www.cbc.ca/news/story/2000/04/13/nf_cashel000413.html; CP. (2003, 24 April). Money for abused Mount Cashel victims offered deal. Retrieved 19 February 2009, from www.canadiancrc.com/Newspaper_Articles/Toronto_Sun_Money_for_abused_24APR03.aspx; Mount Cashel Orphanage (n.d.). Mount Cashel orphanage: Newfoundland's house of horrors. Retrieved 19 February 2009, from www.mountcashelorphanage.com/; Robinson, B.A. (2002, 26 March). Sexual abuse by Catholic clergy: The Canadian situation. Retrieved 19 February 2009, from www.religioustolerance.org/clergy_sex3.htm.

long-term abuse at the hands of Maple Leaf Gardens employees, reports from others started to flood the police call line. The detective in the case observed that 'there is power in numbers' (Brazao & Mascoll, 1997, p. A1), noting that it was clear that once one person had come forward, others felt more comfortable in doing so. The fact that this abuse was not reported to the police for years after it occurred is a strong indication of the stigma that these men felt about the victimization they had experienced.

The second box recounts the events that occurred at Mount Cashel Orphanage in St John's, NL. Although the orphanage was long considered a respectable establishment, it was eventually discovered to be a place of long-term abuse. Media coverage helped to launch an investigation and to expose what was happening at the orphanage. Hundreds of former residents reported that they had been physically and sexually abused while living at Mount Cashel. This scandal is just one of many involving abuse within the Catholic Church; recently, cases have surfaced in the United States, Germany, Belgium, and other countries.

Can We Prevent Sexual Assault?

Over the years, there have been several attempts to explain and to prevent this crime. As previously mentioned, one of the first approaches was to place the responsibility of prevention predominantly with the victim. Early sexual assault cases featured victims being asked whether they had been wearing provocative clothing at the time of the attack, whether they had been drinking alcohol or taking drugs, whether they had consented to the sexual violence, whether they had been aware of the time and/or the location, whether they regularly went out and socialized, whether they had previous sexual experience, and so on. In essence, early explanations of this behaviour not only blamed the victims but also assumed that they were responsible for stopping sexual assault. If victims dressed appropriately, refrained from drinking alcohol, taking drugs, or leaving the house at night unless accompanied by a protector, then sexual assaults could be avoided.

With the advent of the Women's Movement, this explanation was denounced by many groups. Because women were primarily identified as victims of sexual assault, the approach required an unreasonable expectation of women that men did not experience. Women disagreed that following these rules would prevent sexual assault. They also disputed the notion that they should have to follow behavioural rules and thereby accept the responsibility of such crimes. Further, they identified these assumptions as discriminatory, using the responses by the criminal justice system and others to illustrate the daily discrimination that women face.

A secondary response assigns responsibility to the victimizers, who are considered predators in this explanation. The response is to invoke the criminal justice system and to extract these predators from society as well as to deter them from offending again (*primary deterrence*) and to act as a deterrent to others who may be considering committing a similar crime (*secondary deterrence*). It is assumed that the offender will receive medical and/or psychological treatment during incarceration, as those who commit such crimes are usually considered to be unbalanced in some way and in need of behaviour correction. Offenders who are identified as sexual predators are placed on a registry, and their actions are monitored even after release. Although these offenders have served prison sentences and may have taken advantage of treatment, they are never considered fully 'cured'.

Still another explanation of sexual assault crimes places the burden of responsibility on the cultural milieu in which we live. Cultural institutions that maintain traditional gender roles and expectations and the production and dissemination of pornographic material that demoralizes women serve to enhance the idea of women as subordinate and men as dominant. At the heart of this explanation is the assumption that women have been objectified over the centuries and that men have been socialized to exploit women for their own gratification. A second assumption is that these traditional socialization patterns do not serve the betterment of society and that a larger social response is needed. Of particular importance is the need to change socialization practices and to break the barriers for both men and women. Strategies to prevent sexual assault under this model state that not only does education serve a role but that cultural institutions, such as the media, and childhood socialization also need to respond to the crisis. Men need to not objectify women and to consider women an integral part of their lives, as mothers, sisters, wives, friends, colleagues, and employers. To objectify women is self-defeating, in that it limits the ability of society as a whole.

Current Western social norms suggest that society continues to adhere to two of the explanations above. Although our responses seek to deal with the offenders, there is an increasing awareness that sexual assault, and crime in general, is a social ill that does not serve the best interests of its people. Crimes that are predominantly directed towards a specific group, such as the sexual assault of women, are inherently wrong, and the victimizing behaviour is seen more as a collective responsibility forcing several social changes, including more equitable parenting styles, new legislation on the depictions of graphic sexual content, and the encouragement of a diverse workforce.

Summary

In this chapter we have discussed various definitions of sexual assault, as well as some recent trends. Depending on where one looks for data on sexual assault, one can get different estimates of victimization counts. Police data provide a limited understanding of victimization trends, as the UCR looks at only those crimes where the victim has had enough courage to come forward to police. Victimization surveys, such as the GSS, provide a broader picture of victimization by including both crimes that have and have not been reported to police. Overall, trends indicate that the most common forms of sexual assault are minor, with only a small proportion being severe cases.

Despite changes in legislation and research focusing on the occurrence of sexual assault in Canada, this crime remains one of great stigma and therefore is often not reported or discussed. There are several reasons why victims of sexual assault do not report this crime. Currently there are specific services that are offered to women who have been sexually assaulted, but there continues to be a lack of services for men who have experienced this crime. More recent cases, such as the Maple Leaf Gardens scandal and claims of sexual abuse in the Catholic Church, make people aware of the potential for the sexual assault of men and the forms it can take. Regardless of the victim's gender, early prevention attempts placed the responsibility of this crime in the hands of the victim, which also influenced the victim's decision to remain silent. These views have been discouraged in favour of those who see the victimizer as responsible for his or her own actions. More recent anecdotal evidence suggests that society is beginning to view sexual assault as more of a social problem and to seek larger, more institutional responses to the prevention of this crime.

Victims of sexual assault are heroic individuals. Not only do they face the victimization of sexual assault, but they must also consider the ramifications of making this information public. The more formal they make the allegation, the more public scrutiny they must endure. For those who have experienced this crime, or know someone who has, there is an understanding that this is one of the most difficult victimizations an individual can experience. To take actions to formally charge an attacker, understanding that both the offender and the victim will be investigated, is truly courageous. Legislative efforts to reflect the understanding that these crimes are acts of violence, power, and control are slowly working to pave the way for more people to come forward with their experiences. Victimizers continue to victimize if there is no one to identify them and bring their actions to the awareness of authorities. Those victims who do increase this awareness deserve our respect. They are one of the most powerful weapons in the prevention of this crime.

Glossary

longitudinal data   Data collected over a prolonged period of time tracking particular phenomena.

rapare   Latin word meaning 'to take by force'. It is the root of the word 'rape'.

rape   In Canada, prior to 1984, the act of forcing (by using physical threat or coercion) a woman into having sexual intercourse against her will by a man who was not her husband. Historically, and across many cultures, this term referred specifically to the forced sexual intercourse with a woman by a man.

sexual assault level I   Also known as sexual assault. This offence is the least severe form of sexual assault, often comprised of unwanted sexual touching or groping.

sexual assault level II   Also known as sexual assault with a weapon, threats to a third party, or causing bodily harm. Offences of this level are considered more severe than a minor assault and can involve forced sexual intercourse by using threat or force.

sexual assault level III   Also known as aggravated sexual assault. This type is the most severe form of sexual assault and features evidence of severe victim damage, including maiming or wounding.

Critical Thinking Questions

1. Using Table 6.1, list the ways that sexual assault trends are similar to and different from those for robbery and physical assault. Why might these trends be occurring?

2. Compare and contrast experiences that male and female sexual assault victims may have, including most likely victimizer, location, etc., both during and in the aftermath of the assault.

3. Do you agree with the idea that someone can bring about his or her own victimization? Give reasons to support your answer.

4. What are some of the challenges that victims of sexual assault face directly after an assault? What are some of the long-term issues?

CHAPTER 7

Special Topic: Aboriginal Peoples of Canada and Victimization

Learning Objectives

After reading this chapter, you will be able to

- recognize the unique social position of Aboriginal peoples in Canada;
- understand the 'Legacy' of Aboriginal peoples and its implications for future generations;
- examine trends in Aboriginal victimization; and
- identify the unique risk factors that increase vulnerability to victimization among Aboriginal peoples.

Introduction

In this chapter, we will pay special attention to the experiences of Aboriginal peoples in Canada. Aboriginal people include those who identify themselves as Indian, First Nations, Métis, or Inuit, regardless of official status. In many countries, there are populations of peoples that are more vulnerable to victimization than others. For example, many victimization studies in the United States compare African Americans to non-African Americans, as the former group tends to experience significantly higher rates of victimization. In Canada, researchers who have examined the Aboriginal population recognize that people in this group are at a significantly greater risk for victimization than other groups (Brzozowski, Taylor-Butts, & Johnson, 2006). As such, they have been recognized as needing special consideration by the Canadian government. This chapter will examine some of the social factors that cause this higher risk, particularly the

effects of the residential school system on Aboriginal communities. Such systemic victimization has created a group that is uniquely vulnerable to other forms of victimization, the trends of which are also discussed here.

Aboriginal Peoples in Canada

According to the 2006 Canadian Census (Statistics Canada, 2008), 1,172,790 Canadians identify themselves as Aboriginal. This figure represents an increase of 45 per cent from the previous census conducted in 1996 and means that Aboriginal peoples make up 4 per cent of the population of Canada. The largest concentration of Aboriginal peoples are in Winnipeg (68,380), Edmonton (52,100), and Vancouver (40,310). The 2006 census data show that more Aboriginal people (54 per cent) live in urban than in rural locations, with 60 per cent living off-reserve. Aboriginal people are more likely to report living in crowded living conditions, defined as having more than one person per room in the home. Aboriginal people are also three times more likely to live in a home that requires major repairs, representing almost 25 per cent of their population. Aboriginal people living on-reserve were more likely to live in a home that needed major repair compared to those living off reserve.

Aboriginal people are, on average, younger than the non-Aboriginal population (Brzozowski, Taylor-Butts, & Johnson, 2006). Almost half (48 per cent) are below the age of 24, compared with less than one-third (31 per cent) of the non-Aboriginal population. According to Gionet (2009), Aboriginal children 14 years of age and under were more likely to live with a lone parent or guardian when compared to the non-Aboriginal population. In 2006, 45 per cent of children in Aboriginal homes lived with either a lone parent (37 per cent) or another relative (8 per cent). This is more than double the percentage for the rest of the population (17 per cent of non-Aboriginal children live with a lone parent, and less than 1 per cent live with a grandparent or other relative). Children who live off-reserve are more likely to live with a lone parent (41 per cent). Of those children living in urban areas, those with registered Indian status were more likely to live with a lone parent (41 per cent) when compared to those who did not hold this status (35 per cent).

In terms of education and employment, Figure 7.1 illustrates that, in the 2001 census, nearly one-half (48 per cent) of the Aboriginal population had reported not completing high school, compared to nearly one-third (31 per cent) of the non-Aboriginal population. Gionet also reports that 42 per cent of

Aboriginal people had completed school beyond a secondary level. This number is considerably higher for the non-Aboriginal people of Canada; 61 per cent of this group had received at least some education after completing high school. In 2006, only 7 per cent of Aboriginal people reported having a university degree, compared with 21 per cent of the non-Aboriginal population. However, this figure represented an increase from 2001. Just over 60 per cent of Aboriginal people between the ages of 25 and 54 were employed, compared with 81.6 per cent of the non-Aboriginal group. Of those living off-reserve, those with non-registered status were more likely to be employed (71.4 per cent) than those with status (64 per cent). Nearly one-half of people in the same age group living on-reserve were unemployed (48.1 per cent). In 2005, according to Gionet, one-half of Aboriginal people made an annual income of less than $14,517, and this figure was lower for those living on-reserve ($11,224). The median income for non-Aboriginal people was considerably higher ($25,955).

Because Aboriginal peoples in Canada are more likely to have lower levels of income (Gabor, 1994; Maxim, White, Beavon, & Whitehead, 2001; Weinrath, 1999), they are more likely to live in poverty. Pantazis (2000) has documented that poverty is associated with physical situational correlates, such as poor living and working conditions, which accompany low-income living. These conditions, she argues, contribute to an increased risk of victimization. According to Marenin (1992), who comments on crime in Alaskan villages, native communities are a product of many social and structural factors, one

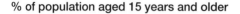

Figure 7.1   Aboriginal People Have Lower Levels of Educational Attainment, 2001

% of population aged 15 years and older

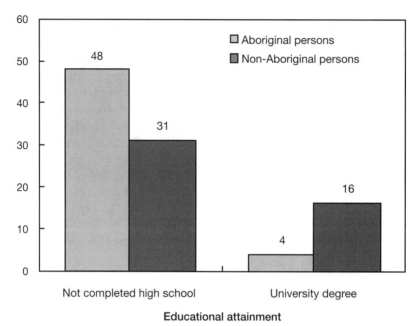

Educational attainment

SOURCES: Brzozowski, J., Taylor-Butts, A., & Johnson, S. (2006). Victimization and offending among the Aboriginal population in Canada. *Juristat, 26*(3). Statistics Canada: Canadian Centre for Justice Statistics, Minister of Industry, p. 3 (Catalogue 85-570-XIE).

of which is higher rates of unemployment. Aboriginal communities have also reported problems with alcohol and substance abuse (Gabor, 1994; Marenin, 1992). Boredom and isolation, accompanied with readily available alcohol, may contribute to the higher crime and victimization rates among Aboriginal community members.

Aboriginal peoples in Canada, as mentioned, often have lower educational attainment, higher unemployment, and substandard living conditions (e.g., lack of safe drinking water, inappropriate sewage disposal, and inadequate heating sources) than other Canadians. In some cases, unemployment rates among Aboriginal peoples mirror third-world countries. As a result of these circumstances, Aboriginal peoples are more likely to experience poor nutrition and higher rates of substance use, homelessness, mental illness, and suicide. A higher rate of alcoholism among this population has led to an increase in children with Fetal Alcohol Syndrome (FAS) and Fetal Alcohol Spectrum Disorder (FASD). Higher rates of certain diseases, including HIV/AIDS, diabetes, and tuberculosis, have also been found in this population. It has been estimated that one Aboriginal person is infected with HIV every day. The life expectancy of Aboriginal peoples is less than the Canadian average.

Along with these problems, this part of the Canadian population also shows high numbers in areas of crime and victimization. Brzozowski, Taylor-Butts, and Johnson (2006) note that, while Aboriginal peoples make up roughly three to four (Statistics Canada, 2008) per cent of the Canadian population, they represent almost 20 per cent of the federally incarcerated population. This statistic suggests that Aboriginal people are less likely to be able to work their way through the system than other groups and that they may be more vulnerable to victimization by the criminal justice system. They also make up a large percentage of those involved in the sex trade. Aboriginal women and children suffer from emotional, sexual, and physical abuse at alarming rates.

Research has increasingly examined the issues facing Aboriginal peoples, specifically attempting to explain why they have such an increased risk for so many factors and have struggled when compared to other groups. Many researchers have argued that this population is in need of support in addressing these problems. Some have also pointed out that the residential school system, one of the leading factors in the history of Aboriginal peoples in Canada and a source of total discrimination against them, provides insight into the victimization of this population.

The Development of the Residential School System

Although the French in New France in the seventeenth and eighteenth centuries had established boarding schools to educate Aboriginal youth, it was not until the early nineteenth century that various religious groups (the Protestants, Catholics, Anglicans, and Methodists) initiated Canada's residential school system. These **residential schools** were attended by Aboriginal students and included industrial schools, boarding schools, homes for students, hostels, billets, schools with day students, and various combinations of these educational delivery systems. Children were enrolled in these schools in order to receive a 'Christian' education and to be protected from their parents' 'backward' influence. School doctrine prohibited the speaking of traditional Native languages and the practising of Native faiths in favour of English or French and Christianity, respectively. Students were also encouraged to adopt patriarchal gender roles; girls were educated in the areas of cleaning, cooking, washing, and ironing, while boys were taught about machinery and agriculture.

Recognizing the importance of this domestic education and religious instruction in assimilating Aboriginal peoples into 'civilized' society, the Canadian government passed the Gradual Civilization Act in 1857, which enfranchised Aboriginal peoples and recognized them not as Aboriginal but as British subjects. By 1920, the government had made attendance of residential schools mandatory for all Aboriginal children between 7 and 15 years of age. As a result of this law, children were forcibly taken from their families by priests, Indian agents, and police officers. By 1931 there were 80 residential schools operating in Canada; in 1948, there were 72 schools with 9,368 students.

Table 7.1	Chronology of the Development of the Residential School System in Canada
1620–80	Boarding schools are established for Indian youth by the Récollets, a French order in New France, and later the Jesuits and the female order the Ursulines. This form of schooling lasts until the 1680s.
1820s	Early church schools are run by Protestants, Catholics, Anglicans, and Methodists.
1847	Egerton Ryerson produces a study of native education at the request of the assistant superintendent general of Indian affairs. His findings become the model for future Indian residential schools. Ryerson recommends that domestic education and religious instruction is the best model for the Indian population. The recommended focus is on agricultural training and government funding will be awarded through inspections and reports.
1857	Gradual Civilization Act passed to assimilate Indians.
1860	Indian Affairs is transferred from the Imperial Government to the Province of Canada. This is after the Imperial Government shifts its policy from fostering the autonomy of native populations through industry to assimilating them through education.
1870–1910	Period of assimilation where the clear objective of both missionaries and government is to assimilate Aboriginal children into the lower fringes of mainstream society.
1920	Compulsory attendance for all children ages 7–15 years. Children are forcibly taken from their families by priests, Indian agents, and police officers.
1931	There are 80 residential schools operating in Canada.
1943	The Department of Indian Affairs superintendent of welfare and training, on receiving from the principal of one of the residential schools a set of shackles that had been used routinely to *chain runaways to their beds* as well as reports of other abuses at school writes, 'I can understand now why there appears to be such a widespread prejudice on the part of Indians against residential schools. Such memories do not fade out of the human consciousness very rapidly.'
1948	There are 72 residential schools with 9,368 students.
1960	Indians finally receive the right to vote.
1962	They first get to exercise this right.
1969	The Canadian government releases its White Paper on Indian Policy, calling for the complete assimilation of First Nations people into Canadian society by eliminating *special status*. The National Indian Brotherhood successfully lobbies Parliament and the public to defeat the White Paper.
1974	The aboriginal education system sees an increase in the number of Native employees in the school system. Over 34 per cent of staff have Indian status. This is after the government gives control of the Indian education program to band councils and Indian education committees.
1975	A provincial Task Force on the Educational Needs of Native peoples hears recommendations from Native representatives to increase language and cultural programs and improve funding for native control of education.

Table 7.1   (continued)

1975	A Department of Indian Affairs and Northern Development publication reports that 174 federal and 34 provincial schools offer language programs in 23 native languages.
1979	Only 15 residential schools are still operating in Canada.
1979	The Department of Indian Affairs evaluates the schools and creates a series of initiatives. Among them is a plan to make the school administration more culturally aware of the needs of aboriginal students.
1979	There are 12 residential schools with 1,899 students.
1980s	Residential school students begin disclosing sexual and other forms of abuse at residential schools.
1984	The last residential school closes.
1985	Bill C-31 passes in Canada to legally eliminate discrimination against Indian women as originally prescribed in the Indian Act.
1986	The United Church of Canada formally apologizes to Canada's First Nations people.
1990	Phil Fontaine, leader of the Association of Manitoba Chiefs, meets with representatives of the Catholic Church. He demands that the church acknowledge the physical and sexual abuse suffered by students at residential schools.
1990	The Oka Crisis takes place. Kanesatake Mohawks take a stand after 270 years of land encroachment by governments, religious, and secular non-Aboriginal groups and in 1990, a golf course developer.
1991	The Missionary Oblates of Mary Immaculate offer an apology to Canada's First Nations people.
1993	The Anglican Church offers an apology to Canada's First Nations people.
1994	The Presbyterian Church offers a confession to Canada's First Nations people.
1995	Dudley George, an unarmed protester occupying Ipperwash Provincial Park, is shot by OPP equipped with riot gear. He was given no medical treatment and died after protesting the failure of the Federal Government to return land that had been temporarily expropriated 50 years earlier.
1996	The report of the Royal Commission on Aboriginal peoples stresses the urgency of addressing the impacts of residential schools.
1996	The last federally run residential school, the Gordon Residential School, closes in Saskatchewan.
1997	Phil Fontaine is elected national chief of the Assembly of First Nations, a political organization representing Canada's Aboriginal people.
1998	The AFN establishes the Indian Residential Schools Resolution Unit.
1998	On 31 March, the Aboriginal Healing Foundation is implemented to promote healing from residential school trauma. It is given a 10-year mandate: one year to set up; four years to disburse the $350-million healing fund on a multi-year basis, and five years to monitor and evaluate the projects.
1998	The litigation list naming the Government of Canada and major Church denominations grows to 7,500.

Table 7.1   (continued)

2001	Canadian government begins negotiations with the Anglican, Catholic, United, and Presbyterian churches to design a compensation plan.
2001	In October, the government agrees to pay 70 per cent of settlement to former students with validated claims.
2001	In December, the Anglican Diocese of Cariboo in British Columbia declares bankruptcy, saying it can no longer pay claims related to residential school lawsuits.
2006	On 10 May, the Government of Canada announces the approval of a final Indian Residential Schools Settlement Agreement.
2007	On 19 September, a landmark compensation deal for an estimated 80,000 former residential school students comes into effect, ending what Assembly of First Nations Chief Phil Fontaine called a 150-year 'journey of tears, hardship and pain—but also of tremendous struggle and accomplishment'.
2007	On 15 December, the class-action deal—one of the most complicated in Canadian history—is effectively settled, when documents are released that say the deal had been approved by seven courts: in Quebec, Ontario, Manitoba, Saskatchewan, Alberta, British Columbia, and the Yukon. The average payout is expected to be in the vicinity of $25,000. Those who suffered physical or sexual abuse may be entitled to settlements up to $275,000.
2008	On 11 June, the Canadian government officially and formally apologizes to the Aboriginal peoples of Canada.

It was not until 1960 that Aboriginal people of Canada were granted the right to vote, and it took another two years before they could exercise that right. By granting this population the right to vote, the Canadian government was recognizing this group as people under the law, and as such the treatment of these people had wide ranging implications. In particular, this marked a turning point in the use of residential schools, given that Aboriginal people could now challenge their treatment under various laws designed to protect all Canadians. Also during this time, thousands of Aboriginal children were taken out of their homes, families, communities, and cultures and placed in white, middle-class homes, instead of residential schools, where they were thought to be

better off. Many children wound up in the United States and some as far away as Europe. Many of these children continue to search for their people.

In the mid-seventies, control of the residential schools was turned over to Aboriginal peoples. As Canadian citizens, Aboriginal groups expressed their desire to teach Aboriginal children and pass on their traditions. They identified various Aboriginal and non-Aboriginal avenues for doing this, including the residential school system. At the same time, the government was losing interest in the program. The schools began hiring more Aboriginal teachers, and they became places for education in Native culture and languages. However, the number of these schools dwindled, leaving only 12 by the end of the decade.

During the 1980s, claims of mistreatment at the residential schools emerged. Victims relayed stories of sexual and physical abuse, neglect, hunger, poor working conditions, and emotional cruelty. This scandal sealed the fate of the residential school system, and the last federally funded school closed its doors in 1996. From the mid-1980s to the late 1990s apologies and other statements of acknowledgement were made to residential school students by the following religious institutions: The United Church of Canada (1986), the Missionary Oblates of Mary Immaculate (1991), The Anglican Church of Canada (1993), and the Presbyterian Church in Canada (1994). These groups and the Canadian government, which apologized in 2008, also compensated the victims. The details of this compensation and the government's apology are discussed on pages 120–1.

As a result of the victimization that occurred within the residential school system, an Aboriginal person who attended such a school is referred to as a **residential school survivor**. In 1991, approximately 13 per cent of the country's Aboriginal population was self-identified as this type of survivor. The ongoing direct and indirect effects of the physical and sexual abuse endured by these survivors and their families, descendants, and communities (including communities of interest) has come to be known as **The Legacy**. These effects may include family violence, substance abuse, physical and sexual abuse, loss of parenting skills, and self-destructive behaviour.

Residential School Victimization

In their book *Stolen From Our Embrace*, Suzanne Fournier and Ernie Crey (1998)

document the experiences of many residential school survivors, including their own. Fournier writes of the effects that the residential school system had on her father and her family. She notes that her father would not talk about his Native heritage, explaining his family's dark hair and eyes as the result of being French Canadian and not Aboriginal. She also states that even though he was a fluent speaker of Halq'emeylem, her father never spoke it at home. As a result, she was never able to fully learn this language that framed her culture and its history. She noted that although there were some survivors who found the schools beneficial, many more found them to be places where the 'killing of the Indian in the child' (p. 47) occurred.

In addition to talking about their own experiences, the authors include stories of sexual and physical assaults, emotional cruelty, neglect, and starvation, such as that of Rose Rice:

> The nightmare began as soon as Emily [Rice] and her sister Rose, then eleven years old, stepped on the small boat that would bear them away. 'I clung to Rose until Father Jackson [a pseudonym] wrenched her out of my arms, . . . I searched all over the boat for Rose. Finally, I climbed up to the wheelhouse and opened the door and there was Father Jackson, on top of my sister. My sister's dress was pulled up and his pants were down. I was too little to know about sex; but I know now he was raping her. He cursed and came after me, picked up his big black bible and slapped me across the face and on the top of the head. (p. 47)

Once children like Emily and Rose Rice had received their education, they were returned home. While this home-coming may have ended the abuse, it presented new problems. The children now spoke English or French, had Christian values, and were often embar-rassed of their families. They found it difficult to readjust to life back on the reserve, but they were not welcome in the non-Aboriginal world. Many resi-dential school children, in addition to facing years of abuse, now had to deal with living without a community or a family. Fournier and Crey state that returning students or 'graduates' were often unable to trust other commun-ity members and, as a result, remained silent about their abuse. The auth-ors also note that many who returned home from a childhood of military-style discipline and abuse experienced symp-toms of Post-Traumatic Stress Disorder (PTSD). Survivors reported many symp-toms, including 'panic attacks, insom-nia, uncontrollable anger, alcohol and drug use, sexual inadequacy or addic-tion, the inability to form relationships, and eating disorders' (p. 63). When residential school survivors became parents, many showed the influence of the school's militant control by becom-ing strict disciplinarians. Others became very lax in their parenting styles. In either case, the traditional Aboriginal methods of parenting were lost to sur-vivors. The lack of trust instilled in sur-vivors also made learning from elders difficult. As a result, elders had no one to pass their knowledge onto, and much of it died with them. Without this trans-fer of information, Aboriginal commun-ities were almost crippled.

Fournier and Crey refer to this pro-cess as the slow and systematic genocide of a people. In an effort to assimilate the Aboriginal people into European Christian doctrine, 'educators' were allowed to strip a people of its knowl-edge, dignity, and humanity. Years of physical, sexual, and emotional abuse had disabled once proud and indepen-dent nations. Traditional knowledge of hunting and gathering food for the winter became dismantled, creating dependence on food sources available to non-Aboriginal people. Much of this food was expensive, highly processed, and led to increased levels of obesity, diabetes, and heart disease. High unem-ployment on reserves forced many into urban centres, where they were not readily accepted. Isolation in these envi-ronments, coupled with experiences of abuse and neglect and few recovery resources, often led to self-medicating as a coping mechanism.

Although difficult, the healing pro-cess was not impossible. Many survivors began to embark on this journey from the moment they left the schools. According to Fournier and Crey (1998), many stu-dents risked beatings by continuing to speak in their first language or practis-ing traditional dances learned from their elders. In essence, these courageous chil-dren were allowing the Aboriginal inside to live, resisting the efforts of 'improve-ment' or being 'civilized'.

Compensation and 'The Deal'

In 1996, the report of the Royal Commission on Aboriginal Peoples stressed the urgency of addressing the impacts of residential schools. One year later, Phil Fontaine, leader of the Association of Manitoba Chiefs and a residential school survivor, was elected national chief of the Assembly of First Nations (AFN), a political organization representing Canada's Aboriginal peoples. One of Chief Fontaine's first priorities was to establish the Indian Residential Schools Resolution Unit. In March 1998, the Aboriginal Healing Foundation was implemented to promote healing from residential school trauma. It was given a 10-year mandate: one year to set up; four years to disburse the $350-million healing fund on a multi-year basis, and five years to monitor and evaluate projects. This fund was supplied by money set aside by the Canadian government to support community-based healing initiatives for residential school survivors. By the end of 1998, the litigation list naming the Government of Canada and major religious denominations had grown to 7,500.

By the last decade of the twentieth century, both the churches and the government faced numerous lawsuits by survivors of the residential school system. Many survivors had engaged in class action suits, acknowledging both the participation of the churches and the government in allowing the abuse at these educational facilities to continue. In 2001, the Canadian government began negotiating with the Anglican, Catholic, United, and Presbyterian churches to design a compensation plan. Although the government agreed to pay 70 per cent of the settlement to former students with validated claims, the lawsuits took a financial toll on various churches around the country. In December of 2001, the Anglican Diocese of Cariboo in British Columbia declared bankruptcy, saying it could no longer pay claims related to residential school lawsuits. This situation caused the Canadian government to take stock of the numerous claims

against it. It became clear to all who were following the issue that the government would have to act to prevent other churches from following suit. On 19 September 2007, a landmark compensation deal for an estimated 80,000 former residential school students came into effect, ending what Chief Fontaine called a 150-year 'journey of tears, hardship and pain—but also of tremendous struggle and accomplishment'. This settlement became known as 'The Deal'. Four different lump sum payment (LSP) options were offered to survivors to compensate them for the suffering they experienced at residential schools.

The first of these options secured LSPs through civil and criminal lawsuits initiated by survivors. This process, which began in the 1990s, was criticized by some survivors as exclusionary, in that it required financial resources, including legal fees, that many people could not afford. This option was also time intensive in addition to being financially and emotionally draining. Survivors going through this process found it less than rewarding.

The second option, Alternative Dispute Resolution (ADR) process, was intended as a less formal, less complicated, and faster alternative to the courts. However, this LSP dealt only with physical and sexual abuse and imposed rigid compensation guidelines for different forms and intensity of abuse. Similar to court cases, survivors following the ADR route needed to prove their claims.

On 10 May 2006, the Government of Canada announced the approval of a final Indian Residential Schools Settlement Agreement. The settlement provided for a Common Experience

Payment (CEP), which compensated survivors based on time spent in one of the listed residential schools identified as abusive. This third LSP plan offered $10,000 for the first school year plus $3,000 for each subsequent school year; the average total payment was approximately $28,000. CEP had additional benefits in that it also included an Independent Assessment Process, which allowed survivors who suffered sexual abuse, serious physical abuse, or other abuse that caused serious psychological effects to apply for further compensation. The settlement agreement also allowed collective measures, including a Truth and Reconciliation Commission, a Commemoration Initiative, and funding for the Aboriginal Healing Foundation and other health support programs. However, the plan is currently limited to direct survivors of the residential school system, ignoring the intergenerational effects that the system had on an entire group of people, such as the children of survivors. Recent extrapolated figures indicate that this group includes approximately 287,350 Aboriginal people.

The final option was the Independent Assessment Process (IAP), a part of the settlement agreement meant to replace the Alternative Dispute Resolution (ADR) process. This option promised to process any residential school abuse claim within a nine-month period. However, there were some attached conditions: to receive compensation through either the CEP or IAP, survivors were required to withdraw any lawsuits they had filed. On 15 December 2007, a class-action deal—which included these four options and was one of the most complicated in Canadian history—was

effectively settled, after being approved by courts in Quebec, Ontario, Manitoba, Saskatchewan, Alberta, British Columbia, and the Yukon. At the time, the average payout was expected to be in the vicinity of $25,000. Those who suffered physical or sexual abuse could be entitled to settlements up to $275,000, through a special application process.

The Apology

Along with receiving the compensation package, Aboriginal peoples made it clear that they also wanted the government to acknowledge its role in the assimilation process. On 11 June 2008, Prime Minister Stephen Harper apologized to the Aboriginal peoples of Canada. Although many survivors had died before this apology was given, it was considered a great step towards the healing of the Aboriginal peoples. The full text of the apology is available in Box 7.1. In Harper's statement, he noted that 'The treatment of children in residential schools is a sad chapter in our history.' He said that this practice was wrong, caused great harm, and had no place in our country (CBC Archives, 2008). Harper acknowledged those who had died before the apology was given and recognized that it was an impediment to the healing of the Aboriginal peoples, in that they were unable to hear the apology and pass the healing of these words to their own children. He recognized that removing children from their families affected the abilities of Aboriginal peoples to parent their own children. He asked for the forgiveness of the Aboriginal peoples and mentioned that the Settlement Agreement and the Truth and Reconciliation Commission represented a way to move forward from this tragic past.

Box 7.1   Full Text of Harper's Apology, Wednesday, 11 June 2008

The prepared text of the apology Prime Minister Stephen Harper delivered in the House of Commons on Wednesday. Paragraphs in parentheses were spoken in French:

Mr. Speaker, I stand before you today to offer an apology to former students of Indian residential schools.

The treatment of children in Indian residential schools is a sad chapter in our history. (For over a century the residential schools separated over 150,000 native children from their families and communities.)

In the 1870s, the federal government, partly in order to meet its obligation to educate Aboriginal children, began to play a role in the development and administration of these schools.

Two primary objectives of the residential schools system were to remove and isolate children from the influence of their homes, families, traditions and cultures, and to assimilate them into the dominant culture.

These objectives were based on the assumption Aboriginal cultures and spiritual beliefs were inferior and unequal.

Indeed, some sought, as it was infamously said, 'to kill the Indian in the child'.

Today, we recognize that this policy of assimilation was wrong, has caused great harm, and has no place in our country.

132 schools financed by the federal government were located in all provinces and territories with the exception of Newfoundland, New Brunswick and PEI.

Most schools were operated as 'joint ventures' with Anglican, Catholic, Presbyterian or United Churches.

The Government of Canada built an educational system in which very young children were often forcibly removed from their homes, often taken far from their communities.

Many were inadequately fed, clothed and housed.

All were deprived of the care and nurturing of their parents, grandparents and communities.

First Nations, Inuit and Métis languages and cultural practices were prohibited in these schools.

Tragically, some of these children died while attending residential schools and others never returned home.

The government now recognizes that the consequences of the Indian residential schools policy were profoundly negative and that this policy has had a lasting and damaging impact on aboriginal culture, heritage and language.

While some former students have spoken positively about their experiences at residential schools, these stories are far overshadowed by tragic accounts of the emotional, physical and sexual abuse and neglect of helpless children, and their separation from powerless families and communities.

The legacy of Indian residential schools has contributed to social problems that continue to exist in many communities today.

It has taken extraordinary courage for the thousands of survivors that have come forward to speak publicly about the abuse they suffered.

It is a testament to their resilience as individuals and to the strength of their cultures.

Regrettably, many former students are not with us today and died never having received a full apology from the Government of Canada.

The government recognizes that the absence of an apology has been an impediment to healing and reconciliation.

Therefore, on behalf of the Government of Canada and all Canadians, I stand before you, in this chamber so central to our life as a country, to apologize to Aboriginal peoples for Canada's role in the Indian residential schools system.

To the approximately 80,000 living former students, and all family members and communities, the Government of Canada now recognizes that it was wrong to forcibly remove children from their homes and we apologize for having done this.

We now recognize that it was wrong to separate children from rich and vibrant cultures and traditions, that it created a void in many lives and communities, and we apologize for having done this.

We now recognize that, in separating children from their families, we undermined the ability of many to adequately parent their own children and sowed the seeds for generations to follow, and we apologize for having done this.

We now recognize that, far too often, these institutions gave rise to abuse or neglect and were inadequately controlled, and we apologize for failing to protect you.

Not only did you suffer these abuses as children, but as you became parents, you were powerless to protect your own children from suffering the same experience, and for this we are sorry.

The burden of this experience has been on your shoulders for far too long.

The burden is properly ours as a government, and as a country.

There is no place in Canada for the attitudes that inspired the Indian residential schools system to ever again prevail.

You have been working on recovering from this experience for a long time and in a very real sense, we are now joining you on this journey.

The Government of Canada sincerely apologizes and asks the forgiveness of the Aboriginal peoples of this country for failing them so profoundly.

(Nous le regrettons.)

We are sorry.

In moving towards healing, reconciliation and resolution of the sad legacy of Indian residential schools, implementation of the Indian residential schools settlement agreement began on September 19, 2007.

Years of work by survivors, communities, and Aboriginal organizations culminated in an agreement that gives us a new beginning and an opportunity to move forward together in partnership.

A cornerstone of the settlement agreement is the Indian residential schools truth and reconciliation commission.

This commission presents a unique opportunity to educate all Canadians on the Indian residential schools system.

It will be a positive step in forging a new relationship between Aboriginal peoples and other Canadians, a relationship based on the knowledge of our shared history, a

respect for each other and a desire to move forward together with a renewed understanding that strong families, strong communities and vibrant cultures and traditions
will contribute to a stronger Canada for all of us.

SOURCE: Apology on Behalf of Canadians for the Indian Residential Schools System, 2008, http://pm.gc.ca/eng/
media.asp?id=2149. Reproduced with the permission of the Minister of Public Works and Government Services,
2010, and Courtesy of the Privy Council Office.

Victimization Trends among Aboriginal Peoples in Canada

Measuring Aboriginal Victimization

One of the difficulties of studying the victimization of Aboriginal peoples is the lack of data regarding their inter-actions with the criminal justice system and their experiences with victimization. Although the current Uniform Crime Report survey (known as UCR2 since a new version was implemented in 1988) contains a section called an 'Aboriginal Indicator', the collection of information on the race or ethnicity of a victim or offender is not required. In fact, with the exception of the corrections intake process, there are no standards for the gathering of such data in the Canadian criminal justice system (Kong & Beattie, 2005). This information is often not col-lected because it is deemed unnecessary to business purposes, its collection con-flicts with internal policy, or its collection is regarded as insensitive or impractical. Where there is an administrative policy to collect this information at the police level, officers may be reluctant to ask the victim or the accused for fear that it could aggravate a situation and possibly hinder an interview or an interrogation. They may, however, report a person's ethnic identity by visual assessment or through contacts with the individual's family or social network. This practice is subject to error and is disputed by national Aboriginal groups. As of 2003, it was reported that only half of the par-ticipating agencies collecting race data for the UCR2 collected information on the accused or the potential accused (Kong & Beattie, 2005).

The issues surrounding the collec-tion of race-based statistics regarding the Aboriginal population have been debated for some time. Julian Roberts (1994) argued that it was dangerous to collect such information, adding that there was no essential need for this data as crime policy at the time had already targeted problem areas and issues within Aboriginal communities. He went on to state that the documentation of crime trends with respect to race could lead to racial discrimination and could in no way aid police beyond finding a suspect.

Alternatively, Thomas Gabor (1994) argued that it was problematic to with-hold this type of information from those involved in dealing with the social prob-lem of crime. While Gabor acknow-ledged that there were dangers posed by collecting race-based statistics, such as racial profiling and cultural stereotyp-ing, he asserted that the benefits of this collection far outweighed the costs. He argued that much of the concern gen-erated about these potential problems was alarmist and paternalistic. To not collect this information due to its sensitive nature allows other, non-Aboriginal groups to define boundaries of crime in special populations without real evidence to support their claims. Further, Gabor added that when there is no open discussion on race and the issues minorities face, negative stereotyping may be more likely to persist. He advocated exploring the social roots of criminogenic factors.

Both Roberts's and Gabor's theories are compelling. Scott and Beaman (2003) agree with the latter argument, offering that by not collecting racial background information, Canadian policy may be reflecting an inherent bias of the racial majority, thereby potentially contributing to the overrepresentation of Aboriginal peoples within the criminal justice system. Crime and victimization policy is often informed by such statistics in order to prevent crime and effect more efficient operation of the criminal justice system. Desperately needed, culturally sensitive, and appropriate programming cannot be developed without the larger scale statistics to prove there is a need. Current programming is based on smaller scale community studies where needs are often assumed in communities where studies have not taken place. Additionally, possible discrimination by criminal justice members cannot be pinpointed unless there are statistics that demonstrate an overrepresentation within the system.

Reporting of Victimization by Aboriginal Peoples

Although information on the victimization of Aboriginal peoples is scarce, the research that is available reveals certain trends. For example, LaPrairie (1990)

states that Aboriginal people are over-represented in the Canadian criminal justice system. Additionally, Aboriginals in both Canada and the United States have a higher rate of violent victimization when compared to other racial groups (Weinrath, 1999; Rennison, 2001).

Other reporting trends are visible in the area of violent victimization and spousal violence. The 2004 General Social Survey (GSS) reported that roughly 6 in 10 violent victimizations were not reported to the police. This holds true for both Native and non-Native Canadian populations. According to Johnson (2006), Aboriginal women are victims of more serious violence than non-Aboriginal women. Looking to spousal violence, only one-third of these cases are reported to police by Aboriginal victims. They are, however, more likely than non-Aboriginals to contact police regarding spousal violence and more likely to use social services. The GSS also reported that another third of women reporting domestic violence stated that their children had witnessed this violence. These statistics hold true regardless of Aboriginal identity. This also holds true even though Aboriginal victims report more serious violence, and more serious injury (Brzozowski, Taylor-Butts, & Johnson, 2006).

The Victimization of Aboriginal Peoples in Canada

Figure 7.2 demonstrates that, overall, victimization rates for Aboriginal peoples are much higher than the rest of the Canadian population (Brzozowski, Taylor-Butts, & Johnson, 2006). According to the General Social Survey (GSS, 2004) two out of every five Aboriginal people reported being victimized over the 12-month period prior to the survey when compared to the non-Aboriginal population (28 per cent). Aboriginal people were twice as likely to report re-victimization (21 per cent) when compared to the non-Aboriginal population (11 per cent). Aboriginal people were also over three times more likely (32 per cent) to report violent victimization, such as sexual assault, assault, and robbery, over the 12-month period when compared to non-Aboriginal groups (10 per cent).

Aboriginal women were found to be at greatest risk for violent victimization, at almost 3.5 times the rate (34 per cent) of non-Aboriginal groups (10 per cent). Aboriginal men, although holding a lower incident rate for violent victimization (29 per cent) were still almost three times more likely to be violently victimized that their non-Aboriginal counterparts (11 per cent). The younger the respondent, the greater the risk for victimization.

Brzozowski, Taylor-Butts, and Johnson

Figure 7.2   Aboriginal Peoples Are More Likely to Be Victims of Violent Crime, 2004[1, 2]

Rate per 1,000 population aged 15 years and older

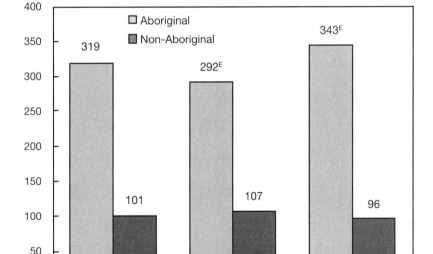

E Use with caution.
1 Includes incidents of spousal physical and sexual assault.
2 Includes sexual assault, assault, and robbery.

SOURCES: Brzozowski, J., Taylor-Butts, A., & Johnson, S. (2006). Victimization and offending among the Aboriginal population in Canada. *Juristat, 26(3)*. Statistics Canada, General Social Survey 2004: Canadian Centre for Justice Statistics, Minister of Industry, p. 5.

(2006) also report that Aboriginal victims were more likely to be accosted by someone they knew (Aboriginal: 56 per cent; non-Aboriginal: 41 per cent) and were twice as likely to be victimized in their own home (Aboriginal: 34 per cent; non-Aboriginal: 17 per cent). Although alcohol was a significant factor in three out of every five crimes, there was no difference between these two populations and alcohol consumption by the perpetrator. The Aboriginal population is also no more likely to be hurt or injured as a result of the victimization. As Aboriginal people are more likely to live below the poverty line, Weinrath (1999) provides evidence that lower levels of income may translate into higher fear of crime rates among this population.

Spousal Violence

Aboriginal people have identified spousal violence as one of the most important issues facing their population (Lane et al., 2003; LaRocque, 1994). Aboriginal communities experience a higher rate of spousal violence than non-Aboriginal communities. Figure 7.3 underscores the findings of the 2004 GSS, namely that while 6 per cent of non-Aboriginal

Figure 7.3   Aboriginal People at Greatest Risk of Spousal Violence, 2004[1, 2]

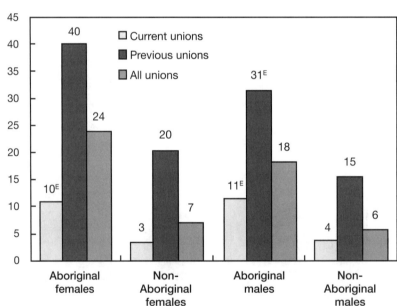

% of females and males

E   Use with caution.
1   Includes common-law partners.
2   Excludes people who refused to state their marital status.

SOURCES: Brzozowski, J., Taylor-Butts, A., & Johnson, S. (2006). Victimization and offending among the Aboriginal population in Canada. *Juristat, 26(3)*. Statistics Canada, General Social Survey, 2004: Canadian Centre for Justice Statistics, Minister of Industry, p. 7.

people reported being victimized by a spouse five years prior to the survey, 21 per cent of Aboriginal people reported the same type of victimization. Rates of spousal violence and spousal homicide are higher for Aboriginal women than for non-Aboriginal women or Aboriginal men (Johnson, 2006). The difference in the rates between Aboriginal and non-Aboriginal women is illustrated in Figure 7.4. Johnson (2006) further reports that summary of the GSS findings state that Aboriginal women experience spousal assault at three times the rate of non-Aboriginal men or women.

Mihorean (2005) reports that the danger of spousal victimization increases when partnerships and marriages have dissolved. Almost 2 of every 5 (37 per cent) Aboriginal peoples

reported victimization by an ex-partner in the five years preceding the GSS, compared with non-Aboriginal groups (18 per cent). More Aboriginal women also reported abuse from a current partner (11 per cent) than their non-Aboriginal counterparts (3 per cent).

Just over two out of every five Aboriginal victims of spousal violence (43 per cent) reported injuries as a result of their victimization experience, and just over one-third reported that the violence was so severe that they feared for their lives. Conversely, in the non-Aboriginal population, just under one-third of spousal violence victims (31.5 per cent) reported injury, and just over one in five (21.5 per cent) of this group reported fearing for their lives. Almost one-half (48 per

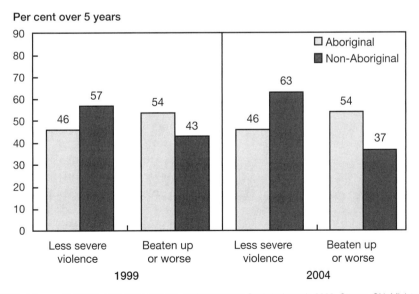

Figure 7.4   Seriousness of Spousal Assaults on Women, by Aboriginal Status, 1999 and 2004

SOURCE: Johnson, H. (2006). Measuring violence against women: Statistical trends 2006. Ottawa, ON: Minister of Industry, p. 65 (Catalogue 85-570-XIE).

cent) of Aboriginal victims of spousal assault reported that their partners had been drinking at the time of assault, compared with 31 per cent in the non-Aboriginal population.

Not only are there differences between Aboriginal and non-Aboriginal communities, but there are also variances between Aboriginal communities. Looking at the territories, where the majority of the population is Inuit, rates of spousal violence are higher, with 12 per cent reporting this type of offence compared with 7 per cent in other Aboriginal areas in the provinces (Johnson, 2006). This same study reported that police consistently recorded higher overall rates of violent crimes in the territories than in the provinces. With respect to the specific crimes associated with spousal violence, people in the territories were more likely than those in other parts of the country to report these offences to police. Victims in the territories were less likely than victims in the provinces to use social services but were more likely to use a shelter.

Homicide

In addition to being at increased risk for victimization overall, and violent victimization more specifically, Aboriginal peoples are also at increased risk for homicide victimization. From 1997 to 2004, where the Aboriginal status of the victim was known, just under one in five (17 per cent) of homicide victims were of Aboriginal descent (Brzozowski, Taylor-Butts, & Johnson, 2006). Figure 7.5 demonstrates that the homicide rate for both Aboriginal males and females is considerably higher than their non-Aboriginal counterparts. Aboriginal

males are over six times more likely (12.2 per 100,000) to be victims of homicide when compared to non-Aboriginal males (1.8 per 100,000 males). The risk of Aboriginal females for homicide victimization is very similar (5.4 per 100,000) compared to non-Aboriginal females (1.8 per 100,000). During this same time period, victims were more likely to be stabbed (44 per cent) or beaten to death (32 per cent) as opposed to shot (13 per cent). Non-Aboriginal populations were at lowest risk for being beaten to death (22 per cent) and were more likely to be stabbed (27 per cent) and most likely to be shot (32 per cent).

In cases of solved homicide, Aboriginal homicide victims were only slightly more likely to know their attackers (88 per cent) than their non-Aboriginal counterparts (83 per cent). Where Aboriginal homicide victims knew their attackers, they were more likely to be killed by an acquaintance (59 per cent) than a family member (41 per cent). Where it was known whether the victim had consumed an intoxicating substance before the homicide, Aboriginal victims were reported to be twice as likely (85 per cent) to have done so compared to non-Aboriginal groups (45 per cent).

Looking specifically at homicides committed between 1980 and 1990 in Ontario, Doob, Grossman, and Auger (1994) found that Aboriginal homicides appear to be significantly higher than those involving non-Aboriginal victims. Further, they found that whether the homicide took place on- or off-reserve made no difference in the victimization rate. They concluded that the high levels of homicide were not specific conditions that occur on- or off-reserve but were consequences of

Figure 7.5   Rates of Homicide Much Higher for Aboriginal Victims, 1997–2000[1,2,3]

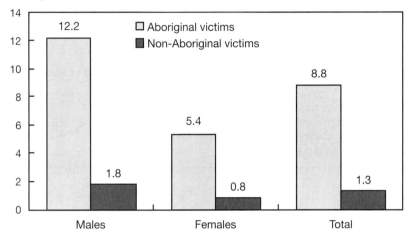

Average rate per 100,000 population

1   Rates are calculated per 100,000 population and are based on the average number of homicides per year, between 1997 and 2000.
2   Excludes homicides where the Aboriginal status of the victim was unknown.
3   Population estimates were derived from 2001 post-censal estimates and 1996 census counts, provided by Statistics Canada, Census and Demographic Statistics, Demography Division.

SOURCE: Brzozowski, J., Taylor-Butts, A, & Johnson, S. (2006). Victimization and offending among the Aboriginal population in Canada. *Juristat, 26*(3). Statistics Canada Homicide Survey: Canadian Centre for Justice Statistics, Minister of Industry, p. 7.

the overall socioeconomic position of the Aboriginal population. The authors suggest that this position is due to the effects of colonization, in that whether Aboriginal people live on- or off-reserve, their collective history is the same and they are equally disadvantaged.

Suicide in Aboriginal Communities

The act of suicide, for many reasons, is somewhat controversial. In victimology, this form of victimization, along with prostitution and drug abuse, is considered a **victimless crime**, a crime in which the victim and the victimizer is the same person. One is, literally, victimizing oneself. In this type of crime, it is assumed that the victim has given consent to the victimizer; the argument has been made that with consent, there is no victimization. Consequently, the term becomes a misnomer, in that it suggests that there is no victim. Clearly this theory is oversimplified. People who commit suicide often suffer from a variety of issues, including addiction and mental illness. To say that they are not victims is to ignore their plight.

Figure 7.6 identifies that Aboriginal people currently experience twice the suicide rate than members of the non-Aboriginal community. According to Kirmayer et al. (2007), while the suicide rate among both groups has declined overall, it has consistently risen in some Aboriginal communities over the past 20 years. Aboriginal females are more likely to attempt suicide, while males are more likely to die at their own hands. In fact, Figure 7.7 demonstrates that Aboriginal males, and youth in particular, are at the highest risk for suicide. Among the northern peoples of Canada, the Inuit rate of suicide ranges from 6 to 11 times

Figure 7.6   Comparison of Suicide Rates of Aboriginal Peoples and General Population in Canada, 1979–2000

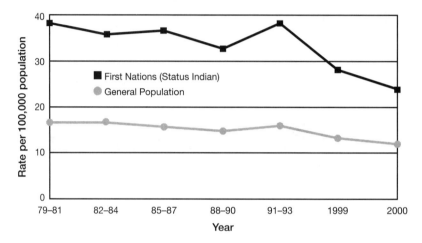

SOURCE: Kirmayer, L. J., Brass, G. M., Holton, T., Paul, K., Simpson, C., & Tait, C. (2007). Suicide among Aboriginal People in Canada. Ottawa, ON: Aboriginal Healing Foundation, p. 14. Reprinted by permission of the Aboriginal Healing Foundation.

Figure 7.7   Comparison of Suicide Rates by Age Group, Aboriginal Peoples and Canadian Population, 1989–1993

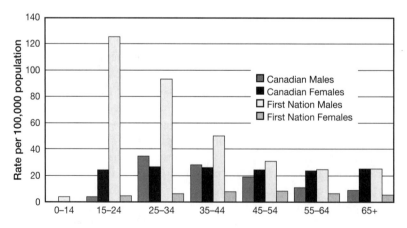

SOURCE: Kirmayer, L. J, Brass, G. M., Holton, T., Paul, K., Simpson, C., & Tait, C. (2007). Suicide among Aboriginal People in Canada. Ottawa, ON: Aboriginal Healing Foundation, p. 22. Reprinted by permission of the Aboriginal Healing Foundation.

the national average. Youth between the ages of 10 and 29 who live on-reserve are five to six times more likely to die from suicide than youth in this same age category who reside off-reserve. One-third of deaths among Aboriginal youths is the result of suicide.

The suicide rate among youth in these communities is of particular concern. Kirmayer and his colleagues (2007) note that the risk factors associated with these statistics are not different from those identified in the general population: feeling depressed or hopeless, having a negative perception of oneself or low self-esteem, abusing alcohol or drugs, experiencing the suicide death of a close friend or family member, having been sexually or physically victimized, living in a home where there is a history of family violence, having parents who do not support or neglect children, being socially isolated or having poor friendships, and not performing well in school settings. However, it is speculated that these risk factors are more prevalent in Aboriginal communities.

For example, statistics show that the suicide rates among youth are significantly higher on reserve. These communities are often very small, so the suicide death of a community member would be felt by many in the community. The suicide death of a close friend or family member, therefore, increases the risk of more suicides in the community. This is also coupled with the fact that, because Aboriginal people tend to die at younger ages, surviving relatives, friends, and other community members tend to witness more death than other groups, which can in turn lead to depression and greater risk of suicide. In essence, this process can be cyclical in some communities.

Kirmayer et al. (2007) report that there are practices that protect or insulate individuals from acts of suicide and suicide attempts. Individuals who report having strong family cohesion, participating in family activities, communicating effectively, feeling understood by one's family, having strong friendships, and doing well in school have a much lower risk of considering or attempting suicide. Programs that would strengthen these qualities and build resilience to suicide would help those who have experienced or are experiencing many of the social problems faced by Aboriginal youth. In other words, helping youth cope with experiences of abuse, addiction, depression, or other mental health issues, would contribute to significantly reducing these rates. Programs that also help students succeed in school, grief counselling, and building confidence and self-worth would serve to insulate not only youth but also many Aboriginal communities against the risk factors associated with suicide.

The Role of Risk Factors

According to Johnson (2006), part of the explanation for these higher rates of victimization among Aboriginal peoples is the prevalence of risk factors among the population. Lower levels of educational achievement, higher levels of unemployment, lower levels of income, and higher levels of single-parent homes are all considered risk factors for both victimization and offending. This population is also younger than the general population and is more likely to engage in alcohol abuse. Aboriginal peoples are also more likely to live in common-law relationships which increase the chances of experiencing spousal violence.

Unique to this population, as discussed earlier in this chapter, are the experiences of the residential school system. Not only were children taken from their homes and forbidden to speak their own language, but they were also often physically and sexually assaulted by the school staff. Because of the lack of parenting in the school system, and the marginalization inflicted on the students, the residential school experience has been attributed as a significant risk factor in the breakdown of Aboriginal family life (Johnson, 2006). Generations of children were raised in an institutional setting designed to eradicate the cultural values taught to them before they entered the system. These experiences were physically and psychologically damaging and, although their effects are waning, they still exist in the memory of many Aboriginal elders. As such, the legacy continues to influence this population.

Summary

This chapter has taken an in-depth look at the victimization of Aboriginal peoples. Unlike any other group in Canada, this population was systematically sought out and their younger members were separated from their families and communities and forced into a regimented and often abusive residential school system. These schools, which operated for generations, served to debilitate an entire population by trying to 'kill the Indian in the child'. The effects of being exposed to these assimilation tactics has come to be known as 'The Legacy' and has contributed to many of the problems faced by Aboriginal peoples.

Although many of these challenges have been placed in a historical context,

the residential school experience has clearly left a lasting social footprint. Aboriginal peoples are some of our most vulnerable citizens, in that they are more likely to be poor, uneducated, and unemployed than other groups. Tied to these living conditions, they are more likely to have problems with addictions and mental illness but less likely to have the resources to deal with them. All of these conditions are risk factors that contribute to increased vulnerability to victimization. Aboriginal people are more likely to be victimized, especially in cases of violent crimes. They are also overrepresented at almost all levels of the criminal justice system.

While some Aboriginal people continue to suffer from the effects of the residential school system, many more have begun the healing process. If we understand the survival of a victimizing act as heroic, this group's survival also brings to light that the recovery process is also one of great courage. For the Aboriginal peoples, this healing involves talking and writing about their experiences so that others can become aware of what they endured. For some this knowledge leads to an understanding of how a group of people can be systematically targeted for abuse. For others who may have attended these schools, it may lead to a realization that their experiences were not unique. The challenges faced by Aboriginal people are not insurmountable. However, in addition to healing their individual wounds, victims of this community must also heal as a collective group. This chapter reinforces that there are many facets to victimization beyond the individual experience that should be considered when studying victimology.

Glossary

Legacy, The The ongoing direct and indirect effects of the physical and sexual abuse endured by students of residential schools and their families, descendants, and communities (including communities of interest).

residential schools A school attended by Aboriginal students and which included industrial schools, boarding schools, homes for students, hostels, billets, schools with day students, and various combinations of these modes of educational delivery systems. The purpose of these schools was to give Aboriginal children a 'Christian' education and to assimilate them into 'civilized society'.

residential school survivor An Aboriginal person who attended a residential school.

victimless crime A crime where the victim and victimizer are the same person, such as prostitution, drug abuse, and suicide. This term is a misnomer, as it implies that there is no victim.

Critical Thinking Questions

1. In this chapter, evidence was provided to show that Aboriginal victims were no more likely to report that they felt alcohol was a factor in their victimization than non-Aboriginal victims. How does this contrast with popular misconceptions about Aboriginal involvement in victimization?

2. Although the Government of Canada has formally apologized to the Aboriginal people and offered them a settlement plan, what other measures could it take to assist in their healing? Do you think further measures are necessary? Why or why not?

3. What contributions did the residential school system make to Aboriginal peoples of today?

CHAPTER 8

Vulnerable Populations and Victimization

Learning Objectives

After reading this chapter, you will be able to

- understand the unique challenges faced by people who are homeless;
- recognize the victimization vulnerabilities of people living in total institutions, such as prisons;
- understand the victimization vulnerabilities of people living with physical disabilities; and
- examine how vulnerabilities affect reporting rates and the implications of not reporting victimization.

Introduction

In this chapter we will examine the unique conditions of three populations which are vulnerable to victimization. We have already learned that a number of characteristics can increase vulnerability of a group of people. For example, we have learned that males and younger people are more likely to be victimized than females and older people, respectively. Females tend to be more vulnerable to particular sets of criminal activity, such as intimate partner violence and/or sexual assault, than are males. As discussed in the previous chapter, being Aboriginal increases a person's overall vulnerability to victimization for a variety of reasons. There are, however, other characteristics that create vulnerability. In this chapter we will look at the following vulnerable groups: people who are homeless, people who are incarcerated, and people who live with disabilities. The people in these groups are similar in that

they are often considered social outcasts; therefore, their victimization is largely unnoticed or disregarded. They also face unique challenges of which victimization is only one part of daily life. Because of their living conditions, members of these groups may have very few resources from which to draw on if they are victimized. Moreover, their existence on the margins of society has implications on their decision to report crime. This chapter will illustrate some of the victimization experiences shared by these groups and how they differ from the majority of victim experiences.

Vulnerable Populations

Most of the victimization literature discussed in this book deals with the general public. It is hoped that such an approach will help you to identify with this material and to give you the sense that almost everyone has been or could be a victim. However, there are certain circumstances that can increase a person's level of victim vulnerability. For example, we know from previous chapters that being younger puts individuals at greater risk for victimization. This phenomenon is often explained by the types of lifestyles younger people lead as compared to their adult counterparts. Another element that increases victimization potential is social marginalization.

People insulate themselves against victimization in a variety of ways. Simple daily activities, such as being with friends and family, living in a home where one feels safe, and having enough resources to live, are protective. People who live on the margins of society are often unable to partake in these activities and become vulnerable as a result. **Marginalization** in a population means that some groups are excluded from mainstream society, which can lead to people in such groups having a lack of power or control in their own lives.

This marginalization can occur in several ways. For example, a person who is homeless must spend all of his or her limited resources on obtaining the basic necessities of life: food, water, shelter, and clothing. He or she is excluded from the general public's perceptions of community, as many view the homeless as not participating members of society. Likewise, a person can be excluded from the community by literally being taken out of society and

Box 8.1 Ralph Klein at the Herb Jamieson Centre for Homeless Men

At a 1982 dinner for newcomers, Calgary's then mayor, Ralph Klein, stated that the city did not like 'bums' and that he would protect Calgary citizens from 'a lot of creeps'. In a press conference later that same week, Klein said that he had not used the word 'bum' but the phrase 'kick ass and get them out of town'. He went on to say: 'If some bank robber from someplace else complains that maybe he was roughed up by a police officer, I'm not going to get too worked up.' Although most of Canada was upset at these comments, they did not seem to harm his political career; Klein remained mayor until he became premier of Alberta in 1992, an office he held for 14 years.

In the early morning of 12 December 2001, Klein was returning home from a dinner party when he asked his driver to stop at a shelter so that he could talk with the homeless and learn about their predicament. Shelter staff reported in their logbooks that Klein was swearing and shouting and asked the men why they did not have jobs. The incident ended with the premier storming out of the centre after throwing a bunch of money on the floor. The next day he stated that he had been drinking and was argumentative that night; he apologized for the 'disruption' and stated that he had quit drinking and was going to write a personal apology to the residents and the centre. In the next election, 200,000 fewer people voted for Klein, but the Conservatives still held on to their majority government. In 2006, Klein announced he would not be seeking re-election.

SOURCES: Mahoney, J. (2001, 15 December). Red-faced Klein sorry for late-night hostel visit. *The Globe and Mail.* p. A1. Lexis Nexis; CBC News. (2006, 12 September). Ralph Klein: Alberta's populist premier. *CBC News In Depth.* Retrieved 4 June 2009, from www.cbc.ca/news/background/klein-ralph/.

placed inside an institution, such as a prison or a home for people with mental or physical disabilities. What if someone is victimized while living in an institution? The options for such a victim are considerably restricted, given that his or her victimizer is more than likely to control the victim's access to the outside world. This chapter will look at three highly marginalized groups—the homeless, prisoners, and people living with disabilities—to illustrate the challenges facing vulnerable populations and the issues relating to victimization.

Victimization of the Homeless

The Importance of Home

Society's handling of homeless people has a long history. Katz (1996) documents some of the earliest policies in the United States, including seventeenth- and eighteenth-century New England Colonial laws that required people without a legal residence in a particular area to leave. In essence, the laws were designed to specifically handle transient people who lived in public spaces. In many ways we have not changed our methods from this time.

Cities often enact bylaws regarding dress codes in public spaces such as malls, with the idea that they can be used to escort people who do not meet a certain standard of appearance off of premises. Although these rules can be used to disrupt activities of youth hanging out in public spaces, they are more often formulated to deal with and directed at homeless individuals who seek refuge indoors, especially as outside temperatures drop. Still other methods include city ordinances that prohibit sleeping in public parks and loitering in public spaces. These rules serve to push the homeless away from public view and into the periphery of public space, marginalizing their existence and further disrupting their already difficult lives. In some cases political leaders have publicly expressed their views of transient workers and the homeless. Box 8.1 illustrates how Ralph Klein clearly made immigrants to Alberta feel unwelcome, publically condoned violence by the state, and verbally assaulted men in a homeless shelter.

Being victimized is a tragic experience for anyone. Karmen (2010) notes that, considering everyday risks, we are three to four times more likely to be injured in some form of accident than we are to have something stolen from us. This difference is largely because a home is a fairly secure place. Further, people who have a home have their persons and their property protected by law enforcement personnel. Neighbours will also often look out for one another, providing an extra layer of protection to daily living. When one does not have home, however, life becomes significantly different, bringing with it desperate living strategies, extreme stress and, sadly, increased vulnerability to victimization (Lee & Schreck, 2005). People who are homeless must carry their possessions with them wherever they go or try and secure them somewhere safe without spending precious financial resources. Homeless populations are often concentrated in neglected areas that feature high crime and victimization rates. While people without a permanent address can receive provincial social assistance, this allowance is considerably reduced because they are not paying rent or a mortgage.

Prevalence of Victimization among the Homeless

Jasinski et al. (2005) observed that homeless women and men are more likely to experience violence than people who have a permanent address. Their study found one alarming outcome: homeless individuals are victimized more in one year than the average individuals in the general population are in a lifetime. The Street Health Report (Ambrosio et al., 1992) recorded that about two in every five of the homeless people surveyed had been assaulted in the year previous to the study. Jasinski et al. (2005) also found that homeless men are more likely than homeless women to be victimized by assault, while homeless women are more likely to be victimized by intimate partner abuse. These gender-specific victimization patterns are consistent with data from non-homeless populations (Statistics Canada, 2005a).

Almost half of the homeless women sampled had been physically assaulted in the year before the study; one-quarter of these assaults were committed by police (Ambrosio et al., 1992). Research in sexual victimization among the homeless population shows that sexual harassment is more often reported by homeless women than men (Hwang, Tolomiczenko, Kouyoumdjian, & Rochelle, 2005). Of the women interviewed, just over two in five (43.3 per cent) had been sexually harassed in the past year, and almost half of those stated that they had experienced the harassment at least five times. More seriously, this same study noted that more than one in five homeless women had been raped in the year previous to the study and more than half had been sexually assaulted at some point in their lifetime.

Another element of homelessness and victimization is mental illness. Simons, Whitbeck, and Bales (1989) suggest that the mental illnesses evident in certain participants in their study may have been one consequence of being homeless and the resulting stress of this lifestyle. It is important to understand which came first: the mental illness or the homeless situation. If the mental illness is present before the individual becomes homeless, the treatment recommendations revolve around providing more mental health and social services to help individuals cope with their situation. If, on the other hand, the problems of mental illness emerge as a result of the stress of being homeless, the strategy changes significantly to finding cheap and affordable housing to reduce the stresses causing the metal illness.

The authors also note that being victimized can cause people to spiral into negative emotions. Their text offers extensive knowledge of the aftermath of victimization. When victimization occurs to someone who is already vulnerable and therefore may be already experiencing the negative cognitive and behavioural consequences of the situation (such as living with the conditions of being homeless), these feelings may intensify and may lead to prolonged bouts of depression, anxiety, feelings of hopelessness, and so on. People who are depressed have trouble making decisions and, therefore, may be unable to change their situation. As a result, victimization can be one of the many factors that contribute to the cycle of homelessness. Figure 8.1 demonstrates that homelessness can lead to increased vulnerability

Figure 8.1   The Cycle of Homelessness and Victimization

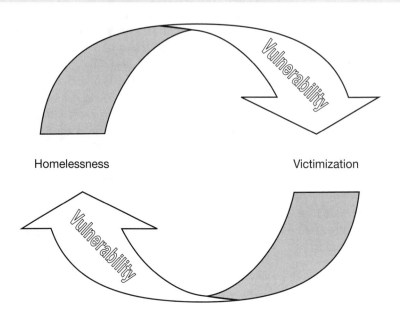

Homelessness   Victimization

to victimization. Victimization can cause increased mental instability and further vulnerability, which leads to feelings of not being able to change their situation. Victimized homeless are now more vulnerable, which increases the odds of being victimized and therefore the cycle continues.

Youth and Homelessness

As stated in the previous section, homelessness is a factor that can increase a person's victim vulnerability. Homeless people are victimized at disproportionately higher rates than their domiciled counterparts. Another well-known fact is that young people are more likely to be both offenders and victims of crime than older people. When we combine these two sets of vulnerabilities, we see even higher rates of victimization (Baron, 2003; Baron & Hartnegal,

1998; Jasinski et al, 2005; Lee & Schreck, 2005).

Baron (2003), in his study of street youth in an unidentified Canadian city, notes that youth who live on the street often arrive there as a result of victimization. The relationship between previous victimization and homelessness increases the likelihood of later victimization. Many of the youth he interviewed not only had experienced victimization but had also committed crimes, and therefore became victimizers, as a means of survival. Baron (2003, p. 37) observes that 'dangerousness and vulnerability can be viewed as "two sides of the same coin," as the factors that contribute to dangerousness also enhance vulnerability' to victimization. In an earlier study (Baron, 1998), this same author observed that where there was a history of victimization in the home, and later on the streets, violence became an accepted way of dealing with conflict. Therefore, depending on the outcome of the violent resolution process, homeless youth are more likely to be a victim of crime.

Gaetz (2004) points to a unique conundrum facing homeless youth, one that is not necessarily faced by their adult counterparts. Youth, and homeless youth in particular, have been often targeted for public efforts to control crime and deviance, primarily because youth are more likely to engage in risky and/or criminal behaviour than adults. The fact that youth are also more likely to be victimized has not been given the same focus. Therefore, any discussions that may have resulted in enhancing community and/or safety have systematically excluded youth, who are seen more as offenders than as one of society's most vulnerable groups. Gaetz argues that, instead of protecting young people, we have actually created legislation focusing on them as offenders. This approach marginalizes street youth when it comes to issues regarding their public safety.

Hate Crimes against the Homeless

Sandra Wachholz (2005) recently published a study looking at the homeless as frequent targets of hate crimes and hate speech. Her findings demonstrate that homeless people must frequently endure hateful acts and language in their daily lives. Wachholz reports that hate speech was most frequently used against homeless people while they were panhandling. When an individual asks for money on the street is it assumed that he or she does not wish to work, that he or she is lazy, and so on. This focus on work takes precedence over all other concerns, such as whether the person may be hungry, ill, or has a family to support.

Respondents report hearing statements such as 'Get a job; Fucking bum; Can you spell work?; You're living off taxpayers, you bum' (p. 148). Racial minorities, usually Aboriginal Americans, reported being shouted at in Spanish with similar language: 'Go back to where you came from, homeless scum,' and 'Homeless piece of shit. I'm calling immigration' (p. 152). Their victimizers usually misidentified their ethnic identity. One respondent reported, 'I have had that done so frequently, I know a little bit of Spanish myself right now' (p. 152). For women, these comments included words of a sexual and derogatory nature, such as 'bitch' and 'slut'. Women were also more likely to be victimized by hate speech than men. One woman in the study recounted how men would stop and honk their horns at her. At one point a man stopped his car and held out change. When she went over to the vehicle she noticed he was masturbating. This experience left the woman shaken and angry. It is suggested that such ideas about and behaviour toward the homeless are not those of an exceptional element but are pervasive in Canadian society (see also Box 8.1).

Respondents in the study reported that, as they aged, the frequency of hate speech and assaults increased. Often times, victimizers would combine acts of hateful speech with physical assault. This would take the form of being insulted while having objects thrown at them from an automobile. Respondents reported being yelled at while being hit with coffee cups, ice cream cones, pennies, and dog food. Although more rare, some reported being 'kicked in the head' and being hit in the face with a closed fist. Respondents said that they were 'hit or knocked down' almost every couple of weeks. For this reason, panhandlers sought to protect themselves by carefully wording their requests so as to not anger or frighten people, working within yelling distance of one another, and sometimes asking someone to come with them to do 'shadow work'. Shadow work involves protecting others who are panhandling by keeping an eye on them and running to their rescue if needed. Box 8.2 relays the story of Paul Croutch, a man who was killed by three reserve soldiers who were heard making hateful comments while they beat him to death (Small, 2008a; 2008b). They then attacked a woman who distracted them from their assault, dragging her through the park and calling her a 'whore', among other names.

Box 8.2 Paul Croutch

Paul Croutch lived in foster homes from the age of six. By the 1960s he had started work at McDonnell Douglas Aircraft in Malton, ON, got married, and, in the last half of the decade, formed his own plastics company with a few partners. When Croutch had a dispute with his partners, they wrote him a letter stating that he was mentally unstable and asking him to get a psychiatric assessment. He never did, but instead moved to Dawson Creek, BC, where he worked as a travelling car salesman and later editor of a local newspaper. At one point he encouraged the local church to keep their food bank open every day and campaigned to help the less fortunate. He eventually had a falling out with his wife, teenage daughter, and his community and subsequently made his way back to Toronto, where he became a homeless person.

On 31 August 2005, Croutch was sleeping in Toronto's Moss Park, as he had been doing for some time. He had covered himself with garbage bags to keep warm and dry. The assistant Crown attorney in the subsequent murder trial stated in court that 'Moss Park was Paul Croutch's bedroom' and the bench he slept on, nestled between two tennis courts and a baseball diamond, 'was his bed'. Croutch slept outside despite his poor health. He had a series of medical problems, including high blood pressure, emphysema, hardening of the arteries, and swollen ankles, suggesting he had trouble with circulation of bodily fluids.

Shortly after 4:00 a.m., Croutch was approached by three reserve members of the Queen's Own Rifles of Canada: Brian Deganis, 24; Jeffrey Hall, 24; and Mountaz Ibrahim, 25. These men were trained as combat soldiers and airborne infantry and were stationed at the Moss Park Armoury. Before they had left the armoury that night, Deganis was allegedly heard making statements about how much he hated homeless people and that he wanted to take them on. At least one of the reservists had consumed alcohol.

The three men attacked Croutch while he was sleeping. He was kicked so hard that his body was lifted off of the ground. During the trial, the Crown stated that he was kicked 'like a football' and that the men yelled that 'bums' were not welcome in Moss Park. Croutch's unconscious body was found several feet away from his bench. The attack was stopped by a witness, Valerie Valen, who threatened to call the police on her cell phone. Although she was bluffing, the three men stopped the assault and approached Valen. She became frightened and started to retreat. The men told her to 'run' but then tripped her as she was trying to get away. She told police that she was beaten and dragged through the park while being called a 'bum' and a 'whore'. They told her to 'Tell all your friends the park is ours. We own it.'

Croutch was taken to hospital, suffering from broken ribs, a torn spleen, and a fatal head injury. He died in hospital. He was 59 years old. All three men eventually pleaded guilty to causing his death and were sentenced accordingly: Deganis and Hall pleaded guilty to manslaughter and were sentenced to 10 years each in a penitentiary; Ibrahim accepted accessory charges and was sentenced to 10 months in jail.

SOURCES: Small, P. (2008a). Homeless man was kicked 'like a football' trial told. *The Toronto Star.* Retrieved 4 June 2009, from www.thestar.com/printArticle/347166; Small, P. (2008b). The real Paul Croutch. *The Toronto Star.* Retrieved 5 June 2009, from www.thestar.com/News/GTA/article/416169; Kraus. K. (2008). Paul Croutch: A casualty of war on the poor. *Rabble News.* Retrieved 3 June 2010, from www.rabble.ca/news/paul-croutch-casualty-war-poor.

Victimization of Prisoners

O'Donnell and Edgar (1998; 1999) have shown that levels of assault, threat, and verbal abuse are perpetrated, received, and witnessed on a fairly regular basis within the prison system. This finding is important as prisoners, by the very nature of the prison system, have little control over their daily routines. They live in what sociologist Erving Goffman (1968) termed a **total institution**, a facility in which all aspects of a resident's daily life are controlled by others. Prisons are particularly good examples of total institutions because inmate control is key to their administration. Prisoners are told when to get up, when and where to eat, when to exercise, how to behave, when to sleep, and so on. Almost every aspect of their lives is directed, controlled, and monitored.

Inmates have few options for recreation and leisure, much of which is available in very short time slots. Likewise, inmates have little control over whom they associate with and when, as prisoners are often herded in groups into various activities. With the exception of where conjugal visits are allowed, visitors are often restricted to a specific area of the facility and often precluded from physical contact with the inmate by some form of barrier. Internal structure and management of prisons also leave little room for escape or defence from victimization. In this type of facility, where large numbers of people, many of whom are incarcerated for violent offences, are forced to interact, the threat of victimization is very real to both those who reside and work behind its walls. Staff members are permitted to use force to resolve conflict, and prisoners often resort to violence as a means of resistance, anger, threats, frustration, entertainment, and so on. As a result, these places are fear inducing, requiring that endurance not only be physical but emotional and intellectual as well.

Measuring Victimization of Prisoners

O'Donnell and Edgar's findings regarding prison violence fit with the general assumption that such violence is common. Many inmates housed in prisons in the United States, for example, are both sexually and physically victimized by other inmates and staff (Gaes & Goldberg, 2004). However, conducting research on and measuring victimization among this population is difficult because it relies on the approval of the institution's administration. This is not to say that corrections staff are not concerned about the welfare of their inmates; there are many reasons why prison studies are not allowed. One is that research by an outside institution such as a university might not put the facility in the best light. Wolff, Shi, and Bachman (2008) have noted that even if a researcher can gain access to prisoners, it is often not a simple matter of asking questions, but how you ask questions that will give the most accurate results. Their study looked at sexual victimization of men and women in prison and found that the rates varied depending on which measures were used. Using questions derived from the American National Violence Against Women Survey, male and female respondents were asked about prison victimization.

Tjaden and Thoennes (2000) found that 0.2 per cent of women and less than 0.06 per cent of men in the general public reported being raped (attempted or completed) during a 12-month period. In comparison, Wolff, Shi, and Bachman (2008) reported that 4.6 per cent of women and 2.7 per cent of men in prison were raped during a 6-month period. This same study reported that rates of physical assault in the general

public over a 12-month period were 1.3 per cent for females and 0.9 per cent for males compared to 22.8 per cent of females and 32.6 per cent of males in prison during a 6-month period. Table 8.1 shows the results of O'Donnell and Edgar's (1999) prison study in the United Kingdom. Participants in this study were asked whether they had been victim of, or been witness to, at least one act of violence in the month prior to the survey. Roughly one-quarter to one-half of the inmates reported being victimized during this time, depending on the facility. The majority of all respondents at all facilities had witnessed the victimization of another.

According to Reed and Morrison (1997), in a study carried out by the Canadian Department of Justice, there were 94 inmate deaths across Canada in 1995–6. Some of the results of this study can be seen in Figure 8.2. These deaths were almost equally split between the provincial inmate population (n=46) and the federal inmate population (n=48).

Table 8.1   Experience of Victimization and/or Incivility and Feelings of Safety (in percentages) in the Month Prior to Survey

Facility	Hurtful verbal assault			Assault		
	Witnessed	Been Victim of	Feel safe from	Witnessed	Been Victim of	Feel Safe From
Feltham (n = 436)	77	58	68	60	32	62
Huntercombe (n = 152)	81	51	77	66	26	70
Bullingdon (n = 408)	63	26	70	54	20	63
Wellingborough (n = 186)	60	26	72	43	17	60

SOURCE: O'Donnell, I., & Edgar, K. (1999). Fear in prison. *The Prison Journal, 79(1)*, 90–99, p. 93. Copyright 1999 by SAGE Publications. Reprinted by Permission of SAGE Publications.

Just over one-quarter of these deaths were suicides (n=28), representing an increase from previous years. The most marked increase occurred in the provincial/territorial population where the number of suicides grew from 18 to 28. These numbers appear small, but when looked at as a rate per 10,000 adults, the inmate suicide rate is more than twice that found in the adult Canadian population (4.0 and 1.7 respectively). Murders by inmates, however, are extremely rare. There were two murders committed within each of the provincial and federal inmate populations in 1995–6. Although there are no specific statistics for violent deaths of corrections officers in the workplace, Figure 8.3 demonstrates that 31 per cent of violent workplace deaths occurred in a hospital, prison, or rehabilitation centre.

Fear and Victimization in Prison

Given the living conditions in prison, it is not surprising that inmates exhibit feelings of fear. Table 8.1 demonstrates that, overall, approximately one-quarter of the inmates in the four facilities studied did not feel safe from verbal assault and approximately one-third did not feel safe from assault. When the researchers probed further, they found that those inmates who had experienced recent verbal or physical victimization were less likely to feel safe from similar actions (see Table 8.2).

What is interesting to note in this study is that inmates felt safe most of the time, except when they were in particular situations or locations in the facility. Inmates reported feeling unsafe when they first arrived at the facility, when they were in the showers or in the segregation unit, and when they had to move between residential wings. However, the feelings of safety varied depending on how the prison was structured and constructed and therefore on which institution inmates were residing in. Two of the

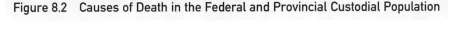

Figure 8.2 Causes of Death in the Federal and Provincial Custodial Population

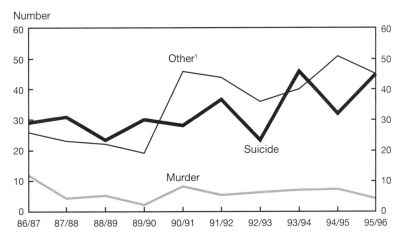

1 Other includes deaths from natural causes, accidents, etc.

SOURCE: Reed, M., & Morrison, P. (1997). Adult correctional services in Canada, 1995–96. *Juristat, 17(4)*. Ottawa, ON: Canadian Centre for Justice Statistics, Minister of Industry, p. 12.

Figure 8.3   Violent Workplace Incidents Most Likely to Occur in Offices, Factories, and Stores, 2004

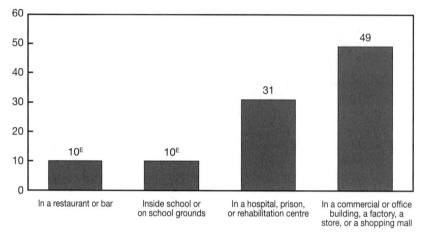

per cent of violent workplace incidents

In a restaurant or bar	10E
Inside school or on school grounds	10E
In a hospital, prison, or rehabilitation centre	31
In a commercial or office building, a factory, a store, or a shopping mall	49

E   use with caution

Note: Only includes violent incidents that occurred at the victim's place of work.

SOURCE: de Léséleuc, S. (2007). Criminal victimization in the workplace 2004. Canadian Centre for Justice Statistics Profile Series. Ottawa, ON: Canadian Centre for Justice Statistics, Minister of Industry, p. 9.

facilities studied had what was termed 'vulnerable prisoner units' (VPUs). These units housed inmates who were targeted by other prisoners and who had to be separated for their protection. Prisoners in these units felt considerably less safe than the other inmates in the study and, in some cases, lived in chronic fear. Additionally, there were conflicts within the VPU between sex offenders and other protected prisoners, such as those who had debts.

Offenders as Secondary Victims

Julius Melnitzer served 18 years as a trial lawyer, including 10 as a criminal lawyer. At his peak, he was considered one of the best lawyers in Ontario. Throughout his career he served as the provincial director of the Ontario Criminal Lawyers Association (Melnitzer, 2002). In 1991

the National Bank of Canada noted that stock certificates that Melnitzer had used as collateral for a $15-million line of credit were forgeries. He had printed over $100 million in blue chip certificates using a local London, ON, printing house. The RCMP also noted that he had defrauded several close friends out of more than $14 million by getting them to invest in bogus property. After pleading guilty to 43 counts of fraud in 1992, Melnitzer was sentenced to nine years in jail. He served two years before being released on day parole and earned full parole in 1995 (Waldie, 2009). While there, he wrote about his experiences and his profession.

As a criminal lawyer, Melnitzer believed that the lawyer's obligation to the client was over when there was either an acquittal or a sentence (Melnitzer,

Table 8.2   Relationship between Fear and Recent Direct Experience of Victimization and/or Incivility (in percentages) in the Month Prior to Survey

	Feltham	Huntercombe	Bullingdon	Wellingborough
Not been insulted and feels safe from insults	70	82	77	76
Been insulted and feels safe from insults	63a	66*	42***	53**
Not been assaulted and feels safe from assault	66	73	66	68
Been assaulted and feels safe from assault	47***	54*	41***	23***

a Not statistically significant.
*p < 0.05. **p < 0.01. ***p < 0.001.

SOURCE: O'Donnell, I., & Edgar, K. (1999). Fear in prison. *The Prison Journal, 79(1)*, 90–99, p. 94. Copyright 1999 by SAGE Publications. Reprinted by Permission of SAGE Publications.

2002). He realized during his time in prison that lawyers need to rethink their commitment to the profession; he also suggested that they need to rethink their role in society. He argued that the civil rights of the prisoner are the lowest common denominator of democracy. Melnitzer saw first-hand the daily violations of basic human rights, including corrections officers being present during discussions between prisoners and their legal counsel. As he claims, the infringement of these fundamental rights serves to undermine everyone.

Melnitzer argues in his book, *Maximum Minimum Medium: A Journey Through Canadian Prisons* (2002), that prisoners continue to need representation while in the prison system to ensure that they receive due process. Although all prisoners must work through their sentences, how and where they do so becomes important. It is assumed within the prison system and perhaps to some degree in the larger populace

that, as a prisoner approaches his or her release date, he or she moves from a maximum security facility to a minimum security one, where there is considerably more freedom and more personal responsibility gained through showing good behaviour. Prison models propose that, if an inmate exhibits 'good behaviour', they will be rewarded by eventually being moved towards a minimum security facility. In essence, they are told that they can 'earn' their way to a better living environment. The quality of life is much better in a minimum security facility, where prisoners are often allowed to wear civilian clothing, are able to move about the facility more freely, and can become eligible for limited passes outside the prison. Completing a full sentence in a maximum security setting, where inmates wear uniforms, can be locked down for 23 hours at a time during normal operations, and are often limited to their cells can be much more stress inducing.

In other words, it is not simply a matter of how much time prisoners must serve, but where and when they have to serve it that can often make the biggest differences to inmate dignity.

Melnitzer noticed that corrections officers often become judges in assessing dispute resolution. Prisoners, therefore, have to defend their rights, which is difficult for those who face illiteracy, lack of education, substance abuse problems, etc. He noted that suspicious behaviour is often documented and never proven. These suspicions can have consequences. He recalls that because of political pressure in one prison, all violent offenders were transferred to a maximum security facility. Often only suspicion of violent behaviour, without proof, resulted in such a transfer. Therefore, minimum security offenders can end up in maximum security designation. The implications of this lack of representation result in prisoners being victimized by the system that is supposed to be rehabilitating them and preparing them for life outside its walls. Prisoners who exhibit good behaviour can be moved and thereby punished by losing freedoms and being placed in maximum security facilities based on political forces outside their control, innuendo, and suspicion instead of evidence evaluated by an impartial judge or jury. If prisoners try to exert their rights, they are threatened with being 'suspicious', which makes living in prison much more difficult. Prisoners under minimum security conditions have the most to lose, as they can be threatened with being moved to a prison with more restrictions.

In his writing, Melnitzer recalled the cases of several inmates who had tried to deal with false accusations and/or assert their legal rights. Melnitzer's own personal experience recounts an incident where he was asked to remove his clothes so he could be 'strip-searched'. He asked if he was suspected of anything, and the corrections officer stated that he was not. When he informed the officer that the search was illegal, the officer called his superior and informed Melnitzer that he had to do it anyway; not consenting to the search was considered grounds for suspicion and therefore grounds for forcing Melnitzer to remove his clothes and be searched. In other words, the policies often suffered from circular or tautological reasoning, in that legally objecting to a search on the basis that there were no grounds for the action to occur became identified as grounds for the search.

Melnitzer also argues that parole boards must be less concerned with the appearance of corrections services policies and procedures and more on principles of law. If we have decided, democratically, that prisoners are entitled to the most basic human and legal rights, then these rights must be upheld or all are in jeopardy. Although controversial, there may be merit to this argument. The methods used to maintain personal rights is also important to this issue. To undermine the basic rights of prisoners erodes the basic rights of those who are not incarcerated. In other words, to victimize prisoners is to indirectly victimize all citizens. If we make it easier to violate the rights of a particular group of individuals, then we essentially make it easier to erode the rights of all citizens, because prisoners are citizens. Although our intention may be to punish this group in a different way, by denying prisoners rights that all Canadians have, we chip away at the protections afforded all Canadians.

Victimization of People with Disabilities

Vulnerability can come in several forms, one of which is disability. Perreault (2009) notes that by signing the United Nations Convention on the Rights of Persons with Disabilities in 2007, Canada recognized that people living with physical disabilities are particularly vulnerable to victimization because of their mobility limitations. He further notes that almost one in seven Canadians (14 per cent) reported in the Participation and Activity Limitation Survey (PALS) that they had at least one physical or mental condition that restricted their daily activities.

Perreault (2009) found that many of the risk factors that increase vulnerability to victimization in the non-disabled population also increase risk for the disabled population. For example, youth was a factor in vulnerability in both groups. Generally, younger respondents (ages 15–44) in the PALS were slightly more likely to report violent victimization, while older adults (ages 45 and over) were just under twice as likely, on average, to report the same type of victimization. Using logistic regression analysis, Perreault was also able to discern that those in the 15–24 age range with a disability were 11 times more likely to be victims of violence when compared to those who were 55 and older and living with a disability. The author also found that those individuals with disabilities were at increased risk for vulnerability if they reported an annual income of less than $15,000. In other words, having a disability compounds the risk for victimization when combined with other individual characteristics such as youth and poverty.

Statistics Canada (Perreault, 2009) also reports that individuals with disabilities are more likely to be victimized by someone they know. Excluding cases of spousal abuse, approximately two out of every three perpetrators of violence against a disabled person was known to the victim. This figure compares with approximately one-half of offenders being known to the victim in crimes among the non-disabled population. In incidents where the victim had a disability, the perpetrator was more likely to be older (48 per cent) than in cases where the victim was not disabled (31 per cent). A larger proportion of victimization of people with disabilities took place in or near the home (31 per cent) than that of people who were not disabled (14 per cent). As discussed in previous chapters, one of the best predictors of future victimization is previous victimization. Almost half (46 per cent) of the respondents who had a disability reported being victimized more than once compared to the non-disabled (36 per cent). This report also shows that victims with disabilities were almost twice as likely to experience spousal violence. They were also two to three times more likely to have been hit with an object, beaten, choked, or to have had a spouse threaten to use a weapon (gun or knife) against them. Interestingly, Perreault (2009) revealed that although it has been found that victims with disabilities were more likely to depend on their spouses for day-to-day activities, a higher proportion reported their violent victimization to police (36 per cent) than in the non-disabled population (25 per cent). Victims with disabilities were more likely to experience more severe

Figure 8.4   Proportion of Persons who Experienced Abuse or Violence by a Spouse

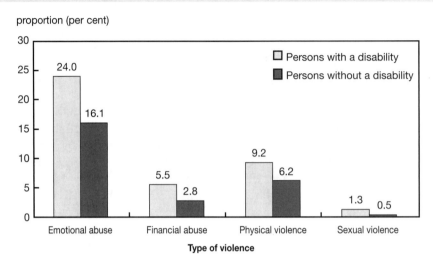

proportion (per cent)

Legend: ☐ Persons with a disability ■ Persons without a disability

Emotional abuse: 24.0 / 16.1
Financial abuse: 5.5 / 2.8
Physical violence: 9.2 / 6.2
Sexual violence: 1.3 / 0.5

Type of violence

SOURCE: Perreault, S. (2009). Criminal victimization and health: A profile of victimization among persons with activity limitations or other health problems. Canadian Centre for Justice Statistics Profile Series. Ottawa, ON: Canadian Centre for Justice Statistics, Minister of Industry, p. 11.

forms of spousal violence, reporting more injury (39 per cent compared with 30 per cent of the non-disabled group). Disabled persons subjected to intimate partner victimization were twice as likely to need medical attention (14 per cent compared with 7 per cent of the non-disabled population) and were more likely to report feeling that their lives were in jeopardy (32 per cent compared with 21 per cent) as a result of this violence. Just under one-third (31 per cent compared with 21 per cent of non-disabled victims) stated that their victimization prevented them from performing daily activities.

Reporting Victimization

The three groups discussed in this chapter all face similar challenges regarding reporting victimization to the police.

Jasinski et al. (2005), in their study of the homeless, found that victimization is seldom reported to authorities. When it is reported, appropriate actions are rarely taken, as police are more often tools of controlling the homeless population rather than crimes occurring within it. As such, the authorities may not be trusted as a source of protection. These circumstances contribute to more and more individuals failing to report occurrences of victimization and to a very unfortunate reality for the homeless population, one that is exacerbated by the location in which they spend most of their time and the lack of capable guardians or social networks to help deal with and/or avoid many of the situations in which victimization of the homeless occurs. Further, Lee and Schreck (2005) offer that victimization becomes a part of the desperate way of living faced by individuals without a home. Under these extreme conditions, victimization can become a way of life.

Reporting victimization while being imprisoned also has significant challenges. Evidence among this population (O'Donnell & Edgar, 1998; 1999) suggests that violence can also become routine in prison. Reporting such victimization may place people in more jeopardy. Over half (56 per cent) of all inmates in O'Donnell and Edgar's studies agreed with the idea that informers 'deserved to be bullied'. Almost three-quarters (72 per cent) of all inmates believed that inmates who were sex offenders should become victims of the same type of crime. If the victimizers are staff at these institutions, they often act as **gatekeepers**, Goffman's (1968) term for anyone who controls access to a particular resource. In the case of the prison population, gatekeepers block inmates from contacting any authority that may serve to punish staff who have victimized inmates. In other words, the victimizer may also be the person who allows access to the outside world. It is also suggested that if the authorities were actually reached, the victims would suffer the same type of response as reported by the homeless: they would be disregarded or taken less seriously. Therefore, not reporting or being unable to report victimization also makes this population uniquely vulnerable.

Clearly, having physical restrictions compounds vulnerability to victimization, especially if we consider the act of self-defence or crime reporting. Victims with disabilities may be less able to physically defend themselves, depending on the nature and severity of their disability. Some may have more difficulty verbally relaying details of the actual victimization.

Although we have focused on physical restrictions in this chapter, people with mental disabilities face many of the same issues. Those who have both physical and mental challenges may be even more at risk than those who have one or the other. As suggested by the statistics given above, perpetrators may find these impairments advantageous and therefore be more likely to target this population.

Explaining High Rates of Victimization among Vulnerable Populations

When a vulnerable person is victimized, the crime seems particularly tragic. Unfortunately, such people may be attractive to victimizers. Rational choice theories (see Chapter 4) state that if we assume that offenders are logical beings who make choices that maximize gain while minimizing cost, we can also assume that they would choose victims who meet this requirement. For example, individuals who do not pose a physical threat to the assailant would be chosen over those who might harm him or her during the attack. Those who lack resources, such as a permanent address or money, may also serve as better target selections because they may not be able to initiate legal proceedings. Likewise, those who would not serve as reputable witnesses to the crime, such as people with severe mental impairments or drug addictions, may also be more preferable as victims than those whose testimony would stand up well in court. Rational choice theories predict that the members of these susceptible groups may be more likely to be selected as targets.

Likewise, lifestyles theory states that if one is more likely to engage in a risky existence, the chances for victimization increase (Hindelang, Gottfredson, & Garofalo, 1978). In particular, this theory states that people become particularly vulnerable when they spend large amounts of time in public spaces, especially during the night. If one is living a life of desperate circumstances, such as living on the street, living on whatever food is available, and dealing with substance abuse issues, lifestyles theory suggests that these activities place individuals at unique disadvantage for victimization. Simons, Whitbeck, and Bales (1989) found support for many of the predictions of this theory. Their study found that those who engaged in risky lifestyles, such as those shared by homeless people, were significantly more likely to be victimized. If this lifestyle included substance abuse, the chances increased. Interestingly, this study did not show a strong relationship between victimization history and history of psychiatric assessments. In other words, a homeless individual with a history of psychiatric disorders was only slightly more likely to be victimized than a person in the non-homeless population who also had a psychiatric problem. Similar findings were reported in a later study by Jasinski et al (2005). Substance abuse problems and lack of employment options were more significant factors contributing to homelessness and the resulting distress.

Although inmate populations also live risky lifestyles, these theories are assumed to explain the victimization vulnerability of people who are not institutionalized. Victimization of those living in a total institution where violence is part of the everyday experience also increases the vulnerability to risk. However, because prisoners are blocked from the outside world and under the total control of the prison system, the factors of their vulnerability are different and therefore the rules under which individuals become more susceptible to victimization are changed. As O'Donnell and Edgar (1999) show, prisoners understand—to some extent—that there are places and times within the institution where they may be more vulnerable. Some inmates live in perpetual fear and require special protection.

Summary

This chapter has looked at the victimization of three unique populations: people who are homeless, people who are incarcerated, and people who live with disabilities. The living conditions of the people in these groups make them more attractive to potential offenders; consequently, their level of victim vulnerability is higher than that of other people. In fact, victimization has become a way of life for many of them. Some members of these groups have experienced so much victimization for so long that often only the most severe cases are reported.

This vulnerability is also increased by society's marginalization of these three groups. Without the basic level of control or power over their own lives, they become subject to those who have control over their lives. People in these groups are often unable to avoid victimization or to involve the criminal justice system. This situation is especially evident in prisons, where all access to the outside world is controlled by the system. If victims do manage to overcome the challenges of filing a police report, they run the risk of that report not being taken seriously for any number of reasons. For example, Crown attorneys may decide not to pursue the case because he or she feels that a victim who is homeless or incarcerated is not a credible witness. For those with physical disabilities, credibility is not a major concern; however, police may have trouble understanding the nature of the report (depending on the level of verbal impairment), and Crown attorneys may have concern about the victim's ability to testify. As a result, these victimizations may be ignored and the offenders unpunished.

Glossary

gatekeeper   Initially coined by sociologist Erving Goffman, refers to anyone who controls access to a particular resource.

marginalization   The exclusion of some groups from mainstream society, which can lead to a lack of power or control.

total institution   Goffman's term for a facility in which all aspects of a resident's daily life are controlled by others. A prison is an example of a total institution.

Critical Thinking Questions

1. Do inmates who are victimized have the same rights to protection as victims who do not reside in a prison? Why or why not?
2. Can the safety of prison inmates be assured? What measures could be taken to achieve this goal?
3. What are some of the similarities and differences between prisoners and homeless people when it comes to being victimized?
4. Think of another type of total institution than prisons. What are the characteristics of the clientele? Do they also share the vulnerability discussed in this chapter? What vulnerabilities might be unique to the group you have in mind?
5. Imagine that you lost the function of your legs or your ability to breathe without medical assistance. How do you think your condition would change the way people interact with you? How do you think it would change your mobility? How and why would this situation make you more or less vulnerable to victimization?
6. Schizophrenia is characterized by the hearing of voices or noises in the mind, sometimes accompanied with tactile or visual hallucinations. This illness generally emerges in individuals from about 15 to 27 years of age. How would a 22-year-old male who had been living with the disease for five years and was currently not taking medication be more vulnerable to victimization than a male who had been living with the disease for longer, was in his late forties, and had a consistent record of managing his illness with medication?

CHAPTER 9

Victimization in Public and Private Spaces over the Life Course

Learning Objectives

After reading this chapter, you will be able to

- understand how victimization, and vulnerability to victimization, can change over the life course;
- understand how environmental factors influence vulnerability to victimization;
- understand how time and place interact to create unique vulnerabilities to victimization; and
- understand how public and private spheres create different types of vulnerabilities.

Introduction

The life course includes various stages. While we are very young, we live primarily in the private sphere of our homes and in the company of our families. As we get older, we spend more time in the public sphere and begin to interact with others at school, university or college, the workplace, and in many other social environments. At some point during our adolescence, we begin to explore more intimate relationships through dating. Most of us leave home at some point and begin to lead more independent lives. We might get married, live common-law or civil union with someone, and/or have children. During middle age, we may also advance in our chosen careers, divorce and remarry, and have grandchildren. Eventually we retire from work and take on new challenges. As we enter our senior years, we may need to rely on others for support, such as our families or assisted living environments.

At all of these stages in our lives, we experience the many highlights of life: having our first kiss, watching our children grow, achieving our career goals, and so on. These stages of our lives are also fraught with major obstacles that we have to overcome, such as illness, the death of a loved one, and, for many, victimization. These types and the associated levels of victimization risk change as we age and as we move between the private and public spheres. In this chapter, we will discuss some of the more common forms of victimization that occur during the life course. We will look at the importance of time and place and how it affects victimization risk and victimization.

The Criminal Event Perspective

The criminal event perspective, as outlined by Sacco and Kennedy (2002), extends the discussion of criminal activity beyond the short period of time in which the crime actually occurs. Earlier in this text (see Chapter 4) we talked about the importance of not only viewing the transaction theoretically but also understanding the events leading up to the transaction (precursors) and the events that follow it (aftermath). Sacco and Kennedy also discuss the significance of looking at how being in the public or private sphere affects the types of victimization we may experience. For example, the risk for certain types of victimization increase when we are at home, including being victimized by a family member. When we leave home this risk diminishes, but other forms of victimization risk increase, such as being in a traffic accident or being harassed in our workplaces or school environments.

Figure 9.1   Illustration of Elements of Sacco and Kennedy's Criminal Event Perspective

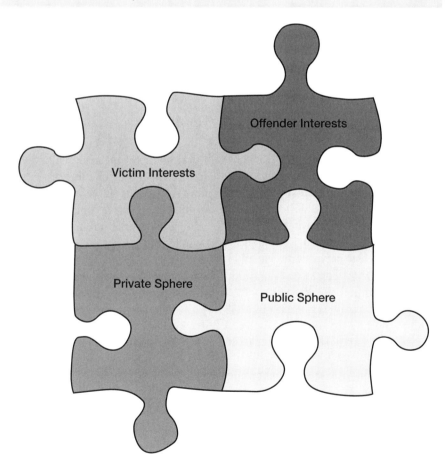

SOURCE: Sacco, V. T., & Kennedy, L. W. (2002). *The criminal event perspective: Perspectives in space and time* (2nd ed.). Toronto: Nelson Thomson Learning.

Perceived and Actual Risk of Victimization over the Life Course

There is often a sharp difference between the fear that people have about victimization and the actual threat of victimization. When we talk about fear of crime, we are sometimes referring to the perceived risk of being victimized, which is often a lot higher than the actual risk. For example, ask yourself the following question: 'What, in your opinion, is the most dangerous city in Canada?' In my class, students tend to think that the answer is Toronto. Many of my students live in or near the city and watch or listen to local newscasts. They hear about crimes in Toronto and are concerned about the number of homicides in that city. Toronto accounted for approximately one in every six homicides in the country in 2008, with a total of 103 homicides in the Toronto Census Metropolitan Area (Beattie, 2009). The city's homicide rate is calculated to be 1.9 homicides per 100,000 residents, which is just slightly above the national average of 1.8 for that year. Trends show consistently that the western Canadian cities are the most dangerous. In 2008, Winnipeg topped the list with a rate of 4.1, followed by Regina (3.8) and Edmonton (3.4). In this case, the students' fear of homicide is greater than their risk.

Fear of crime will be examined more closely in Chapter 10. For the purposes of this chapter, it is important to note the relationship between fear and actual threat. Our risk for victimization is highest when we are younger and then declines over our lifetime. However our fear of victimization declines until about middle age (age 40–50) and then increases as we continue to age (Ferraro, 1996). This correlation is illustrated in Figure 9.2.

Victimization in the Private Sphere

For many of us, the home is a place of safety. Although we all have our issues with our family members, for the most part our home is a place where we take refuge from the rest of the world. It is a place where we try to relax and spend time with our friends and family. However, not all homes are safe from victimization. Predators can work both within and outside the family. Patterns within private sphere victimizations can be shaped by the close-knit relationships that exist between the victim and the victimizer.

Child Abuse

In historical and contemporary societies all around the world, children have been and are treated as chattels or personal property (Kadushin & Martin, 1988). Parents can exploit their children for labour, sell their children, and even kill them if it is deemed necessary (Kadushin & Martin, 1988). The act of killing a child, or infanticide, occurs for a variety of reasons: parents lack the resources to provide for the child; the child is deformed, ill, or cries often; or the child is of an undesired sex (usually a girl). In some cases of twin births, one or both may be abandoned and left to die, depending on the strength of the babies and other belief systems about multiple births.

Although most parents no longer view their children as property, they do hold considerable control over them until they reach adulthood. Some parents enforce this control through

Figure 9.2 Changes in Perceived Risk and Actual Risk of Victimization over the Life Course

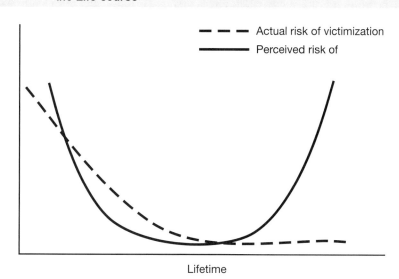

Lifetime

traditional forms of corporal punishment, adhering to the following adages:

Spare the rod and spoil the child.
Children should be seen and not heard.

The Bible also includes several passages that support these ideas:

He who withholds his rod hates his son, but he who loves him disciplines him diligently. (Proverbs 13:24)

Foolishness is bound up in the heart of a child; The rod of discipline will remove it far from him. (Proverbs 22:15)

Do not hold back discipline from the child, Although you strike him with the rod, he will not die. You shall strike him with the rod and rescue his soul from Sheol. (Proverbs 23:13–14)

The rod and reproof give wisdom, But a child who gets his own way brings shame to his mother. (Proverbs 29:15)

The use of corporeal punishment, such as spanking, to control a child is a topic of current debate. For some, spanking is a preferable form of discipline; for others it is a form of child abuse. Establishing the difference between these two terms is difficult, especially because the definition of child abuse is somewhat elusive. Although most of us have a basic understanding of what it means to abuse a child, the meaning is not uniform and can change depending on the situation. Consider these questions:

1. Were you ever spanked as a child?
2. Would you spank your own children?
3. Do you feel spanking is a legitimate form of discipline for children?

Responses to these questions vary depending on a variety of factors. One prominent factor is the family environment in which individuals are raised. Parents often model parenting style for their children. In other words, how someone is raised has a strong influence on how he or she raises his or her own children. Another factor is the culture in which families live. In some cases, a culture may dictate the most appropriate way to deal with children. Both familial and cultural environments can encourage or discourage the use of physical punishment. A third factor is time. As we move through generations, we change the way we think about child discipline. For example, in my parents' generation it was considered normal to punish a child using spanking. Although from different backgrounds, both of my parents had this experience as children. My parents, however, were influenced by the 'Hippie Generation' of the 1960s and chose to ignore their collective upbringings regarding how to raise their children in favour of a more open environment where spanking was rarely ever used. As a child, I watched the effectiveness of this idea and, as an adult, do not adhere at all to the spanking method, choosing options that I have had more success with, such as using 'time outs' and privilege systems. However, others have had different experiences, which will be reflected in their answers to the questions above.

For most, there is a general agreement that **child abuse** features certain characteristics. It is a deliberate act or set of actions that is considered maltreatment of a child. According to Brzozowski (2004), this mistreatment includes acts of physical abuse, sexual abuse, neglect, and emotional abuse, as well as witnessing family violence. She also points out that there is no one measurement system used to estimate the prevalence of child abuse in Canada. However, looking at a variety of data sets, we can get a good

idea of how often this type of victimization occurs. The data presented in this chapter considers the term 'children' to mean all individuals under the age of 18.

According to Nemr (2009), data captured by the Uniform Crime Reports (UCR2) indicate that adolescents are the most vulnerable to physical and sexual victimization when compared to all other age groups (see Figure 9.3). This study reports that children, as a group, are more vulnerable to physical and sexual abuse (833/100,000 people) than adults (761/100,000 people). The highest rate evidenced was for youth between the ages of 12 and 17; statistics show this population as being physically and sexually victimized at a rate of 1,628/100,000 Canadians, nearly four times the victimization rate for children ages 11 and under. Nemr also states that most of the differences between the rates of children and adults can be attributed to the higher incidence of reporting sexual assault crimes against children. Cases of sexual assault against children are reported to police at a rate of 193/100,000 individuals, approximately five times the reporting rate for adults (37/100,000). The majority of these reports (83 per cent) concerned the most minor form of assault: sexual assault level I. Adults tended to report physical assaults more than children, with the exception of adolescents, whose reporting rate of 1,333/100,000 is double the adult rate. Child and youth victims were less likely to report physical injury if they were abused by a non-family member (Nemr, 2009). The report elaborates that 4 in 10 children victimized by a family member sustained physical injuries, compared to those who were assaulted by non-family members (48 per cent). Almost

Figure 9.3   Rates of Sexual and Physical Assault Highest among Youth Aged 12–17

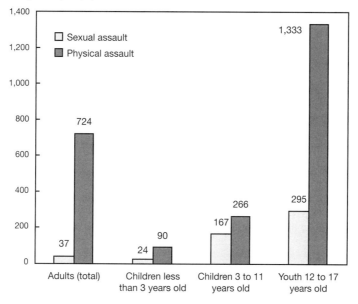

rate per 100,000 population

□ Sexual assault
■ Physical assault

1,333

724

266
167
295

37   24   90

Adults (total)   Children less than 3 years old   Children 3 to 11 years old   Youth 12 to 17 years old

Note(s):   Includes children and youth under the age of 18. Excludes incidents where the relationship between the victim and the accused was unknown. Data are not nationally representative. The Incident-based Uniform Crime Reporting Survey collected data from 153 police services representing approximately 94% of the population of Canada in 2007. Hamilton Police Service is excluded from the analysis due to the data quality of the relationship variable. Rate per 100,000 population for the geographic areas policed by the Incident-based Uniform Crime Reporting Survey respondents, based on population estimates provided by Demography Division, Statistics Canada.

SOURCE: Nemr, R. (2009). Fact sheet—Police-reported family violence against children and youth. *Family violence in Canada: A statistical profile 2009*. Ottawa, ON: Canadian Centre for Justice Statistics, Minister of Industry, p. 33.

all (97 per cent) of the injuries reported required no medical treatment and were considered minor.

Nemr (2009) found that children were most likely to be victimized by an acquaintance (55 per cent) as opposed to a family member (30 per cent). The majority (57 per cent) of children in the latter group were assaulted by a parent. Parents were more likely to physically assault their children (92/100,000) than to sexually assault them (24/100,000). The breakdown of these relationships is

illustrated by Figure 9.4, which shows the rate per 100,000 population of both physical and sexual assaults for various known assailants, broken down by the gender of the victim.

Figure 9.4 shows that physical assault on a male or female child is most likely to be carried out by a parent. Teenage girls reported a slightly higher rate (149/100,000) than adolescent boys (133/100,000). As children move into adolescence, their rate for physical violence increases significantly. Adolescent females are most at risk for physical abuse by a family member, with the highest threat occurring at age 17 (364/100,000). Males carried out most (71 per cent) of the physical assaults on family members. Almost half of these perpetrators were fathers (44 per cent); significantly fewer brothers (13 per cent) and extended family members (10 per cent) were responsible for physical familial abuse against children and youth.

Looking at the crime of sexual assault, this figure demonstrates that female victims are as likely to be victimized by a parent as they are by a member of their extended family. They are, however, four times more likely than boys (107/100,000 compared with 25/100,000, respectively) to be victimized by a relative. Girls are most vulnerable to this type of victimization between the ages of 12 and 15. Ninety-five per cent of familial sexual assaults were committed by males, with just over 33 per cent being non-family members, 32 per cent being fathers, and 27 per cent brothers.

Intimate Partner Violence

While males are more likely to be victimized by an acquaintance, women are more likely to be victimized by someone they know well. In her analysis of the 2004 General Social Survey (GSS), AuCoin (2005) estimated that 7 per cent of all Canadians over 14 years of age have experienced abuse by a current or former partner (marital or common-law) in the previous five years. Intimate partner violence, also referred to as spousal violence, occurs when a person in a current or former common-law or married relationship is deliberately assaulted in some way by his or her partner. Since 1998, spousal violence in Canada has experienced a

15 per cent decline, which is similar to trends in other violent crimes. Taylor-Butts (2009) reported that there were 75,779 incidents of spousal violence reported to police in 2007, with over 80 per cent involving a female victim. Incidents of spousal assault accounted for just over 1 in 10 (12 per cent) violent crimes reported to police in Canada and over half (53 per cent) of all family violence reports. Police reports however, only account for reported crime. Although we do not have an estimate for unreported crime for 2007, Mihorean (2005), using the 2004 GSS, states that only 28 per cent of victims of intimate partner violence reported the crimes to police. Recall that this is possible because the GSS is a victimization survey and not only accounts for all reported crime but can also ask respondents about crimes which they did not report to police.

The people at the greatest risk for this crime are between the ages of 25 and 34 (371/100,000) and between 35 and 44 (321/100,000). The risk for spousal violence declines sharply after age 45. The majority of crimes committed against the victim were *assault level I*, or *common assault* (62 per cent), followed by *assault level II* (*assault with a weapon or causing bodily harm*), and *assault level III* (*aggravated assault*) (15 per cent). Level I assaults consist of shoving, hitting, slapping, and punching; they do not involve serious injury or the use of or threats with a weapon. Assault levels II and III, on the other hand, involve serious injury and/or the use of a weapon to threaten, coerce, or injure. The three types of assault are also defined in the Criminal Code of Canada:

Assault
265 (1) A person commits an assault when

Figure 9.4   Rates of Family Violence, Especially Sexual Assault, Higher for Girls Than for Boys

rate per 100,000 population

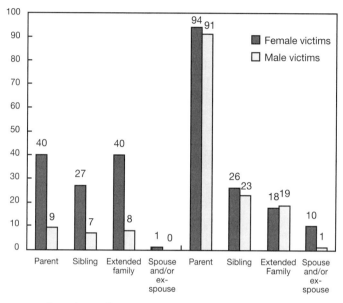

Sexual assault   Physical assault

Note(s):   Includes children and youth under the age of 18. Excludes incidents where the relationship between the victim and the accused was unknown. Data are not nationally representative. The Incident-based Uniform Crime Reporting Survey collected data from 153 police services representing approximately 94% of the population of Canada in 2007. Hamilton Police Service is excluded from the analysis due to the data quality of the relationship variable. Rate per 100,000 population for the geographic areas policed by the Incident-based Uniform Crime Reporting Survey respondents, based on population estimates provided by Demography Division, Statistics Canada.

SOURCE: Nemr, R. (2009). Fact sheet—Police-reported family violence against children and youth. *Family violence in Canada: A statistical profile 2009*. Ottawa, ON: Canadian Centre for Justice Statistics, Minister of Industry, p. 34.

(a) without the consent of another person, he applies force intentionally to that other person, directly or indirectly;

(b) he attempts or threatens, by an act or a gesture, to apply force to another person, if he has, or causes that other person to believe on reasonable grounds that he has, present ability to effect his purpose; or

(c) while openly wearing or carrying a weapon or an imitation thereof, he accosts or impedes another person or begs.

Assault with a weapon or causing bodily harm

267 Every one who, in committing an assault,

(a) carries, uses or threatens to use a weapon or an imitation thereof, or

(b) causes bodily harm to the complainant, is guilty of an indictable offence and liable to imprisonment for a term not exceeding ten years or an offence punishable on summary conviction and liable to imprisonment for a term not exceeding eighteen months.

Aggravated Assault

268 Every one commits an aggravated assault who wounds, maims, disfigures or endangers the life of the complainant.

Figure 9.5 outlines the types of abuse that occurs between a victim and a current or former spouse. While current spouses are more likely to assault or seriously assault

their victims, ex-partners are more likely to stalk or harass their former partners. Of all intimate partner violence reports made to police, almost all (93 per cent) were cleared by police, usually with a charge (78 per cent).

While men are more likely to be victimized outside the home, it appears that women are more vulnerable to violence within the home. Furthermore, women's risk for spousal or intimate partner violence increases until about

Figure 9.5   Level I Assault the Most Common Offence against Current and Former Spouses, Criminal Harassment and Threats More Common among Ex-Spouses, 2007

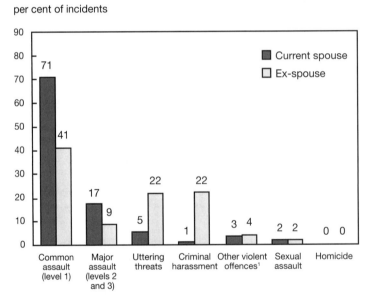

per cent of incidents

1 Includes robbery, unlawfully causing bodily harm, discharge firearm with intent, assault against peace-public officer, criminal negligence causing bodily harm, other assaults, kidnapping, hostage-taking, explosives causing death/bodily harm, arson, and other violent violations.

Note(s): Percentages may not total 100% due to rounding. Data are not nationally representative. The Incident-based Uniform Crime Reporting Survey collected data from 153 police services representing approximately 94% of the population of Canada in 2007. Hamilton Police Service is excluded from the analysis due to data quality of the relationship variable. Excludes incidents where the sex and/or age of the victim was unknown. Includes victims aged 15 to 98. Current spouse includes legally married and common-law partners. Ex-spouse includes separated and divorced partners.

SOURCE: Taylor-Butts, A. (2009). Fact sheet—Police-reported spousal violence in Canada. *Family violence in Canada: A statistical profile 2009.* Ottawa, ON: Canadian Centre for Justice Statistics, Minister of Industry, p. 26.

age 45, then begins to decline. This is in stark contrast to the patterns that males experience. Males are most vulnerable to victimization when they are young, between the ages of 13 and 17, but as they move into intimate relationships, their chances of victimization decline. In other words, while men are insulated from victimization by engaging in a relationship, this same life course decision for women increases their vulnerability to victimization by their spouses.

In a recent study, Warner (2010) examined the risks associated with being female and the likelihood of experiencing violence by an intimate. Warner found that women were more than four times more likely than men to experience violence from an intimate partner. Women were also more likely to experience violence from an intimate partner than from any other perpetrator. Men, however, were more likely to experience violence from someone outside the home. When women were victimized by an intimate, they were usually more likely to be injured. Therefore, these results demonstrate that the risk for spousal violence for women is much more severe than it is for men.

Elder Abuse

Violence against older adults has only recently been identified as a social problem. It is not that this form of victimization was not occurring, but it was more of a 'hidden' form of family violence. Recently, however, we are seeing awareness campaigns regarding this form of violence. In the area of elder abuse, like in many other forms of victimization, few studies have looked beyond incidents of physical violence. This lack of information is largely due to the fact that other types of abuse, such as neglect,

financial abuse, and emotional/psychological abuse, is more difficult to measure. Added to this is Ogrodnik's (2007) estimation, based on the 2004 GSS, that approximately half of the victimizations of seniors are not reported to police.

According to Vaillancourt (2009), the victimization of seniors (those 65 and older) represented 2 per cent of all incidents of violent victimization reported to police. This figure is 15 times lower than the most vulnerable age group, those from 15 to 24. Of these crimes, just over one-third (35 per cent) were perpetrated by a family member; the same amount were committed by a friend or acquaintance. In other words, if the offender was known to the victim, there is an almost one in two chance that the former was a family member.

Of those seniors who reported abuse to police, victimizers were identified most commonly as adult children of the victim (men: 15/100,000; women: 16/100,000). According to Vaillancourt (2009), 83 per cent of these reports involved offending sons. Female seniors were more likely than males to report that the perpetrator of their victimization was a current or former spouse (17/100,000 compared to 9/100,000). The number of reports declined, per capita, as the age of the victim groups increased. Vaillancourt suggests that the reason for this decline may be that people over the age of 75 are more likely to live alone or in an institutional setting. Living away from family members may be protective against vulnerability to abuse. Health conditions, such as illnesses that impair the brain, may also be a reason for not reporting victimization. This study also cites the problem of increasingly diminishing social networks as individual age. Because the number of people that a senior may rely on is small, there may be a willingness to tolerate the abuse in exchange for continued support. For example, if a elderly person lives with an adult child who is abusive, he or she may decide to tolerate the abuse because his or her income could not support living outside the abusive environment.

Seniors were most likely (52 per cent) to report assault level I offences, followed by threats (19 per cent) and assault levels II or III (16 per cent). Female seniors were more at risk for common assault (28/100,000) than males (21/100,000), but male and female seniors were equally at risk for most other forms of victimization. Forty-five per cent of victims reported that their victimization resulted in injury. Almost all (91 per cent) of these injuries were considered minor, requiring basic first aid. In cases where the injury was serious, just over three-quarters (77 per cent) were the result of physical force. Of those who sustained severe injury, male seniors were more likely (12 per cent) than females (6 per cent) to be victimized with a weapon.

Looking specifically at the abuse of women age 60 and older, Fisher and Regan (2006) were interested in how the abuse experience affected the overall health of the victim. They surveyed 842 women who had visited an Ohio health clinic, the results of which are presented in Table 9.1. The researchers asked the women about different types of abusive situations. Nearly half (47 per cent) reported being the victim of at least one form of abuse since the age of 55, including physical, sexual, controlling behaviour, and/or psychological/emotional abuse. A third of the women (32 per cent) who had reported physical abuse stated that it was recurring. Just over one in five

(21 per cent) of sexual abuse reports also admitted that there were repeated incidents, as did almost half (47 per cent) of the women who reported psychological/emotional abuse. Almost all (97 per cent) of those women who reported physical abuse reported emotional abuse as well. Looking at the relationship of the victimizer to the victim in specific types of abuse, sexual abuse and controlling behaviour were most often carried out by a spouse or boyfriend (73 per cent and 56 per cent, respectively), while 73 per cent of those who had been threatened were victimized by a family member other than a partner. Forty-five per cent of cases of physical abuse were carried out by a relative, and slightly less (39 per cent) were perpetrated by an intimate partner. The older the respondent in the study, the more likely they were to report multiple forms of abuse.

Victimization in the Public Sphere

As we get older, we tend to become more engaged with the world and more involved with the public sphere. As we move from childhood to adolescence and to adulthood, we spend more time away from home and eventually establish our own residences. Being away from a strong and cohesive family network can leave us susceptible to other types of vulnerabilities. As we get older, we stay out later with our friends, and we may experiment with drugs and alcohol. All of these activities, although relatively common, increase our victimization risk potential. Most trends in victimization types tend to decrease as we leave our youth. However, victimization patterns change as we change. As we move into

Table 9.1   Abuse over 55 Years Old: Types of Abuse and Extent and Frequency of Abuse of Women 60 and Older

Type of Abuse, Specific Behaviour[a]	Extent of Abuse in % (number)		
	Abuse Victim[b]	Repeat Abuse	Abuse Occurring often[c]
Psychological/Emotional	44.6 (372)	47.3 (176)	57.3 (212)
Called you a name or criticized you	30.2 (245)		
Shouted or swore at you	25.3 (209)		
Been possessive or jealous of someone close to you	17.6 (139)		
Control	4.1 (34)	29.4 (10)	88.2 (30)
Routinely checked up on you in a way that made you afraid	2.5 (21)		
Put you on an allowance	1.7 (14)		
Not letting you go to work or social activities or see or talk with your friends	1.3 (12)		
Threat	11.7 (98)	23.5 (23)	48.0 (47)
Said things to scare you	6.0 (50)		
Threw, hit, kicked, or smashed something	8.5 (71)		
Physical	3.8 (38)	31.6 (12)	40.6 (13)
Pushed, grabbed, or shoved you	2.6 (22)		
Slapped, hit, or punched you	1.7 (14)		
Hit you with an object	1.0 (8)		
Choked or attempted to drown you	0.7 (6)		
Sexual	3.4 (28)	21.4 (6)	46.4 (13)
Pressured you to have sex in a way you did not like or want	2.9 (24)		
Physically forced you to have sex	1.1 (9)		
Attacked the sexual parts of your body	0.5 (4)		

a   The items listed under each type of abuse are the specific behaviours that comprise the respective type of abuse measure.

b   Respondents who refused to answer or reported 'don't know' to a form of abuse question were not included in forms of abuse calculations. Only those who refused to answer or reported 'don't know' to all the forms of abuse questions within a respective type of abuse were excluded from the type of abuse estimates.

c   Per cent represents those women who responded that at least one form of abuse within the specific type of abuse happened occasionally, frequently, or very frequently.

SOURCE: Fisher, B. S., & Regan, S. L. (2006). The extent and frequency of abuse in the lives of older women and their relationship with health outcomes. *The Gerontologist, 46(2)*, p. 204. Reprinted by permission of Oxford University Press.

areas of the public sphere, such as school, workplace, or care institutions, our risks for other types of victimization increase.

Bullying at School

According to Taylor-Butts and Bressan (2008), 13 per cent of the drug and Criminal Code violations in 2006 occurred on school grounds. Of those reported to police, approximately one-quarter (27 per cent) occurred outside regular school hours, with the majority (73 per cent) occurring while kids were in school. The authors caution that this disparity in these figures may be the result of recent 'zero tolerance' programs, which target violence in schools and may lead to a much higher reporting rate of victimization during school hours. Likewise, there may be under-reporting of criminal activity on school grounds when students and staff are not on the premises. However, much of the bullying that goes on in schools often goes unreported, and therefore does not make it into these official types of statistics.

Kids Help Phone (2010), an organization that helps kids cope with victimization, defines **bullying** as the deliberate use of verbal or physical acts that are hurtful, often over a long period of time. Although we most often think of acts of physical harm, which is also the focus of the majority of current research in this topic, there are many forms of bullying. Table 9.2 lists the examples included in the Kids Help Phone's definition. These forms clearly show that there is more to bullying than just physical harm.

Reviewing the characteristics of typical bullying victims, Lawrence and Adams (2006) identified three possible types. The first are those who are considered submissive and less aggressive than most. These are kids who are identified as 'sensitive' and are often quiet, anxious, and insecure. Another victim type includes those children who, while more aggressive, are considered agitating in some way. It is suggested that some of these children may suffer from Attention-Deficit Hyperactivity Disorder (ADHD). Although they are more likely to fight back, they cause tension and irritability in their classmates. Finally, children who are very popular, bright, or talented may also be targeted because it is thought that these individuals intimidate bullies in some way.

In Frisen, Jonsson, & Persson's (2007) anonymous survey of school-aged children, the authors found that more boys (44 per cent) reported being victims of bullying than girls (34 per cent). Boys and girls were almost equally likely to report being a **bully** (someone who engages in deliberate acts of harm, often over a long period of time), but roughly 1 in 10 girls (11 per cent) and more than 1 in 6 boys (15 per cent) reported being both a victim of bullying and a bully during the reference period of the study. These trends are illustrated in Table 9.3. These authors also examined at what age bullying was the largest problem; the results are featured in tables 9.4 and 9.5. Children between the ages of 7 and 9 were most likely to report being a target of bullying, followed by 10–12 year olds. Bullying behaviour, however, was most likely to be reported by students in the 10–12 range, followed by 13–15-year-olds. It would appear then, that older bullies tend to target younger kids for acts of aggression.

One suggested explanation of bullying is that it is the result of one person exhibiting power and control over

Table 9.2   Types of Bullying

Type	Description	Examples
Physical bullying	Physical bullying means hurting someone's body or their stuff. This includes:	Hitting, slapping, punching Kicking Shoving Spitting Stealing or destroying someone's belongings, like their clothes, MP3 player, bike, or even homework
Verbal bullying	Verbal bullying includes anything you say to hurt someone. This means:	Hurling insults Name calling Making fun of someone, especially in front of others (ridiculing) Threatening to hurt Put downs about clothing, hair, habits Sexist, racist, or homophobic statements
Social bullying	Social bullying involves using your friends or other relationships against someone. Some examples are:	Spreading rumours Excluding someone from the group Trash-talking behind someone's back Ganging up Breaking up friendships on purpose
Cyber bullying	Cyberbullying involves using any kind of technology, like a computer or cell phone, to hurt someone. Here are some examples:	Sending cruel e-mails and texts Posting embarrassing photos of someone, or doctoring photos and putting them on a website Creating websites to mock others Rating people's appearance online Using someone else's name online to damage their reputation in the real world
Racial bullying	Racial jokes and stereotypes are not funny; they are forms of racial bullying. Other examples are:	Making fun of a person's racial, ethnic, or cultural background Teasing a person about the way they dress Saying that the food someone eats is gross Mocking a person's accent or style of speech Leaving people out because of their race or culture
Sexual harassment	Sexual harassment includes saying or doing something to make a person feel uncomfortable about their body or sexuality. Here are some examples:	Touching someone in a sexual way when it's uninvited or unwanted Making sexual comments about someone's body Rating someone's appearance Making fun of someone for being Gay, Lesbian, Bisexual, Transgender, or Questioning Spreading rumours about someone's sexual reputation Forcing someone into an intimate act, like kissing or touching

Table 9.2	*continued*	
Dating violence	Not all relationships are healthy. It might seem strange, but even boyfriends and girlfriends can bully each other. This kind of bullying is called relationship violence. Here are some examples:	Ridiculing a boy/girlfriend for his/her 'weaknesses' Sharing private, personal information with others Hitting, pinching, slapping Forcing a boy/girlfriend to do things that he/she doesn't want to do Verbal insults
Homophobic bullying	Homophobic bullying includes verbal or physical harassment of someone whose sexual orientation is lesbian, gay, bisexual, transgender, transsexual, two-spirit, questioning, or queer (LGBTQ). Here are some examples:	Making jokes about LGBTQ people Pushing, shoving, kicking, or being violent in any other way against a LGBTQ person Making sexual comments about a LGBTQ person Touching a LGBTQ person intimately when the touching is uninvited

SOURCE: Kids Help Phone. (2010). It's Time to Stop Bullying. Teens Info Booth. Retrieved 18 May 2010, from www.kidshelpphone.ca/Teens/InfoBooth/Bullying/24-hours-of-bullying-text-version.aspx. Reprinted by permission of Kids Help Phone.

Table 9.3   Percentage of Adolescents That Reported Being Victims of Bullying, Bullies, or Both Bullies and Victims (Bully–Victim) during Their School Years

	Total (N=119)	Boys (N=71)	Girls (N=48)
Victim of bullying	39%	46%	34%
Bully	28%	29%	27%
Bully–victim	13%	15%	11%

SOURCE: Frisen, A., & Persson, C. (2007). Adolescent's perception of bullying: Who is the victim? Who is the bully? What can be done to stop the bullying? *Adolescence, 42(168)*, p. 752. Reprinted by permission of Libra Publishers, Inc.

Table 9.4   Time Period in School during Which Bullied Students Are Bullied

Age	Total (N=46)	Boys (N=22)	Girls (N=24)
7–9	23	11	12
10–12	18	10	8
13–15	12	3	9
16–18	3	1	2

SOURCE: Frisen, A., & Persson, C. (2007). Adolescent's perception of bullying: Who is the victim? Who is the bully? What can be done to stop the bullying? *Adolescence, 42(168)*, p. 753. Reprinted by permission of Libra Publishers, Inc.

Table 9.5	Time Period in School during Which Bullying Students Bullied Others		
Age	Total (N=33)	Boys (N=24)	Girls (N=19)
7–9	11	4	7
10–12	22	8	14
13–15	16	10	6
16–18	3	2	1

SOURCE: Frisen, A., & Persson, C. (2007). Adolescent's perception of bullying: Who is the victim? Who is the bully? What can be done to stop the bullying? *Adolescence, 42(168)*, p. 754. Reprinted by permission of Libra Publishers, Inc.

another. A popular conception about bullying is that it is carried out by older, stronger individuals from other classes. This idea is supported by the study conducted by Frisen et al. However, Chan's (2009) study, which used a survey that allowed respondents to identify themselves and the bullies who target them, found that a majority of bullying incidents were carried out by the victims' peers. Chan's study shows that although students may be exhibiting power and control over others, they are often targeting victims who are in close proximity.

Rodkin and Berger (2008) found that popularity played an influential role in the victim–bully relationship in American elementary schools. Where the bully and the victim were of the same gender, the bully was often popular and aggressive, while the victim was less popular. When the bully was identified as both unpopular and male, they were more likely to choose popular girls as their targets. This study found that regardless of popularity or gender, all bullies were disliked.

Savoie (2007) notes that those who have been victimized by bullying are more likely to have reported multiple incidences. As with other forms of victimization, increased vulnerability to bullying is the result of prior victimization of this type. Two-thirds of respondents in Savoie's study who had reported bullying victimization stated that they had been targeted more than once; 16 per cent stated that they had been targeted 12 times or more. With regard to severity of injury, 60 per cent stated that on one occasion they had been hit so hard that they required medical attention.

Although bullying may seem like typical schoolyard antics to some, victims of bullying can experience hardships later in life. Lawrence and Adams (2006) note that evidence shows that children bullied in their younger school years often have trouble adjusting as they move through the education system. They are more likely to have trouble with their studies and more likely to drop out of high school. Some bullied children may even become bullies themselves. Finally, the hardships experienced by bullying victims may also lead to acts of suicide.

Workplace Bullying

When we think of bullying, our thoughts tend to gravitate to the schoolyard. However, workplace bullying is a growing social concern, and an increasing number of researchers are focusing on this behaviour. Table 9.6 provides examples of what constitutes workplace bullying.

Research in this area pays particular attention to employees who are 'toxic' and how they affect workplace operations. Cavaiola and Lavender (2000) note that workers who are identified as having **Antisocial Personality Disorder (APD)** are some of the most dangerous. According to the *Diagnostic and Statistical Manual of Mental Disorders IV* (American Psychiatric Association, 2000), people with this condition act and lie compulsively and exhibit a lack of remorse and inability to plan. While they seem charming and give the impression that they are capable, their job performance is often weak. They may interview well, but their lack of work consistency begins to show over time. These workplace

Table 9.6   Examples of Behaviours Involved in Workplace Bullying

- spreading malicious rumours, gossip, or innuendo that is not true
- intimidating a person
- undermining or deliberately impeding a person's work
- physically abusing or threatening abuse
- removing areas of responsibilities without cause
- constantly changing work guidelines
- establishing impossible deadlines that will set up the individual to fail
- withholding necessary information or purposefully giving the wrong information
- making jokes that are 'obviously offensive' by spoken word or e-mail
- intruding on a person's privacy by pestering, spying, or stalking
- assigning unreasonable duties or workload which are unfavourable to one person (in a way that creates unnecessary pressure)
- underwork—creating a feeling of uselessness
- yelling or using profanity
- criticizing a person persistently or constantly
- belittling a person's opinions
- unwarranted (or undeserved) punishment
- blocking applications for training, leave, or promotion
- tampering with a person's personal belongings or work equipment
- any form of public humiliation
- personal insults and name-calling
- freezing out, ignoring, or excluding
- constantly undervaluing effort
- removing areas of responsibility
- deliberately sabotaging or impeding work performance
- refusing to delegate
- over-monitoring, especially with malicious intent
- using lengthy memos to make wild and inaccurate accusations
- instigating complaints from others to make individual appear incompetent

SOURCES: Canadian Centre for Occupational Health and Safety. (2010). *Bullying in the workplace*. Retrieved 29 January 2010, from www.ccohs.ca/oshanswers/psychosocial/bullying.html; Shaw, S. (1998, 20 March). From the playground to the workplace, bullying happens because it's allowed: Understanding bullying in the workplace. *The Ring: The University of Victoria Newspaper*. Retrieved 29 January 2010, from http://ring.uvic.ca/98mar20/Bullying.html.

bullies can easily move from one workplace to the next because of their impressive interview abilities.

APD is often confused with the term 'psychopathy', the definition of which is problematic. According to Rafter (1997), the meanings of 'psychopathy' (a concept borrowed from German psychiatry) and 'psychopath' have varied considerably over the last century; therefore, the literature on this topic is imprecise about the diagnostic phenomenon. Rafter argues that criminological texts gave this concept life, taking advantage of the fact that people generally assume consensus about the definition, despite the fact that it continues to be debated.

Hare (1996), who is considered the leading authority on psychopathy and psychopathy research, views the **psychopath** as an 'interspecies predator' who works to satisfy selfish desires by using skills such as charm, manipulation, violence, and intimidation. These predators are not constrained by social norms and violate social expectations without feelings of guilt or remorse. He asserts that they represent between 15 and 25 per cent of all prisoners and are a significant proportion of repeat and serial offenders as well as those who involve themselves in legal but morally questionable behaviour. Further, psychopaths are well established in the corporate and business environment, especially during restructuring or times of change within the organization (Babiak & Hare, 2006).

By analyzing the results of a small case study sample, Babiak (1995) investigated the idea that there are certain legitimate venues where people with psychopathic tendencies are more likely to fit in. In particular, he notes that organizations going through hectic change, such as restructuring, high employee turnover, and so on, may be more conducive and more attractive to those who express these personality traits. The instability of the workplace environment allows less monitoring of employee behaviour, thereby allowing someone with psychopathic tendencies to operate with less supervision. Facts are less likely to be checked, and bad behaviour in an unstable environment may be ignored rather than reported. Babiak administered Robert Hare's Psychopathy Checklist-Revised (PCL-R) (Hare, 1991) to workers at various organizations. The PCL-R is conducted using a semi-structured interview technique rating individuals on a 20-item clinical rating scale. The scale ranges from 0–40, with the average rating of about 22–24 for the non-psychopathic population. A score of 30 or over indicates presence of psychopathic traits. The scale consists of two factors. Factor 1 measures items such as egocentricity, manipulativeness, callousness, and lack of remorse, while Factor 2 measures more behaviour manifestations of the personality trait, such as degrees of impulsivity, anti-social or unstable lifestyles, and social deviance (Hare, 1996). Babiak (1995) found that some workers exhibited psychopathic traits, in that they showed all the signs of a traditional psychopath (charming, glib, acting without conscience or remorse, etc.) but without acting illegally.

To illustrate how victims can be affected by these types of individuals, Babiak (1995) documents the case of 'Dave', who despite interviewing very well, exhibited performance problems after he was hired. Many of his co-workers initially liked him, but they eventually found that he was creating problems within the office; many had to pick up work that he had not completed. Although his direct supervisor, Frank, noted that Dave often lied and promised work that he could not do, he continued to try to work with him. Eventually, however, he reported Dave to his superiors. Dave, as it turns out, had not only already been in contact with Frank's superiors but had also made a favourable impression and had warned them that Frank would make false allegations against him. Dave was eventually promoted over Frank, as he was felt to have management potential. Babiak argues that Dave looked to forge alliances with the organization's powerful and important people in order to achieve his goals. Once these relationships were made, he would abandon those that were no longer useful. In this way he was able to advance his career. Although he did not directly bully Frank, he did undermine his ability and the ability of others to do their work in order to be promoted. This behaviour created untold hardship for almost all who came in contact with him.

In another study on workplace bullying, Coyne, Craig, and Chong (2004) asked 288 firefighter personnel about their experiences in this area. In particular they were interested in how the presence of bullying, or the experiences of victimization, affected group cohesion. The researchers asked the firefighters to disclose if they had been a victim of bullying or had bullied other workers. They also asked the respondents to identify the bullies and the victims of bullying in their group. Overall, this study found that the firefighters preferred to work with victims of workplace bullying rather than the bullies. It was also found that victims of bullying were more likely to be identified as stars in the group. However, one-quarter of victims were isolated from their peers and therefore rejected by many of the team. Bullies, and those who were both bullies and victims, were more likely to be socially isolated from the group. Even though it is important for firefighters to work as a cohesive unit, much more so than many other jobs, there still exists this type of workplace victimization within this profession. Lack of cohesion in a workplace can make working conditions difficult. For firefighters, reduced solidarity may affect their ability to do their jobs, which often involve the team working effectively to save lives.

Institutional Elder Abuse

As we get older, we may become less able to take care of ourselves. Older adults who find themselves in this predicament then have to make choices about how they can both maintain independence and meet the increased challenges of self-care. As stated earlier, many senior citizens move in with family members, often an adult child, to receive the care that they need. Others find an assisted living or a complete care facility more preferable, especially if family members are unable to provide suitable accommodation. In most cases, although the elderly person may not like having to move, his or her quality of care is improved, especially when 24-hour assistance is required. However, in some cases, the vulnerability of these individuals makes them targets for abuse by other residents of the facility or by the staff who are charged to care for them.

Box 9.1   Abuse by Nursing Home Staff

Norma Stenson was a frail 87-year-old woman who had suffered a series of strokes. She was moved to Charlotte Villa Retirement Home in Brantford, ON. Her supplemental caregiver, Jean Bowen, had recommended the home, which was reputed to be one of the best in the city. Although Stenson had trouble communicating because of her strokes, her low opinion of her new home was evident. Assuming it was just because she was unhappy with the new environment, Bowen asked her to give the facility a chance.

Bowen recalled that it quickly became clear that Stenson was being abused. 'She indicated by using my arms [that] she was shaken and tossed. . . . By March it was getting worse—she wasn't being shaken anymore, she was being maybe hit somehow—just little bruises to start with. She indicated at one point that she was hit in the stomach, and I honestly believe she was because she could hardly move for a couple of weeks.'

After the bruises kept appearing, Lesley Anthony, Stenson's other supplementary caregiver, approached the home's administration about her concerns. She was offered suspicious explanations. The director stated that Stenson was lying and that she had fallen from a wheelchair and had hit herself on her own bedrail. Anthony was berated, accused of being 'too good to this woman' and was told that 'this lady gets treated the way the rest of them thought she should get treated.' Later, employees of the home made their own complaints. Amanda LaPierre reported that Stenson had kicked her in the stomach and had said, 'I want to kill your unborn baby child.' Bowen and Anthony realized that these statements had to be false, given that Stenson had not been able to speak in full sentences for years. Bowen said, '[I]f she could talk, she would talk to me everyday.' She also remarked that Stenson's physical frailty rendered her physically incapable of kicking someone in the stomach.

Stenson's supplemental caregivers took photos of the bruises and showed them to police, who told them that because Stenson was unable to speak for herself, there was really nothing they could do. The two women then placed a hidden camera in Stenson's room to catch the abusers in the act. When they checked the tape eight days later, they saw Stenson being threatened with a slipper and fists, screamed at, and thrown into bed by staff members. The footage also showed staff taking money from her wallet and eating her food. Both caregivers were shocked and sickened by what they saw and took the evidence to police, who decided that they had enough to open a case and assigned it to Det. Dave Wiedrick.

Charges were eventually laid against two employees, including LaPierre, who claimed self-defence but pleaded guilty to two counts of theft and four of assault. She was sentenced to 240 hours of community service. The second employee, Shelley Grisdale, was charged with two counts of theft and one of assault. She was acquitted on the assault charge, and the two charges of theft were stayed. Both LaPierre and Grisdale were fired from their jobs.

After the abuse was exposed, Stenson was moved to another facility, Versa Care, which was owned by the same company but, unlike Charlotte Villa, had government regulation. Sadly, Stenson started to make the same complaints shortly after arriving at the new home. Acting quickly, Bowen and Anthony installed the hidden camera in her room. Upon reviewing the tape, they saw one episode where, in the middle of the night, Stenson was shaken and tossed into her wheelchair, slamming her arm against the chair. The resulting bruise took weeks to heal. They also saw a theft and an incident where a staff member had placed a pillow over Stenson's face and left the room. Again, the caregivers approached police. This time, the police did not feel that this behaviour was sufficient grounds for an investigation because the Criminal Code did not define these behaviours as crimes. This conclusion differed strongly from the training that both Bowen and Anthony had received: 'As a caregiver, you're taught from day one, abuse is anything from verbal—you cannot threaten verbally; you cannot intimidate; you cannot shake; you cannot toss; you can't even tip them up from a prone position to a standing position without stopping. All those are supposed to be abuse and criminal.'

When the television news show *W5* became involved and asked Versa Care's director for an interview, she declined. Eventually, the vice president of Central Park Lodges, who owned both facilities, viewed the footage and promptly 'sent home' the staff who had committed the acts on the video.

SOURCES: W5: Help me: Elder abuse in Canada. (2004, 6 February). *CTV News*. Retrieved 3 February 2010, from http://www.ctv.ca/servlet/ArticleNews/story/CTVNews/1076082613040_71491813/?hub=Wfive; Caregiver in W-FIVE video acquitted of assault. (2004, 9 March). *CTV News*. Retrieved 30 April 2010, from www.ctv.ca/servlet/ArticleNews/story/CTVNews/20040309/elderly_abuse_video_040309?s_name=&no_ads=.

Box 9.1 illustrates some of the forms of abuse that seniors can experience at the hands of nursing home staff. This story highlights the victim's communication problems, which made reporting significantly more difficult. Although her supplemental caregivers initially attributed her complaints to her being unhappy about living in a home, they soon began to suspect abuse. When individuals become heavily reliant on others for their well-being, this dependence also makes them increasingly vulnerable to the abuse of the trust they have given to their caregiver. The more fragile the victim, the higher the risk of victimization and the greater the potential impact of that victimization on the victim. Although the use of cameras in the case above eventually identified the culprits who were victimizing Stenson, she had to endure the abuse for a considerable amount of time before her communications could be understood and acted upon. Preventative measures such as employee screening, as opposed to reactive measures such as the measures used here to catch the abusers, may be more beneficial to the long-term health of people who depend heavily on others for their day-to-day needs.

Summary

This chapter has examined the dynamics of public and private spheres and their role in victimization risk over an individual's lifetime. As we age, our victimization risk generally increases throughout childhood and into adolescence but then decreases as we reach adulthood. However, there are certain victimization risks that increase in adulthood, such as those regarding intimate partner violence. Moving outside the relative safety of our homes and our families and into public domains also changes the type of victimization risk we encounter. Younger people travel in different circles and have different responsibilities and relationships than older people. Therefore, even though our victimization risk for most crimes begins to decline as we enter our twenties, this risk can increase depending on where we spend our public lives.

Glossary

Antisocial Personality Disorder (APD) A diagnosis in the *Diagnostic and Statistical Manual* IV (DSM), which is often confused with the term 'psychopathy'. People with APD exhibit many symptoms in common with psychopathy, including compulsive acting and lying, lack of remorse, and an inability to plan.

assault level I Also known as common assault. This offence involves intentionally threatening or applying force onto a person without his or her consent.

assault level II Also known as assault with a weapon or causing bodily harm. Offences of this type are more serious than common assault and describe cases where the assailant carries, uses, or threatens to use a weapon or imitation or causes physical harm to the victim.

assault level III Also known as aggravated assault. This level is the most serious type of assault and includes wounding, maiming, disfiguring, or endangering the life of the victim.

bully One who engages in deliberate acts of harm, often over a long period of time.

bullying The deliberate use of verbal or physical acts that are hurtful, often over a long period of time.

child abuse A deliberate act or set of actions that is considered maltreatment of a child. This mistreatment includes acts of physical abuse, sexual abuse, neglect, and emotional abuse, as well as witnessing family violence.

psychopath Described by Hare (1996) as an 'interspecies predator' who works to satisfy selfish desires by using skills such as charm, manipulation, violence, and intimidation. These predators are not constrained by social norms and violate social expectations without feelings of guilt or remorse. This term is often confused with APD. According to the DSM IV, psychopathy is not an appropriate diagnosis and does not reflect an illness.

Critical Thinking Questions

1. What types of victimization occur more often during childhood but less often during adolescence? Other than the ones covered in this chapter, what are some patterns of victimization that are more likely to occur at certain times in our lives than others? What patterns are more likely to occur in specific places?

2. Do you think we experience a greater risk of victimization when we go to a bar? What are some of the protective behaviours that we can engage in to reduce that risk?

3. Do you think that people with impairments (physical, mental, developmental) or disabilities are more or less at risk for victimization than those who do not have these characteristics? Why or why not?

4. What types of physical environments create the most vulnerability to

victimization? What characteristics make these environments more dangerous?

5. What types of physical environments are most protective? What are some common characteristics of these safer environments?

6. Men are more likely to be victimized in public spaces, while women are more likely to be victimized in private spaces. Why do you think this pattern exists? Do you think that this pattern is changing? How and why?

7. Consider the following four situations in which an individual comes up behind you and touches your buttocks in an inappropriate way.

    a. In your home, by a friend whom you've invited for dinner.
    b. In the workplace, by your boss.
    c. In a nursing home while visiting a family member, by one of the residents.
    d. In a hospital, by a stranger wearing a stethoscope.

8. Would you report the behaviour identified in Question 7? If so, to whom would you report it? Would your answers be different depending on the person's gender?

CHAPTER 10

Special Topic: Fraud

Learning Objectives

After reading this chapter, you will be able to

- understand the differences in victimization experience between people who experience violent crime and those who experience fraud victimization;
- examine different types of fraud;
- analyze trends in fraud victimization; and
- recognize technology's role in increasing vulnerability for this specific type of crime.

Introduction

To this point in our discussion, we have focused on violent forms of victimization. We tend to fear these forms more and to consider them more serious than the non-violent types. It is often assumed that non-violent victimization creates less damage because the victim is not physically hurt. Consequently, these forms are often overlooked, even though they are more common. One such non-violent victimization is fraud, which has traditionally been considered a white-collar crime. This chapter examines various types of and trends in fraud victimization, including the influence of technology. The chapter will conclude with some common techniques used by fraudsters and some tips on how individuals can exercise caution when confronted with these offenders.

White-Collar Crime

Victimology tends to focus on violent crime. Although there are fewer studies on other forms of victimization, many victimology courses demonstrate a growing interest in the area of white-collar crime. The term **white-collar crime** was first coined by famous criminologist Edwin Sutherland (1949) in his book of the same name. Sutherland defined the crime as one 'committed by a person of respectability and high social status in the course of his occupation'; it currently includes non-violent crimes committed for financial gain, including tax evasion, embezzlement, counterfeiting, insider trading, and various types of fraud. The term refers to those criminals who act alone or as part of organizations seeking to commit crimes such as fraud and theft.

Curious about how criminal acts were learned, Sutherland researched how the techniques, rationalizations, and 'tricks of the trade' were passed from one person to another. He included his findings in *Criminology* (1924) and later published *The Professional Thief* (1937), a qualitative study of a local confidence man, or 'con artist', who explained to Sutherland how he learned his trade. *White Collar Crime* was published the year before Sutherland died. In it, he criticized the American government for not collecting information on white-collar crimes and argued that our knowledge about crime and criminality (and victims) was incomplete because it was derived from theories of violence.

Most of the literature on white-collar crime focuses on overviews of crimes committed by organizations and corporations rather than the more common forms of fraud. **Fraud**, unlike the types of victimization that we have examined in this book, is generally non-violent but uses deception to achieve financial or material gain. Figure 10.1 shows that fraud victimization represents only 8 per cent of all property crime. The lack of violence in this crime by no means suggests that the effects of fraud victimization cannot have severe repercussions for the victim.

Moore and Mills (1990) provide evidence that white-collar crime victimization is overshadowed by other types of victimization, both in American public policy and research literature. Rebovich, Layne, Jiandani, and Hage (2000) found that most Americans believe white-collar crime to be less serious than most street crimes and its victims less likely to be college-aged and -educated. In the United States the National Crime Victimization Survey (NCVS) and the National Incident-Based Reporting System (NIBRS) do not specifically

Figure 10.1 Minor Thefts Account for Over Half of Property Crimes[1], 2005

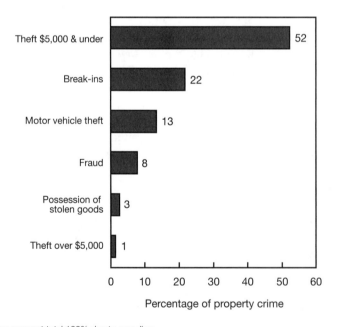

Percentage of property crime

1 Percentages may not total 100% due to rounding.

SOURCES: Gannon, M. (2006). Crime statistics in Canada, 2005. *Juristat, 26(4)*, p. 8. Statistics Canada: Canadian Centre for Justice Statistics, Uniform Crime Reporting Survey.

include information about fraud victimization. Shichor (2002) notes that this situation harms the field of victimology because white-collar crime can be as devastating—if not more so—as violent crime in terms of economic and emotional impact.

Prevalence of Fraud Victimization

According to Titus, Heinzelmann, and Boyle (1995), nearly one-third of Americans are victims of fraud attempts every year; one-half of these attempts are successful. In addition, undergraduate and graduate students, because of their youth, their educational attainment, and their income levels are more vulnerable

to being victims of fraud. In Canada, the number of fraud victimizations reported to police has decreased from 130,559 in 1986 to 102,052 offences in 1996 and 92,599 reports in 2006 (Statistics Canada, 2008). Canadians were victimized by fraud at a rate of 267.4/100,000 people in 2007. As with violent victimization rates, the highest rates of fraud victimization are in western Canada while the lowest are in the east (Statistics Canada, 2009). Table 10.1 demonstrates these reported victimization rates across the country.

With respect to victimization, Ogrodnik (2007) reports that seniors appear to be particularly vulnerable to telemarketing fraud. This study also recognizes that there are no national statistics on this type of fraud. This study states that the Canadian Anti-Fraud Centre (CAFC), formerly PhoneBusters, reports that 84 per cent of the total dollar loss through various telemarketing schemes was lost to those who were over 60 years of age. Reasons for this vulnerability vary but include the perception that seniors have substantial savings and therefore are more likely to be targeted by this type of victimizer, that seniors are more polite and trusting of strangers, and that seniors are more likely to have limited contact with family and therefore are less protected by others. Aboriginal people tend to be more vulnerable to fraud victimization if they reside off-reserve. The reported crime victimization rate for Aboriginal people who reside on-reserve is substantially below the national average at 215/100,000 population, while those who live outside the reserve system have a much higher rate (329/100,000 [Statistics Canada, 2006b]).

Table 10.1 Reported Fraud Victimizations in Canada, 2007

	Rate /100,000
Canada	267.7
Newfoundland and Labrador	225.4
Prince Edward Island	181.1
Nova Scotia	267.4
New Brunswick	234.7
Quebec	204.3
Ontario	266.0
Manitoba	185.2
Saskatchewan	320.1
Alberta	359.1
British Columbia	335.5
Yukon	325.9
Northwest Territories	265.0
Nunavut	218.6

SOURCE: Statistics Canada. (2009). Summary tables: Crimes by offences, by province and territory. Retrieved 22 April 2009, from www40.statcan.gc.ca/l01/cst01/legal04d-eng.htm.

Difficulties in Measuring Fraud Victimization

One of the central issues about discussing fraud is that there are competing definitions of what should be included in this crime (Statistics Canada, 2006a). In Canada, there is no systematic way of documenting the various and complex crimes that fall under the guise of fraud. The legal definition is offered in Box 10.1. It is clear from examining this section of the Criminal Code that a wide array of crimes can fall under this umbrella definition. Additionally, even if a violation can be classified as fraud under the legal definition, there can be further issues that complicate determining how often the crime occurs and what its victim pool may look like.

Box 10.1 The Criminal Code of Canada's Definition of 'Fraud'

380. (1) Every one who, by deceit, falsehood or other fraudulent means, whether or not it is a false pretence within the meaning of this Act, defrauds the public or any person, whether ascertained or not, of any property, money or valuable security or any service,

(a) is guilty of an indictable offence and liable to a term of imprisonment not exceeding fourteen years, where the subject-matter of the offence is a testamentary instrument or the value of the subject-matter of the offence exceeds five thousand dollars; or

(b) is guilty

(i) of an indictable offence and is liable to imprisonment for a term not exceeding two years, or

(ii) of an offence punishable on summary conviction, where the value of the subject-matter of the offence does not exceed five thousand dollars.

Affecting public market

(2) Every one who, by deceit, falsehood or other fraudulent means, whether or not it is a false pretence within the meaning of this Act, with intent to defraud, affects the public market price of stocks, shares, merchandise or anything that is offered for sale to the public is guilty of an indictable offence and liable to imprisonment for a term not exceeding fourteen years. R.S., 1985, c. C-46, s. 380; R.S., 1985, c. 27 (1st Supp.), s. 54; 1994, c. 44, s. 25; 1997, c. 18, s. 26; 2004, c. 3, s. 2.

Sentencing — aggravating circumstances

380.1 (1) Without limiting the generality of section 718.2, where a court imposes a sentence for an offence referred to in sections 380, 382, 382.1 and 400, it shall consider the following as aggravating circumstances:

(a) the value of the fraud committed exceeded one million dollars;

(b) the offence adversely affected, or had the potential to adversely affect, the stability of the Canadian economy or financial system or any financial market in Canada or investor confidence in such a financial market;

(c) the offence involved a large number of victims; and

(d) in committing the offence, the offender took advantage of the high regard in which the offender was held in the community.

Non-mitigating factors

(2) The court shall not consider as mitigating circumstances the offender's employment, employment skills or status or reputation in the community if those circumstances were relevant to, contributed to, or were used in the commission of the offence. 2004, c. 3, s. 3.

SOURCE: Department of Justice, Canada. Criminal Code of Canada

Canadians rely on police-reported data to examine the prevalence of fraud, which requires that the police be notified that such a crime has been committed. One of the confounding issues when trying to capture the amount of fraud activity is that victims of fraud are often not aware that they have been victimized until significant time after the crime has occurred. In some cases, victims are unaware of the victimization at all. As with other crimes, even when the victim is aware of the victimization, he or she may not go to the police. Further, as seen in Figure 10.2, data show that incidents of fraud appear to be decreasing, which Statistics Canada (2006a) suggests is due to the changing nature of fraud. The falling numbers may be a reflection of a drop in the more traditional types of fraud, such as cheque fraud, but may not capture the newer forms of fraud that involve computers and other electronic systems, such as credit card fraud and Internet scams.

Figure 10.3 provides information on specific types of fraud. The data here show that cheque fraud experienced a 77 per cent drop between 1977 and 2004, while credit card fraud increased. One explanation for this shift is that we now use credit cards more often than cheques when buying everyday items. The change may be lowering the overall fraud rate, which dropped 38 per cent

over the same time period. Although credit and debit cards have increased security measures in place to protect against fraud, new technologies that can steal card numbers and record personal identification numbers (PINs) are of constant concern to cardholders and the financial institutions that encourage the use of these cards. Therefore, although the new security features have reduced fraud overall, new advances in technologies used by offenders must be considered in these numbers.

Statistics Canada (2006a) understands that current data on fraud comes from a variety of sources and is provided in piecemeal format at best. For example, if a business owner uses profits from his or her own publicly traded company to make a series of investments that turn out to lose value, it is difficult to determine if he or she just has bad business sense or if he or she deliberately sought to defraud investors. Furthermore, such a crime would be more likely to be reported to a business regulatory body than to a criminal authority. If the former found a criminal issue, it may turn the case over to the latter.

Letter, Phone, and Internet Scams

Conning victims out of their valuables has a long history. One of the earliest and

Figure 10.2 Police-Reported Data on Fraud Suggest Fraud Decreased Substantially, 1991–2001

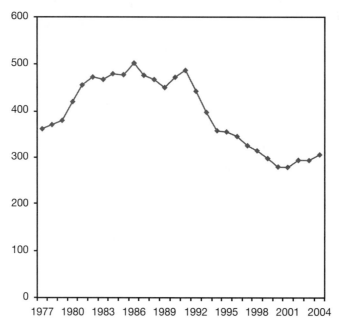

Rate per 100,000 population

SOURCE: Statistics Canada (2006). A feasibility report on improving the measurement of fraud in Canada, 2005. Ottawa, ON: Centre for Justice Statistics, Minister of Industry, p. 8.

most recalled examples is the Spanish Prisoner scam. As near as many can tell, the earliest documentation of this scam dates back at least to the middle of the nineteenth century (Aycock & Aycock, 2008), although many unreferenced sources use a start date of 1588. The basic premise of the scam is that a potential victim is told by a con artist that he or she is in contact with a very wealthy Spanish prisoner, whose identity must remain a secret for fear of putting him in danger. The potential victim is assured that the prisoner can buy his freedom if he can get to his personal wealth. The potential victim is permitted to help by paying a guard to access the prisoner's

money and is promised to be compensated financially for this assistance (some sources make reference to the promise of marriage to the prisoner's beautiful daughter as well). The potential victim supplies the money and becomes vested in the process. The victimizer then asks for more money as there is now a new obstacle (guards must be bribed, transportation must be secured, fees have to be paid, etc.). The victim is slowly bilked out of funds until he or she realizes that he or she is being victimized.

The Spanish Prisoner is just one method of defrauding someone. There are many ways that people can solicit valuables, money, and/or information

Figure 10.3 Police-Reported Data Suggest Rate of Cheque Fraud Falling while Credit and Debit Card and Other Fraud Have Increased Slowly in Recent Years

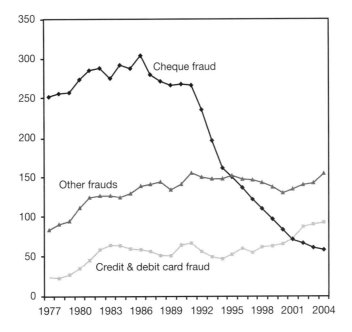

Rate per 100,000 population

SOURCE: Statistics Canada (2006). A feasibility report on improving the measurement of fraud in Canada, 2005. Ottawa, ON: Centre for Justice Statistics, Minister of Industry, p. 9.

from an individual. Day-to-day activities require that we divulge some personal information to various people in order to buy products, get services, and interact with others. We hand it out to banks and online stores and include it in job and credit card applications. Many of us give our phone numbers or e-mail addresses to big box retailers when asked in the checkout line. In discussions with others we reveal facts about ourselves so that they may get to know us. In many cases, the passing of information to an individual who is offering a service is legitimate and is even needed in order to accomplish certain tasks: banking,

purchasing a home, a car, or groceries, and so on. Companies also like to collect information for marketing purposes. However, the collection of information and requests for money may sometimes be for illegitimate purposes. The problem for the potential victim is to work through each request on a daily, sometimes hourly, basis, to assess it on its merit, and to reach a decision on its legitimacy. Below is a series of descriptions of various Internet and phone scams which are specifically designed to gain the trust of a potential victim so that he or she will part with cash, valuables, and/or personal information.

Identity Theft

Identity theft refers to all types of crime in which someone illegally acquires and uses another person's personal and identifying information, usually for financial gain. Although most forms of this fraud are perpetrated for individual gain, it can also be carried out on behalf of members of organized criminal groups or networks and terrorists and/or terrorist organizations. There are indications that identity theft is on the rise (Public Safety Canada, 2004) due, in large part, to the increasing sophistication of technology in developing communication tools such as those provided by the Internet and enhanced phone services. For example, many companies encourage their customers to do business online, often to reduce costs such as mailing information or maintaining a physical retail space. Banks are one such company: the customer is told about the convenience of on-demand banking wherever and whenever he or she needs it, and the bank reduces costs by not producing or mailing paper bills. It also do not have to maintain as many bank locations, given that the use of such sites is anticipated to decline with the online service. Although extensive measures may be used to secure the bank's website, if the customer is using a wireless connection that is not sufficiently encrypted or protected in some other way, his or her information can be stolen in transit from the computing device (such as the computer or a cell phone) to the website.

From 2002 to 2003, it is estimated that the total identity theft-related losses to individuals and businesses in the United States were approximately USD$53 billion. In Canada the losses for 2002 were estimated at approximately

Table 10.2   Number of Victims and the Total Loss to Victims Reported to Canadian Anti-Fraud Centre, 2007, 2008

	1 January–31 December 2007	1 January–31 December 2008
Mass Marketing Fraud		
Based on complaint date		
Canadian Victims	4,471	5,898
Canadian Victims — Dollar Loss (CDN)	$19,304,955.75	$23,515,110.92
Identity Theft		
Based on complaint date		
Canadian Victims	10,327	11,335
Canadian Victims — Dollar Loss (CDN)	$6,447,099.75	$9,581,105.05
West African Letter Fraud		
Based on complaint date		
Canadian Victims	166	123
Canadian Victims — Dollar Loss (CDN)	$5,337,593.14	$3,284,509.23

SOURCE: Canadian Anti-Fraud Centre. (n.d.). *Statistics on fraud.* Retrieved 25 March 2009, from www.phonebusters.com/english/statistics.html.

CAD$2.5 billion. In 2007, the CAFC received 10,327 complaints of identity theft from Canadians reporting total losses of $6,457,099.75 (see Table 10.2). In 2008, this same agency reported an increase in identity theft complaints of 9.25 per cent to 11,380 and even greater losses of $9,599,885.05.

Although there is an increased awareness of identify fraud, very few studies

---

Box 10.2 The Case of Norman Gettel: Victim of Identity and Mortgage Fraud

Norman Gettel had worked as a printer for Pacific Press for many years when he decided to retire in the late 1990s, a few years after he had paid off the mortgage on his Richmond, BC, bungalow. In 2008, this retiree in his seventies did not receive his annual assessment in the mail, so he decided to call the British Columbia Assessment Authority, who told him that he did not own the property anymore. Perplexed, he made his way to the Land Titles Office and was told the same information. Gettel recalls the confusion of the situation when he told the employee, 'I hate to differ with you, but I didn't sell it.' The papers that Gettel was shown offered a different story. Not only was Gettel's home sold for over $600,000 in July 2007 without his knowledge, but the 'buyer' had also put a $400,000 mortgage on it, which had gone into default. The victimizers in this case had redirected the mail for this transaction to an address in Burnaby, BC.

Upon further investigation, it was discovered that someone claiming to be Gettel went to a Surrey law office to sign property transfer papers after selling the house, signing away Gettel's $607,600 home for '$1.00 and natural love and affection' to the alleged new owner of the home, Oleg Balan. Balan then immediately took out a $400,000 mortgage on the property but did not show up to claim the property, as is the pattern with this type of scam. The 'buyer' and the 'seller' are also thought to be working together on defrauding the banks and the owner of the property.

Gettel eventually received a copy of a lawyer's letter to the supposed new owner, dated 1 February 2008. The mortgage was in default and a lawyer for CIBC Mortgages Inc. demanded payment in full of $403,034.95 plus interest at $53.18 per day plus legal expenses of $375. The letter further stated that CIBC Mortgages Inc. was giving notice that it 'intends to enforce its security' on Balan's property.

During this ordeal, Gettel could not pay his property taxes because, at the time, he technically did not own his home. He was also dealing with chronic obstructive pulmonary disease and has been re-victimized by having to pay a lawyer $10,000 to get his own home back. At the time the article covering this story was written, the case had not made it to court, although Gettel's lawyer had filed a notice of pending litigation. However, the BC Supreme Court made a ruling recently that the true owner of a property can regain the title if it was fraudulently transferred.

SOURCE: Shaw, G. (2008, 20 June). Con artist sell homes without owners knowing. *The Vancouver Sun*. Retrieved 18 January 2009, from www.canada.com/vancouversun/news/story.html?id=929a42de6d51-46d2-87a7-debc8924db79&p=3; *Vancouver Sun*. (2008, 20 June). Con artists sell homes without owners knowing: When the annual assessment for Norman Gettel's home didn't arrive in the mail this year, he phoned the BC Assessment Authority. Retrieved 7 June 2010, from http://www.canada.com/story_print.html?id=929a42de-6d51-46d2-87a7-debc8924db79&sponsor=.

have looked at the actual victims of this crime. Most of what we have come to understand about the consequences for these victims comes from other media such as documentaries and newspapers. One such case that caught national attention was the identify theft and mortgage fraud of Normal Gettel (see Box 10.2). Fraudsters had obtained enough private information about Gettel to actually sell his house without him knowing about it. The few clues that he was the victim of fraud were that he had not received his yearly assessment and the copy of the letter he obtained from CIBC Mortgages Inc. demanding the supposed new owner to pay the outstanding mortgage that was in default. Although it is rare for victims of identity fraud to also be victims of mortgage fraud, they usually become victims of a secondary crime. However, one does not actually have to have his or her identity actually stolen to experience the effects, as illustrated in the case of James below.

The Case of James

Furnell (2007) examines the problems of identity impairment even in mild cases of identity theft. He recites the true story of James, a resident of the United Kingdom. When a statement for a declined credit card arrived at his address, James found out that someone had been applying for credit in his name. This was unexpected as James was very cautious about his information, shredding documents, soaking bank statements until the documents were degraded and unreadable, and so on. All applications by the impersonators were declined for a variety of reasons; however, James's credit rating had dropped because it had been

queried a number of times. If he needed credit, he could be declined because of this lower score.

When James reported the first fraudulent attempt to Bank A, they asked him for his personal information (name, date of birth, etc.), but when James asked the customer service representative to verify the bank's authenticity, he could not. The bank could not offer solutions on confirming its identity or advise James on measures that he could take to do so. James now wondered if the letter he received was part of another scam to get information from him.

After repeated calls to Bank A, James eventually found out that he could register his address and credit information with a fraud prevention service to scrutinize applications for fraudulent attempts. He later learned that this service does not stop the applications from being made. Continued applications served to lower his credit score even further. After a month of phone calls and countless hours of communicating with banks and credit bureaus, he eventually had the fraudulent attempts to obtain credit removed from his records. Because the attempts had not been successful, no crime of identity theft actually occurred, leaving Furnell (2007) to conclude that although James's identity was never stolen, the value of his identity was compromised.

Furnell goes on to say that even though the bank was aware that there were fraudulent attempts on James's account, it was James who had to take the time to get them removed from his record. The bank did not do this automatically. It also warned that it could take up to a month to finally have them removed, even after the request was made. Therefore, if a fraudulent credit request was made once a month, a credit score could be permanently impaired. The bank would not share the details of the fraud attempts with James, citing that it had, ironically, to protect the privacy of the fraudsters. Although he eventually secured this information from the bank, to see what information the impersonators actually had, James later found out that the bank made a series of mistakes on the report, further adding to confusion and risking his credit score. During this whole period, James did not report the crime to police, as victims are encouraged to report such incidents to the bank.

Characteristics of Identity Theft Victims

Stuart, Schuck, and Lersch (2004) note that in a municipal sample of Florida cases, victims of identity theft tended to be white males who were victimized by people they did not know. Victims had a wide age range, suggesting that all ages were susceptible to this crime. Offenders tended to be African-American females who worked alone. These authors compared their results on race to a national data set and found that, when looking at financial crimes, these trends were highly unusual. They also noted that while the crime of identity theft is on the increase, clearance rates for these crimes are decreasing.

Public Safety Canada (2004) reports that victims come from a diverse range of backgrounds, but many have in common good or potentially good credit ratings. Victims are approached by identity thieves in varying ways depending on their access to technology. Electronically, individuals may be approached by e-mails and/or websites designed to solicit their personal information. People may be asked for bank account numbers, PINs, social insurance or social security numbers, birthdates, pets' and children's names (these are often used for account passwords) and so on. Such information, however, can also be obtained by more 'old-fashioned' methods, such as searching through someone's wallet or garbage.

However the information is obtained, the outcome is often the same. Public Safety Canada (2004) reports that victims of identity theft frequently suffer financial loss and damage to their credit rating and reputation, as well as emotional distress. Some victims report having credit cards and (less often) mortgages taken out in their name; others state that their impersonator accumulated a criminal record! As with the case of James above, many are also left with the complicated and sometimes arduous task of clearing their records. An American survey on identity theft conducted by the Federal Trade Commission (2004) found that victims had spent a total of 300 million hours in the preceding year to resolve problems created by this crime. Identity theft has become a source of particular concern for law enforcement agencies as it is a possible **gateway offence**, an offence that creates opportunities for other, often more serious, crimes to be committed. Some of these are listed below.

Phishing

A **phishing scam** is designed specifically to solicit personal information by creating a website or e-mail that looks exactly like one a victim might use. The idea is that the person who is solicited is conned into giving out personal bank information, which can later be used to commit fraud using the victim's identification and access information. The e-mails and web pages that are replicated to look like legitimate pages are used as 'lures' to 'bait' potential victims. This process has also been called 'brand spoofing' in that the victimizer uses electronic replications of genuine brands of various products and services that a potential victim may be interested in. Phishers ask for a number of personal details, including phone numbers, date of birth, bank account numbers, PINs, social insurance or social security numbers, and credit card numbers, making the victim think that he or she is providing this information to a legitimate company or agency. This information allows victimizers to access bank accounts and credit cards, forge false identities, and so on.

Many of these requests are quickly identified as fraudulent by internet users. Often there is an unusual phrasing of terms or the requests are strange and bizarre, such as a promise to provide millions of dollars for the short-term use of a bank account. Offers are usually 'too good to be true'. The Internet has made access to potential victims easy and inexpensive; victimizers can contact thousands of people at once and need only one to respond to be successful.

Advance Fee Fraud

There are several variations to the **advance fee fraud**. However, the basic premise is that a potential victim is asked for money or personal information in advance of a substantial payout, which is never received. Examples of the more widespread forms of this crime are discussed below.

419/West African/Nigerian Letters

Advance fee letter fraud has been in existence for a long time but has become increasingly popular over the last decade. This type of scam is also referred to as the 419 scam, or West African or Nigerian letters. The term '419' refers to the section of the Nigerian Criminal Code that these offers violate. However, the Nigerian government often does not prosecute, blaming the victim for getting involved in a scheme that breaks the law of the scammer's country.

In the **419 scam**, individuals and businesses in wealthier countries, such as Canada and the United States, receive letters (via e-mail, regular post, or fax) expressing the urgent need for the recipient to carry out a 'business transaction'. The letters usually relay some story of inheritance, the theft of money from the government, or an unclaimed estate that needs to be moved to the recipient's country. The sum of money is usually extremely large, often in the millions of dollars. The recipient is usually asked to provide bank account numbers, some other personal information, and a phone number where he or she can be reached; in exchange for this assistance, he or she will receive a percentage of the funds. The senders of such letters often use titles such as 'doctor', 'high commissioner', 'parliamentary secretary', 'chief executive officer', or 'prince/princess' to entice the reader into believing in the legitimacy of the often bizarre offer. The writer is often from Nigeria, or another West African nation, and often mentions the desire to evade either prosecution or taxation by the government of that country. The letters often stress confidentiality of the transaction, the importance of honesty and trust, and/or the strong religious belief or background of the sender. Two examples of this scam are offered in boxes 10.3 and 10.4.

Although the first takes advantage of the recent recession by offering employment in a China-based company, the second is a more traditional offer.

Box 10.3   Example of Advance Fee Fraud E-mail Offering Employment

From: [name and e-mail withheld]
Sent: Monday, 13 April 2009 11:57 PM
Subject: ([company name withheld]) Job offer Recession bailout

FROM THE DESK OF (President & CEO)
[name withheld]
[company name withheld]
[address withheld]

Good Day Sir/Madam,
This message is sent in English for universal Understanding.

A company, [company name withheld] Imports and Exports based in People Republic of China, is in need of representatives in Australia, Europe and North America to represent its Interests. We would want you to put your best in the job offer, we want the best of service from you, Please note that you should have no fear dealing with us as these job opportunity is 100% risk free and it demands no financial obligation from you.

Our company [company name withheld], a small consultant Company in P.R. of China has been mandated to seek Individuals in Europe and North America for this Purpose.

We are able to get your email address with the help of marketing research based on your location, The representatives will act as a receiving payment Agents and also placing orders for goods and products from customers, You will be compensated with 10% for your service.

We guarantee you a minimum of $2,000(1,750 Euros) monthly part time and can reach $20,000 (17,500 Euros) based on the volume and Experience as time goes on, This is a good opportunity with a good company with more potential for you in the future.

If you are interested and for more information, contact our company consultant Mr. [name withheld]. through his email :[email withheld]

Box 10.4   Example of Advance Fee Fraud: 419 Scam

From: [name and e-mail address withheld]
Sent: Wednesday, 15 April 2009 12:20 PM
Subject: Dear,

Dear,

I am so happy for your health may almighty God be with you by understanding this message. I want to tell you that I really want to been relationship with you. Though we've not met before now but it takes one day for two to be together in unity and peaceful life, I'm Miss [name withheld] the only child/daughter of late Mrs [name withheld] Address: [address withheld]

I am 20years old girl. I lost my parent, and I have an inheritance from my late mother, My parents were very wealthy farmers and cocoa merchant when they were alive, After the death of my father, long ago, my mother was controlling his business until she was poisoned by her business associates which she suffered and died. Before the death of my mother on October 2004 in a private hospital here in Coted'ivoire where she was admitted, she secretly called me on her bed side and disclosed to me about the sum of Eight million five hundred US dollars ($8.5million) she left in suspense account in one of the bank here in Abidjan.

It was the money she intended to transfer oversea for investment before her sudden death,She also instructed me that I should seek for a foreign partner in any country of my choice who will assist me transfer this money in oversea account where the money will be save and invested wisely, Because of the current political problem here in Ivory Coast I decided to transfer the money to abroad where it will be save and invested, therefore, I am crying and seeking for your kind assistance in the following ways:

(1) To provide a safe bank account into where the money will be transferred for investment.

(2) To serve as a guardian of this fund since I am only 20 years old.

(3) To make arrangement for me to come over to your country to further my education and to secure a resident permit for me in your country.

I have decided to offer you 20% of the total amount for your willingness to help me, Please kindly response to my mail immediately with your full personal information, telephone number so that I can call and speak with you on the telephone.

Thanks for your understanding.

Miss [name withheld]

[E-mail withheld]

If the recipient responds to the initial request, the victimizer asks for further information to complete the transaction, usually stating that there are some fees involved in order to move the money. These fees must be paid by the victim, as the victimizer's money is unavailable until it is released by a holder (such as a bank, lawyers, the government, etc.). These types of requests continue, often increasing in value, until the victim realizes that he or she has been scammed, in some cases losing thousands of dollars.

Advance Fee Loans

Advance fee loans are offered by companies advertising guaranteed loans regardless of the applicant's credit history. The advertisements often appear in newspapers, in the back of magazines, or as spam e-mails. Once a victim contacts one of these companies, he or she finds out that the loan requires an advance service fee that can range from a few hundred to a few thousand dollars. The victim never receives the loan and cannot get the fee refunded.

Inheritance Schemes

In this scheme, potential victims are contacted (usually by e-mail) by someone claiming to have become very wealthy as the result of an inheritance. This person usually has some problem getting the money out of the country and asks the recipient to assist with the banking matters (and possibly to pretend to be a long-lost relative of the deceased) in exchange for a share of the wealth. This scam is essentially a form of advance fee fraud combined with a phishing scheme; victimizers seek to get the victim's personal information but also ask for various fees in order to secure the funds. An inheritance scheme can be quite elaborate. Victimizers will often draw up false websites demonstrating 'proof' of the wealthy person's death and create Certificates of Deposit for a safety deposit box as 'evidence' of the inheritance. Other tactics are used, including making references to foreign diplomats who will help with the transfer of funds.

Lottery or Sweepstakes Schemes

This type of scheme is another example of an advance fee fraud combined with a phishing scam. In these schemes, a potential victim is contacted by a supposed lottery corporation stating that it has chosen the victim because of a 'winning e-mail' or a 'winning draw'. Regardless of how the potential victim is chosen, all of these schemes claim that he or she has won funds from a contest or lottery that he or she did not enter. An example of this type of fraud is offered in Box 10.4. In this scam, the potential victim is asked to contact the person responsible for handing out the funds. As the scam progresses, he or she is asked for fees to release the funds, process the funds, and so on. As with all advance fee frauds, the amount of these fees increases as the scam moves forward. Often the victim is told to keep the award secret, to avoid unnecessary publicity, and to contact a mobile number so that the victim and the con artist can keep in closer contact. According to the CAFC (n.d.), this type of scam is an ever-growing problem, securing an increased number of victims. Education and prevention information stress the importance that lottery corporations do not contact people by e-mail or ask for money to receive money. They also advise people to be wary of prizes offered for draws and contests that they have not entered.

Box 10.5   Example of Lottery Advance Fee Fraud Solicitation

From: SOUTH AFRICA 2010 WORLD CUP BID LOTTERY AWARD [mailto: e-mail withheld]
Sent: Monday, 20 April 2009 9:39 PM
Subject: {Spam? 5} PRIZE AWARD NOTIFICATION

SOUTH AFRICA 2010 WORLD CUP BID LOTTERY AWARD.
PRIZE AWARD NOTIFICATION

We announce today the external draw #7011 of the South Africa 2010 World Cup Bid Lottery Award draw held on the 30th March, 2009 in the Republic Of South Africa.

You have been approved for payment the sum of US$2,400,000.00 (Two Million Four Hundred Thousand United States Dollars) this is from the total prize money of US$31,200,000.00 shared among the thirteen (13) international winners in the Second Category credited to file with REF: NUMBER: GML-S343-KKT-8871 and BATCH NUMBER: 56T-DTH78-SAR79.

To file for your claim, please contact our fiduciary claim Agent;

_____

Dr. [name withheld]
Email: [e-mail withheld]
Tel: [phone number withheld]

_____

Please remember to quote your Reference and Batch Numbers along with the following details:

NAME:.........
MAILLING ADDRESS:........
EMAIL:..........
COUNTRY:..........
PHONE/FAX NUMBER:......
AGE:.......
SEX;........
OCCUPATION:......

Congratulations!!!

Sincerely,
Mrs. [Name withheld]
Zonal Co-ordinator

A variation of this scam is called a 'prize pitch', whereby a potential victim is contacted stating that he or she has been randomly (or specifically) selected to receive a particular luxurious prize or one of a certain number (three or five) of prizes available. These prizes often include boats, cars, all-expense paid trips, and/or large amounts of cash. The victimizer asks the potential victim to buy a product such as a pen, coin, or other type of 'valuable' collection—paying in advance—in order to secure the winnings. The products are often cheaply made and highly overpriced, and the unfortunate victim also does not win the lottery prize. After the prize pitch, another victimizer may contact the victim, offering to get the money back that was fraudulently taken. This second victimizer may claim to be an official who has seized the assets of the fraudulent company and is seeking to get the victim his or her prize. As with the initial scam, the prize recovery also requires a fee which must be paid in advance. This scam is particularly tragic, as victims are re-victimized when they are already vulnerable.

Puppy Scams

According to the CAFC, operated by the Ontario Provincial Police (OPP), there seems to be an increasing number of scams targeting dog lovers. Victimizers place a classified ad for puppies (often purebred varieties) at a very attractive price, especially to people who want a specific breed. This scheme is another variation of an advance fee scam, this one involving the promise of a puppy when all the necessary fees are paid. The lure in the advertisement states that the owner of the puppies has recently moved, is moving, or currently resides in another country. The victimizer often uses photos of puppies from the Internet and claims that these are the animals for sale. The victimizer does not actually have these dogs but will ask for money in advance for the animal, shipping, customs charges, and so on. The victim is instructed to pay these fees via a money wiring service such as Western Union or Money Gram. The animal never arrives, and subsequent calls or e-mails to the 'seller' are not returned.

Investment, Ponzi, Pyramid, or Chain Letter Schemes

In these types of schemes, victimizers provide a potential investor with an 'opportunity' to participate in a (non-existent) investment with a high rate of return. The rates of return offered in the initial pitch are often much higher than those of more traditional investment companies. If the potential victim is interested, the investment structure is explained, often in very complex terms. The victimizer will often use strong sales tactics, mentioning that there is a limited-time offer available and that the potential victim 'must act quickly' to take full advantage of the offer. The victimizer, upon receipt of the money, will often disappear, and the victim never receives his or her return.

A variation on this type of scheme is the **Ponzi scheme**, named after Charles Ponzi, an Italian immigrant who became very rich very quickly in Boston *circa* 1920 and was soon after arrested and imprisoned for fraud. In this scheme, potential victims are lured by a high-return investment. The money that they receive is from subsequent waves of investors, demonstrating a 'significant return' but not one from profit earned on the venture. When the initial victims begin receiving funds, they often recommend the victimizer to friends so that they can share in the opportunity. In doing so, the scheme is extended. Eventually, the scheme ends with the victimizer absconding with the money. A recent example of the use of this scheme is the Bernard Madoff case, which occurred in the United States in 2008.

This form of investment fraud is also called a **pyramid scheme**, or a chain letter fraud, in which victims are selected and rewarded in the hopes that they will tell their friends and that these subsequent 'investments' will then be used to pay the initial investors. More potential victims are needed with every new wave of victims brought into the scam. Because there are significantly more victims at the bottom than at the top as the scam progresses, the shape of the victim pool looks like a triangle or pyramid. Such schemes can continue for years as

Figure 10.4 How a Ponzi Scheme Works

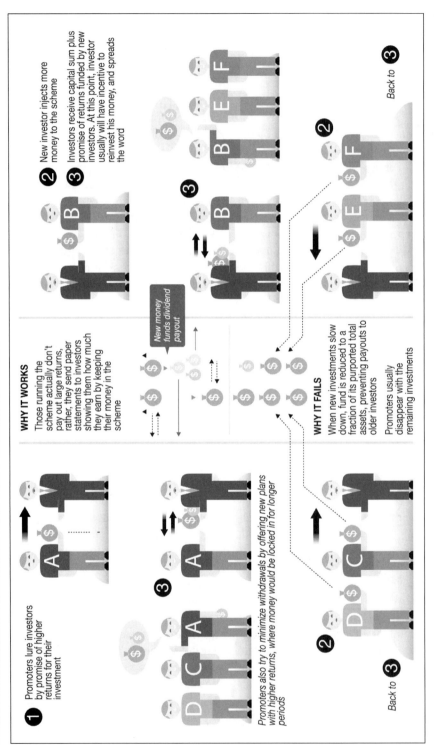

SOURCE: Graphic: How a Ponzi Scheme Works (2009, 18 September). Adapted from *Calgary Herald*. Retrieved from www.calgaryherald.com/news/Graphic+Ponzi+scheme+works/1993414/story.html.

long as there are new investors. Madoff managed to continue his scheme for over 20 years by paying out small sums of money as 'profits' from investments to the initial key and influential investors. His victims were in the thousands, and many were from respected families. He was eventually caught because victims started to become suspicious and to talk among themselves.

Other Types of Scams

Phone Number Spoofing

Almost anyone who has Caller ID has experienced phone number **spoofing**. In this scam, the potential victim notices that the incoming phone number is odd, such as 123-456-7890, 000-000-0000, or 777-777-7777. The victimizer has used a device that programs a different phone number into the system rather than the actual number where the call is originating from. Although the phone message from this number may be legitimate, it should be considered with caution as a legitimate service would not want to obscure its information from a potential client.

Cheque Overpayment Fraud

In this scam, the victim receives a cheque as payment for products sold or services provided. The cheque is usually forged but looks like a valid personal, certified, or corporate cheque and is often for more than what was originally owed. The victim is told that the overpayment is just an oversight or clerical mistake and that he or she must return the overpayment by cashing the cheque and returning the excess funds. As the counterfeit cheque often takes weeks to verify, especially if the issuing bank is in a foreign country, the victim often receives the cash for the note but eventually finds out that the cheque was forged and that he or she has to return the money to the bank. The victim, therefore, is not only out the money owed to him or her but also the personal funds that were used to 'repay' the victimizer. This type of fraud can be combined with advance fee fraud and prize pitches where victims are asked to return 'excess prize winnings' or 'overpayments' on loans.

False Charities

In this scam, victims are contacted by phone, e-mail, or regular post and asked to make a donation to what appears to be a legitimate charity. These organizations often have names that sound very similar to more legitimate charities, but the proceeds are pocketed. These victimizers have peak operations during the time of other legitimate charities, such as the end of the year, when many start their funding drives. In some cases the fake charity will request that donations be sent via a money transfer service so that the funding can be used 'immediately'.

Office Supplies or Business Directory Schemes

This rather old scam seeks to victimize companies. Companies are enticed into buying low-priced, or 'bargain', photocopier/fax toner, office supplies, or directories over the phone. The e-mail or person on the phone applies a common pressure tactic stating that the prices will 'be going up soon', that this is a 'special offer', and that the company must purchase these products 'today'. The purchased product may arrive, but it may be substandard or poorly made, and the price is often not the one offered in the initial contact or includes additional fees for 'delivery' or 'processing' of the order, making the item substantially overpriced.

900 Scams

The **900 scams** try to entice victims, through various methods, to call a 1-900 number for various reasons. These numbers are used by businesses which provide services over the phone for a fee. Callers who use them agree to pay so many dollars, often per minute, to obtain information, vote on particular issues, engage in sex talk, and so on. Scammers will send an enticement either through e-mail or more traditional mail services, encouraging the reader to call a specific number. Often the enticements state that the reader has won a prize, such as cash, cars, boats, and/or trips, and that he or she must call the number to receive more information.

These offers often state that the cost per minute is about five dollars and that the average phone call is about six to eight minutes long. However, the 1-900 line is answered by a computer which usually prohibits the user from speeding up the call. When the victim does get to the end of the message, his or her prize is often a very small cash amount, such as one or two dollars. This means that a victim paid 30 to 40 dollars, often with additional taxes, to collect a few dollars.

Common Elements of Phone and Internet Fraudulent Solicitations

Regardless of the type of scam, the solicitations all have certain facets in common that serve to warn prospective victims against being victimized:

- Victims often have a first impression that the offer is too good to be true, and it probably is. Victimizers will appeal to a victim's desire to either save or make money, offering significant savings or funds/prizes as part of the enticement.

- The contact is often from a complete stranger stating that the potential victim was either specifically chosen or randomly selected.

- Victimizers will often use high-pressure sales tactics, where one is pressured into buying 'today' or giving an 'immediate response'. This approach is meant to make the potential victim anxious about missing out on a prospective opportunity. The tactic serves to encourage him or her to make a rash decision.

- Victimizers may also use spiritual beliefs to appeal to their potential victim, in an attempt to convey that the sender is a religious and therefore honest person.

- Victims are asked to keep information secret, often accompanied by a request for 'privacy', 'discretion', and 'confidentiality'.

- Victims may be asked for an up-front fee, often payable through a parallel money transfer system such as Western Union.

- Victimizers will often not disclose their location, their phone numbers, etc. If contact is made, it is usually via a cell phone number to make the victimizer easily accessible to the victim. Any address or phone number is usually false and may frequently change as the victim moves through the scam. Once the scam has been taken as far as it can go, the cell phone number is discarded, making the tracking of the victimizer almost impossible.

- Victimizers will often pepper offers with high-ranking titles to make them seem more legitimate. Examples of such titles include doctor, diplomat, high commissioner, chief financial officer, vice president, president, count/countess, prince, princess, and solicitor.

- Many e-mail fraud solicitations have grammatical and spelling errors, typos, and generic labels for the person they are contacting (Sir, Sir/Madam, Inheritor, Award Winner, Kind Person, Trusted One, Dear, etc.).

Vulnerabilities to Fraud Victimization

A study carried out by Schoepfer and Piquero (2009) attempted to determine if there were any risk factors associated with becoming a victim of certain kinds of fraud. In addition to looking at various demographics (age, race, educational attainment, employment, and income), the authors also looked at whether the individual was a financial risk taker. The following questions were posed to respondents (p. 212):

1. Have you ever responded to a mailing other than Publisher's Clearinghouse by purchasing an item in order to become ELIGIBLE FOR A FREE PRIZE?
2. Have you ever responded to a mailing, WITHOUT purchasing something to become ELIGIBLE FOR A FREE PRIZE (other than Publisher's Clearinghouse)?
3. Have you ever given someone, other than a family member, your PIN [personal identification] number such as an ATM code or telephone calling card code?
4. Do you find it hard to resist a telephone sales pitch?
5. Do you check into the background of contractors, such as roofers, driveway pavers, or remodelling contractors, who work for you?

6. Before you discard credit card solicitations you receive in the mail do your tear them up?
7. Do you give personal information such as your credit card number or social security number over a cordless phone?

To form conclusions from these questions, answers to the first three were coded as either 'yes' or 'no'. The remaining questions were answered on a 4-point Likert scale (1 = always, 4 = never). If respondents said 'never' it was re-coded as 'no' and all other answers were coded 'yes'. The number of 'yes' answers were then added up to create a risk score. The higher the number, the more financial risk an individual was willing to take. Respondents were also asked about the number of credit cards they carried in their wallet or purse. It was assumed that the more credit respondents reported carrying with them, the higher the risk they were taking if their wallet was lost or stolen. This study found that there was a strong and significant relationship between the variables measuring risk and whether the respondent reported fraud victimization. The only other significant finding was that the younger the respondent, the more likely he or she was to be victimized in this way. Other demographics, including race, educational attainment, employment status, and income, neither increased nor decreased one's risk of fraud victimization.

Prevention: The Role of Target Hardening

The crime of identity theft is increasing, as is the difficulty in catching the perpetrators. Explanations offered by routine activities theory may offer some solutions for this situation. Recall from earlier chapters that Cohen and Felson (1979) theorized that there were three main elements to a criminal event: a motivated offender, a suitable target, and a lack of capable guardianship. This theory suggests that one can have an effect on criminal events by reducing criminal motivation and the number of suitable targets and by increasing capable guardianship. In terms of identity theft, various companies have enhanced capable guardianship with advances in technology.

An example of this new technology is the security chip now available in most credit cards. By using these chips, banks and credit card companies reduce the chances of the card being used fraudulently; chips are easier to track and offer the additional security feature of a PIN instead of a signature, which can be forged. Other cards include a picture of the owner for easy verification. Companies are also taking measures to make identity documents more difficult to forge. Most companies now understand the importance of establishing properly identified clients and are now implementing stricter requirements on obtaining credit and other services. Although these measures are largely increasing the guardianship of this information, they also reduce the motivation of the offender by making the acquisition and production of identity documents more difficult. However, because identity theft is still new and changing with the advancements in technology, prevention for potential victims is still one of the more widespread approaches to reducing this crime.

Target hardening, or the process of making victims appear less suitable to offenders, is a prime strategy in the fight against fraud victimization. The primary tool in this fight is the education of the public. Box 10.6 demonstrates some of the tips that can be found on many websites encouraging people to be careful and guarded with their information. A similar feature of these tactics is that people should trust their instincts when approached for personal information. If one is feeling pressured, or thinks that an offer is too good to be true, it usually is. If one is concerned about having information taken, then he or she should refuse to give it out and make sure that documents are destroyed so that they do not fall into the wrong hands. All of this is good advice.

However, as illustrated with the case of James, whose story was relayed earlier in the chapter, there can still be

Box 10.6 Tips to Protect Potential Victims from Identity Theft

- Proceed with caution if a marketer asks you to send personal or financial information before he or she discloses an offer, if you're promised a valuable prize in return for a low-cost purchase, if you're required to send money to take advantage of a deal or to obtain a loan, or if an offer sounds too good to be true.
- Proceed with caution if you're asked to call a special number. The number is often long-distance that results in your being billed at a costly per-minute rate.
- Buy gift cards from a clerk if possible—it is safer than buying them off the rack. Also, opt for gift cards that have a protective backing, and keep your receipts.

- Pay attention to your billing cycles. Follow up with creditors if your bills don't arrive on time.
- Review credit card statements carefully. Be suspicious of unfamiliar charges.
- If denied credit, find out why.
- Put only your name and address on cheques.
- When using a payment card, ensure that your card is swiped only once and in the proper card reader.
- Cut up expired and unused credit and debit cards. The card may have expired, but the number may still be valid.
- When shopping and banking online, make sure that the merchant has a secure transaction system before you give your credit card number or other financial information.
- Never reply to spam e-mail, avoid posting your e-mail address in an open forum, and protect your computer with anti-virus and anti-spam software, as well as a firewall.
- Do not donate to a charity in cash, ask for a copy of the charity's annual report, and confirm the charity's authenticity by checking the list of Canada's registered charities.
- Before you reveal any personal information, find out how it will be used and if it will be shared.
- Do not give out personal information on the phone, through the mail, or over the Internet unless you have initiated the contact or know whom you're dealing with.
- Do not carry your SIN card—leave it in a secure place. Also, give your SIN only when necessary; ask to use other types of identifiers when possible.
- Guard your mail. Deposit outgoing mail in post office collection boxes or at your local post office. Promptly remove mail from your mailbox after delivery. Ensure that your mail is forwarded or re-routed if you move or change your mailing address.
- Avoid using easily available information like your mother's maiden name, your birth date, the last four digits of your SIN, or your phone number as your PIN or password.
- Minimize the amount of identification information and number of cards you carry on your person.
- Keep items with personal information in a safe place. Be sure to tear or shred receipts, copies of credit applications, insurance forms, physician statements, credit offers, and any other documentation which contains personal information.
- If any of your key documents (such as your birth certificate, driver's license, passport, bank card, or credit card) are lost or stolen, notify the issuer immediately.
- Lock your household mailbox if possible. If you are going to be away, arrange for a trusted neighbour to pick up your mail. You can also go to your local post office (with identification) and ask for Canada Post's hold mail service, which is available for a fee.
- Find out how your employer makes sure your personal information is private.
- When you receive a renewal or replacement for a document or certificate that contains identity information (such as your driver's licence or vehicle registration), make sure you return or destroy the old one.
- Protect your computer with a start-up password that is a combination of letters (upper and lower case), numbers, and symbols. Don't use an automatic login feature that saves your user name and password.
- Disable file-sharing software to prevent unauthorized access to your computer and its data.

- Even though you've deleted files from folders, remnants may still be on the computer's hard drive, where they may be easily retrieved. Make sure personal information is really deleted before you sell, recycle, or discard your computer.

SOURCES: Consumer Protection Branch of the Ministry of Justice and Attorney General. (n.d.). *Tips for reducing the risk of identity theft.* Retrieved 18 January 2009, from www.safecanada.ca/identitytheft_e.asp; Government of Ontario. (2006). *What is identity theft?* Retrieved 18 January 2009, from www.gov.on.ca/MGS/en/ConsProt/STEL02_045992.html; Office of the Privacy Commissioner of Canada. (2005). *Five key steps to reduce the risk of identity theft.* Retrieved 18 January 2009, from www.privcom.gc.ca/fs-fi/02_05_d_27_e.asp; Winnipeg Police Service. (2008). *Crime prevention: Identity theft – Could it happen to you?* Retrieved 18 January, 2009, from www.winnipeg.ca/police/TakeAction/identity_theft.stm.

difficulties even when one is diligent. After James finally got his bank to part with the fraudulent information provided to it, he found out that the impersonators had only his first name, middle initial, last name, and current address (Furnell, 2007). Although this fact may explain why the applications for extra credit were denied, these details can be found in most phone directories. Even with this small amount of information, James was victimized. Further, not everyone can be on guard with all of their information all of the time. To insist that people do so is in many ways blaming the victim. If someone becomes a victim of fraud, will he or she be held partially to blame for not following every possible precaution?

Summary

This chapter examined a number of ways that people can become victims of fraud and the experiences of some of those who have gone through this particular form of victimization. Because of the non-violent nature of this fraud, it is tempting to assume that it is a less severe crime than those that feature violence; however, it is clear that its effects can be harmful and long-lasting. It must also be remembered that some fraud victimizations can lead to other, often more serious, forms.

The key to protecting ourselves from fraud is prevention. Averting this crime can be achieved in various ways, including increasing security measures on identity documents and credit applications, making it more difficult for victimizers to obtain or reproduce such items, and educating people about this type of victimization. Significant effort has gone into providing the public with information about this crime, in the hopes that people will be more protective of their information and therefore less likely to be victimized. This approach, albeit a sound one, has the added danger of blaming the victim if he or she does not take all of the precautions that they are aware of. When we increase the victim's responsibility for crime, we inadvertently also decrease the culpability of the offender. Most would agree that we, as a society, should not head in this direction.

Glossary

419 scam   A type of advance fee fraud that is most commonly associated with Nigeria or other West African countries and named for the section of the Nigerian criminal code that it violates. Also known as the West African or Nigerian letter, this scam asks potential victims to supply banking information in order to transfer a large sum of money. In return, the potential victim is promised a percentage of the funds. This scam is carried out throughout the world and is a derivation of the Spanish Prisoner scam.

900 scam   A scam in which a potential victim is enticed to call a 1-900 number to receive information, a prize, or a service. Although the cost per minute of these numbers is advertised as being low, the calls are prolonged to increase the fee.

advance fee fraud   A generic type of scam which has several variations. These scams involve an offender asking a potential victim for money in advance of a substantial payout, which is never received.

fraud   A non-violent crime that uses deception to achieve financial or material gain.

gateway offence   An offence that creates opportunities for other, often more serious, offences to be committed. For example, identity theft allows someone to commit further crimes while impersonating another person and thereby decreasing the chances of being detected.

identity theft   A form of fraud in which someone illegally acquires and uses another person's personal and identifying information, usually for financial gain.

phishing scam   A scam in which a potential victim is 'hooked' into divulging personal information, which is used by the offender for identity theft, credit card fraud, or other illegal purposes.

Ponzi scheme   Named after fraudster Charles Ponzi, a scam that involves individuals investing in an opportunity created by the offender. Promised a high return, the investors are paid from the proceeds of subsequent investors, who are often referred to the offender by the initial investors. Because this type of fraud requires a constantly increasing victim pool to sustain itself, it is also known as a pyramid scheme.

pyramid scheme   A type of scam that requires a growing number of people to invest in a non-existent investment opportunity. Monies are paid to initial investors in the hopes of receiving referrals to more potential victims. These subsequent 'investments' are used to continue to pay the other investors. Because there are more victims at the bottom of the scheme than at the top, the shape of the victim pool looks like a pyramid.

spoofing   The process of hiding one's originating information, such as a phone number or e-mail address, from potential victims. False or no information can be offered instead of the genuine details.

white-collar crime   A term first coined by criminologist Edwin Sutherland, who defined it as a 'crime committed by a person of respectability and high social status in the course of his occupation'. The definition has been broadened over time and currently refers to non-violent crimes committed for financial gain, including tax evasion, embezzlement, counterfeiting, insider trading, and various types of fraud.

Critical Thinking Questions

1. Look at the tips offered in Box 10.6 and answer the following questions.
   a. How many of these tips do you actually do to protect your identity?
   b. How many more could you be doing?
   c. Could you follow these tips all the time? Is it reasonable to expect you to do so? Why or why not?
2. Answer the same questions that were asked in the study by Schoepfer and Piquero (2009) mentioned earlier in this chapter. Count up the number of 'yes' responses you had to the question set. Your answers can range from zero (zero questions answered 'yes') to seven (all questions answered 'yes'). What was your score? Make sure to answer honestly and not the way you think you should after reading this chapter. Are you a risk taker with your personal information?
3. Think about the last time you were asked for personal information. Was the request legitimate? Did you give them the information anyway? If so, why? What motivated you to do so? If not, what did you do? How was your refusal taken?
4. Why do you think e-mail scams are successful?
5. Which of the following do you think should be required to obtain a credit card? Give reasons for your answers.
   a. Filling out an application.
   b. Providing numbers of existing credit cards you may have.
   c. Providing proof of identity with government documents. (If yes, should these be the originals given in person or photocopies sent in the mail?)
   d. Providing a reference. (If yes, what kind?)
   e. Receiving a telephone call from the bank or credit card company to confirm the application and the information received.
   f. Being able to change the mailing address during the application process.
   g. Being able to have statements sent to a post office box.
6. What other measures should the bank or credit card company employ to protect the information gathered during the application process?
7. Is the victim of fraud truly blameless? Why or why not?

CHAPTER 11

Aftermath and Recovery

Learning Objectives

After reading this chapter, you will be able to

- understand some of the experiences that victims can have following victimization;
- examine the symptoms of Post-Traumatic Stress Disorder as it relates to victimization;
- identify other types of stress experienced by the victim; and
- understand what aids in the process of victimization recovery.

Introduction

The aftermath of victimization for the victim, those who know him or her, and others who hear about the event is an area worth exploring. While a victimizing incident often takes no more than a few minutes, the aftermath can last considerably longer. This chapter will examine how the effects of victimization vary for each individual and are based on a variety of factors, including the type, intensity, and duration of the victimization, the injury, damage, or loss of property involved, the support systems in place, the previous victimization experience of the victim, the response of police, and the outcome for the offender. In particular, we will examine the fear that is felt by various types of victims and the effects of Post-Traumatic Stress Disorder (PTSD) and other forms of stress experienced by the victim and his or her support systems. Finally, we will look at a relatively new trend in the study of trauma: the role of resilience and victim recovery.

Victimization and Secondary Victimization

Although the actual victimization incident can often last no more than three minutes, the after-effects of victimization can continue for days, months, or even years. Often after the criminal victimization experience, the victim may choose to report the incident to police. Once the police are called, the victim puts him- or herself at risk for re-victimization by the criminal justice system as it investigates his or her allegations. The victim can be re-victimized by the justice system if it treats the victim with mistrust or suspicion and/or questions his or her credibility (Burt, 1980; Cann, Calhoun, Selby, & King, 1981; Schwendinger & Schwendinger, 1974). As mentioned in earlier chapters, a victim may also be blamed for the attack. This situation is a form of **secondary victimization**, whether it is committed by members of the criminal justice system, the medical system, or the victim's support network of friends and family. This term should not be confused with 'secondary victims' (see Chapter 2).

Although anyone can be subjected to the processes of secondary victimization, they are most pronounced with victims of sexual assault. This tendency is largely because, unlike most other crimes, determination of whether a sexual assault occurred centres on issues of the victim's consent. If the victim consented to the sexual activity, then a sexual assault did not occur. For this reason, the criminal justice system spends a lot of time questioning the victim, as well as the offender, to establish if consent was given.

Consent comes into question in cases of sexual assault because the act of violence included a sexual component. For example, if a person was punched in the face and then reported the assault to the police, there would be little question as to whether an assault occurred, as it is assumed that no one would consent to being punched. When that same assault is accompanied with a sexual assault, investigators must determine whether the assault was perceived as a desirable sexual act (despite the violence). The believability of the victim plays a key role in the perception of others when trying to establish whether the criminal act occurred. Looking back to our example, one could say that a person who is physically attacked is assumed to be more truthful than a person who reports a sexual attack.

How, when, and where a victim of sexual assault reports the crime is of key importance to first responders. Winkel and Koppelaar (1991) argue that if the victim is calm, cool, and collected, he or she is less likely to be believed. However, a highly emotional victim is often perceived to be more likely to have exhibited caution before the attack and less likely to be responsible for the situation. The authors state that this difference may be because individuals have a preset idea that victims should respond to victimization with hysteria. The further a victim moves away from that ideal response, the less likely he or she is to be considered not responsible for the victimization.

To combat this process, police, medical personnel, and court staff are often given specialized training to use with victims. This training has helped to lessen the stress experienced by victims as they report the crimes committed against them. Although the system is moving towards more sensitivity for victims, and especially sexual assault victims, secondary victimization is still an issue. In a study of rape survivors, Campbell (2005) interviewed victims who sought out medical and police services; the interviews took place before the victims were discharged from the hospital. Overall, victims often reported that offensive comments were made and that the process was a lot more stressful than the first responders acknowledged. This result is important, as most of these groups have received training to deal with the unique circumstances facing sexual assault victims when they first contact the medical or criminal justice system.

Reactions to Victimization: Fear

Defining 'Fear of Crime'

Consensus has not been reached as to a definition of **fear of crime**. Generally, people agree that it is a response to a threat and the fear of being harmed. However, 'crime' is a very generic term;

this explanation might be more aptly called 'fear of victimization'. Fear of crime varies with respect to the type of fear being considered (Ferraro, 1996). Ferraro and LaGrange (1987, p. 73–74) suggest that it is better to ask respondents about fear of specific crimes, such as homicide, robbery, or sexual assault, rather than asking about fear of crime more generally.

Fear of crime and risk of victimization are concepts that are slightly different but are often confused. Many agree that fear of crime is more immediate, while actual risk is less emotional and pertains to the actual chance of victimization. The essential difference is that while people are constantly saying that crime is going up and that they fear victimization, their actual risk of victimization is going down. Canada has been experiencing a downward trend in reported crime since 1992, and homicides have been declining steadily since the mid-1970s (Bunge, Johnson, & Balde, 2005).

It has been suggested that multiple measures to assess fear levels be used, in addition to using measures in multiple hypothetical situations. It is also recognized that most fear of crime studies use a single crime measure, asking the question: 'How safe do you feel (or would you feel) being out alone in your neighbourhood at night?' This question may actually be a measure of judgment about crime, not the emotional response to crime (or fear).

The terms 'worry' and 'concern about crime' have been used interchangeably in fear of crime research. Levy and Guttman (1985) suggest that 'fear' of crime actually refers to fear of violent crime whereas 'concern' or 'worry' about crime refers to fear of property offences. There is agreement that these terms are not identical, although they continue to be debated. In the Canadian Violence Against Women Survey (VAWS, 1993), the term 'worry' was chosen because it was felt to be a more valid instrument of measurement in estimating fear of crime among women.

In the VAWS, female respondents were asked whether they were worried, somewhat worried, or not at all worried in four hypothetical situations. Using different scenarios to assess fear is considered a good measure of fear of crime, in that it demonstrates that fear can change depending on the situation of a potential victim. Scott (2003) and Johnson (1996) documented that three of every five women (61 per cent) who responded to the VAWS stated that they were worried about walking in their neighbourhood after dark, while even more (75 per cent) reported

Table 11.1   Descriptive Statistics on Both Precursory and Protective Behaviour by Responses of Female Respondents: Fear

Fear: Somewhat or Very Worried	N	%
Walking alone in neighbourhood at night	10,641	61.0
Using public transport alone at night	5,447	75.4
Using parking garages alone at night	7,724	81.3
Being home alone at night	12,156	39.0

SOURCE: Scott, H. (2003). Stranger danger: Explaining women's fear of crime. *Western Criminology Review,* *4*(3), p. 206.

being worried or somewhat worried using public transportation after dark. Women continue to be most fearful while in parking garages after dark (81 per cent). What is surprising is that almost two in every five women reported being somewhat or very worried about being alone in their own home (39 per cent). Although this study did not ask males these same questions, it is suggested that men are less fearful in these situations.

Fear of Strangers

What compounds these measurement issues is that some have recognized that fear of crime is, in fact, strongly tied to fear of strangers (Baumer, 1979; Scott, 2003). This connection creates a dilemma for many who fear crime. It is widely recognized that people are most likely to be victimized by people they know. It has been suggested by Baumer that perhaps it is not just the fear of all strangers but rather some specific type of stranger that is paramount in this fear.

Social Consequences of Fear

As one of our strongest emotions, fear serves to warn us of danger, prepare ourselves to meet this danger, and generally makes us more aware. However, it can also have negative effects. Fear is complex and is often accompanied by stress and anxiety. People may restrict their activities inside and outside of their homes as a result of intense fear of the potential for victimization.

Most criminologists agree that victimization as a social problem was acknowledged in the late 1960s in the United States. By the 1970s, fear of crime became a national problem (Silver, 1974) and polls ranked it as the primary problem facing American society

(Furstenberg, 1972). In 1986, Skogan noted that fear, along with other factors, could be a strong contributor to neighbourhood decline. This process of decline occurred through what he termed **positive feedback**, whereby fear can not only enable decline but can also continue to add to the process. Although the overall reaction to fear is negative, the process is considered a positive form of feedback, as it is additive. For example, fear can lead to behavioural changes such as reducing time spent outside the home, which can lead to lack of community cohesiveness, which can lead to increased crime rates in the neighbourhood, which can lead to more fear, and so on. Specifically, Skogan (1986, p. 215) identified the following six stages in the feedback process:

1. physical and psychological withdrawal from community life;
2. a weakening of the informal social control processes that inhibit crime and disorder;
3. a decline in the organizational life and mobilization capacity of the neighbourhood;
4. deteriorating business conditions;
5. the importation and domestic production of delinquency and deviance; and
6. further dramatic changes in the composition of the population.

For these and other reasons, fear has been thought of by some to have a **contagion effect**. That is, the effects of fear can spread from one person to another or one community to another. For example, people may choose not to go into an area of a community or city because it is perceived to be dangerous and therefore represents an increased risk of victimization. This perception also means that people living in these parts of the community or city may become isolated, which leaves them vulnerable to victimization. Dangerous neighbourhoods may experience decreased response times for emergency services and, therefore, may increase the chances of victimization for people who live in those communities. This, in turn, can generate more fear within the community and its surrounding areas.

People who fear crime may also spend money to enhance their safety. There are a multitude of products and services based on this fear, including alarm systems, dog breeding, noisemakers, whistles, self-defence classes, security doors and latches, ironworks to place bars on windows and doors, cell phones, alert systems (personal and city), HAS-MAT training, pharmaceuticals, and last (but certainly not least), the firearms and weapons industry.

There are several ways that fear has been conceptualized. Moriarty (1988) notes that fear can be generated by contact with **significant others**, a term initially coined by George Herbert Mead (1934) to refer to those people who serve as an individual's close support network and whose opinions he or she values. Examples of significant others are immediate family members such as parents and siblings, spouses, children, close friends, mentors, and so on. In other words, if those who influence you are fearful, then you are also likely to become fearful and, in turn, generate these same fears in others.

The Power of Fear

Fear is a common reaction to a perceived threat. Threats can be tangible, in that one can react to an immediate risk of harm, or they can be more abstract, in the perception that the possibility of being hurt has increased. As a result, fear has the potential to modify behaviour. In other words, fear can motivate individuals to restrict a variety of movements and, therefore, freedoms. Tables 11.2 and 11.3, which were taken at the time of the VAWS (1993) survey, illustrate some restrictions that women have placed on themselves.

Table 11.2 shows that 10 per cent of survey respondents had taken a self-defence course. Almost 16 per cent of women always or usually carry a self-defence weapon with them. Nearly one-third (31.5 per cent) stated that they avoided walking by groups of boys and men and over three-fifths (62.4 per

Table 11.2   Descriptive Statistics on Both Precursory and Protective Behaviour by Responses of Female Respondents

Current Protective Behaviour	N	%
Taken a self-defence course	12,300	10.0
Always/usually carry defence weapon	12,300	15.9
Always/usually avoid walking by boys/men	11,939	31.5
Walks alone after dark < 1/wk.	10,652	62.4

SOURCE: Scott, H. (2003). Stranger danger: Explaining women's fear of crime. *Western Criminology Review, 4(3)*, p. 206.

Table 11.3   Descriptive Statistics on Both Precursory and Protective Behaviour by Responses of Female Respondents: Current Protective Behaviour

Current Protective Behaviour	N	%
Uses public transport alone after dark < 1/wk	5,459	78.1
Always/usually locks car doors when alone	9,757	63.5
Always/usually checks back seat of car	9,757	61.6
Uses parking garages alone after dark < 1/wk	7,738	75.4

SOURCE: Scott, H. (2003). Stranger danger: Explaining women's fear of crime. *Western Criminology Review, 4(3)*, p. 206.

cent) stated that they walk alone less than once a week. Table 11.3 demonstrates that even more women (78.1 per cent) restrict their behaviour by reducing their use of public transportation to less than once a week. Almost two-thirds (63.5 per cent) stated that they lock their doors when they are home alone in the evening. If driving, the majority of women (61.6 per cent) check the back seat before getting in the vehicle, and three-quarters of women (75.4 per cent) stated that they restrict their use of parking garages after dark to less than once a week.

The implications of these restrictive behaviours are far-reaching. In essence, when women, who are one-half of the population, choose to not leave the house or to not use public facilities after dark, they are not participating in the world in the same way as men. They are not taking advantage of employment or social activities, which can often lead to social and economic networking and can benefit families. Women may take lower-paying jobs with daytime hours because they do not feel safe being out at night. This self-restrictive behaviour of women has come to be known as an informal, self-imposed form of **'curfew'**. This curfew, born out of the fear of being assaulted,

limits the ability to take advantage of opportunities afforded to men who hold less fear engaging in activities at night. Women understand that, for a myriad of reasons, they are at increased risk for violence because of their average smaller size, their gender, and so on.

Types of Fear

There are different ways of thinking about fear. One is **direct fear**, which occurs as a result of actual victimization. There is also fear that results from indirect victimization, known as **indirect fear**. This form of fear is less intense and does not involve being directly exposed to the victimization. Baumer (1979, p. 256) states that there is a **ripple effect** of fear that occurs when people hear about the victimization of others. Given that there are more people who hear about a particular victimization than actual victims, it is assumed that indirect fear is the more common of the two forms.

Writing about the concepts of fear, Carl Keane (1995) made the distinction between 'concrete' and 'formless' fear. **Concrete fear** is the fear of specific events, such as fear of specific criminal victimization. For example, Ferraro (1996) and Warr (1984) noted that women are most likely to fear sexual assault, while men are most likely to fear being killed. **Formless fear** is a more general, unfixed fear of victimization. This type can be interpreted as an overall anxiety about victimization, one that is unconnected to any specific victimization experience or threat.

Perspectives on Fear

Researchers have categorized victimization, understanding its role in fear production, to look at it in several ways. Each concept is useful, depending on the perspective that is needed. Most researchers agree that these categorizations produce different reported levels of fear, which were previously of little interest to scholars and not understood. Recently, however, there has been a change.

Fear can be produced from the effects of either direct or indirect victimization. **Direct victimization** produces fear in the moment, in response to a specific situation. **Indirect victimization** occurs as the result of direct victimization to another. Those who witness or hear of the victimization become indirectly victimized as they react to the event. The fear that results from this type of victimization is less immediate and is not in response to a specific victimizer; it often occurs to supporting members of a victim, who have more fear for the direct victim than for themselves. A similar category is the idea of fear resulting from actual victimization, where the victim actually experiences a victimizing event, and a vicarious victim, where the victim feels victimized by learning of the victimization of another. Although the differences are subtle, they can be illustrated with the following example (see also Table 11.4).

Suppose there is a report on campus of a person being violently and sexually assaulted. Different victims emerge from this situation. First, there is the **actual direct victim** who experiences the actual victimization. This person experiences fear in response to the situation at hand and may also experience fear after the assault. This person will probably suffer from PTSD (see page 226), as well as any physical injuries that were inflicted on him or her.

Another type of victim is one who witnesses the assault and is traumatized by it, experiencing fear for him- or herself but not in a direct response to an actual victimization. Such a victim is called an **actual indirect victim**. Using our example of a sexual assault on campus, an actual indirect victim may have seen part of the assault and was upset by what he or she saw. This type of victim is often less afraid than the person who experienced the assault directly and usually does not suffer any physical injury as a result of the attack.

A third type of reaction to this crime is the **vicarious direct victim**, who has no direct exposure to the victimization but is so strongly affected by learning of the event that he or she experiences the same intensity of fear and many of the same symptoms as the direct victim. A vicarious direct victim can suffer many of the same type of PTSD symptoms as the actual direct victim. He or she may be fearful of going outside, have interrupted sleep patterns, and so on. In some instances, he or she may share the same fears as the direct victim, such as being victimized by the same attacker. Although the fear level can be similar to an actual direct victim, there is no physical injury and no direct exposure to the victimizer. This type of response to victimization is rare.

Finally, there is the **vicarious indirect victim**, an individual who was not present at the victimization scene but hears of the victimization of another and learns from the event. In our example, this victim would be someone who read about the assault in a school or local newspaper or heard about it via discussions with others. This person may or may not change behaviour as a result of hearing of the victimization. Unlike the vicarious direct victim, there is no fear that this victim is at risk from the original victimizer, but there is an acknowledgement that he or she should learn from this incident and perhaps take some precautions moving forward in life. The resulting fear levels are lowest among this group, although these are the most numerous victims.

Another victimization pattern that can affect fear depends on whether the victimization was carried out in a more common manner than other forms. For example, victimization that occurs as a result of a bar brawl is somewhat predictable in the sense that observers can see the beginnings of a fight, anticipate that there is a potential for others to get involved, and so on. Observers can rationalize and have time to react to the situation. Less traditional forms of victimization, such as random acts of violence, produce tremendous anxiety for both the direct victim and the indirect victim. People often fear random acts of violence by strangers, as they are less predictable than those carried out by people they know. There may be the perception that known attackers may be able to be reasoned with using common experiences as a starting point, while strangers have no known commonalities and therefore offer no initial negotiation position.

Finally, fear will vary depending on whether the actual victimization occurred to a person or to a piece of property, such as a car, house, or building. Although individuals may fear the loss or damage of property, they are more concerned for their own well-being. Therefore, the threat of direct, personal victimization elicits more fear than the victimization of an object.

Williams and Akers (1987) have incorporated the element of time into their typology of victimization, represented by the following classifications: lifetime, recent, remote, vicarious, and anticipated. In short, these authors suggest that fear patterns change over time as well as the proximity to the offender. For example, we tend to feel that we are

Table 11.4   Model of Victimization Exposure and Response

	Direct	Indirect
Actual	Victim has first-hand experience of the victimization by the victimizer and is directly affected by it.	A witness sees the victimization first-hand and is inadvertently victimized by witnessing someone else being victimized.
Vicarious	A non-witness learns of the victimization of another, but experiences similar experiences as the direct victim even though he or she was never actually victimized.	A non-witness learns of the victimization and is indirectly affected by the learning of the event. This person may change his or her behaviour in certain circumstances, warn others, etc.

at a lower risk of victimization when we hear of victimizations in another country than of those that occur closer to our personal residences. We also have more immediate fear reactions when the victimization incident occurs in the recent past, as opposed to a victimization experience that happened 20 years ago.

Reactions to Victimization: Stress

Stress is a common reaction to many experiences, including victimization. The symptoms associated with stress are varied, and for this reason severe stress reactions are sometimes difficult to identify. Because everyone is different, some people may engage in behaviours as a result of a stressful incident because they find them enjoyable, while others may engage in them as a response to trauma. A good example of this pattern is the behaviour of eating. Most people eat food because they find it pleasurable. Some individuals, however, eat in response to being stressed. Table 11.5 is a list of common stress reactions.

Good stress, which is called **eustress** (Lazarus, 1974), is a form of stress that brings about positive change. For example, many of us get stressed because of an upcoming mid-term or exam. Still others get stressed when we are meeting someone for the first time, such as a first date or a new boss. These experiences can be trying, but overcoming them can be positive and empowering, allowing us to build confidence which can help us handle new stressors, or opportunities, that may come our way. Although experiencing some amount of stress may be unavoidable and good, too much stress is dangerous.

How much stress each person can handle varies depending on the individual. According to Cooper (2000) and Kahn and Byosiere (1992), stress is an imbalance between the resources and supplies that individuals believe they possess and the perceived threats or demands related to a given situation. Stress results when there are fewer resources, both physiologically and psychologically, than are needed to deal with a perceived threat, harm, or challenge. **Stress**, therefore, can be defined as a physical and/or psychological set of reactions to demanding situations. The demanding or threatening situations (or stimuli) that produce stress (or response) are called **stressors**. According to the Canadian Centre for Addiction and Mental Health ([CAMH], n.d.,) the stress response has three physical stages:

Stage 1: Mobilizing Energy
At first, your body releases adrenaline, your heart beats faster, and you start to breathe more quickly. Both good and bad events can start this reaction: the night before your wedding or the day you lose your job.

Stage 2: Consuming Energy Stores
If, for some reason, you do not escape from the first stage, your body begins to release stored sugars and fats from its resources. At this stage, you will feel driven, pressured, and tired. You may drink more coffee, smoke more, and drink more alcohol than is good for you. You may also experience anxiety, memory loss, catch colds or get the flu more often than normal.

Stage 3: Draining Energy Stores
If you do not resolve your stress problems, the body's need for energy will

Table 11.5   Fifty Common Signs and Symptoms of Stress

1. Frequent headaches, jaw clenching or pain	26. Insomnia, nightmares, disturbing dreams
2. Gritting, grinding teeth	27. Difficulty concentrating, racing thoughts
3. Stuttering or stammering	28. Trouble learning new information
4. Tremors, trembling of lips, hands	29. Forgetfulness, disorganization, confusion
5. Neck ache, back pain, muscle spasms	30. Difficulty in making decisions
6. Light headedness, faintness, dizziness	31. Feeling overloaded or overwhelmed
7. Hearing ringing, buzzing, or 'popping' sounds	32. Frequent crying spells or suicidal thoughts
8. Frequent blushing, sweating	33. Feelings of loneliness or worthlessness
9. Cold or sweaty hands, feet	34. Little interest in appearance, punctuality
10. Dry mouth, problems swallowing	35. Nervous habits, fidgeting, feet tapping
11. Frequent colds, infections, herpes sores	36. Increased frustration, irritability, edginess
12. Rashes, itching, hives, 'goose bumps'	37. Overreaction to petty annoyances
13. Unexplained or frequent 'allergy' attacks	38. Increased number of minor accidents
14. Heartburn, stomach pain, nausea	39. Obsessive or compulsive behaviour
15. Excess belching, flatulence	40. Reduced work efficiency or productivity
16. Constipation, diarrhea	41. Lies or excuses to cover up poor work
17. Difficulty breathing, sighing	42. Rapid or mumbled speech
18. Sudden attacks of panic	43. Excessive defensiveness or suspiciousness
19. Chest pain, palpitations	44. Problems in communication, sharing
20. Frequent urination	45. Social withdrawal and isolation
21. Poor sexual desire or performance	46. Constant tiredness, weakness, fatigue
22. Excess anxiety, worry, guilt, nervousness	47. Frequent use of over-the-counter drugs
23. Increased anger, frustration, hostility	48. Weight gain or loss without diet
24. Depression, frequent or wild mood swings	49. Increased smoking, alcohol or drug use
25. Increased or decreased appetite	50. Excessive gambling or impulse buying

SOURCE: The American Institute of Stress. (n.d.). *Effects of stress*. Retrieved 3 April 2009, from www.stress.org/topic-effects.htm. Reprinted by permission of The American Institute of Stress.

become greater than its ability to produce it, and you will become chronically stressed. At this stage, you may experience insomnia, errors in judgement, and personality changes. You may also develop a serious sickness, such as heart disease, ulcers, or mental illness.

Others have conceptualized the physiological response to stress in another way. **General Adaptation Syndrome (GAS)** is an influential model introduced in the 1930s by endocrinologist Hans Selye (1936/1998). The central theme behind GAS is that individuals are biologically programmed to react to threats in three stages:

Alarm
This stage has come to be popularly known as the 'fight-or-flight' response. In times of stress, the individual

responds to an external stressor by dealing with it (fight) or by removing him- or herself from the stressful situation (flight). The body becomes energized physiologically in order to make the appropriate response. Adrenaline may increase, along with hearing and visual acuity, as well as reaction time to potential threats. When threatened with harm, one can choose to escape the dangerous situation, or stay and defend oneself.

Resistance
In this stage, the body adjusts to cope with the perceived threat. The increased energy levels become normal and sustainable while the person is feeling threatened.

Exhaustion
This heightened state of energy can be sustained only for short periods of time. Once resources are depleted, the body becomes exhausted and 'gives up'.

Although this theory is still somewhat influential, modern research suggests that cognitive reactions are also important. According to Lazarus and Folkman (1984), it is not only the event itself that elicits a stressful response, but the individual must also perceive the situation as stressful. This process is called **cognitive appraisal** and is defined as the process by which we perceive our environment to be either dangerous or safe. Each person's reaction to a situation is different. Depending on how we assess our situation, we will react accordingly. Lazarus (1991, p. 3) states that 'stress is not a property of the person, or of the environment, but arises when there is a conjunction between a particular kind

of environment and a particular kind of person that leads to a threat appraisal.'

A Gendered Response to Stress

While the 'fight-or-flight' response has received wide attention over the years, Shelley Taylor and her colleagues have effectively argued that it has largely been the male response to stress (Taylor, Klein, Lewis, Gruenewald, Gurung, & Updegraff, 2000). Males and females have a significantly different behavioural response to stress. Women, according to the authors, 'tend to befriend', while males 'tend to defend'. In other words, while men respond to stress by escaping or facing a stressor, women tend to befriend others or to engage in nurturing activities towards their children in response to stress. It is argued that these behaviours, found in studies of both humans and animals, serve to protect both the female and her offspring.

Stress Experienced by University and College Students and Non-Postsecondary Students

Renner and Macklin (1998) devised a scale that looked at the stress of college and university students using many common experiences that occur throughout their academic careers. Within this scale are also rare events, such as victimization, for comparison. Table 11.6 lists these stressors and their scores. On the left are stressors identified by adults who were sampled from all stages of life (Holmes & Rahe, 1967) and on the right are stressors specifically identified by university and college students (Renner & Macklin, 1998).

According to Holmes and Matsuda (1973), higher stress scores relate to increased stress levels. Higher stress levels increase your chances of becoming ill or having an accident. The premise is that people who are under a lot of stress tend to be more distracted and less careful, factors that are associated with an increased likelihood of having accidents (Sherry, 1991). Holmes and Rahe (1967) asked individuals to check off whether any of the events listed in Table 11.6 had happened to them in the last 12 months and to add up the 'life change units' associated with each event. The scoring system for either scale is below:

- below 150: no significant problems
- 150–199: considered 'mild life crisis'—associated with a 33 per cent increase in the chance of accident or illness
- 200–299: 'moderate life crisis'—associated with a 50 per cent increase in the chance of accident or illness.
- Over 300: 'major life crisis'—associated with an 80 per cent increase in the chance of accident or illness.

Give the scale a try and check your stress levels.

Post-Traumatic Stress Disorder (PTSD)

Post-Traumatic Stress Disorder (PTSD) is one of the few disorders for which there is a known cause. PTSD is caused by exposure to extremely traumatic and stressful situations that fall outside the realm of normal, everyday individual experiences. Common triggers for PTSD include rape/sexual assault, combat exposure, childhood neglect, childhood physical abuse, sexual molestation, natural disasters, terrorist attacks, acts of war, and so on. When PTSD symptoms emerge in rape victims specifically, it has been referred to as Rape Trauma Syndrome

(Frazier & Borgida, 1992; Giannelli, 1997). For example, Box 11.1 outlines the case of 'L', who continued to have fear and anxiety responses some time after she was abducted and sexually assaulted. Months after being attacked, she was still easily frightened and experienced tremendous fear when approaching certain areas in her home where the abduction took place. She was also seeing a counsellor to help her deal with the after-effects of her trauma.

The *Diagnostic and Statistical Manual of Mental Disorders* ([DSM-IV-TR] APA, 2000) lists six criteria (see Table 11.7) used to identify this disorder. What is interesting to note is that this symptoms-based classification uses medical terminology, implying that the cause of this PTSD is internal to the victim. People with PTSD experience a variety of symptoms, including flashbacks (commonly in the form of recurrent memories or nightmares of the traumatizing and stressful event), inability or restricted ability to feel emotions, feelings of apprehension, and sudden and/or uncontrolled outbursts of anger, sadness, and/or laughter. Because of these symptoms, PTSD is treated as an anxiety disorder. Although most people develop the disorder soon after a traumatic event, response can sometimes be delayed for months or, in some cases, even years. Symptoms of the disorder can become so severe that the individual finds it difficult to function in day-to-day situations.

According to the Canadian Mental Health Association ([CMHA], n.d.), 1 in 10 Canadians suffer from some form of PTSD. Victims can develop the disorder as children or adults. A study by Breslau et al. (1997, 1999) found that women are twice as likely to develop the syndrome. This risk becomes even more

Table 11.6 Sample Items from the Social Readjustment Rating Scale ([SRRS], left) and the College Undergraduate Stress Scale ([CUSS], right)

SSRS Major Life Event		CUSS Event	
Death of a spouse	100	Being raped	100
Divorce	75	Finding out you are HIV-positive	100
Marital separation	65	Death of a close friend	97
Jail term	63	Contracting an STD (other than HIV)	94
Death of a close family member	63	Concerns about being pregnant	91
Personal injury or illness	53	Finals week	90
Marriage	50	Oversleeping for an exam	89
Dismissal from work	47	Flunking a class	89
Marital reconciliation	45	Having a boyfriend or girlfriend cheat on you	85
Pregnancy	40	Financial difficulties	84
Death of a close friend	37	Writing a major term paper	83
Change to different line of work	36	Being caught cheating on a test	83
Change in number of arguments with spouse	36	Two exams in one day	80
Major mortgage	31	Getting married	76
Foreclosure of mortgage or loan	30	Difficulties with parents	73
Begin or end school	26	Talking in front of class	72
Change in living conditions	25	Difficulties with a roommate	66
Change in work hours or conditions	20	Job changes (applying, new job, work hassles)	65
Change in residence/schools/recreation	19	A class you hate	62
Change in social activities	18	Confrontations with professors	60
Small mortgage or loan	17	Maintaining a steady dating relationship	55
Vacation	13	Commuting to campus, or work, or both	54
Christmas	12	Peer pressures	53
Minor violations of the law	11	Being away from home for the first time	53
		Getting straight As	51
		A fraternity or sorority rush	47
		Falling asleep in class	40

SOURCES: Holmes, T. H., & Rahe, R. H. (1967). The Social Readjustment Rating Scale. *Journal of Psychosomatic Research, II,* 213–18; Renner, M. J., & Macklin, R. S. (1998). A stress life instrument for classroom life. *Teaching of Psychology, 25,* 47.

Box 11.1   Sexual Assault of 'L'

In the summer of 2000, 11-year-old 'L' (whose real name is withheld to protect her privacy) was kidnapped from her family home in Morinville, AB. She was sexually assaulted for many hours, until she managed to escape from her attacker. Even though her assailant was arrested and incarcerated, the impact and suffering continued to affect 'L'. For her, being a victim of sexual assault was more than the hours of counselling she received or the years her attacker spends behind bars. As her aunt described, 'She [was] scared more, I think, of people in general . . . she [was] scared of being alone; she [was] scared of walking past rooms in her house where she was abducted; and she [was] frightened to be in her own home. She [was] frightened of everyone around her.'

SOURCE: Family says young sexual assault victim scarred for life. (2001, 16 January). *CBC News Online.* Retrieved 19 January 2008, from www.cbc.ca/news/story/2001/01/16/sex160101.html.

Table 11.7   DSM-IV-TR Criterion for Post-Traumatic Stress Disorder (PTSD)

Diagnostic criteria for PTSD include a history of exposure to a traumatic event meeting two criteria and symptoms from each of three symptom clusters: intrusive recollections, avoidant/numbing symptoms, and hyper-arousal symptoms. A fifth criterion concerns duration of symptoms and a sixth assesses functioning.

Criterion A: stressor

The person has been exposed to a traumatic event in which both of the following have been present:

1. The person has experienced, witnessed, or been confronted with an event or events that involve actual or threatened death or serious injury, or a threat to the physical integrity of oneself or others.

2. The person's response involved intense fear, helplessness, or horror. Note: in children, it may be expressed instead by disorganized or agitated behaviour.

Criterion B: intrusive recollection

The traumatic event is persistently re-experienced in at least one of the following ways:

1. Recurrent and intrusive distressing recollections of the event, including images, thoughts, or perceptions. Note: in young children, repetitive play may occur in which themes or aspects of the trauma are expressed.

2. Recurrent distressing dreams of the event. Note: in children, there may be frightening dreams without recognizable content.

3. Acting or feeling as if the traumatic event were recurring (includes a sense of reliving the experience, illusions, hallucinations, and dissociative flashback episodes, including those that occur upon awakening or when intoxicated). Note: in children, trauma-specific re-enactment may occur.

4. Intense psychological distress at exposure to internal or external cues that symbolize or resemble an aspect of the traumatic event.

5. Physiologic reactivity upon exposure to internal or external cues that symbolize or resemble an aspect of the traumatic event.

Criterion C: avoidant/numbing

Persistent avoidance of stimuli associated with the trauma and numbing of general responsiveness (not present before the trauma), as indicated by at least three of the following:

1. Efforts to avoid thoughts, feelings, or conversations associated with the trauma

Table 11.7   *continued*

2. Efforts to avoid activities, places, or people that arouse recollections of the trauma

3. Inability to recall an important aspect of the trauma

4. Markedly diminished interest or participation in significant activities

5. Feeling of detachment or estrangement from others

6. Restricted range of affect (e.g., unable to have loving feelings)

7. Sense of foreshortened future (e.g., does not expect to have a career, marriage, children, or a normal life span)

Criterion D: hyper-arousal

Persistent symptoms of increasing arousal (not present before the trauma), indicated by at least two of the following:

1. Difficulty falling or staying asleep

2. Irritability or outbursts of anger

3. Difficulty concentrating

4. Hyper-vigilance

5. Exaggerated startle response

Criterion E: duration

Duration of the disturbance (symptoms in B, C, and D) is more than one month.

Criterion F: functional significance

The disturbance causes clinically significant distress or impairment in social, occupational, or other important areas of functioning.

Specify if: Acute: if duration of symptoms is less than three months

Chronic: if duration of symptoms is three months or more

Specify if:

With or Without delay onset: Onset of symptoms at least six months after the stressor

SOURCE: American Psychiatric Association (2000). Reprinted with permission from the Diagnostic and Statistical Manual of Mental Disorders. Text revision, Fourth Edition (Copyright 2000).

pronounced if the traumatic victimization they experienced happened before the age of 15. According to the DSM-IV (APA, 2000), approximately 8 per cent of Americans suffer from this same disorder. The Canadian Armed Forces states that, although numbers vary on the source, roughly 13–20 per cent of soldiers who have worked on peacekeeping missions currently suffer or have suffered from PTSD (NDCF Ombudsman, 2002).

Other After-Effects of Victimization

Gannon and Mihorean (2005) queried individuals who had been victims of violence to see how the experience had affected them. In particular, they looked at how violent victimization influenced the ability to carry out main activities, such as work, school, childcare, and so on. They found that one-quarter of the victims in their study had difficulty carrying out their main activity. Incidents of robbery were most likely to disrupt a person's main activity. In slightly more than one-third of robbery incidents (35 per cent), victims found it difficult to carry out their main activity compared to 25 per cent of sexual assaults and 22 per cent of physical assaults.

Among those victims who had difficulty carrying out their main activity, 37 per cent said that it was for one day, while a further 39 per cent indicated it was for two to seven days. Sixteen per cent of victims who had their main activities disrupted said that they were having trouble carrying out their main activity more than two weeks after the incident. While not all violent incidents resulted in physical injury, many left emotional scars. Of the emotions that the incidents did evoke, feeling angry (32 per cent); upset, confused, or frustrated (20 per cent); and fearful (18 per cent) were the most prevalent. For about 1 in 10 incidents, victims said that their experience made them more cautious or aware (9 per cent). Yet in about one-quarter (26 per cent) of incidents, victims said that the incident did not affect them much. For other common reactions, see Figure 11.1.

Having difficulty performing a main activity that generates income can have other ramifications, including loss of income and possible loss of employment, which can further increase stress. Loss of income may translate into a loss of resources to help cope with stress, such as money to pay for medications, certain

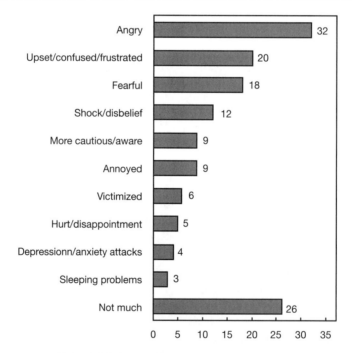

Figure 11.1 Anger Is the Most Common Reaction among Victims of Violent Victimization, 2004

Note: Figures may not add up to 100% due to multiple responses. Excludes incidents of spousal sexual and physical abuse.

SOURCE: Gannon, M., & Mihorean, K. (2005). Sexual offences in Canada, 2004. *Juristat, 25(7)*. Ottawa, ON: Centre for Canadian Justice Statistics, Minister of Industry, p. 12.

psychological and medical care, childcare, and so on. Students who have difficulty getting to classes and/or concentrating on their studies may get lower grades than usual or fail a course. This in turn can affect scholarships and other rewards that come with doing well at school.

Arias and Corso (2005) looked at the differences in direct costs of intimate partner violence, committed by a partner of a different gender, to male and female victims. They also looked at how many times services were accessed by these victims. Intimate partner violence often involves many different types of victimization experiences and therefore serves as a good example for cost estimation of violent victimization. Significantly more women than men reported being physically victimized by their partner and suffering related injuries. Women were more likely to use medical facilities, such as emergency departments, in-patient hospital admissions, and physician services, to deal with their injuries. A greater proportion of women than men also reported seeking mental health services and, on average, made more visits as a result this victimization.

Women were also more likely than men to take time off from work, childcare, and/or household responsibilities because of their injuries. When looking at direct financial cost to the victim, women who had experienced at least one physical victimization by an intimate partner had more than twice the average per person cost ($948.00) than men who had experienced at least one incidence ($387.36). These estimates by Arias and Corso (2005) do not include many other subsequent costs of victimization, such as legal fees, court room time, therapeutic intervention for children, incarceration of the offender,

and so on. These costs are significantly higher than the figures given here.

Stockholm Syndrome

Depending on the intensity and type of abuse experienced by a victim, another possible outcome—although rare—is **Stockholm Syndrome**, defined as a psychological and emotional process whereby a victim (usually a hostage or an abused person) identifies with and feels a strong attachment toward his or her victimizer. The syndrome was initially identified as the result of events during a bank robbery in Stockholm, Sweden, on 23 August 1973, in which four bank employees (Birgitta Lundblad, Elisabeth Oldgren, Kristin Ehnmark, and Sven Safstrom) were held captive by Jan-Erik Olsson and Clark Olofsson, who both had criminal histories. Over the six-day hostage period, the captives came to hold empathetic and protective feelings towards the two men and eventually viewed police as more threatening than the robbers. In some cases, the relationship between the victims and their captors continued for years after the robbery. This initial identification of a post-traumatic relationship between a previously unknown abductor and his or her victim has come to be known as Classic Stockholm Syndrome (Strentz, 1982; Kuleshnyk, 1984; Graham, Rawlings, & Rigsby, 1994). Indicators of Stockholm Syndrome include positive feelings by the captives towards their captors; negative feelings by the captives towards the police and other authorities trying to win their release; and positive feelings by the captors toward their captives (Kuleshnyk, 1984).

Daniel Lang (1974), a reporter who documented the case in great detail, noted that the hostage takers acted with both brutality and kindness. A commissioner who entered the bank to check on the hostages a few days into the ordeal noted that the environment was peculiar; the hostages were hostile towards him and almost comfortable with their captors, engaging in banter and light conversation and even smiling. After the ordeal, the hostages reported that the small kindnesses afforded them were seen as gifts and they were appreciated. They saw their captors as merely responding to the threat of police. Hostages later reported confusion in these feelings of gratitude, even though at the time they seemed rather genuine. Graham, Rawlings, and Rigsby (1994) propose 10 paradoxes of the syndrome, which are reproduced in Table 11.8.

Despite the harmful affects of

Table 11.8   Paradoxes That Are Stockholm Syndrome

Hostage perspective	Outsider's perspective
• Feel gratitude towards their captor for letting them live (or giving them their lives back).	• Believe no one had the right to willfully threaten or take another's life
• Find it difficult to feel anger towards captors; instead feel gratitude.	• Expect hostages to feel rage at captors for jeopardizing hostages' lives and subjecting them to terror.
• See captors as kind. Psychological impact of captor's small kindnesses supersedes psychological impact of terror.	• See captors as indifferent to hostages' and others' suffering.
• An open door does not look like an open door.	• Find it difficult to comprehend why hostages don't escape when they apparently have the opportunity to do so.
• Won't try to escape if given opportunity if captor might be killed in the escape attempt.	• Don't understand why hostages would be concerned about whether a captor is killed during an escape attempt; wouldn't death be a just punishment for captor?
• See captors as 'good guys' who are protecting them and police as 'bad guys' who are trying to kill them.	• See captors as 'bad guys' and police as 'good guys'.
• Are sympathetic to the politics of their captors.	• The hostages should be politically polarized against their captors.
• May refuse to testify against captors; seek leniency and may develop defence funds to help get captors off.	• Expect hostages to want their captors to receive maximum prison sentence possible for hostage taking.
• Remain loyal to captors following release, not feeling safe enough to be disloyal without expecting retribution.	• Don't understand why hostages remain loyal to their captors following release; feel the sympathy and loyalty hostages expressed while captives surely weren't real.
• Don't feel safe following release. Fear captors coming back to hold them captive again.	• Think former hostages are safe once released.

SOURCE: Graham, D. L., Rawlings, E. I., & Rigsby, R. K. (1994). *Loving to survive: Sexual terror, men's violence, and women's lives*. New York, NY: New York University Press, 12. Reprinted with permission.

Stockholm Syndrome, Turner (1990) suggests that its presence in an actual hostage negotiation situation is encouraging. It means that the victim has been somewhat successful in bonding with his or her captor and has therefore increased his or her chances of survival.

Building on these ideas, Graham, Rawlings, and Rigsby (1994) applied the idea of Stockholm Syndrome to other groups where there was an identified victim and the presence of intense, long-term abuse. They reviewed records of concentration camp prisoners, cult members, civilians in Chinese Communist Prisons, pimp-procured prostitutes, incest victims, physically and/or emotionally abused children, battered women, prisoners of war, and hostages to determine if there was evidence of similar facets of the syndrome. Although this list is not meant to be exhaustive, Graham (1987) added other victims that were not within the realm of this study, including prisoners, children, and partners of alcoholics. These additional groups, she offered, also exhibited signs of identifying with their guards and/or abusers, respectively. In all groups, there was evidence of bonding in the presence of four conditions. First, there was a genuine perceived threat to one's own survival and a strong belief that the captor was willing to carry out his or her threats. Second, the captive perceived some small kindness by the abuser. Third, captives were isolated from views other than those of the captor. Fourth, the victim had a genuine belief that he or she could not escape.

Secondary Victims of Crime and Support Networks

Unlike secondary victimization, secondary victims are those who are close to the victim, who witnessed or heard about the victimization, and/or who are at risk of becoming negatively affected by the damage inflicted on the victim (see Chapter 2). These victims are often forgotten, as they have not directly experienced the crime but have only dealt with the injured party. However, knowing that a close friend or relative has been harmed can cause emotional pain. In cases where the victim is incapacitated either emotionally and/or physically, the people who offer support find that their lives are also changed by the victimization. For example, Box 11.2 outlines the case of Julianne Courneya, who is severely disabled as a result of being victimized. She is cared for by her parents, secondary victims who not only deal with their daughter's victimization but also struggle with the demands of caring for a an injured family member. Although Courneya's identity was initially protected, her parents lobbied to have her name released, in order to help in fundraising efforts for therapies for her recovery (Banff assault victim identified, 2005).

Secondary victims are extremely important, as they are often part of the victim's support network. It is ironic that those who help victims are also victimized. Although support systems are available for direct victims of crime, similar services are often not offered to secondary victims. This deficiency may have strong implications for first responders, such as police, paramedics, and firefighters, who regularly see victimization as part of their jobs. Although this work can be exceptionally rewarding, people in these fields are often encouraged to seek out regular counselling as part of the coping strategy for doing this type of work. Table 11.9 illustrates some

Box 11.2   The After-Effects of Violent Crime on Victims: The Case of Julianne Courneya

In July 2005, Julianne Courneya was 21 years old, engaged, and six weeks pregnant. On her way home from a party in Banff, AB, she was sexually assaulted; she was found partially clothed and brutally injured. Moved to Ottawa to be with her family, Julianne was left in a vegetative state, unable to speak, control her muscles, or feed herself. Doctors have said that she will likely never recover from the attack. 'She is trapped and this is absolutely heartbreaking to witness,' her father said.

Although Julianne's attacker has been imprisoned indefinitely, the family's 'living hell' continues. They cling to hope and believe that the little things make a difference. Julianne's father reads her Harry Potter books, tucks her into bed every night, opens her window blinds every day, plays the radio, and takes her outside to feel the sun. 'I want her back,' he says. The family rallied to get the publication ban of their daughter's face and name lifted in order to elicit sympathy and financial support for a treatment in Florida known as hyperbaric oxygen therapy. Her father explains that 'Just by her picture you can see that this girl is a beautiful soul who wouldn't do anything to harm anyone, and this should never have happened to her, or anyone like her . . . she's everyone's daughter.' As of the beginning of 2008, thousands of dollars have been raised to support this treatment, but Julianne remains in a vegetative state. 'We have made a commitment to our daughter to do everything in our power to help her,' her father has said.

The assault has obviously affected Julianne's life and the life of her family. They continue to be optimistic, hoping for small improvements.

SOURCES: Banff assault victim 'everyone's daughter'. (2006, 3 November). *CBC News Online*. Retrieved 19 January 2008, from www.cbc.ca/canada/ottawa/story/2006/11/03/banff-ban.html; Zickefoose, S. (2006, 16 August). Family in 'living hell' after attack. *Calgary Herald*. Retrieved 19 January 2008, from www.canada.com/calgaryherald/news/story.html?id=63769aa2-9ccb-4ec6-8940-3d76038d51e5.

effects experienced by supporters who had different relationships with victims. This chart shows that the closer the supporter is to the victim, the more likely they are to have elevated fear levels and to take precautions at home and, to a lesser extent, outdoors.

According to Friedman et al. (1982), approximately 6 out of every 10 victim-identified supporters assisted victims on the day of the victimization. In some cases, bystanders were the first to offer support. Many victims commented that this help was unexpected and therefore greatly appreciated. Those who had experienced more serious crimes, such

as robbery, assault, and burglary were more likely to rely on an impersonal support system, such as neighbours, acquaintances, bystanders, and strangers. Friedman and colleagues suggest that this is because more violent crimes place individuals in an immediate crisis that forces them to rely on whomever is available at the moment of need.

Both Friedman et al. (1982) and Davis et al. (1999) found that the emotional support provided by the informal network of people surrounding the victim was more common than the use of more formal support systems, such as victim assistance programs. As

Table 11.9   Effect of Crime on Supporters of Strength to Ties to Victim

	Elevated fear of crime	Took precautions at home	Took precautions outdoors
Propinquity			
Lived in same neighbourhood	53%	73%	26%
Lived in different neighbourhood	34%	54%	2%
Relationship			
Intimate/blood relative	47%	68%	14%
Less close relationship	33%	49%	13%
Emotional ties			
Close ties to the victim	47%	69%	17%
Loose ties to the victim	22%	39%	0%

SOURCE: Friedman, K., Bischoff, H., Davis, R., & Person, A. (1982). *Victims and helpers: Reactions to crime.* Washington, DC: National Institute of Justice.

victims moved through the aftermath of victimization and their needs became more specific and more technical, they tended to rely more on these formal systems. Brickman (2003) found that when victims chose someone to talk to about their experiences, they chose friends or family 70 per cent of the time. Victims who reach out to these informal systems are also more likely to eventually employ more formal systems to help them cope (Ruback & Ivie, 1988).

Recovery and Resilience

Reaction to trauma, and the eventual recovery process, differs from individual to individual. Reaching out to informal support systems, such as close friends and family members, appears to have some influence on the recovery of the victim. When the victim seeks help, studies are mixed as to whether or not this helps the victim. For instance, Friedman et al. (1982) noted that, while there was little difference between victims and non-victims when dealing with crime related problems, they did find that victims reported fewer problems four months after the victimization event when they felt that they had received 'all the help they needed' from family and friends. This result is supported by Rienick, Mulmat, and Pennell (1997), who found that victims of violent crimes reported less emotional problems one month post-assault.

Traditional responses to analyzing the effects of victimization have emphasized the negative aspects of trauma. Trauma, albeit negative, generates different responses from individuals. As previously mentioned, some people can find an act of victimization severely disturbing, while others report only minor effects. The idea that some victims are more resilient than others has become a recent focus of study. In particular, some researchers are not only interested in the effects of trauma but also in why some victims seem to recover more quickly than others. Instead of studying the negative aftermath of victim experience, they attempt to understand what makes some people less vulnerable to the effects of victimization.

The Positive Psychology Movement

The positive psychology movement (Seligman & Csikszentmihalyi, 2000; Sheldon & King, 2001) allows researchers to conduct research and clinical practice in both the negative and positive aspects of the human condition, including the areas of well-being, hope and optimism, and affirmative emotions. Within this positive category, researchers are beginning to look at encouraging and protective responses to crime such as capacities for love, courage, interpersonal skill, perseverance, forgiveness, and wisdom. They also seek to understand civic virtues such as responsibility, nurturance, altruism, civility, and tolerance (Peterson & Seligman, 2004; Seligman & Csikszentmihalyi, 2000).

Violence and trauma tend to challenge people's core values and raise questions about their meaning and purpose in life (Janoff-Bulman & Frantz, 1997). As a result, many who have experienced adversity and/or trauma have either sought out spirituality for the first time or turned to pre-existing beliefs. Those who have strong religious or spiritual faith understand that these can bring comfort in times of distress. Ai, Peterson, and Huang (2003) suggest that spiritual faith can be a strong internal motivating resource bolstering mental resources available to the victim. Therefore, another area of interest in this movement is the role of spirituality and religion in coping with adversity (Hill & Pargament, 2003; McCullough,

Hoyt, Larson, Koenig, & Thoresen, 2000; Pargament, 1997; Peterson & Seligman, 2004).

According to Ai and Park (2005), both of these emerging areas seem to be signalling a strong change not only in the study of victimology but also in the way we look at victims. Rather than seeing victimization as exclusively negative, it may soon be more likely to be seen as a critical point to understanding what makes us stronger. They provide opportunities to more completely understand survivors of violence and trauma by looking at both the negative and positive aspects of the victimization experience. Attention is given to the potentially positive aspects of protection, resilience, and growth that many survivors also experience. Ai and Park assert that the first studies coming out of this movement suggest that general expectancies, such as a victim having hope and being optimistic about a positive outcome, play a role in aiding post-traumatic recovery. Religiosity and spirituality can also influence post-traumatic adjustment. Trauma may also affect religious experience and spirituality. For example, individuals may adopt a religious ideology or become more intense in their belief system after an assault, perhaps attributing spiritual meaning to the event. Others may abandon their faith in response to the trauma they have experienced. Finally, positive life changes and growth can occur following traumatic experiences which, in turn, may help in adjusting to victimization.

Summary

This chapter has examined various aftereffects of victimization. What happens after victimization in terms of victim experience is not well documented, partly because being a victim is a very sensitive issue. The more personal and/or stigmatizing the victimization, the more difficult it is for individuals to disclose this information to researchers. However, victimologists continue to seek out details from a variety of disciplines to aid in our understanding of this process.

Victimization can include loss of property or personal injury. More traumatic injury, or series of injuries, can result in more serious reactions to the experience. In severe cases of victimization, victims may exhibit patterns of behaviour collectively known as Post-Traumatic Stress Disorder (PTSD). In more rare cases, where the victimization is prolonged, some individuals may develop another complex of symptoms known as Stockholm Syndrome. Beyond psychological reactions to crime, victims can experience social consequences and financial loss that continue to create challenges long after the event.

These trends all appear to be extremely negative. For the most part, however, people recover from these experiences and go on to live fulfilling and happy lives. Victimization may not be as damaging as our studies have led us to believe. Not all victims become irreparably damaged; if they did, society would not be able to function. Helping others through negative times can also be an exceptionally rewarding experience. There is some evidence that strong familial, social, and even spiritual support networks may serve to protect individuals from the most negative aspects of victimization. Researchers are not only attempting to understand the negative effects of victimization, but they are also seeking to understand what personality and social aspects of individuals protect against the long-term mental and physical damage caused by victimization.

Glossary

actual direct victim An individual who experiences an actual victimization.

actual indirect victim An individual who is traumatized by witnessing an actual victimization. This type of victim fears for him- or herself but not in a direct response to an actual victimization risk.

cognitive appraisal The process by which an individual perceives his or her environment to be dangerous or safe.

concrete fear The fear of specific events, such as fear of specific criminal victimization.

contagion effect The spread of the effects of fear from one person to another or from one community to another.

'curfew' A self-restrictive behaviour of women, born out of the fear of being assaulted, which limits the ability to take advantage of opportunities afforded to men who hold less fear engaging in activities at night.

direct fear A form of fear that occurs as a result of actual victimization.

direct victimization Victimization that produces fear in the moment, in response to a specific situation.

eustress A term originally coined by psychologist Richard Lazarus which refers to a type of stress that has positive or beneficial effects.

fear of crime Generally, a response to a threat and the fear of being harmed.

formless fear A more general, unfixed fear of victimization which can be interpreted as an overall anxiety about victimization unconnected to any specific victimization experience or threat.

General Adaptation Syndrome (GAS)
An influential model of the physiological response to stress introduced in the 1930s by endocrinologist Hans Selye. The central theme behind GAS is that individuals are biologically programmed to react to threats in three stages: alarm, resistance, and exhaustion.

indirect fear A less intense form of fear that does not involve being directly exposed to victimization.

indirect victimization Victimization that occurs as the result of witnessing or hearing of the direct victimization of another.

positive feedback The process of neighbourhood decline occurs through *positive feedback*, whereby fear can not only enable decline, but can continue to add to the process. This process is considered 'positive' because the process is additive; preconditions add to subsequent conditions, and so on.

Post-Traumatic Stress Disorder (PTSD) A disorder caused by exposure to extremely traumatic and stressful situations that fall outside the realm of normal, everyday individual experiences. These situations include severe accidents, acts of war, sexual assault, child abuse, severe intimate partner abuse, and natural disasters.

ripple effect The spreading of fear that occurs when people hear about the victimization of others.

secondary victimization The process whereby the victim is victimized by the criminal justice or medical systems through the process of investigation of the reported victimization incident. This subsequent victimization occurs when the victim is treated with mistrust or suspicion and/or his or her credibility is questioned. Members of these systems may also attempt to blame the victim for his or her own victimization.

significant others Coined by George Herbert Mead, a term that refers to those people who serve as an individual's close support network and whose opinions he or she values.

Stockholm Syndrome A rare psychological and emotional process whereby a victim (usually a hostage or an abused person) identifies with and feels a strong attachment toward his or her victimizer.

stress A physical and/or psychological set of reactions to demanding situations.

stressors The demanding or threatening situations (or stimuli) that produce stress.

vicarious direct victim An individual who has no direct exposure to a victimization but is so strongly affected by learning of the event that he or she experiences the same intensity of fear and many of the symptoms as the direct victim.

vicarious indirect victim An individual who hears of the victimization of another and learns from the event. The resulting fear levels are lowest in this type of victim, who may or may not change his or her behaviour.

Critical Thinking Questions

1. In what ways has fear restricted the behaviour of individuals? Organizations? Governments?

2. What are some of the implications of studying only the damage caused by victimization?

3. What do the following statements have in common? How can they be applied to victimization experiences?

    I am not a victim, but a survivor.

    That which does not kill you, makes you stronger.

    Every cloud has a silver lining.

4. Can symptoms associated with Stockholm Syndrome explain some victims' reactions to intimate partner violence? Why or why not?
5. How are the symptoms of PTSD unique to victims of crime as opposed to victims of other kinds of trauma?

CHAPTER 12

Resources for Victims in the Criminal and Civil Justice Systems

Learning Objectives

After reading this chapter, you will be able to

- examine options made available to victims as they move through the criminal and civil justice systems, using the illustration of those who have experienced intimate partner violence;
- examine the roles, benefits, and unintended consequences of victim impact statements;
- comprehend the physical, emotional, and financial costs of exercising these options, many of which must be exercised simultaneously; and
- examine the issues in creating a victims' bill of rights.

Introduction

A crime victim is faced with a number of resources offered by the criminal and civil justice systems to deal with victimization. The availability of these options depends on the type of crime experienced and, in many cases, whether the victim chooses to exercise them. This chapter will examine the advantages and disadvantages of several of these resources and how they often must be used simultaneously. While these options can be applied to most crimes, our focus will be on intimate partner violence. Awareness of this crime forced the system to respond to its victims' unique needs and helped to initiate some of the options included here. We will also discuss the efficacy of victim impact statements, victims' satisfaction with their justice system experiences, and efforts to create a victims' bill of rights in Canada.

What the Criminal Justice System Can Offer the Victim

At present, the criminal justice system is limited in what it can offer the victim, largely because it is a vast and, for the most part, cumbersome structure. As a system of interrelated parts (which are often out of sync), its concerns are primarily with the accused. The victim, although intrinsic to the process of identification, apprehension, and punishment of those who victimize, is often treated as secondary. He or she is a key witness, in many cases essential to the successful prosecution of an accused, but is often given less attention. Nowhere is this more clearly evident than in cases of domestic violence, and more specifically intimate partner violence.

Traditionally, we have referred to the violence between heterosexual couples as domestic violence. However, this term did not encapsulate all partner types and was often confused with other forms of violence in the home, such as child abuse, elder abuse, and so on. Therefore, **intimate partner violence (IPV)** is now the preferred term for violence between individuals who are living in, or who have lived in, an intimate relationship. IPV can occur between partners who are currently living or who have previously lived in a common-law, married, or civil union partnership. In particular, IPV is a more encompassing term which also captures violence that occurs between those people who are divorced, separated, or have ceased to live in an intimate partnership. The term also includes the more rare violence that can exist in partnerships involving more than two individuals. **Domestic violence** now refers to all violence that occurs within the home, most often between family members. This master category includes intimate partner violence as well as all other forms of violence that can take place under domestic circumstances, such as child abuse, elder abuse, and violence between siblings and/or between other family members.

Victims of IPV have reported a number of crimes committed against them, including physical assault, sexual assault, sexual harassment, stalking, economic deprivation, verbal degradation, and ongoing emotional abuse. In the extreme, many have identified being subjected to 'intimate terrorism' (Graham-Kevan & Archer, 2003; Johnson, 2000), a term that refers to a process of severe abuse similar to that experienced by prisoners of war. **Intimate terrorism** is a process where physical and/or sexual violence are some of the many tactics used with the explicit desire to control one's partner,

often completely. Under the process of intimate terrorism techniques, the partner of the abuser becomes a prisoner of the relationship, whereby all aspects of daily activity are controlled and can be accompanied by circumstances of extreme economic, nutritional, and/or physical deprivation.

Special Case: Intimate Partner Violence

Most common-law systems assume that all are equal before the law. Put another way, it is assumed that everyone who uses the system is afforded the same level of service and protection, regardless of race, gender, religious beliefs, sexual orientation, and so on. For the most part, the Canadian criminal justice system attempts to uphold these principles.

There are some cases, however, that have challenged the system by demonstrating an inherent flaw within it. The law has traditionally assumed that all *men* are equal before the law. Thinking about this statement more critically reveals that the law assumed that women are the same as men in all ways and operate the same way in varying situations. This includes the idea that men and women are physically of the same stature and strength. Therefore, under common law, one should only respond with like force if threatened. This puts women at a unique disadvantage if under physical and/or sexual threat.

For example, if a man is attacked by another, he is allowed to defend himself, but only to the point of deterring his attacker. In other words, if the men exchange words but no physical action is initiated by the victimizer, the victim cannot use physical force. If unprovoked physical force is used by the target of verbal threats, he risks being charged if the police are called, as his level of force in response to a perceived threat was considered excessive.

Although all are recognized as equal before the law, the assumptions of physical equality stem from these older ideas of androcentric, or male-centred, law. In a more traditional system, men were the primary participants in the legal system, both as those who worked within it and those who were subject to it. Violence patterns recognized under the law were usually those committed by males, in that the victim and the victimizer were more likely to be strangers or acquaintances, younger, and so on. As women and other minorities were given the right to vote in Canada, the law also included them as equal citizens. However, it often failed to recognize the different concerns of women, including the victimization patterns they experienced. Women were less likely to be involved in stranger or acquaintance interactions and were more likely to be victimized by their intimate partners. In cases where women were feeling threatened, their unequal physical strength, as well as their position in a patriarchal society, were initially not taken into consideration. Women essentially were treated like men under the law but lacked the physical attributes and the social opportunities of men, leading to inherent inequality between the sexes.

With the rise of the Civil Rights and Women's movements in both Canada and the United States came the recognition of the equal but different rights of women. Essentially, it was acknowledged that it was important for the law to treat women and minorities as

equal and to be *equitable* where there were needs not being addressed by the criminal justice system. In other words, women and minorities are considered equal, *but different.* As with the earlier example, women who are involved in a physical altercation are also permitted to use the physical force needed to deter their victimizer. However, because of their often smaller stature, women may not be able to use the same amount of physical force against a male victimizer. If a woman in an abusive relationship is dependent on her partner's wage-earning, she may have difficulty in taking steps to deter the abuse.

The case of intimate partner violence is a good example when considering the options available to people who are feeling threatened. The recognition of the unique dynamics of IPV has spurred several initiatives and new programs to help women in this situation. In essence, these additional measures recognize that more traditional legal methods have been ineffective and have not served the special circumstances of the victimizer being within the close-knit circle of the family.

Responses for Victims of Intimate Partner Violence

IPV victims who require a more formal response from the criminal justice system may find that it is somewhat awkward in dealing with their specific needs. The irony is that because the victimizers are family, many of the standards of dealing with this situation create problems for the system. For example, in an assault where the perpetrator is not a family member, the crime is usually reported by the victim or a witness. The system is engaged and the police begin the process of investigation. However, when the victimizer is an intimate partner, the normal routes for bringing the victimization event to the attention of the criminal justice system become somewhat hindered. Victims of IPV may choose not to report the crime for various reasons, including fear of retribution and/or further violence, promises from the victimizer that the abuse will stop, fear that they will not be believed, fear of economic hardship, and the disturbance of the family unit (Department of Justice, 2001). Often women who are victims of IPV report being victimized several times before the police were eventually called (Statistics Canada, 2007).

People who witness intimate partner violence also tend not to report the victimization. Strangers to the family unit may not want to get involved. Family members who witness the abuse may be too young, as in the case of children, to act to protect the victim. As a result, the normal social systems that detect victimization falter when the victimizer is the intimate partner of the victim. Because the violence occurs in the context of family, many dismiss it as a private matter.

Therefore, the system depends on the victim or a witness to report abuse in order for it to react. Without detection or reporting, there is no chance of eventual punishment of the victimizer. When the system does not become involved to resolve an abusive situation and attempt to protect the victim, the violence continues until it is no longer feasible. This result can happen in one of three ways. First, the victimizer may simply stop abusing the victim because he or she realizes that it is no longer desirable. Such an outcome is rare, unless there is an outward motivator such as a witness or a legal response. Second, the victim can

successfully evade the abuser and escape the situation; however doing so is often a difficult response, as the victim may have to consider other family members (such as children) in the escape plan. This result is the most common response to this situation. Finally, the victim may eventually succumb to his or her injuries. The criminal justice system is called into action when the death is detected.

Options for Victims of Intimate Partner Violence within the Criminal Justice System

In many ways, the criminal justice system has been forced to deal with the needs of special victims, such as those who suffer from violence at the hands of someone they love. When confronted with an intimate partner violence situation, the victim can choose from several options, which are either legitimate or illegitimate. **Legitimate options** are those options where the recourse does not harm the victim. **Illegitimate options** are those that may hurt those who have called for help. For each option, the underlying cause of the reaction to the intimate partner violence is explored. Although these options are discussed in terms of intimate partner violence, they are, either in whole or in part, available to all crime victims, depending on the specific situation.

Option One: The Victim Can Ignore the Situation

The first option for the victim is to simply ignore the abuse. The victim may choose to do this for several reasons, but the outcome is the same: the violence stays between the victim and the victimizer with no outside influences. This option is an illegitimate one because it serves to enable the victimizer to continue the abuse. The relationship between the two parties remains intact unless acted upon by one or the other. The victim is at a unique disadvantage in this situation if the relationship uses violence or intimidation as a form of communication. He or she continues to be intimidated by violence, or the threat of violence, and has few options for self-protection.

In this option, the victim decides to manage the victimizer's behaviour to the best of his or her ability, often at personal peril. The police are not involved, and the violence will more than likely continue. This option is frequently the first response to a violent situation. When the violence does not stop, other options are often explored.

Option Two: The Victim Can Handle the Violence Informally

The second option is that the victim can acknowledge the violence but seek to resolve the situation through a multitude of informal methods which do not involve initiating a police response. For example, the victim can threaten the offender with action, such as leaving, telling family members, or calling the police. The effectiveness of these threats can vary. Another possibility under this option is that the IPV victim can call members of his or her support system, such as family members and friends, and ask for their assistance. This support system can react in several ways. First, they can encourage the victim to ignore the violence. This response assumes that the relationship is paramount and that to bring attention to the violent behaviour within it will threaten its stability. A second set of responses includes verbally

counselling the offender against violence or (in some cases) using threats or acts of physical violence to deter the abuser from continuing to use violence against the victim. The more severe the response, the greater the assumption by the support network that the violence should not continue. Informal responses have different degrees of effectiveness.

Option Three: The Police Are Called but Choose to Ignore the Situation

If informal responses fail to stop IPV, a third option available to victims is police intervention. In this option, the police are eventually involved, either by the victim or someone else who detects that a crime is being committed. This step is a crucial one because the criminal justice system is being called into action. It cannot react without a complaint. Officers assess the situation and, in cases of IPV, may determine that there is evidence of spousal violence. They then have several options on how to react to the situation. The first of these is to do nothing.

The underlying cause of doing nothing at entrance into the criminal justice system is based on the police officers' perception that action will be ineffective. In many ways, the police act as what Goffman (1963) called a 'gatekeeper', or as an entry point into the criminal justice system. If they decide to ignore the situation, the criminal justice system will cease in its reaction. Officers may choose this option for several reasons. In the case of IPV, they may feel that there will be no long-term change or that calling the police is simply part of the fundamental dynamics of an abusive relationship. They may also feel that arresting the victimizer will ultimately be ineffectual; the victimizer will just return to the household, and the victim will let him or her back in. Option three is an illegitimate option because the response by the police allows for the risk of violence against the victim to continue.

Option Four: The Police Are Called and Choose to Counsel the Participants

If the police intervene in a domestic situation but find no evidence of abuse, they may consider counselling the couple a legitimate option. When done properly, this option offers participants specific information. For example, the victimizer is warned against the possibility of arrest if the police are called back to the location. Officers may also offer other precautions against continued violence such as professional counselling, therapy, and self-help courses such as anger management classes.

When officers offer the option of counselling instead of more punitive measures, the underlying assumption is that the relationship should be preserved. This option is often chosen because, while it is clear that there has been some sort of dispute, there is no clear evidence that violence has occurred. The service is offered with the understanding that one participant may initiate a breakup at any time. The problem with this approach is that it is somewhat inappropriate. Often the offending participant will not be violent or intimidating toward his or her partner in front of an officer. Although this option used to be thought of as a legitimate response to intimate partner violence calls for service, offering a non-punitive solution is currently considered an illegitimate response because it continues to place the person who is

being abused at risk by leaving him or her in a relatively unchanged situation.

Option Five: The Police Are Called and Choose to Send One Party Away

Like options three and four, this option involves police intervention. In this case, however, police may attempt to resolve the dispute by sending one party, usually the identified abuser, away from the scene of the abuse for a period of time, typically anywhere from 12 to 24 hours. There are various ways in which this option can be exercised. A more punitive response is to detain the offender for 24 hours. By removing the offender, the victim has an opportunity to leave if he or she desires. The police can also encourage the victim to find another place to stay 'for a little while'. One or all of these responses can be used, depending on the assessment of the situation by the responding police unit.

These extraction methods used to be considered legitimate responses to intimate partner violence. However, they have fallen into disfavour for many of the same reasons as identified for option four. All of the strategies presume that the victim, once separated from the victimizer, will be able to exercise choices that he or she could not with the abuser present. Although this assumption appears to have value on first examination, it ignores some serious practical issues. For example, a victim dealing with the effects of the abuse and the police response may have difficulty making complicated and life-changing decisions in a single day. In addition, there are often no financial means to follow up on relocation plans, even if they were available in such a short period of time. If children are involved, their lives must also be taken into consideration—such as the effects of pulling them from one school and placing them in another, disrupting the family unit, and so on—which may severely complicate any relocation response by the victim. Additionally, if the victim is encouraged to find another living accommodation for some period of time, he or she experiences the additional penalty of being uprooted after being victimized.

The underlying assumptions in this option are the same as in option four: the relationship, although in crisis, will more than likely remain intact and may benefit from the parties spending time away from one another. Officers may feel that nothing will come of arresting the offender and/or the victim. Some officers understand that arresting someone who is the household's sole wage earner may also harm the family and therefore choose not to disrupt the relationship.

Option Six: Arrest

Arresting the presumed offender is currently the preferred legitimate method of dealing with domestic violence. Most police services in Canada have a **mandatory arrest policy**, which requires officers to arrest offenders of this crime. The initial extraction can be anywhere from three to four hours to three to four days, potentially giving the victim more time to decide on leaving the situation. The victim may be assisted with relocation, although this usually does not occur without agency involvement. The option of going to a shelter with children is available only to women escaping IPV. Shelters for men currently do not accept men with children. If a female victim is willing to go to a public facility, her ability to do so will depend on availability of spaces and

the location of that facility. Small towns and rural communities do not often have these services and may require the victim, and any children she may have, to travel significant distances. Men who are escaping violence and who have children have to make alternative arrangements.

Under the mandatory arrest policy, the criminal justice system asserts that the relationship could benefit from a separation of the victim and the victimizer (either temporary or permanent). Officers may feel that the imposed change is more symbolic than substantive. Although this response is more formal than the others, the victim still faces many of the obstacles mentioned above. This response does have the added advantage that the system decides to make the arrest. In the third, fourth, and fifth options mentioned above, a victim who wants to pursue more formal punishment options, such as arrest, has to press charges against the abuser. The abuser, in turn, could try to get the victim to withdraw the charge by negotiating with him or her, usually using threats and/or violence.

Another alternative to this option is a **dual arrest policy**. These policies currently do not exist across Canada but are used in parts of the United States. Dual arrest policies instruct officers to arrest both parties in a dispute. This policy can be applied to intimate partner violence but also other forms of physical disputes, such as two men fighting in a bar. If both parties are fighting in front of witnesses and/or at the time of the initial response and investigation by police, then both parties are arrested. Likewise, in some cases, if both parties clearly have physical signs of having been violent but are not violent in front of investigating officers or witnesses, both may be arrested. In this process, the system treats the victim and the victimizer in the same way. This policy is currently not considered a legitimate option because the fear of arrest may deter victims from calling the police when they are being threatened. If arrested, the victim is punished for calling for help.

Option Seven: Restraining Orders (ROs), Peace Bonds, and Terms of Release

A **restraining order (RO)** is a legitimate response that is initiated after arrest and prolongs separation between a victim and his or her offender. In the United States, there are similar orders called 'orders of protection'. In essence these orders are a 'stay away for a while' mandate for the victimizer. An RO must be issued by a judge in a court hearing and can last anywhere from a few days to a few months or even longer. These orders are valid only in the province in which they were made and can often take several months to obtain, as evidence must be gathered and presented before the court. Both the victim and the abuser can present this evidence to support or challenge the order, respectively. In order for an RO to be issued, the judge must believe that the victim's fear is reasonable.

In Canada, if the victim feels immediately threatened and does not want to wait for an RO, he or she can receive an interim order known as an *ex parte order*, which can be issued without the presence of the accused abuser and if the judge agrees that the concern for safety is immediate and reasonable. *Ex parte* orders are issued for between 24 hours and 1 week so that the victim will be safe while the victimizer is notified and allowed to respond to the order.

The RO is not effective until the offender has been officially served with a copy of the order.

Restraining orders can be made more permanent if both parties appear before a judge in a formal hearing. New evidence, which often includes the arrest of the victimizer, must be provided to assure the court that an extension of the order is required. Extensions may also be granted if one or both parties are not able to appear at the hearing. If the offender is arrested as a result of police investigations, he or she may be served in jail. If the offender evades arrest, service may not be possible for some time.

A more permanent restraining order serves to prolong separation of the victim and offender, formalizes the distance between the two parties, and announces that their relationship is in the process of dissolution. The terms of the order may also be extended to include items such as financial support or child custody and support. In small towns where there is no clerk or clergy, this order may function as a legal separation or divorce, effectively ending cohabitation. When these orders are granted it is assumed that the relationship is beyond repair and that, for the safety of all involved, cohabitation should end.

According to Fraser (n.d.), **peace bonds** are granted via the courts and can be enforced anywhere in Canada. The issuance of a peace bond means that the provisions of the Criminal Code were used to make the request and not those of the Family Law Act; as a result breaking the terms of a peace bond constitutes a criminal code offence. The offender must keep the peace by meeting the requirements of the bond until such time as it expires. He or she may also be asked for a financial assurance of up to $1,000—violation of this bond results in a forfeiture of the money with the possibility of further fines or a term of imprisonment. In some cases, the courts can issue **mutual peace bonds**, whereby both the victim and the offender are prohibited from contacting one another. The underlying assumption with this type of bond is that the victim may provoke the victimizer and thereby be partially responsible for the victimization or for the breaking of the bond.

Terms of release are requirements that an offender must meet in order to be released from jail. These terms are set out in a hearing that usually takes place within a few days of the victimizer's initial arrest. In cases of intimate partner violence, the judge may require that the abuser stay away from the victim. There also may be other requirements issued at this time. For example, the offender can be ordered to refrain from using drugs or alcohol or to refrain from associating with others with a criminal record. Terms of release expire when the victimizer has been found guilty or not guilty, either by trial or plea.

Restraining orders, peace bonds, and terms of release are thought to be mechanisms that a victim can use for further protection. He or she is advised of the initial option of a restraining order if it is felt that he or she is at increased risk for further violence. However, their value is often not appreciated by those who apply for them. It is often felt that they are symbolic gestures; after all, they are only pieces of paper. Fraser (n.d.) claims that these orders are also often poorly enforced. Legally, however, they do provide impetus to police to remove the offender before further violence occurs.

Penalties vary from province to province and state to state. Many of these cases are handled in Family Court in both Canada and the United States, although some states prosecute such offences in criminal court.

Option Eight: Civil Court Options

In addition to the options mention above, the victim has several legitimate **civil court options** available to him or her, which involve a series of actions that take place in the civil, as opposed to the criminal, court system. This option can also be exercised outside or in tandem with any of the seven other options. Options for victims are vast, and are made in consultation with a civil attorney. They can include filing a small claims application or filing a more substantial financial claim. In the case of IPV, additional options available to the victim include filing for legal separation and dissolution of the marriage. Filing the documents required for separation and beginning the process of dissolving the relationship may involve the negotiation of assets or debt, as well as any custody considerations that must be brought before the court. In Canada, a couple is legally separated once they are living in separate living accommodations and apart from one another. Reconciliation is still an option at this point.

Legally dissolving a marriage, which usually occurs after a legal separation, is another legitimate civil option that a victim can employ to remove him- or herself from IPV. Canadian law requires that one of the following situations be present as grounds for divorce: the couple has been living separately for more than one year, one or both partners have committed adultery, or one or both partners have been mentally or physically cruel toward the other or toward each other. In some cases, perpetrators of IPV have used this civil process, in particular the separation/custody/divorce proceedings, to prolong their ability to inflict emotional abuse and financial hardship on the victim by using delay tactics such as not showing up for court appearances, not filing papers on time, and so on. Divorce ends the relationship on a permanent basis but without spatial restrictions unless accompanied by a restraining order, peace bond, and/or terms of release.

Option Nine: Prosecution

Prosecution is a legitimate **criminal court option** for individuals who have been victimized. This process is often long and drawn out. Under common law, the accused is presumed innocent until proven guilty in a court of law. As such, the court will make provisions to allow the accused to live a life with a minimal amount of disruption if the Crown does not express a fear for public safety and/or the safety of the victim or that the accused may not appear at the next proceeding. If the offender is released on his or her own recognizance while awaiting trial, with or without conditions, the victim may be at considerable risk. As with civil proceedings, the legal fees for this process are expensive for both parties. However, where the Crown is involved, lawyer fees are handled by the state. Other costs, such as the costs of counselling, time spent away from work, childcare costs if needed, and so on, are not covered and are expected to be paid by the victim. In cases of IPV, as with civil court options, the accused may use the trial to prolong the relationship, by delaying court dates, making unreasonable requests, and so on.

Effectiveness of the Options Offered by the Criminal Justice System for IPV Victims

Currently many of the options discussed in the previous section must be exercised by the victim. He or she is often the person who brings in the police and gives them the evidence needed to arrest the attacker. If the victim is reasonably fearful for his or her safety, he or she must find legal counsel to initiate the process of getting a restraining order and then follow up on that order by getting other bonds and terms of release documents. If the couple is cohabitating and these processes are being used, it is also likely that the victim must secure a residence separate from the victimizer and start the separation, divorce, and/or custody processes. These actions must all be done while coping with the victimization and managing any children that the victim may have.

Another criticism has been launched at the use of restraining orders and the assumptions by those who administer and enforce them. Postmus (2007) has identified four common myths associated with these orders: women who seek restraining orders are not really abused but want a quick way to get custody of their children; battered women rarely follow through with the hearing and waste the court's time; compared to men, battered women are awarded unfair stipulations and benefits in restraining orders because of judicial bias and the presence of an attorney; and restraining orders are not effective and may cause more problems for victims. These misconceptions, according to Postmus, all assume that restraining orders have become a tool of relationship management. These attitudes can have serious implications for enforcement of these orders.

For example, officers often report to a call for service to find the target of the restraining order in the victim's home. Even though the victimizer is often there at the victim's invitation, the victim allegedly requires his or her removal because their discussions of a future relationship have come to an impasse. Officers view this behaviour as 'self-violating' and feel that the RO should become invalid if the victim violates its terms. Furthermore, the victim is obviously not afraid of the offender but is simply using the RO to gain an upper hand in the relationship. Advocates find this type of thinking faulty. The RO is not taken out against the victim, therefore he or she cannot be found in violation of its terms. It is the victim's right to try to re-establish a relationship if he or she sees fit. Although there may be cases of 'pseudo-victims' who use the legal system as a relationship management tool, these cases are rare. Regardless, they become the standard by which other, genuine cases are measured.

The adoption of a mandatory arrest policy in some parts of Canada and the United States over the last few decades represents an option that removes much of the responsibility for arrest from the victim and has been considered by many as a positive step forward in the fight against IPV (Miller, 2001). The purpose of this policy is to increase the number of arrests stemming from domestic violence and to reduce police discretion when dealing with complaints of this nature (Frye, Haviland, & Rajah, 2007; Miller, 2001). There is some evidence to suggest that this approach is having a positive effect. In the United States, the National Crime Victimization Survey (Dugan, 2003) found that in states with mandatory arrest policies female householders self-report fewer experiences with domestic violence. Salazar et al. (2003) also found that this policy may be having an effect on social attitudinal norms regarding domestic violence. In other words, Salazar stated that the results imply that the tolerance for IPV is decreasing, forcing potential abusers to rethink their options before considering violence against an intimate partner.

Although there may be benefits to the policy, other studies suggest that there are also some unintended effects for the victim, such as creating the impetus to implement 'dual arrest' policies and therefore the possibility of increasing the proportion of arrests of women (Hirschel & Buzawa, 2002; Jones & Belknap, 1999; Martin, 1997). Most experts agree that the 'escape and terminate' option is ultimately the healthiest option for all involved. If the victim can leave the violent relationship at the earliest opportunity, with or without pressing charges or following any of the subsequent steps, he or she is most likely to experience less injury. Ironically, it is this very action of leaving the relationship that may put the victim at the greatest risk for increased violence.

Victim Impact Statements

Historically, the victim has moved from being active in small tribal communities to passive in early common-law systems and back to active in the 1970s with the growth of the Victim's Movement. In the 1970s articles appeared in law journals about the rights of victims and the needs of their families. Western nations saw the advent of rape crises centres, domestic violence shelters, crisis hotlines, and victim impact statements.

A **victim impact statement (VIS)** is a written or oral statement presented in court that allows the victim to go beyond the visible harm caused by the victimization and to describe the impact of the victimization, including additional physical, financial, and/or emotional hardships that he or she has experienced. The victim may also be permitted to make a sentencing recommendation as part of his or her statement. VISs can be prepared by or in concert with the victim. Victims may not be able to attend court to make the VIS for a variety of reasons, including severe physical or mental illness, emotional inability to attend, fearfulness, or (in the case of victims of homicide) death. If the victim cannot make the statement, a representative (such as his or her attorney, a surviving family member, a parent/guardian, a spouse, a close relative, or a dependent) can create one on his or her behalf. An example of a VIS form issued in Manitoba is shown in Box 12.1.

VISs can be introduced at various

Box 12.1   Manitoba Victim Impact Statement Form

When completed please forward to the Crown attorney's office.

Name of victim: _____

Police Incident Number: _____

Date of Offence: _____

Police agency the incident was reported to: _____

Charges (if known): _____

Name of offender (if known): _____

Town, city or community where the incident occurred: _____

Relationship to the offender (if any): _____

You can ask to read your statement in court. If you would like to do so, please check the following box:

☐ **I wish to read my statement aloud in court.**

Please Note: The court will be informed if you wish to read your Victim Impact Statement in court; however, if you are not present at the hearing, sentencing will proceed.

If you are not the direct victim, please indicate why you have completed this statement and your relationship to the victim.

Name: _____

Relationship to the victim: _____

Reason: _____

_____

Ces renseignements sont également offerts en français.

PLEASE COMPLETE THE FOLLOWING SECTIONS

(Please print or write clearly. If you need more space, please attach additional pages.)

1. Emotional Impact:

Please describe how the crime has affected you emotionally.

Consider the effect of the crime on your life. For example:

- emotions, feelings and reactions
- spiritual feelings
- lifestyle and activities
- relations with your partner, spouse, friends, family or colleagues
- ability to work, study or attend school
- counselling or therapy provided

_____

_____

_____

_____

_____

_____

2. Impact:

Please describe any physical injuries or disabilities that you suffered because of the crime. For example:

- pain, hospitalization, surgery you have experienced because of the crime
- treatment, physiotherapy and/or medication you have received
- ongoing physical pain, discomfort, illness, scarring, disfigurement or physical restriction
- need for further treatment, or expectation that you will receive further treatment
- permanent or long-term disability

_____

_____

_____

_____

_____

3. Financial Impact:

Please describe any financial or property losses that resulted from the crime. For example:

- the value of any property that was lost or destroyed and the cost of repairs or replacement

- insurance coverage and the amount of the deductible you paid
- financial loss due to missed time from work
- the cost of medical expenses, therapy or counselling
- any costs not covered by insurance

_____

_____

_____

_____

_____

_____

This is not an application for financial compensation or restitution. If you wish to inquire about compensation, contact the Compensation for Victims of Crime Program at (204) 945-0899 (Winnipeg) or toll free: 1-800-262-9344.

4. Other Comments or Concerns:

Please describe any other concerns that have arisen as a result of the crime. For example:

- other ways your life has changed because of the crime
- how you feel about contact with the offender

_____

_____

_____

_____

_____

_____

IMPORTANT:

When you submit your Victim Impact Statement to the Crown attorney, your statement will be disclosed. This means a copy of your statement will be forwarded to the offender and/or the offender's lawyer.

The statements that I have made above are true to the best of my knowledge. I understand that this information will be submitted to the offender or the offender's lawyer and may be submitted to the court if there is a sentencing hearing. I understand that I may be called upon to testify in court if any information in this Victim Impact Statement is questioned. I also understand that if this statement is filed in open court, it becomes a public document and discussions around the content of the statement may be presented and recorded on the court record. I am submitting this statement voluntarily.

Signature of Victim: _____ **Date:** _____

> **Please complete the following if translation services were provided in the preparation of this statement:**
>
> I did faithfully and to the best of my ability translate and interpret in the _____ language, the contents of this Victim Impact Statement to the victim named herein, who indicated an understanding of the said contents.
>
> Name: _____ Occupation: _____

Note: Community and Youth Correctional Services may use your Victim Impact Statement when writing Pre-Sentence Reports, or for other case management purposes. Pre-Sentence Reports are used by the judge when deciding an appropriate sentence for the offender.

Notice about personal information and personal health information.
The personal information and personal health information on this form is collected by the Prosecutions Branch of Manitoba Justice under the authority of the Criminal Code (Canada) and The Victims' Bill of Rights of Manitoba. It will be used and disclosed as stated on this form.

Your personal information and personal health information are protected by The Freedom of Information and Protection of Privacy Act (FIPPA) of Manitoba and The Personal Health Information Act (PHIA) of Manitoba. We cannot use your information for any other purpose without your consent, unless the law permits it or requires it. We cannot share your information outside Manitoba Justice without your consent, unless the law permits or requires this.

If you have any questions or concerns about your Victim Impact Statement, contact a Crime Victim Services Worker or a Crown attorney at the number(s) provided on the Personal Information Sheet

SOURCE: Manitoba Justice. (n.d.). Victim impact statement form. Retrieved 14 June 2010, from www.gov.mb.ca/justice/victims/pdf/victimimpactstatementform.pdf. Permission to reproduce this form is provided by the Queen's Printer for Manitoba. The Queen's Printer does not warrant the accuracy or currency of the reproduction of this information.

stages of the legal process. In Canada and in many parts of the United States, they are allowed at sentencing and, in some instances, at bail hearings, plea bargaining sessions, and parole hearings. In Canada, the VIS is used only after an offender is found or has pleaded guilty. These statements have been rendered in the sentencing process and to a lesser extent are an option during plea negotiation.

The Criminal Code of Canada specifically allows victims to present VISs at sentencing:

722 (1) For the purpose of determining the sentence to be imposed on an offender or whether the offender should be *discharged* pursuant to section 730 in respect to any offence, the court shall consider any statement that may have been prepared in accordance with subsection (2) of a victim of the offence describing the harm done to, or loss suffered by the victim arising from the commission of the offence.

722 (2) A statement referred to in subsection (1) must be prepared in

writing in the form and in accordance with the procedures established by a program designed for that purpose by the lieutenant governor in council of the province in which the court is exercising its jurisdiction; and filed with the court.

According to the CCC, victim impact statements are not mandated by law. The victim can choose not to present one; however, if a statement is made, the judge *must* consider it in sentencing.

Benefits of VISs

Victim impact statements have many benefits. They have a positive impact on court dispositions, increasing the use of restitution and compensation orders. They show that the victim is involved and committed to the court process. Through a VIS, the victim gets to tell how the crime affected him or her socially, financially, and emotionally. The statement allows the court to understand that the victim is a human being (Summer, 1987). Recognizing the victim as an important participant in the process raises his or her self-confidence, restores his or her dignity, and reduces his or her feelings of powerlessness. A VIS also allows the court to see how the offender's behaviour has impacted the life of the victim, thereby allowing better evaluation of the offender's action for sanction purposes. In other words, the VIS helps to make the sentence more appropriate (Erez, 1990, 1994; Erez & Rogers, 1999). This outcome can increase the victim's satisfaction with the criminal justice system.

Unintended Consequences of VISs

Along with the benefits of VISs are possible detriments. While a VIS can contribute to fair sentencing, it can also lead to an overly harsh sentence. A victim is subjective; his or her statement may also make the court subjective in its consideration of punishment. This result interferes with the objectivity of the court, which should not be influenced by outside persons and/or public (political) pressure. In Australian courts, VISs have been found to influence sentencing to some degree, both positively and negatively (Erez, Rogers, & O'Connell, 2000). In Canada, the statement is also collected in various ways, depending on the province, creating a non-standardized procedure for letting the victim know that this option is available. For example, in some jurisdictions police may give the victim a form explaining a VIS, while in others police may refer him or her to a Victim Services Unit. In other areas, the Crown collects VISs.

In all cases, a copy is given to the offender, and the victim may be questioned by defence counsel regarding the statement. This questioning may harm the victim because he or she may have to answer questions about these statements and about the harm that has already been done to him or her. This is because the participation of the victim, in creating a VIS, might affect the offender's right to a fair trial. Of concern is that victim impact statements are evidence of sorts, introduced after the fact (i.e., at sentencing). Traditionally, evidence is supposed to be presented during the court process, after which a sentence is rendered. Proponents of these ideas claim that the VIS offers no new information; the reporting of victim damage is already built into the judicial system. Further, it has been argued (Sebba, 1996) that these statements serve only to facilitate a philosophical movement toward a more retributive, punitive approach to justice. This has led some to suggest that the VIS should be able to be cross-examined, as it is introducing new material for consideration and can affect the sentence of the offender. Alternatively, supporters of VISs argue that the VIS should not be challenged, especially if that statement suggests that there was a physical and emotional need that was created. To do so would further harm the victim.

There are also safety and protection issues to consider. The judge must take into consideration the danger an offender may pose to society and must listen to the VIS in order to do so effectively. This argument assumes that the judge is incapable of carrying out this task and imposing the suitable sentence by looking at the evidence, the offender's record, and the victimization incident. Ideologically, criminal offences are crimes against the state. As such, sentencing should reflect public interest as it relates to the case, not the interests of any one particular victim. The state has a vested interest in maintaining consistency in its treatment of offenders. Citizens have a right to expect certain punishments for certain offences. In fact, sentencing cannot be arbitrary under common law. Its objectivity increases public perception of fairness by the state and the public's confidence in the criminal justice system.

It can also be argued that, if a VIS demonstrates victim participation and commitment to sentence outcome, lack of one may convey exactly the opposite (Ashworth, 1993). Ashworth states that the victim may be further harmed by recalling how they were victimized. In essence are we not asking the victim to relive the experience for the convenience of the court? If the victim does not show up for such a painful event, will the court assume that the victim is not hurt, not worthy, or not vested in the judicial process? In other words, will the offender receive a lighter sentence if the victim does not make a statement?

Finally, the level of psychological stress may also be an important factor in determining the advantages of VISs. Why subject the victim to make a statement when some studies show that they have little effect or are ignored? Decisions should be based on fact, not human emotion. Does requiring this additional step not elongate the process of the trial, creating more emotional stress for the victim and additional expense to an already overburdened system?

Victims' Bill of Rights

Recent trends in the United States and Canada demonstrate a push to support a victims' bill of rights. Under the Clinton administration, a Victims' Bill of Rights was established in the United States. In Canada, there is a Victims' Bill of Rights in Manitoba (1998) and Ontario (1996) only. Manitoba's bill (see Box 12.2) is considered the most thorough because it specifies prescriptive rights as opposed to provisions and identifies the specific responsibilities of each service provider.

At issue with the establishment of such a bill is that it may interfere with the rights of the offender. As Box 12.3 shows, these rights are protected by sections 7 through 14 of the Canadian Charter of Rights and Freedoms, which serve to protect all citizens against unreasonable arrest. Once arrested, the importance of being treated fairly becomes paramount.

Box 12.2 Manitoba Victims' Bill of Rights, Prologue and Contents for Sections 1 through 5.

(Assented to 29 June 1998)

WHEREAS victims of crimes and other offences have needs, concerns and interests that deserve consideration in addition to those of society as a whole;

AND WHEREAS all victims should be treated with courtesy, compassion and respect;

AND WHEREAS victims should have access to appropriate protection and assistance, and should be given information regarding the investigation, prosecution and disposition of crimes and other offences;

AND WHEREAS it is in the public interest to give guidance and direction to persons employed in the justice system about the manner in which victims should be treated;

AND WHEREAS persons employed in the justice system should consider the rights and views of victims in a manner that does not unreasonably delay or prejudice investigations or prosecutions, that is consistent with the law and the public interest, and that is reasonable in the circumstances of each case;

PART 1

DECLARATION OF VICTIMS' RIGHTS

DEFINITIONS

1(1) Definitions
1(2) Exercise of rights by corporation or other entity
1(3) Registered common-law relationship

VICTIMS' RIGHTS AND ACCESS TO SERVICES

2(1) Victims' entitlement to services by request
2(2) Minister may approve a form of request
2(3) Reasonable effort to be made to locate victim

LAW ENFORCEMENT AGENCIES

3 Right to information from police agency
4 Right to give opinion on alternative measures and release
5 Right to interview by same gender in sexual offence

6 Right to confidentiality
7 Right to information about investigation of offence
8 Right to information about escape from police custody
9 Right to return of property
10 Minister may make agreement for services
11 Right to information about prosecution office

PROSECUTIONS

12 Right to information about prosecutions
13 Right to information about status of prosecution
14 Right to be consulted about prosecution
15 Right of victim to have restitution requested
16 Right to information about corrections office

COURT ADMINISTRATION

17 Right to information about court administration
18 Right to separate waiting area at court

SURCHARGES

44(1) Surcharge payable by person guilty of offence

44(2) Amount of surcharge

44(3) Collection of surcharge

44(4) Justice may reduce or waive surcharge

PART 5

COMPENSATION FOR VICTIMS OF CRIME

45(1) Definitions

45(2) Definition of 'victim'

46(1) Eligibility for compensation

46(2) Charge or conviction not required

47 Compensation for victim's injury

48 Compensation for dependants of deceased victim

49 Manner of payment of compensation

50(1) Who may apply for compensation

50(2) Application for person under 18

50(3) Application for mentally incompetent person

51(1) Time limit for applying

51(2) Extension of time

52(1) Director to evaluate applications

52(2) Director may request information

53 Reports from attending professionals and hospitals

54 Director may refuse or reduce compensation

55 Director may vary compensation

56 Certain amounts to be deducted from compensation

57(1) Applicant to advise director of recovery or action

57(2) Applicant may be required to take action

57(3) Director to approve settlement of action

57(4) Compensation may be reduced or revoked

58(1) Application of money from person causing injury or death

58(2) Reduction or discontinuance of periodic payment

59(1) Director to give written notice of decisions

59(2) Notice to include information on reconsideration

59(3) Right to request reconsideration

59(4) Director to give written notice of reconsideration

60(1) Right to appeal decision made on reconsideration

60(2) Extension of time

61 L.G. in C. may appoint or designate appeal body

62 Appointment of Compensation Appeal Board

63 Remuneration and expenses of board members

64(1) Powers of appeal board

64(2) Powers of inquiry

65 Appeal board may request assistance of experts

66 Appeal board to give written notice of decision

67(1) Appeal to Queen's Bench

67(2) Grounds for appeal

68 Garnishment of compensation

SOURCE: Victims' Bill of Rights. (1998). Province of Manitoba, Canada. Retrieved 24 February 2009, from http://web2. gov.mb.ca/laws/statutes/ccsm/v055e.php. Permission to reproduce this text is provided by the Queen's Printer for Manitoba. The Queen's Printer does not warrant the accuracy or currency of the reproduction of this information.

All of these Charter rights are subject to limitation under section 1 that can reasonably restrict one's freedom. It is important to note that while both victims and victimizers are protected under the Charter, the rights of only the latter are expressly written into the document. This absence of the victims' rights could be viewed as meaning that the rights of the citizen who may be falsely accused are more important than those of the citizen who is victimized.

Box 12.3   Legal Rights under the Canadian Charter of Rights and Freedoms

Life, liberty and security of person
7. Everyone has the right to life, liberty and security of the person and the right not to be deprived thereof except in accordance with the principles of fundamental justice.

Search or seizure
8. Everyone has the right to be secure against unreasonable search or seizure.

Detention or imprisonment
9. Everyone has the right not to be arbitrarily detained or imprisoned.

Arrest or detention
10. Everyone has the right on arrest or detention
   a) to be informed promptly of the reasons therefore;
   b) to retain and instruct counsel without delay and to be informed of that right; and
   c) to have the validity of the detention determined by way of *habeas corpus* and to be released if the detention is not lawful.

Proceedings in criminal and penal matters
11. Any person charged with an offence has the right
   a) to be informed without unreasonable delay of the specific offence;
   b) to be tried within a reasonable time;
   c) not to be compelled to be a witness in proceedings against that person in respect of the offence;
   d) to be presumed innocent until proven guilty according to law in a fair and public hearing by an independent and impartial tribunal;
   e) not to be denied reasonable bail without just cause;
   f) except in the case of an offence under military law tried before a military tribunal, to the benefit of trial by jury where the maximum punishment for the offence is imprisonment for five years or a more severe punishment;
   g) not to be found guilty on account of any act or omission unless, at the time of the act or omission, it constituted an offence under Canadian or international law or was criminal according to the general principles of law recognized by the community of nations;
   h) if finally acquitted of the offence, not to be tried for it again and, if finally found guilty and punished for the offence, not to be tried or punished for it again; and
   i) if found guilty of the offence and if the punishment for the offence has been varied between the time of commission and the time of sentencing, to the benefit of the lesser punishment.

Treatment or punishment

12. Everyone has the right not to be subjected to any cruel and unusual treatment or punishment.

Self-crimination

13. A witness who testifies in any proceedings has the right not to have any incriminating evidence so given used to incriminate that witness in any other proceedings, except in a prosecution for perjury or for the giving of contradictory evidence.

Interpreter

14. A party or witness in any proceedings who does not understand or speak the language in which the proceedings are conducted or who is deaf has the right to the assistance of an interpreter.

SOURCE: Canada. Canadian Charter of Rights and Freedoms. Ottawa ON: Department of Justice. Retrieved 10 March 2009, from http://laws.justice.gc.ca/en/charter/#juridiques.

The Effectiveness of the Criminal Justice System

Evaluating the effectiveness of the Canadian criminal justice system can be difficult. Table 12.1 illustrates some findings of the most recent General Social Survey (GSS) in regards to personal safety and perceptions of the criminal justice system. These data suggest that the police fair better than the courts when it comes to dealing with those who enter into the criminal justice system either as victims or offenders. These results have also been charted in Figure 12.1. The majority of respondents felt that the police were doing a good job in being approachable (65 per cent), ensuring neighbourhood safety (61 per cent), law enforcement (59 per cent), and treating people fairly (59 per cent). Given that the police are often the first contact for victims with the criminal justice system, these figures are encouraging. It is even more interesting when one considers that approximately 30 per cent of violent crimes do not get cleared and/or remain unsolved (see Figure 12.2).

The public seems less satisfied with the court and prison system as people move through the criminal justice system. Only 1 in 5 (20 per cent) GSS respondents felt that the courts did a good job in treating victims fairly. Even less (15 per cent) were of the opinion that justice was served quickly. Although almost one-third of respondents (31 per cent) felt that the criminal justice system was doing a good job in controlling prisoners, less than one in five (18 per cent) felt that the prison system was doing a good job in producing law-abiding citizens. Figure 12.3, however, illustrates that the public's view on the prison system has improved since 1999. Overall, the public had the least confidence in the parole system, where only one in six respondents (17 per cent) felt that the parole board was releasing people who were not likely to re-offend and even less (15 per cent) felt that it did a good job in supervising parolees.

With respect to intimate partner violence issues in particular, Russell and Light (2006) found that in cases where

Table 12.1   Perception of Job Being Done by Police and Courts by Canadians 15 and Over

	Good job	Avg. job	Poor job	DK/not stated
Local police: enforcing laws	59	31	6	4
Local police: responding to calls	52	23	8	18
Local police: being approachable	65	19	5	11
Local police: supplying information on reducing crime	50	28	11	11
Local police: ensuring neighbourhood safety	61	28	5	6
Local police: treating people fairly	59	25	7	10
Courts: providing justice quickly	15	37	36	12
Courts: helping victims	20	37	28	16
Courts: determining guilt or innocence of accused	27	43	15	16
Courts: providing a fair trial	44	35	8	13
Prison system: prisoner supervision and control	31	32	14	23
Prison: helping prisoners become law-abiding	18	35	23	24
Parole: releasing offenders who are not likely to reoffend	17	37	31	16
Parole: supervising parolees	15	33	32	20

SOURCE: Statistics Canada. (2005). General Social Survey, cycle 18 overview: personal safety and perceptions of the criminal justice system, 2004. Ottawa, ON: Minister of Industry.

Figure 12.1 Majority of Canadians Believe Police Are Doing a Good Job, 2004

% of population 15 years and older who perceive police as doing a *good* job

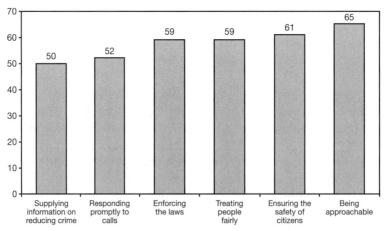

1 Only the percentage who perceive local police force as doing a good job is shown.

SOURCE: Gannon, M. General Social Survey on Victimization, Cycle 18: An Overview of Findings, 2004. Statistics Canada, Social and Aboriginal Statistics Division. Minister of Industry, p. 13.

Figure 12.2 Police Clearance Rates[1] for Violent and Property Crimes Have Decreased Just Slightly Since the Early 1990s

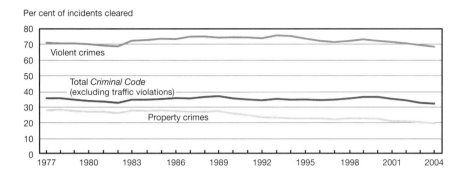

Per cent of incidents cleared

Violent crimes

Total *Criminal Code*
(excluding traffic violations)

Property crimes

1 The clearence rate is the number of incidents cleared (i.e., solved) by police during the year divided by the number of incidents during the year.

SOURCE: Gannon, M., Mihorean, K., Beattie, K., Taylor-Butts, A., & Kong, R. (2005). Criminal justice indicators, 2005. Statistics Canada: Minister of Industry, p. 84.

Figure 12.3 Canadians' Assessments of Prisons Have Improved since 1999

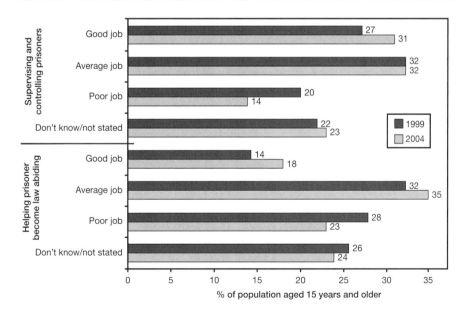

SOURCE: Gannon, M. (2004). General Social Survey on victimization, Cycle 18: An overview of findings, 2004. Statistics Canada, Social and Aboriginal Statistics Division, Minister of Industry, p. 12.

RCMP officers arrested a male victimizer, the victims reported feeling empowered by the offender being apprehended and charged. However, the arrest sometimes depended on whether the police felt that the victim was deserving of their efforts. **Deserving victims** had serious injuries, and assailant culpability was easily identified. **Undeserving victims** were evidenced to have less serious injuries and thought to be complicit in the assault. Other factors that affected perceptions of a victim's status were substance abuse and repeated calls for service at the same address. Less-deserving victims, who were often most in need of intervention, were more likely to receive minimal investigations and informal responses instead of an arrest of their offender. Victims who had become 'less deserving' reported that they were aware of receiving less than standard service from the police; they reported increased dissatisfaction with police response to their calls for service.

Victim Satisfaction with the Criminal Justice System

As mentioned in the previous chapter, a victim can experience secondary victimization (re-victimization by the criminal justice system) as he or she seeks justice. Fenwick (1997) and Smith, Watkins, and Morgan (1997) suggest that participation in the criminal justice system, such as in the preparation and deliverance of victim impact statements can reduce this consequence. Young (2001) has reported that victims may gain a sense of control by participating in the sentencing process which can ultimately aid in their healing. Furthermore, according to Fenwick (1997), Wemmers (1999), and

Young (2001), increased victim participation in the court process by preparing documents such as VISs increased victim satisfaction with sentencing outcome of their cases. Kilpatrick, Beatty, and Howley (1998, pp. 7–8) made two significant observations regarding factors that increased victim satisfaction: victims who were informed of their rights were more satisfied with the justice system than those who were not, and victims who thought that their participation had an impact on their cases were more satisfied with the system.

Some studies, however, found that not all victims who involved themselves in the process experienced more positive outcomes. Tobolowski (1999) found that engaging in the process did little to help with victims' anxiety experienced during the process and that the increased amount of information they received did not result in higher levels of victim satisfaction. In other words, rather than giving a sense of control in the process and reducing anxiety, involvement in the process only intensified these negative feelings. Additionally, Giliberti (1990) found that victims who prepared and delivered VISs were not necessarily happy with their own specific case outcome but did report higher levels of satisfaction with the process. This difference may be due to victims noticing that their participation had no real effect on the sentencing outcome (Erez & Rogers, 1999).

Kennard (1989) asserts that as victims are more likely to support the justice system as they become increasingly satisfied with it. As a result, they are more likely to use the system and to co-operate with its various parts. Sanders, Hoyle, Morgan, and Cape (2001, pp.

448–9) have suggested that there are certain benefits to victim participation in the criminal justice system:

1. Giving a victim 'a voice' for therapeutic purposes;
2. Enabling the interests and/or views of victims to be taken into account during decision- making;
3. Ensuring that victims are treated with respect by criminal justice agencies;
4. Reducing stress for victims in criminal proceedings;
5. Increasing victim satisfaction with the criminal justice system; and
6. Increasing victim co-operation, as a result of any of the above objectives.

Despite these assertions, almost 90 per cent of cases that move through the Canadian criminal justice system are negotiated by plea (Verdun-Jones & Tijerino, 2002). Furthermore, this process of plea negotiation or bargaining in Canada is not open to public scrutiny, prohibiting the victim from becoming involved when this option is used by a victimizer. As a result, VISs can be used only once this process is over, and sentence has often been determined. In some parts of the United States, victims have been allowed to participate in this pre-trial process. In Kennard's (1989) study of cases in Florida, it was found that victims who were allowed to participate in the pre-trial process reported increased satisfaction with the criminal justice system. This result occurred even though victimizers were given less jail time in favour of other forms of punishment.

Summary

The justice system provides a systematic way to deal with a host of disputes. This chapter has analyzed several of the options available to victims of crime, particularly those victimized by an intimate partner. While the law has recognized that such victims have specific needs and has made more options available, the system itself remains large and bureaucratic. It is often a one-size-fits-all network that overwhelms and disappoints the victims who attempt to use it. Their needs and the needs of the system are often out of sync. To help combat this problem, several groups around the country continue to lobby for more effective and inclusive responses to all forms of family violence.

As awareness of victims as clients of the system grows, so do efforts to make the system more approachable for victims. One method is to make the victim a more active participant in the process, through such means as victim impact statements. Victims who can engage with the system generally report having a more positive experience. The next chapter will discuss other ways of including the victim in the judicial process.

Glossary

civil court options for victims Actions that can be taken in civil court in addition to, or in lieu of, any criminal or informal response to victimization. An example of a civil action is the launch of a civil suit for damages caused by the offending party. In the case of IPV, options can include filing for legal separation or divorce, in addition to filing lawsuits against the victimizer.

criminal court options for victims Actions that are taken in criminal court where the Crown, representing the Queen or King, takes action on behalf of the victim to exact punishment on the accused for the transgressions against the victim.

deserving victim In cases of intimate partner violence, a victim who police determine merits their services. This type of victim is more likely to have serious injuries than an undeserving victim. The victim's partner is also easily identified as the abuser.

domestic violence Violence that occurs between family members. Forms of domestic violence can include elder abuse, child abuse, intimate partner violence, and violence between siblings.

dual arrest policy A policy that dictates arresting both parties in a dispute. This policy can be applied to intimate partner violence and to other incidents, such as two men fighting in a bar. Dual arrest treats the victim and the victimizer in the same way.

ex parte **orders** An interim restraining order issued to victims who have reason to feel immediate danger. This type of order does not require the accused abuser to be present at court. *Ex parte* orders are issued for only 24 hours to 1 week so that the victim will be safe while the victimizer is notified and allowed to respond to the order.

illegitimate options for victims A response to victimization that may perpetuate harm to the victim. Ignoring the situation is an example of an illegitimate option.

intimate partner violence (IPV) Violence that occurs between people who are or have been in an intimate relationship, such as living common-law, married, or in a civil union.

intimate terrorism A severe form of intimate partner violence using a process where physical and/or sexual violence are some of the many tactics used with the explicit desire to control one's partner,

often completely. Under the process of intimate terrorism techniques, the partner of the abuser becomes a prisoner of the relationship, whereby all aspects of daily activity are controlled and which can be accompanied by circumstances of extreme economic, nutritional, and/or physical deprivation.

legitimate options for victims A response to victimization that does not harm the victim. Divorce is an example of a legitimate option for ending intimate partner violence.

mandatory arrest policy A requirement in most municipal areas of Canada that identified offenders of intimate partner violence be arrested.

mutual peace bond Issued by the court, a type of peace bond in which both the victim and the offender are prohibited from contacting one another.

peace bond An order from the court to keep the peace. The issuance of a peace bond means that the provisions of the Criminal Code of Canada were used to make the request and not those of the Family Law Act. Breaking the terms of a peace bond constitutes a criminal code offence.

restraining order (RO) Essentially a court-ordered 'stay away for a while' mandate for an accused victimizer. An RO can last days, months, or longer and is valid only in the province where it is issued. This type of order requires that evidence be given in court, which can be a long process, and that the fear of the victim is reasonable.

terms of release Requirements that an offender must meet in order to be released from jail. These terms are set out in a hearing that usually takes place within a few days of the initial arrest of the victimizer and expire when he or she is found guilty or not guilty.

undeserving victim In cases of intimate partner violence, a victim who police determine does not merit their services.

This type of victim is less likely to have serious injuries than a deserving victim. He or she is thought to be complicit in the assault and may have made repeated calls for service and/or have issues with substance abuse, and may continue to communicate or reside with his or her abuser.

victim impact statement (VIS) A written or oral statement presented in court by a victim or victim representative. A VIS allows the victim to go beyond the visible harm of the victimization and to describe the economic and/or emotional hardship. In some cases, this statement can include a sentencing recommendation.

Critical Thinking Questions

1. How do the rights of the victim create problems for the rights of the offender?
2. What policies do you think work and do not work with respect to deterring violence? How could the latter policies be fixed?
3. Does the offender have the right to challenge information presented in a victim impact statement? Why or why not?
4. Why is victim satisfaction with the criminal justice system important? What are the implications of feeling that the criminal justice system is meeting one's needs?

CHAPTER 13

New Initiatives for Victim Inclusion in the Criminal Justice System: Restorative Justice Practices

Learning Objectives

After reading this chapter, you will be able to

- examine how restorative justice systems differ from other types of criminal justice systems;
- discuss ways in which restorative justice practices are practised; and
- understand the strengths and pitfalls of a restorative justice practice inside a common-law system.

Introduction

Throughout this text, we have explored the various ways in which victims have been treated, and often mistreated, by various individuals and by the criminal justice system. We have also discussed the process of secondary victimization, in which victims may be blamed, in whole or in part, by the criminal justice system. Although it is designed to help victims, this system is primarily concerned with the apprehension and the protection of rights of the alleged victimizer. Consequently, victims are often neglected in this process, while continuing to serve the function of being witnesses in their own victimization. They are an absolute necessity to the criminal justice system in Canada but in many ways are not considered equal partners in this process.

In this final chapter we will look to the justice system alternatives available to victims. In particular, we will examine some of the newer elements of restorative justice systems and practices that are being integrated into the common-law system

here in Canada and throughout the world. Restorative justice practices are designed to combine the roles of the victim and the offender beyond witness and victimizer, respectively. We will begin our discussion by defining several types of justice systems and will then consider both the strengths and weaknesses of restorative justice.

Types of Criminal Justice Systems

Canada, the United States, Britain, and many other nations employ a **common-law system**, which creates law through court decisions rather than legislative or executive action. In this system, laws are also enacted by the courts and are applied to each case by an impartial judge or jury. Where there is no appropriate application of the law, such as in cases that are rare or that involve emerging legal trends, judges may set a **precedent**, a legal decision which establishes legal principles or rules. When a precedent has been set, all other similar cases must follow the decision set out by the original case.

Like many other common-law systems, Canada's is an **adversarial justice system**, one which pits the victim and the victimizer against one another. The idea of this arrangement is that the opposing sides enter into the criminal justice system and engage in legal combat until one is declared the winner. Ideally, justice is achieved when one side convinces a judge or jury to believe its version of events.

In contrast, France, many countries, provinces, and territories with French colonial heritage (provincial law in Quebec, state law in New Orleans, many African and South American countries), as well as Germany, Japan, Mexico, and other countries engage in a civil law system. A **civil law system** is a system whereby laws are written for the people and are the codification of a system of values, beliefs, and so on. This is in contrast to a **case law system**, which is more akin to our common-law system, where law is decided by judges using case examples to address legal disputes. Civil law systems include an **inquisitorial system**, in which the laws are comprised of abstractly written codes and the court serves not as an impartial body but as one that actively engages in deciding the best application of the codes. In this type of system, both the victim and the victimizer are engaged in the system by providing evidence. Both parties can be questioned by the judge, in order that the appropriate application of law is made. This practice is in contrast to common-law systems, where the victim and/or the offender can choose not to testify on their behalf if their respective lawyer does not feel it would benefit their case. The goal of the inquisitorial system is to be active and seek justice while simultaneously representing the best interests of the state, rather than to convince an impartial body of a particular version of events.

Comparing Restorative and Retributive Systems

Another distinction between systems is that between restorative and retributive criminal justice systems. Technically, the systems mentioned below can work well under either a common- or civil law system. However, for the purposes of this text, we will examine them under the common-law system, which most Western readers are familiar with. A **retributive justice system** systematically punishes citizens who have been found to have violated a law or norm, on the grounds that the crime has created an imbalance in the social order that must be restored by taking action against the criminal. The inherent assumption of this type of system is 'an eye for an eye' (see Chapter 1). This punishment can involve fines, probationary sentencing, incarceration or, in some countries, death of the offender.

A **restorative justice system** is a response to wrongdoing that promotes mediation and emphasizes healing the wounds of those affected by conflict and crime, including victims, offenders, and communities. Also known as a communitarian, redemptive, or reintegrative justice system, this type attempts to restore balance by encouraging the participation of all parties involved in order to reach a resolution that satisfies everyone and that will achieve reconciliation and harmony. Restorative justice sessions often take place in informal settings, with the results being offered as a recommendation to the judge in the case. There are no juries in this system; the judge, in ideal circumstances under common law, remains impartial and implements the recommendation. Restorative justice programs are typically offered as an alternative in non-violent crimes and/or crimes involving a juvenile offender. This tendency may be because of the perception that such programs are more effective in these types of cases.

Transformative justice occurs when restorative justice is applied beyond the domain of criminal justice, such as in bankruptcy law, corporate law, environmental law, and family law. The basic principle of this perspective is that the law and its implementation are used both to explore options available within the various justice systems and alter the parties' perceptions of one another in order to reach a greater understanding of the dispute (Bush & Folger, 1994). For example, in a retributive system, someone caught purchasing heroin is fined or imprisoned. In a transformative system, efforts are made to find alternative definitions or explanations of the behaviour under question. The individual can be seen as having a substance abuse problem and/or coping with addiction. Borrowed from a health care model, this concept recasts the offender into a form of victim. He or she may not need incarceration but health-promoting alternatives, such as drug treatment and/or counselling. The situation, therefore, becomes transformed, allowing for more options than just retributive ones.

Acceptance of Restorative Justice in Canada

One of the largest challenges in exploring or adopting alternatives for both offenders and victims is determining how they will be integrated into the existing system. One of the public's chief concerns surrounds the issue of sentencing. How does a restorative recommendation and implementation accommodate the public's need for perceived punishment, especially in cases that do not include incarceration?

In 1996 the Criminal Code of Canada was amended to add sentencing principles, which include providing reparations for harm done to victims or the community and promoting a sense of responsibility in offenders, as well as an acknowledgement of the harm they have done. The Supreme Court of Canada recognized the importance of this approach in its landmark decisions *R v. Gladue* and *R. v. Proulx*, which are included in boxes 13.1 and 13.2.

Box 13.1   Case Law: *R. v. Gladue*

The accused, an aboriginal woman, pled guilty to manslaughter for the killing of her common law husband and was sentenced to three years' imprisonment. On the night of the incident, the accused was celebrating her 19th birthday and drank beer with some friends and family members, including the victim. She suspected the victim was having an affair with her older sister and, when her sister left the party, followed by the victim, the accused told her friend, 'He's going to get it. He's really going to get it this time.' She later found the victim and her sister coming down the stairs together in her sister's home. She believed that they had been engaged in sexual activity. When the accused and the victim returned to their townhouse, they started to quarrel. During the argument, the accused confronted the victim with his infidelity and he told her that she was fat and ugly and not as good as the others. A few minutes later, the victim fled their home. The accused ran toward him with a large knife and stabbed him in the chest. When returning to her home, she was heard saying 'I got you, you fucking bastard.' There was also evidence indicating that she had stabbed the victim on the arm before he left the townhouse. At the time of the stabbing, the accused had a blood-alcohol content of between 155 and 165 milligrams of alcohol in 100 millilitres of blood.

At the sentencing hearing, the judge took into account several mitigating factors. The accused was a young mother and, apart from an impaired driving conviction, she had no criminal record. Her family was supportive and, while on bail, she had attended alcohol abuse counselling and upgraded her education. The accused was provoked by the victim's insulting behaviour and remarks. At the time of the offence, the accused had a hyperthyroid condition which caused her to overreact to emotional situations. She showed some signs of remorse and entered a plea of guilty. The sentencing judge also identified several aggravating circumstances. The accused stabbed the deceased twice, the second time after he had fled in an attempt to escape. From the remarks she made before and after the stabbing it was clear that the accused intended to harm the victim. Further, she was not afraid of the victim; she was the aggressor. The judge considered that the principles of denunciation and general deterrence must play a role in the present circumstances even though specific deterrence was not required. He also indicated that the sentence should take into account the need to rehabilitate the accused. The judge decided that a suspended sentence or a conditional sentence of imprisonment was not appropriate in this case. He noted that there were no special circumstances arising from the aboriginal status of the accused and the victim that he should take into consideration. Both were living in an urban area off-reserve and not 'within the aboriginal community as such'. The sentencing judge concluded that the offence was a very serious one, for which the appropriate sentence was three years' imprisonment. The majority of the Court of Appeal dismissed the accused's appeal of her sentence.

Held: The appeal should be dismissed.

SOURCE: Canada, Supreme Court. (1999) R. *v.* Gladue. *Judgments of the Supreme Court of Canada*. 1 S.C.R. 688. Retrieved 4 May 2009, from http://csc.lexum.umontreal.ca/en/1999/1999rcs1-688/1999rcs1-688.html.

Box 13.2   Case Law: *R. v. Proulx*

After a night of partying involving consumption of some alcohol, the accused decided to drive his friends home even though he knew that his vehicle was not mechanically sound. For a period of 10 to 20 minutes, the accused, who had only seven weeks of experience as a licensed driver, drove erratically, weaving in and out of traffic, tailgating, and trying to pass other vehicles without signalling, despite steady oncoming traffic and slippery roads. As the accused was trying to pass another vehicle, he drove his car into an oncoming lane of traffic, side-swiped a first car and crashed into a second one. The driver of that second vehicle was seriously injured. The accident also claimed the life of a passenger in the accused's car. The accused was in a near-death coma for some time, but ultimately recovered from his injuries. The accused entered guilty pleas to one count of dangerous driving causing death and one count of dangerous driving causing bodily harm. He was sentenced to 18 months of incarceration, to be served concurrently on both charges. The sentencing judge concluded that a conditional sentence pursuant to s. 742.1 of the *Criminal Code*, which would allow the accused to serve his sentence in the community, would not be appropriate because it would be inconsistent with the objectives of denunciation and general deterrence. The Court of Appeal allowed the appeal and substituted a conditional custodial sentence for the jail term.

    Held: The appeal should be allowed.

SOURCE: Canada, Supreme Court. (2000) *R. v. Proulx. Judgments of the Supreme Court of Canada.* SCC 5. Retrieved 4 May 2009, from http://csc.lexum.umontreal.ca/en/2000/2000scc5/2000scc5.html.

In both of these cases, the Supreme Court ruled that the unique circumstances of the individual (i.e., Aboriginal heritage and living circumstances) must be considered when delivering sentences. In *R. v. Gladue*, the accused pleaded guilty to manslaughter and initially was not offered any special provisions because she was living off-reserve. During the appeal, the special case of Aboriginal peoples in Canada was brought up. The court effectively argued to the Supreme Court of Canada that all alternatives had to be explored when considering sentencing, and the Supreme Court agreed. What this meant for all Canadians is that alternatives to traditional retributive sentencing, which is the most common route used in this country's criminal justice system, should be explored where there are special circumstances and an opportunity to be more effective in the victimizer's rehabilitation. The effects of the colonization of Canada on the Aboriginal peoples is an excellent example of such circumstances.

In *R. v. Proulx*, the defendant appealed the right to have a conditional sentence placed upon him rather than a term of incarceration. The court recognized that there were both punitive and rehabilitative aspects to this type of sentencing and stated that these types of sentences have demonstrated effectiveness. It was noted that compared to probation, a primarily rehabilitative tool, conditional measures such as house arrest had more punitive effects. Judges must consider the dangerousness of the offender and exclude those who have a sentence with a mandatory minimum jail time, such as sentencing at the federal level (where offenders receive mandatory sentences of at least 2 years plus 1 day). The decision stated that it should be the norm to consider less punitive measures, with the exception of these two factors. In other words, these options are not available to individuals who have received a federal sentence and/or who are considered violent to the extent that he or she may be a threat to public safety. Time served in the community was both rehabilitative and restorative, in that it allowed the community to acknowledge the offender's actions and aid in the offender's possible rehabilitation and reintegration into the community.

Further government support for restorative justice was received with the publication of the Law Commission of Canada's *From Restorative Justice to Transformative Justice* (1999). The government's commitment to 'launch a program of restorative justice to help victims overcome the trauma of crime and provide non-violent offenders with a chance to help repair the damage caused by their actions' was stated in the Speech from the Throne of the Second Session of the 36th Parliament in October 1999. Additionally, the principles and substantive provisions of the Youth Criminal Justice Act, passed in 2002, endorse the use of restorative justice in youth crime and offer a statutory framework for its development.

Models of Practice

There are several ways to undertake rehabilitative measures. All models include the community coming together to make a decision about a victimizing behaviour. Members of the community include the victim and the victimizer but may also include others who wish to be involved, such as family members of the victim and the victimizer, who are often the primary support system that help both parties through this difficult time. In some cases, friends of either party or community elders may want to participate. The group reaches a decision regarding the appropriate rehabilitation effort and then acts upon it in various ways, depending on where the recommendation was granted. This section will look in detail at three popular methods of restorative justice practice: family group conferencing, victim–offender mediation, and sentencing circles.

Family Group Conference (FGC)

This concept is similar to family counselling in that family members gather to discuss a particular issue, usually one having to do with the children of that family. However, this model may also feature family mediation and therefore a wider group of participants, including community representatives. **Family Group Conferencing (FGC)** is a unique process that involves a shift from a decision-making process that is 'expert based' to one that is family based. The roots of this process trace back to traditional Aboriginal cultures in which the care and decision-making for children was considered the natural responsibility of the extended family and community.

FGC is an effective process in empowering families to take control of their future. Families develop a plan for the care and safety of their children that is endorsed and supported by the child, welfare agency, and the court rather than having one imposed on them by those agencies. A Family Group Conference is a special meeting of parents, children, extended family, and those that feel like family. The purpose of the meeting is to create a plan that considers the child's physical, emotional, mental, and spiritual needs and that will protect a child from harm.

The FGC method gives families the opportunity to participate in the decision-making and care of their children. This objective is carried out by offering a collaborative model that emphasizes the strengths within the family as opposed to what it does not have. As a result, FGC is thought to be a more culturally sensitive approach to helping families. Although community service agencies are involved, agency personnel are used as neutral facilitators rather than as people who are acting on behalf of an organization. The family is empowered to make decisions regarding the difficulties they are facing and is encouraged to create realistic, achievable, and long-term plans. Because the children are also involved in this process, the FGC model enables them to strengthen relationships and vital attachments with their families, communities, and cultures. The central idea, as with all restorative justice methods, is to restore balance and harmony for families and promote understanding of all perspectives held within that family unit.

Victim–Offender Mediation

Victim–offender mediation (VOM) programs, also known as victim–offender reconciliation, victim–offender meetings, or victim–offender conferencing programs, are a relatively recent process. The most common form of mediation occurs when two parties attempt to resolve a dispute with the assistance of a trained mediator (Wright & Galaway, 1989). The VOM process is a strictly voluntary and informal one that encourages the victim and offender to resolve their dispute in a mutually agreeable manner; the mediator has no decision-making authority. This concept runs contrary to more traditional methods, where victim and offender participation is often mandated and the process is fraught with many rules and regulations. In these conventional approaches, disputes are resolved through an arbitration process, where a third party hears complaints from both sides and makes a decision about what occurred and how it should be handled.

In a VOM, there must be only one central dispute to resolve, one that both the offender and the victim agree is an issue. Matters that are raised during the process are considered confidential, and the mediator cannot testify against either party in any future legal action. In the event that an agreement is reached, both parties must agree to abide by it. Family members and other interested parties may also be involved in this process as long as they agree to the conditions set forth by the VOM process.

Studies on VOM programs suggest that victims are often much more satisfied with the outcome of this process than with more traditional methods. Mark Umbreit (1994) evaluated victim–offender mediation programs in four American juvenile courts. In all, interviews were conducted with 1,153 victims and offenders. Victim–offender programs resulted in very high levels of satisfaction among both parties. Victims were twice as likely to report satisfaction with the outcome (80 per cent) than those who used more traditional methods of resolution (38 per cent). In just over 90 per cent of mediation cases, a plan for restitution to compensate the victim was agreed upon by both parties. In 80 per cent of cases, offenders complied with their restitution obligations. More significantly, the VOM programs helped reduce fear and anxiety among crime victims.

Umbreit (1998) also suggests that the VOM process teaches victimizers to take the victim's perspective and to empathize with the victim experience, which may be a factor in reducing recidivism. Those who were identified as victimizers were also more likely to believe that justice had been done. However, some evaluations of VOM has shown no significant difference between recidivism rates of offenders who went through the process and those who exercised non-mediation options (Niemeyer, 1996).

Sentencing Circles

The use of sentencing circles to deal with dispute resolution has evolved from traditional Aboriginal methods. **Sentencing circles**, often called peacemaking or rehabilitation circles, commonly involve elders of the community, along with various court representatives such as the Crown attorney and the defence counsel, the victim, the offender, their family members and close friends, and other members of the community. Their purpose is to allow individuals to tell their stories about how the victimization affected them and to reach a consensus as to what the victimizer and the community can do to restore balance to all parties. These programs can be used at the sentencing stage or following incarceration to assist with an offender's reintegration into the community.

Figure 13.1 demonstrates a common sentencing circle structure. The victim and victimizer sit in the middle of the circle, along with the mediator, a neutral person who does not impede the dialogue between the two parties but who ensures that the rules of the circle are followed and may act as a facilitator between them, as well as between others attending the circle. Surrounding the victim, offender, and the mediator are members of the court, family members, and sometimes close friends. These people can also participate in the process and share their perspectives. The next group is comprised of individuals from the community who would like to participate. Finally, the outer circle represents the community as a whole, which may have been affected by the victimization as a unit. Although there may not be individuals actually sitting in this circle, the community is always kept in mind during the process.

Sentencing circles in particular are a method of dealing with members of the community who have broken the law. This type of circle is available in all provinces and territories in Canada. It is often conducted after the victimizer has had experience with the common-law criminal justice system and has been

Figure 13.1 General Structure of Restorative Justice Circles

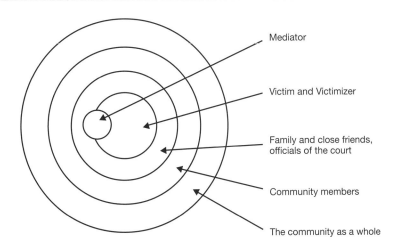

Mediator

Victim and Victimizer

Family and close friends, officials of the court

Community members

The community as a whole

found guilty or has accepted guilt and is willing to assume responsibility for his or her actions. The sentencing circle encourages the victimizer to acknowledge the harm that he or she has done to society and to victims. The community is also encouraged to accept its responsibility in this process, as well as to aid in the rehabilitation and reintegration of both the victim and the offender.

According to McCold (2000), the sentencing circle represents a partnership between the community and the criminal justice system. Using a directed process, community members develop a consensus on the steps necessary to build an appropriate sentencing plan using a traditional ritual and structure in a caring and respectful environment. Although members of the criminal justice system may be present (such as lawyers for both parties, police service members who attended to the case, etc.), all participants and observers are assumed to be of equal power in the circle. All members sit facing one another. In some cases, two circles are formed, one inside the other. The inner circle involves those mentioned above, while the outer circle can involve people who have specific information that may help in the healing process, such as agency personnel and other professionals or interested community members.

Because sentencing circles borrow from Aboriginal teachings, the guidelines surrounding their operation resemble the beliefs and practices of this group. The circle is often opened with a prayer, and everyone is welcomed and asked to introduce themselves. The guidelines of the circle are explained. Often a sacred object, such as an eagle feather, is passed around,

and the holder of the object offers his or her point of view about the problem. The object moves around the circle several times. Although not all circles are conducted in an identical manner, the following similar themes are often reproduced:

- introducing the participants;
- expressing the desire for the promotion of healing as a result of the circle;
- participants expressing concern for the victim and offering support to the victim and the victim's family;
- listening to the victim;
- participants expressing concern for the offender and offering support for the offender and the offender's family;
- listening to the offender;
- listening to the community members who were also affected by the situation; and
- making a group recommendation to the court about appropriate sentencing.

Many of these themes can be combined into various passes of the sacred object. The basic idea is that all points of view are heard and that everyone recognizes that all participants are not alone but are acting and seeking help as a community. The circle closes with a summary of what was agreed and/or disagreed upon, and often participants are asked if they would like to make any closing comments. Participants are thanked for their caring and participation, and often a short prayer is offered to end the meeting.

According to Green (1998), sentencing circles have several criteria which must be met in order to ensure that the process includes willing and voluntary participants in the process (see Box 13.3). Not only must all parties be present, or be represented, but they must do something to help the healing, take responsibility for the victimization, and/or responsibility for some other part of the process. Each participant should be able to state how the victimization has affected him or her and to identify how he or she can engage in the healing process.

During the recommendation stage of the circle procedure, the victim, the offender, court officials, and the

Box 13.3 Criteria for the Establishment of Sentencing Circles

- The accused must agree to be referred to the sentencing circle.
- The accused must have deep roots in the community in which the sentencing is held and from which the participants are drawn.
- There are elders or respected non-political community leaders willing to participate.
- The victim is willing to participate and has been subjected to no coercion or pressure in so agreeing.
- The court should try to determine beforehand, as best it can, if the victim is subject to Battered Women's Syndrome. If she is, then she should have counselling and be accompanied by a support team in the circle.
- Disputed facts have been resolved in advance.
- The case is one for which a court would be willing to take a calculated risk and depart from the usual range of sentencing.

Rules Governing a Sentencing Circle

- There are no special powers or privileges for anyone in the circle.
- There are no interruptions while a person is speaking. In a sentencing circle, a person may speak only in turn. The laws of the Creator shall govern the person speaking. Those laws are honesty, sharing, kindness, and respect.
- In the circle, decisions are made on the basis of consensus.
- At all times during the proceedings of a sentencing circle, the chairperson will maintain the order and the process of the circle.

Sentencing Circle Exclusions

- For purely punitive sanctions or where a term of incarceration in excess of two years is realistic, the sentencing circle is *not* appropriate. The circle is not appropriate where:
- there have been frequent repeat offences or the offence is indictable;
- the attitude of the offender prohibits his or her involvement;
- there are no community sentencing options available to the circle; and
- the community is not prepared to be involved in the circle.

Involvement: Judge, Lawyer, and Police

- Representatives of the criminal justice system must be willing and able to participate.
- The decision as to whether a sentencing circle will be granted is the judge's alone but must take into consideration all the criteria as to whether or not to grant a sentencing circle and whether the court is prepared to take a calculated risk with respect to the offender.

- After the circle has reached a consensus as to the sentence for the offender, the judge then steps back into his judicial role and may choose to impose or reject the sentence that the circle has recommended. However, the sentence is rarely rejected by the judge.

Involvement: Community

Community participants must

- be willing and able to participate and provide follow-up;
- be willing to organize the circle and provide translation services if necessary (anyone can organize a circle, i.e., probation officer, social worker, First Nation Justice Committee member, Band Councilor, or an elder);
- be willing and able to mobilize community resources so as to assist the offender and his or her family in the process of rehabilitation and recovery if necessary; welcome the participants, if possible provide coffee, milk, Kleenex, lunch, and transportation for the elders if needed;
- be totally supportive of the process and be familiar with the proceedings;
- feel free to ask questions, express their opinions as their views are important and more valid than those of people from outside the community, but people should refrain from counselling the offender or talking in excess;
- be involved in ongoing supervision, reintegration of the offender into the community, and evaluation of the offender's progress on a regular basis.

Involvement: Offender

The offender must be willing to

- participate and accept responsibility for his or her actions;
- face his or her victims and make whatever amends may be necessary;
- participate in traditional or Christian ceremonies to initiate the healing process;
- spend time with an elder and participate in any preparations the elder recommends at his or her home reserve or one of his or her choice; and
- make whatever legal amends necessary to the victim and do whatever is necessary to the victim to reconcile the negative relationship created between him- or herself, the victim, and the community as a result of the offence.

Involvement: Victim

The victim must be

- involved in the sentencing circle process directly or through the aid of a representative or surrogate victim (when that is realistic);
- given as much consideration and respect as possible in recognizing compensation and/ or restitution for him or her or a community service agency of his or her choice; and
- willing to become involved with the community in some way to facilitate the healing of the offender.

SOURCE: Green, R. G. (1998). *Justice in Aboriginal communities: Sentencing alternatives.* Saskatoon, SK: Purich Publishing. p. 76.

community collectively decide on what steps should be taken to resolve the dispute. According to Green (1998), all parties must agree on the recommendations, including the offender. The parties must reach an agreement that satisfies not only the community but also the court requirements of a just and appropriate sentence. Circle participants can consider a variety of choices, including peer counselling, restitution or compensation to the victim(s), community service work, mediation, compulsory school or work attendance, referral to specialized programs (i.e., anger management, sexual abuse awareness training), referral to counselling or drug or alcohol treatment, Aboriginal spiritual activities (i.e., sweats, forgiveness/sacrifice ceremonies), Aboriginal cultural activities (i.e., event security, event volunteer, elders' assistant, cleaning grounds, distributing food), talking and healing circles, curfew rules, regulations respecting residency, requirements not to associate with peers who are perceived to provide a negative influence, keeping the peace and remaining on good behaviour (as required by the court), counselling for offender and family, speaking/teaching (e.g., to students), and traditional sentences (i.e., fines, incarceration, probation, house arrest, electronic monitoring).

Threats to Restorative Justice Practice

According to Latimer, Dowden, and Muise (2001), who conducted a large study on several restorative justice programs, such programs, when used in appropriate cases, are a more effective method of improving satisfaction for both victims and offenders. In addition to this conclusion, restorative justice programs may increase offender compliance with restitution and decrease recidivism when compared with more traditional criminal justice measures.

However, there have been obstacles to establishing and maintaining these types of programs in various communities. The same study found that a single person can obstruct this process. For example, if there is a restorative justice program in a community that the Crown prosecutor or some other crucial participant in the process believes is ineffectual, he or she is less likely to agree that it is an appropriate course for the offender. As a result, although the offender, the offender's family, and the victim may want to engage in this process as a diversion from a more traditional punitive sentence, this person may not wish to make the recommendation to the court. Due to the lack of unanimous agreement, the offender will be sentenced with traditional measures. Where this type of resistance is prevalent, the programs can cease to exist.

These programs are also vulnerable to changes in governmental policies. Deukmedjian (2008) documented the changes that affected Community Justice Forums, a restorative justice measure adopted by the RCMP. Communities gain RCMP support for restorative justice practices by engaging in grassroots enrolment of community members willing to participate in the process. In the early to mid-1990s the government funded a national program that allowed RCMP officers to participate in this new and successful program. However, when the RCMP changed its mandate and started to restructure these forums after the turn of the century, many of the original players were excluded from the new processes, and community members and agencies felt unwanted. The process of consultation that is inherent in restorative justice practices had not been used effectively, leaving many regular community participants feeling isolated. As a result, some communities experienced mistrust of these RCMP forums. The program leadership that was needed from these communities and within the RCMP began to falter. Eventually, the RCMP was forced to cut the program funding for this initiative and revert to more traditional ways of handling disputes.

Other factors that can affect restorative justice programs include the importance of community acceptance. Although there may be an interest in supporting such a program, it is the community and the willingness to participate as a group that can determine whether a program can successfully emerge or be sustained. Where a restorative justice option exists, it is susceptible to the public perception of its effectiveness. If a client of the program re-victimizes the community and it receives wide-spread public attention, the validity of the program may be called into question regardless of its success rate. Once a community loses faith in a program, the program will suffer. Communities are also often concerned about the amount of tax dollars spent on this type of program. If the program is perceived as less effective than more traditional forms of justice, the use of public dollars can become an issue which may gain the support of local politicians.

Effectiveness of Restorative Justice Programs for Victims

Wemmers and Canuto (2002) identify several key factors that affect the success of restorative justice programs. Their study found that victims were more likely to give positive evaluations of programs where participation was voluntary. Victims felt that the process held their victimizers accountable for their actions in a way that was not offered by more traditional systems. Further, the process itself allowed for the request for restitution and recognized the victim's stake in the outcome of the case. Victims reported that they also liked that the restorative process kept victims notified of case developments.

This same study found that regardless of victimization experience, victims who wish to participate in restorative justice programs do so for fairly consistent reasons (Wemmers & Canuto, 2002). Often victims used the process because it provided an avenue to seek reparation. Some victims also reported that they had a desire to help the offender. Others wished to confront the offender with the seriousness of the victimization by telling him or her their story. In many cases, victims wanted to know from the victimizer why he or she committed the offence, and the restorative justice options allowed for this type of discussion.

Likewise, when victims declined to be part of the restorative justice process, their reasoning was also fairly consistent. In many cases victims did not participate because they felt that their loss was too small or trivial to make the effort worthwhile. Wemmers and Cunuto (2002) also report that studies showed that some victims refused to participate because they were afraid and/or feared the offender. Some victims reported being unable to partake in the process because they were still too angry about the victimization. They also reported that they did not think they could believe that the victimizer was sincere in his or her efforts.

Overall, Umbreit (1994) reports that both victims and offenders were satisfied with the experiences they had during restorative justice programs; however, the latter were the more satisfied groups. In a subsequent study, Umbreit (1995) talked to 323 victims in his analysis of victim–offender mediation programs in four Canadian cities (Ottawa, ON; Winnipeg, MB, Calgary, AB, and Langley, BC). Over half (56.7 per cent) of the victims participated in a mediation program, while the others were referred to a program but chose not to participate. Victims who did agree to participate were more satisfied with the outcome (78 per cent) than those who used other methods to deal with the issue (48 per cent).

It is tempting to say that the results found in Umbreit's (1995) study were due to the mediation treatment. However, Umbreit states that because his study could include people only after they had completed treatment, there is no real way to understand what caused the two groups to choose the way that they did. Therefore, although it is suggested that the mediation experience is more likely to elicit a positive criminal justice experience for the victim, we cannot conclusively confirm this outcome from the study results.

This lack of verification has lead Wemmer and Canuto (2002) to suggest that the restorative justice process is not a panacea for all victims. They further remark that their analysis sheds little light on those victims who chose not to participate in the process. Therefore, we really do not understand whether or not this group is fundamentally different in victimization experience or some other factor that would make a traditional option more appropriate. Further, we do not know whether victims who rejected the restorative option were satisfied with the alternative that they chose. Overall, Wemmer and Canuto concluded that more attention must be paid to victims as they move through this process. Although restorative justice measures do allow for this type of effort, the process still favours the concerns of the offenders. This consistent focus on the offender by the criminal justice system may lead to lower satisfaction ratings by victims who use it.

Restorative Justice and Secondary Victims of Homicide

Although restorative justice programs are more commonly used in non-violent crimes and/or in cases where the offender is a juvenile, there have been smaller studies that examine the effectiveness of these programs in more severe forms of victimization. For example, Umbreit and Vos (2000) interviewed five participants (three family members of murder victims and two murderers) involved in cases where the offenders had received the death penalty as a result of their actions. The study was conducted in Texas, where the two offenders had each raped at least one woman and engaged in at least one act of murder or attempted murder after the sexual assault had taken place. Offender 1 explained that his crime was one of opportunity. At the time of his criminal actions, Offender 2 had an irrational motive spawned by the recent dissolution of his marriage (Umbreit & Vos, 2000, p. 70):

I decided I would rape and make women love me, and if I could practice this and get real good at it, I could do it to my wife and then everything in my personal life would be great again, and normal. . . . I can't comprehend it. I know that is where my thought patterns were at; I can't comprehend it today.

Offender 2 killed his target and her roommate when she tried to intervene and attempted to kill the roommate's boyfriend. While Offender 1 did not use drugs or alcohol during his criminal activities, Offender 2 did and was reportedly higher than he had ever been in his life when he committed these crimes. Both offenders had experienced healing journeys as a result of being placed on death row and had come to view religion and religious experience as important. Offender 1 entered into the victim–offender mediation program because he was on a healing journey and wanted to apologize for his actions. Offender 2 wanted his victims to heal and to give back, in a way, something he had taken with his murderous actions.

The three family members of the victims spoke initially of the shock of losing their loved ones in such a brutal manner. All three family participants shared that they wanted to meet the killer of their loved one. They wanted to 'look him in the eye' and wanted him to 'look [them] in the face' (p. 71). Each family member also had other motives for meeting the offenders. Two wanted specifics about the crime (e.g., how the victim was selected, was the victim scared, how did he lure the victim, and so on). Two wanted to let the offender know about the impact his actions had on their lives.

Two wanted to hear the victimizer take responsibility for his actions, and one stated that she wanted to be involved for her own personal healing journey.

All five participants reported that the program was a powerful and healing experience that offered them a sense of relief and feeling of being renewed. One of the victim's granddaughters reported that she felt that 'energy was kinda lifted out of me' and that she felt 'exhausted' (p. 78). Family members reported feeling 'good' and 'at peace' as well as feeling more 'alive'. All three family members reported that their negative feelings, especially anger, had lessened towards the offender in their respective case. Both offenders reported that they felt better because they were able to do something, no matter how small, to improve the situation that they had created. Offender 1 stated that 'it actually makes it a lot easier to face the execution . . . that you've done something positive, that at least something positive will come out of this' (p. 82).

This study was conducted because there was a strong will on the part of the secondary victims and the offenders to participate in a victim–offender mediation program. All of the victims' family members realized that this process 'was not for everyone' (p. 83). Unfortunately, this study was unable to verify the offenders' accounts beyond their own reports, which were made just weeks before the men were executed. However, both offenders stated that they agreed with the victims that the healing process they participated in should be made available to others. Offender 1 reported (p. 84):

Maybe it can open up a lot more awareness as far as opening up and learning . . . instead of working as just a straight penal facility, that it can actually become a correctional facility, that there actually can be attempts made at rehabilitation instead of just a thing of holding prisoners until their time is served.

These findings were echoed in an earlier study conducted by Flaten (1996), who interviewed 7 of 11 victim–participants who entered into a similar program after being victims of violent offences. Victims in that study were satisfied with the outcomes and felt that this restorative justice method was appropriate and should be made available to more victims in their situation.

Radelet and Borg (2000) have strongly criticized Umbreit and Vos's study because it was conducted a short time before the offenders' deaths. They claim that these circumstances make it difficult to weed out the effects of the mediation and the effects of being faced with imminent execution. The death of the offenders gives neither the victims nor the offenders time to grow through the restorative and healing process.

Criticisms of Restorative Justice Methods

Takagi and Shank (2004) identify several flaws of the restorative justice process. First, they point out that the concepts of restorative justice have developed into an industry unto itself. For example, the ideas of restorative justice have been turned into tribunals and special courts and have been used to attract students to restorative justice specialties. Second, the authors argue that, despite the popularity of the concept, success measures have not clearly been defined. Some programs

measure victim satisfaction, while others measure recidivism. Many studies are based on small sample sizes, meaning we cannot generalize about the successes or failures of these programs.

This problem is further complicated by the fact that these programs are not implemented in any standard form. Some programs engage in programs without participation of the victim, while others will not use various components of programs but what is often easier to implement. Takagi and Shank note that in Australia, where restorative justice methods are inspired by the community work done by the Maori people, many restorative justice programs do not involve a public shaming, which is often integral to the Maori way of restoring justice. The effect of removing parts of the process is unknown.

Summary

This chapter has examined the role of restorative justice as a model that encourages victim participation. Common-law systems, as discussed throughout this text, rarely consider the victim as a true participant in the process of achieving justice. Often the offender is the focal point for the state, which attempts to establish guilt in a criminal wrongdoing and/or to exact a sentence on the offender. The victim, in this process, is often viewed as merely a witness in his or her own victimization.

Restorative justice methods, which stem from a more community-based system of justice borrowed from Aboriginal ways of restoring social balance, offer an alternative to the traditional systems available in Canada. In restorative systems, the victims are not only witnesses to their victimization, but they are also allowed to participate in the process by sharing their stories, asking questions of various parties (including the offender), and requesting restitution from the offender.

The system is not without its challenges. In Canada and many other countries, restorative justice systems must attempt to exist inside established common-law systems. This effort can often lead to confusion about how recommendations from either system can be harmonized into one series of actions that restore justice. In this situation, the conclusions of any mediation, counselling session, or restorative sentencing recommendation must be offered to the court which may choose to ignore it and thereby create tension between the two systems.

Studies show that, for the most part, victims appear to be more satisfied with the restorative process. There is some scant evidence to show that this finding also holds for victims who have experienced violent crime. Offenders and victims in these studies who have entered into a restorative justice process have commented that this type of justice activity is appropriate, although not for all victims. Many have suggested that these options should be made available to more people, in an effort to help healing and restore balance after victimization experiences.

Glossary

adversarial justice system A justice system found in countries that use common law. In the adversarial system, the victim and the victimizer are engaged in a process that pits them against one another. Ideally, justice is achieved in this system when one side convinces a judge or jury to believe its version of events.

case law system A system of law where legislation is made by judges, using cases to set precedent. Principles of common law are a good example of this type of system.

civil law system A system of law whereby laws are written for the people and are the codification of a system of values, beliefs, and so on. Principles of inquisitorial law are a good example of this type of system.

common-law system A legal system whereby laws are created through court decisions, rather than via legislative or executive action.

family group conferencing A restorative justice practice that is similar to family counselling in that family members gather to discuss a particular issue, usually one having to do with the children of that family. This model also features family mediation and therefore a wider group of participants, including community representatives.

inquisitorial justice system A justice system found in countries that use civil law. In this system, laws are comprised of abstractly written codes and the court serves not as an impartial body but as one that actively engages in deciding the best application of the codes. The underlying assumption of the inquisitorial system is to find the truth.

precedent A legal decision that establishes legal principles or rules. A judge may set a precedent where there is no appropriate application of the law, such as in cases that are rare or that involve emerging legal trends. When a precedent has been set, all other similar cases must follow the decision set out by the original case.

restorative justice system A response to wrongdoing that promotes mediation and emphasizes healing the wounds of those affected by conflict and crime, including victims, offenders, and communities. Restorative justice sessions often take place in informal settings, with the results being offered as a recommendation to the judge in the case. There are no juries in this system; the judge, in ideal circumstances under common law, remains impartial and implements the recommendation. Restorative justice programs are typically offered as an alternative in non-violent crimes and/or crimes involving a juvenile offender. This system is also called a communitarian, redemptive, or reintegrative justice system.

retributive justice system A system of justice that systematically punishes who have been found in violation of a law or norm, on the grounds that the crime has created an imbalance in the social order that must be restored by taking action against the criminal. The inherent assumption of this type of system is 'an eye for an eye'. This punishment can involve fines, probationary sentencing, incarceration or, in some counties, death of the offender.

sentencing circles Also called rehabilitation or peacemaking circles, a type of alternative dispute resolution that commonly involves elders of the community, along with various court representatives such as the Crown attorney and the defence counsel, the victim, the offender, their family members and close friends, and other members of the community. Circles may be used at the sentencing stage or following incarceration to assist an offender's reintegration into the community. Their purpose is to allow individuals to tell their stories about how the victimization affected them and to reach a consensus as to what the victimizer and the community can do to restore balance to all parties.

transformative justice A form of justice that occurs when restorative justice is applied beyond the domain of criminal justice, such as in bankruptcy law, corporate law, environmental law, and family law. The basic principle of this perspective is that the law and its implementation are used both to explore options available within the various justice systems alter the parties' perceptions of one another in order to reach an greater understanding of the situation under dispute.

victim–offender mediation (VOM) A restorative justice practice, also known as victim–offender reconciliation, victim–offender meetings, or victim–offender conferences. The most common form of mediation occurs when two parties attempt to resolve a dispute with the assistance of a trained mediator. The VOM process is a strictly voluntary and informal one that encourages the victim and offender to resolve their dispute in a mutually agreeable manner; the mediator has no decision-making authority. This process runs contrary to more traditional methods, where victim and offender participation is often mandated and the process is fraught with many rules and regulations.

Critical Thinking Questions

1. Given the strong evidence regarding victim satisfaction with restorative justice programs, do you think that a victim should be forced to participate in such a program? Why or why not?

2. In what circumstances do restorative justice practices seem to deal with crime more effectively than traditional criminal justice practices?

3. If you were a victim of a crime and had an opportunity to talk with your offender, would you? What factors would affect your decision?

4. How important is apologizing to a victim? Does it really make a difference to either the victim or the offender? Do you think victimizers who apologize are sincere? Why or why not?

5. Are restorative justice practices truly different from any other type of criminal justice practice? Give reasons for your answer.

6. Should restorative justice measures be used with victims and offenders involved in violent crimes? Try to envision a program that would allow victims of severe violence to talk with their victimizers and discuss whether victims should have this opportunity.

Glossary

419 scam A type of advance fee fraud that is most commonly associated with Nigeria or other West African countries and named for the section of the Nigerian criminal code that it violates. Also known as the West African or Nigerian letter, this scam asks potential victims to supply banking information in order to transfer a large sum of money. In return, the potential victim is promised a percentage of the funds. This scam is carried out throughout the world and is a derivation of the Spanish Prisoner scam.

900 scam A scam in which a potential victim is enticed to call a 1-900 number to receive information, a prize, or a service. Although the cost per minute of these numbers is advertised as being low, the calls are prolonged to increase the fee.

actual direct victim An individual who experiences an actual victimization.

actual indirect victim An individual who is traumatized by witnessing an actual victimization. This type of victim fears for him- or herself but not in a direct response to an actual victimization risk.

advance fee fraud A generic type of scam which has several variations. These scams involve an offender asking a potential victim for money in advance of a substantial payout, which is never received.

adversarial justice system A justice system found in countries that use common law. In the adversarial system, the victim and the victimizer are engaged in a process that pits them against one another. Ideally, justice is achieved in this system when one side convinces a judge or jury to believe its version of events.

aftermath of crime The third and final stage in the criminal event perspective. This particular stage spans a considerably long period of time and looks at the offender's, victim's, and public's reaction to the criminal transaction.

Antisocial Personality Disorder (APD) A diagnosis in the *Diagnostic and Statistical Manual IV (DSM)*, which is often confused with the term 'psychopathy'. People with APD exhibit many symptoms in common with psychopathy, including compulsive acting and lying, lack of remorse, and an inability to plan.

assault level I Also known as common assault. This offence involves intentionally threatening or applying force onto a person without his or her consent.

assault level II Also known as assault with a weapon or causing bodily harm. Offences of this type are more serious than common assault and describe cases where the assailant carries, uses, or threatens to use a weapon or imitation or causes physical harm to the victim.

assault level III Also known as aggravated assault. This level is the most serious type of assault and includes wounding, maiming, disfiguring, or endangering the life of the victim.

bias Error that is either known or unknown and created by flaws in study design, such as in the development of the measurement instruments, sample selection, study implementation, or study questions.

bully One who engages in deliberate acts of harm, often over a long period of time.

bullying The deliberate use of verbal or physical acts that are hurtful, often over a long period of time.

case law system A system of law where legislation is made by judges, using cases to set precedent. Principles of common law are a good example of this type of system.

celerity of punishment In deterrence theory, one of the three components of effective punishment. This part claims that the punishment for a crime should be measured and specific to the offence and that the offender and the public must perceive it to be appropriate.

certainty of punishment In deterrence theory, one of the three components of effective punishment. This part states that the offender and the public must perceive that the chance for being punished for a particular deviant act is high, thereby deterring the act from being committed again.

child abuse A deliberate act or set of actions that is considered maltreatment of a child. This mistreatment includes acts of physical abuse, sexual abuse, neglect, and emotional abuse, as well as witnessing family violence.

civil court options for victims Actions that can be taken in civil court in addition to, or in lieu of, any criminal or informal response to victimization. An example of a civil action is the launch of a civil suit for damages caused by the offending party. In the case of IPV, options can include filing for legal separation or divorce, in addition to filing lawsuits against the victimizer.

civil law system A system of law whereby laws are written for the people and are the codification of a system of values, beliefs, and so on. Principles of inquisitorial law are a good example of this type of system.

cognitive appraisal The process by which an individual perceives his or her environment to be dangerous or safe.

common-law system A legal system whereby laws are created through court decisions, rather than via legislative or executive action.

compliant victim A victim who complies with the demands of the victimizer in order to protect him- or herself or another who has been threatened. This type of victim is assumed innocent.

concrete fear The fear of specific events, such as fear of specific criminal victimization.

contagion effect The spread of the effects of fear from one person to another or from one community to another.

criminal One who commits a crime.

criminal court options for victims Actions that are taken in criminal court where the Crown, representing the Queen or King, takes action on behalf of the victim to exact punishment on the accused for the transgressions against the victim.

criminal event perspective The idea that criminal activity has three phases: criminal precursors, criminal transaction, and the aftermath of crime.

criminality Behaviours associated with law violation.

criminal precursors The first stage in the criminal event perspective. This stage includes the experiences, demographics, etc. that occur before the crime and influence its transaction and aftermath.

criminal transaction The second stage in the criminal event perspective. In this stage, the offender engages in a criminal event, which usually lasts only a few minutes.

criminology The study of crime and criminals in context.

critical perspectives A set of theories that seeks to explain the biases occurring in social systems. When applied to victimology, these theories investigate the role of power in its various forms and its influence on crime patterns, differential experiences of crime and victimization, as well as the social responses to victimization and victimological thinking.

'curfew' A self-restrictive behaviour of women, born out of the fear of being assaulted, which limits the ability to take advantage of opportunities afforded to men who hold less fear engaging in activities at night.

deserving victim In cases of intimate partner violence, a victim who police determine merits their services. This type of victim is more likely to have serious injuries than an undeserving victim. The victim's partner is also easily identified as the abuser.

deterrence A concept aimed at exacting justice and dissuading the offender from doing harm again. Deterrence assumes that witnesses to the punishment will also be discouraged from ever committing the harm.

deterrence theory The theory that criminal acts are prevented by appropriate sanction. According to this theory, there are two forms of deterrence (specific and general) and three components of punishment (celerity, certainty, and severity).

deviance The study of any action, group, and/or members of that group that are considered to be outside a prescribed set of cultural norms.

direct fear A form of fear that occurs as a result of actual victimization.

direct victimization Victimization that produces fear in the moment, in response to a specific situation.

domestic violence Violence that occurs between family members. Forms of domestic violence can include elder abuse, child abuse, intimate partner violence, and violence between siblings.

dual arrest policy A policy that dictates arresting both parties in a dispute. This policy can be applied to intimate partner violence and to other incidents, such as two men fighting in a bar. Dual arrest treats the victim and the victimizer in the same way.

ethnic cleansing The process whereby a group of people is identified as different based on ascribed characteristics and is systematically targeted and removed, usually by death, from a population.

eustress A term originally coined by psychologist Richard Lazarus which refers to a type of stress that has positive or beneficial effects.

event outcomes Larger social effects of victimization that can be either negative or positive.

ex parte **orders** An interim restraining order issued to victims who have reason to feel immediate danger. This type of order does not require the accused abuser to be present at court. *Ex parte* orders are issued for only 24 hours to 1 week so that the victim will be safe while the victimizer is notified and allowed to respond to the order.

family group conferencing A restorative justice practice that is similar to family counselling in that family members gather to discuss a particular issue, usually one having to do with the children of that family. This model also features family mediation and therefore a wider group of participants, including community representatives.

fear of crime Generally, a response to a threat and the fear of being harmed.

feminist perspectives A gendered set of theories used to explain women's experiences. When applied to victimology, these theories attempt to reveal the gendered patterns of crime and victimization, as well as the lack of explanations of these experiences in traditional male-dominated criminological thinking.

first-degree murder A type of homicide where the victim has been killed deliberately, killed while being the victim of another serious crime, or killed as the result of carrying out duties associated with the protection of the state, such as those performed by a police officer, judge, prison warden, or corrections officer.

formless fear A more general, unfixed fear of victimization which can be interpreted as an overall anxiety about victimization unconnected to any specific victimization experience or threat.

fraud A non-violent crime that uses deception to achieve financial or material gain.

gatekeeper Initially coined by sociologist Erving Goffman, refers to anyone who controls access to a particular resource.

gateway offence An offence that creates opportunities for other, often more serious, offences to be committed. For example, identity theft allows someone to commit further crimes while impersonating another person and thereby decreasing the chances of being detected.

Gemeinschaft A state of social existence in small, tightly knit communities where traditional family and kinship values predominate.

General Adaptation Syndrome (GAS) An influential model of the physiological response to stress introduced in the 1930s by endocrinologist Hans Selye. The central theme behind GAS is that individuals are biologically programmed to react to threats in three stages: alarm, resistance, and exhaustion.

general deterrence A form of deterrence in which the public is indirectly deterred from criminal activity as a result of seeing sanction against an offender.

Gesellschaft A more rational and less personable form of relationship based on interdependence between the parts of society.

hate crime A crime where a particular person or group is targeted for victimization because of minority status, such as racial or ethnic identity and/or sexual orientation.

homicide Literally, 'the killing of man', refers to the killing of a person by another.

homicide victim According to the Canadian Criminal Code (s. 222.1), a person whose death is caused by another person, either directly or indirectly, by any means.

identity theft A form of fraud in which someone illegally acquires and uses another person's personal and identifying information, usually for financial gain.

illegitimate options for victims A response to victimization may perpetuate harm to the victim. Ignoring the situation is an example of an illegitimate option.

indirect fear A less intense form of fear that does not involve being directly exposed to victimization.

indirect victimization Victimization that occurs as the result of witnessing or hearing of the direct victimization of another.

infanticide Literally, the killing of infants or very small children. In legal terms, infanticide is a form of manslaughter in which a newborn child is killed, either deliberately or through an act of omission, by his or her biological mother. It is assumed that the mother suffers from a mental defect caused by childbirth.

inquisitorial justice system A justice system found in countries that use civil law. In this system, laws are comprised of abstractly written codes and the court serves not as an impartial body but as one that actively engages in deciding the best application of the codes. The underlying assumption of the inquisitorial system is to find the truth.

intimate partner violence (IPV) Violence that occurs between people who are or have been in an intimate relationship, such as living common-law, married, or in a civil union.

intimate terrorism A severe form of intimate partner violence using a process where physical and/or sexual violence are some of the many tactics used with the explicit desire to control one's partner, often completely. Under the process of intimate terrorism techniques, the partner of the abuser becomes a prisoner of the relationship, whereby all aspects of daily activity are controlled and which can be accompanied by circumstances of extreme economic, nutritional, and/or physical deprivation.

labelling theory Credited to Edwin Lemert, a social reaction theory that examines how the deviant identity is formed out of the reaction of others to the actor.

Legacy, The The on-going direct and indirect effects of the physical and sexual abuse endured by students of residential schools and their families, descendants, and communities (including communities of interest).

legitimate options for victims A response to victimization that does not harm the victim. Divorce is an example of a legitimate option for ending intimate partner violence.

lex talonis Legal retaliation, more popularly known by the Old Testament phrase 'an eye for an eye'.

lifestyles theory A rational choice theory claiming that certain behavioural patterns create an opportunistic structure for criminals.

longitudinal data Data collected over a prolonged period of time tracking particular phenomena.

mala in se Offences that are in and of themselves wrong or said to go against nature.

mala prohibita Acts that are against laws.

mandatory arrest policy A requirement in most municipal areas of Canada that identified offenders of intimate partner violence be arrested.

manslaughter A type of homicide where the offender is found to have killed the victim in the heat of passion or when the victim is found to have provoked the offender before he or she was killed.

marginalization The exclusion of some groups from mainstream society, which can lead to a lack of power or control.

mass murder The act of killing many people in a single murderous event with very little time between murders.

mariticide A type of homicide in which a person kills his or her spouse.

murder A culpable homicide in which the victim's death is deliberately caused or was the result of reckless or negligent behaviour.

mutual peace bond Issued by the court, a type of peace bond in which both the victim and the offender are prohibited from contacting one another.

obtrusive methods Research methods whereby the researcher, or observer, has direct contact with the participant.

peace bond An order from the court to keep the peace. The issuance of a peace bond means that the provisions of the Criminal Code of Canada were used to make the request and not those of the Family Law Act. Breaking the terms of a peace bond constitutes a criminal code offence.

penal couple The relationship between the victim and the offender.

phishing scam A scam in which a potential victim is 'hooked' into divulging personal information, which is used by the offender for identity theft, credit card fraud, or other illegal purposes.

Ponzi scheme Named after fraudster Charles Ponzi, a scam that involves individuals investing in an opportunity created by the offender. Promised a high return, the investors are paid from the proceeds of subsequent investors, who are often referred to the offender by the initial investors. Because this type of fraud requires a constantly increasing victim pool to sustain itself, it is also known as a pyramid scheme.

positive feedback The process of neighbourhood decline occurs through *positive feedback*, whereby fear can not only enable decline, but can continue to add to the process. This process is considered 'positive' because the process is additive; preconditions add to subsequent conditions, and so on.

Post-Traumatic Stress Disorder (PTSD) A disorder caused by exposure to extremely traumatic and stressful situations that fall outside the realm of normal, everyday individual experiences. These situations include severe accidents, acts of war, sexual assault, child abuse, severe intimate partner abuse, and natural disasters.

precedent A legal decision that establishes legal principles or rules. A judge may set a precedent where there is no appropriate application of the law, such as in cases that are rare or that involve emerging legal trends. When a precedent has been set, all other similar cases must follow the decision set out by the original case.

primary deviance Coined by Edwin Lemert, the initial participation in a deviant act. In victimology, primary deviance occurs during a victimizing event.

primary victims Individuals or institutional entities directly affected by harm.

psychopath Described by Hare (1996) as an 'interspecies predator' who works to satisfy selfish desires by using skills such as charm, manipulation, violence, and intimidation. These predators are not constrained by social norms and violate social expectations without feelings of guilt or remorse. This term is often confused with APD. According to the DSM IV, psychopathy is not an appropriate diagnosis and does not reflect an illness.

pyramid scheme A type of scam that requires a growing number of people to invest in a non-existent investment opportunity. Monies are paid to initial investors in the hopes of receiving referrals to more potential victims. These subsequent 'investments' are used to continue to pay the other investors. Because there are more victims at the bottom of the scheme than at the top, the shape of the victim pool looks like a pyramid.

rapare Latin word meaning 'to take by force'. It is the root of the word 'rape'.

rape In Canada, prior to 1984, the act of forcing (by using physical threat or coercion) a woman into having sexual intercourse against her will by a man who was not her husband. Historically, and across many cultures, this term referred specifically to the forced sexual intercourse with a woman by a man.

rational choice perspective Widely associated with Derek Cornish and Ronald Clarke, a rational choice theory that seeks to explain the victimizer's motivation and decision-making process. This perspective claims that victimizing behaviour is the process of successful rationalization based on the offender weighing the pros and cons of committing crime.

rational choice theories A set of theories, including lifestyles, routine activities, deterrence, rational choice perspective, and situated transaction, in which the offender is assumed to be a rational and active person who makes choices based on the presence or absence of potential gain and the cost of committing the crime.

residential schools A school attended by Aboriginal students and which included industrial schools, boarding schools, homes for students, hostels, billets, schools with day students, and a combination of any of these types. The purpose of these schools was to give Aboriginal children a 'Christian' education and to assimilate them into 'civilized society'.

residential school survivor An Aboriginal person who attended a residential school.

restorative justice system A response to wrongdoing that promotes mediation and emphasizes healing the wounds of those affected by conflict and crime, including victims, offenders, and communities. Restorative justice sessions often take place in informal settings, with the results being offered as a recommendation to the judge in the case. There are no juries in this system; the judge, in ideal circumstances under common law, remains impartial and implements the recommendation. Restorative justice programs are typically offered as an alternative in non-violent crimes and/or crimes involving a juvenile offender. This system is also called a communitarian, redemptive, or reintegrative justice system.

restraining order (RO) Essentially a court-ordered 'stay away for a while' mandate for an accused victimizer. An RO can last days, months, or longer and is valid only in the province where it is issued. This type of order requires that evidence be given in court, which can be a long process, and that the fear of the victim is reasonable.

retribution The process by which a person, either the victim or the victim's representative, exacts punishment in retaliation for harm that has been done to a victim.

retributive justice system A system of justice that systematically punishes who have been found in violation of a law or norm, on the grounds that the crime has created an imbalance in the social order that must be restored by taking action against the criminal. The inherent assumption of this type of system is 'an eye for an eye'. This punishment can involve fines, probationary sentencing, incarceration or, in some counties, death of the offender.

ripple effect The spreading of fear that occurs when people hear about the victimization of others.

routine activities theory (RAT) A rational choice theory that posits that three elements must be present in order for a criminal event to occur: a motivated offender, a suitable target, and a lack of capable guardianship. If one or more of these elements are missing, a crime will not occur.

secondary deviance Coined by Edwin Lemert, describes an individual's acceptance of the label of deviance or 'otherness' and his or her subsequent engagement in the social world as a deviant. In victimology, secondary deviance occurs when an individual accepts the label of victim.

secondary victimization The process whereby the victim is victimized by the criminal justice or medical systems through the process of investigation of the reported victimization incident. This subsequent victimization occurs when the victim is treated with mistrust or suspicion and/or his or her credibility is questioned. Members of these systems may also attempt to blame the victim for his or her own victimization.

secondary victims Individuals or institutional entities indirectly affected by harm done to a primary victim but who are in close social proximity to the primary victim.

second-degree murder Any type of murder not classified as first-degree.

sentencing circles Also called rehabilitation or peacemaking circles, a type of alternative dispute resolution that commonly involves elders of the community, along with various court representatives such as the Crown attorney and the defence counsel, the victim, the offender, their family members and close friends, and other members of the community. Circles may be used at the sentencing stage or following incarceration to assist an offender's reintegration into the community. Their purpose is to allow individuals to tell their stories about how the victimization affected them and to reach a consensus as to what the victimizer and the community can do to restore balance to all parties.

serial murder The act of killing people individually and sequentially, with long 'cooling-off' periods between homicide events.

severity of punishment In deterrence theory, one of three components of effective punishment. In this part, the offender and the public should perceive that the punishment is neither too lenient nor too harsh, in order to maximize the benefit of deterring criminal activity.

sexual assault level I Also known as sexual assault. This offence is the least severe form of sexual assault, often comprised of unwanted sexual touching or groping.

sexual assault level II Also known as sexual assault with a weapon, threats to a third party, or causing bodily harm. Offences of this level are considered more severe than a minor assault and can involve forced sexual intercourse by using threat or force.

sexual assault level III Also known as aggravated sexual assault. This type is the most severe form of sexual assault and features evidence of severe victim damage, including maiming or wounding.

significant others Coined by George Herbert Mead, a term that refers to those people who serve as an individual's close support network and whose opinions he or she values.

situated transaction theory Developed by David Luckenbill to explain homicide, a theory that seeks to locate crime in time and place. In this theory, the offender and victim often go through six stages of engagement before the criminal activity is completed.

snowball sampling A sampling method by which participants in a research study are asked to refer other members to the study.

social Darwinism Developed by Herbert Spencer, the idea that social dynamics are governed by evolutionary principles. This theory is also encapsulated by the phrase 'survival of the fittest'.

social interactionist theory Developed by sociologists Charles Horton Cooley and George Herbert Mead, the idea that people base their individual identities on how others perceive them.

social reaction theories Initially developed to explain deviance, a set of theories that examine the various reactions to a person being identified as belonging to a particular group. In victimology, the concept is used to examine how a person comes to accept or reject being labelled as a victim.

specific deterrence A form of deterrence in which the offender is directly deterred from criminal activity as a result of experiencing sanction for an offence.

spoofing The process of hiding one's originating information, such as a phone number or e-mail address, from potential victims. False or no information can be offered instead of the genuine details.

spree murder The act of killing one of more individuals in multiple locations, over relatively short periods of time. Spree killers share characteristics of mass murderers, in that multiple people may be targeted in one location, but there is a short cooling-off period while the killer moves to another location with another set of targets.

stigma From the Greek, meaning a physical mark or spot on the body that can lead to disgrace, embarrassment, and/or reproach. In sociology, the term refers to any characteristic that causes these effects.

Stockholm Syndrome A rare psychological and emotional process whereby a victim (usually a hostage or an abused person) identifies with and feels a strong attachment toward his or her victimizer.

stress A physical and/or psychological set of reactions to demanding situations.

stressors The demanding or threatening situations (or stimuli) that produce stress.

symbolic interactionism A theory asserting that human interaction is based solely on the interpretation of symbols, such as language and behaviour, communicated between individuals.

target hardening The process by which a potential victim is educated, or 'hardened', about the way offenders operate and is encouraged to take protective measures against victimization.

terms of release Requirements that an offender must meet in order to be released from jail. These terms are set out in a hearing that usually takes place within a few days of the initial arrest of the victimizer and expire when he or she is found guilty or not guilty.

tertiary victims Individuals or institutional entities that have no relationship with the primary victim but who suffer as a result of knowing about the victimization experience.

total institution Goffman's term for a facility in which all aspects of a resident's daily life are controlled by others. A prison is an example of a total institution.

transformative justice A form of justice that occurs when restorative justice is applied beyond the domain of criminal justice, such as in bankruptcy law, corporate law, environmental law, and family law. The basic principle of this perspective is that the law and its implementation are used both to explore options available within the various justice systems alter the parties' perceptions of one another in order to reach an greater understanding of the situation under dispute.

undeserving victim In cases of intimate partner violence, a victim who police determine does not merit their services. This type of victim is less likely to have serious injuries than a deserving victim. He or she is thought to be complicit in the assault and may have made repeated calls for service and/or have issues with substance abuse, and may continue to communicate or reside with his or her abuser.

unobtrusive methods Research methods whereby the researcher, or observer, has indirect contact with the participant through surveys, attitude questionnaires, and so on.

uxoricide A type of homicide in which a man kills his wife.

vicarious direct victim An individual who has no direct exposure to a victimization but is so strongly affected by learning of the event that he or she experiences the same intensity of fear and many of the symptoms as the direct victim.

vicarious indirect victim An individual who hears of the victimization of another and learns from the event. The resulting fear levels are lowest in this type of victim, who may or may not change his or her behaviour.

victim One who is killed, injured, or otherwise harmed by another.

victimal Coined in 1963 by Beniamin Mendelsohn, a term that means the opposite of the word 'criminal'. As an adjective it is used to describe the behaviour of a victim (e.g., victimal conduct).

victimal receptivity An individual's unconscious propensity to being victimized, which exists in varying degrees.

victim blaming The process of assigning some level of responsibility to the victim for his or her own victimization.

victim facilitation The concept whereby a victim is said to create circumstances, through neglect or carelessness, that increase his or her potential for victimization.

victimia A consecrated animal.

victim impact statement (VIS) A written or oral statement presented in court by a victim or victim representative. A VIS allows the victim to go beyond the visible harm of the victimization and to describe the economic and/or emotional hardship. In some cases, this statement can include a sentencing recommendation.

victimity According to Beniamin Mendelsohn, the opposite of criminality. Victimity refers to the quality or state of being a victim or that which constitutes being a victim.

victimize The act of offending against someone and making him or her a victim.

victimless crime A crime where the victim and victimizer are the same person, such as prostitution, drug abuse, and suicide. This term is a misnomer, as it implies that there is no victim.

victim–offender mediation (VOM) A restorative justice practice, also known as victim–offender reconciliation, victim–offender meetings, or victim–offender conferences. The most common form of mediation occurs when two parties attempt to resolve a dispute with the assistance of a trained mediator. The VOM process is a strictly voluntary and informal one that encourages the victim and offender to resolve their dispute in a mutually agreeable manner; the mediator has no decision-making authority. This process runs contrary to more traditional methods, where victim and offender participation is often mandated and the process is fraught with many rules and regulations.

victimologist A researcher who studies both victims and the context in which victims exist.

victimology The study of victims and the social context in which victims exist.

victim precipitation Also sometimes referred to as victim blaming or victim facilitation, the idea of shared responsibility in victimization between the offender and the victim. Behaviours that can be interpreted as contributing to victim precipitation are those actions that bring about, in whole or in part, a person's victimization.

victim provocation The notion that the victim has incited or instigated his or her own victimization.

victim responsibility The idea that there is a level of shared participation and culpability between the victim and the offender in the victimizing event.

victim vulnerability The risk of victimization that is attributed to an individual or group.

white-collar crime A term first coined by criminologist Edwin Sutherland, who defined it as a 'crime committed by a person of respectability and high social status in the course of his occupation'. The definition has been broadened over time and currently refers to non-violent crimes committed for financial gain, including tax evasion, embezzlement, counterfeiting, insider trading, and various types of fraud.

References

2nd woman says Smith never told her about HIV. (2007, 31 January). *CTV News.* Retrieved from www.ctv.ca/servlet/ArticleNews/story/CTVNews/20070131/trevis_smith_070131?s_name=&no_ads=.

400 potential cases of food poisoning linked to popular British restaurant. (2009, 7 March). *National Post,* p. A16.

Adler, F., Mueller, G. O. W., & Laufer, W. S. (1998). In memoriam: Marvin Wolfgang (1924–1998). *The Criminologist, 23*(3), 1, 19.

Ai, A. L., & Park, C. L. (2005). Possibilities of the positive following violence and trauma: Informing the coming decade of research. *Journal of Interpersonal Violence, 20*(2), 242–250.

Ai, A. L., Peterson, C., & Huang, B. (2003). The effect of religious coping and positive attitudes of adult Muslim refugees from Kosovo and Bosnia. *The International Journal for the Psychology of Religion, 13,* 29–46.

Alphonso, C. (2007, 7 March). Pepper-sprayed at U.S. border, man seeks apology. *The Globe and Mail,* p. A7.

Ambrosio, E., Baker, D., Crowe, C., & Hardill, K. (1992). *Street health report. A study of the health status and barriers to health care of homeless women and men in the city of Toronto.* Toronto, ON: City of Toronto.

American Institute of Stress. (n.d.). *Effects of stress.* Retrieved 3 April 2009, from www.stress.org/topic-effects.htm.

American Psychiatric Association. (2000). *Diagnostic and statistical manual of mental disorders* (DSM-IV-TR) (4th ed.). Washington, DC: Author.

Amir, M. (1971). *Patterns in forcible rape.* Chicago, IL: University of Chicago Press.

Appleby, T., & Cheney, P. (2009, 7 March). Accused in Davis slaying appear in court. *The Globe and Mail,* p. A14.

Arias, I., & Corso, P. (2005). Average cost per person victimized by an intimate partner of the opposite gender: A comparison of men and women. *Violence and Victims, 20*(4), 379–91.

Ashworth, A. (1993). Victim impact statements and sentencing. *Criminal Law Review, 7,* 498–509.

Associated Press. (2004). Little sympathy for Kobe case prosecutors; Blame for dropping process shifted to victim: Legal expert. *The Hamilton Spectator.* Retrieved 10 April 2008, from ProQuest.

Attorney General of British Columbia [AGBC]. (n.d.) *Victim impact statement: An information guide.* Retrieved 25 February 2009, from the Ministry of the Attorney General website, Criminal Justice Branch: www.ag.gov.bc.ca/public/criminal-justice/StatementGuide.pdf.

AuCoin, K. (Ed.). (2007) *Family violence in Canada: A statistical profile 2007* (pp. 13–32). Ottawa, ON: Canadian Centre for Justice Statistics, Minister of Industry.

AuCoin, K., & Beauchamp, D. (2007). Impacts and consequences of victimization, GSS 2004. *Juristat, 27*(1). Ottawa, ON: Canadian Centre for Justice Statistics, Minister of Industry.

Aycock, J., & Aycock, A. (2008). Why I love/hate Wikipedia: Reflections upon (not quite) subjugated knowledges. *Journal of the Scholarship of Teaching and Learning, 8*(2), 92–101.

Babiak, P. (1995). When psychopaths go to work: A case study of an industrial psychopath. *Applied Psychology: An International Review, 44,* 171–88.

Babiak, P. (2000). Psychopathic manipulation at work. In C. B. Gacono (Ed.), *The Clinical and Forensic Assessment of Psychopathy: A Practioner's Guide* (pp. 287–312). Mahwaw, NJ: Lawrence Erlbaum Associates.

Babiak, P., & Hare, R. D. (2006). *Snakes in Suits: When Psychopaths go to Work.* New York, NY: HarperCollins.

Banff assault victim 'everyone's daughter'. (2006, 3 November). *CBC News Online.* Retrieved 19 January 2008, from www.cbc.ca/canada/ottawa/story/2006/11/03/banff-ban.html.

Banff assault victim identified. (2005, 7 March). *The Ottawa Citizen.* Retrieved 10 June 2010 from www.canada.com/ottawacitizen/news/city/story.html?id=64cfaaf5-0137-4167-9471-172275e79938&k=30530.

Barnes, H., & Teeters, N. (1943). *New Horizons in Criminology.* New York, NY: Prentice Hall.

Baron, S. (2003). Street youth violence and victimization. *Trauma, Violence, & Abuse,* 4(1), 22–44.

Baron, S., & Hartnegal, T. F. (1998). Street youth and criminal violence. *Journal of Research in Crime and Delinquency, 35*(2), 166–192.

Baumer, T. L. (1979). Research on Fear of Crime in the United States. *Victimology,* 3(3/4) 254–64.

Beattie, S. (2009). Homicide in Canada, 2008. *Juristat, 29*(4). Ottawa, ON: Statistics Canada, Minister of Industry.

Becker, H. (1963). *Outsiders: Studies in the sociology of deviance.* New York, NY: Free Press.

Bentham, J. (1789). *An introduction to the principles of morals and legislation.* Oxford, England: Clarendon Press.

Blatchford, C. (2009a, 7 March). There is much Canadians don't know about their fallen. *The Globe and Mail,* p. A2.

Blatchford, C. (2009b, 7 March). Girl's blithe comments after fatal stabbing of teen gave detectives the chills. *The Globe and Mail,* p. A8.

Blatchford, C., Friesen, J., & Appleby, T. (2005, 29 December). Slain teenager veered blithely into crossfire: Dead victim in Yonge Street shootings has been identified as Jane Creba. *The Globe and Mail.* Retrieved from www.theglobeandmail.com/servlet/story/RTGAM.20051228.wcreba1228a/BNStory/National/.

Blumer, H. (1969). *The Chicago School of Sociology.* Chicago, IL: University of Chicago Press.

Bonoguore, T. (2009, 7 March). Mattress workers seek assurance of wages. *The Globe and Mail,* p. A15.

Boy hurt in foster care to be taken off life support. (2009, 7 March). *The Globe and Mail,* p. A11.

Brazao, D., & Mascoll, P. (1997, 26 February). Sex scandal at Gardens 'snowballs'. *The Toronto Star,* Final Ed. p. A1. Retrieved from Lexis Nexis.

Brazao, D. (2007, 5 May). Maple Leafs owners to face new round of sex-abuse claims: Man seeks $4M for alleged molesting by usher in '70s; lawyer says 5 more on way. *The Toronto Star.* Retrieved 27 May 2010, from www.thestar.com/news/article/210749.

Breslau, N., Chilcoat, H. D., Kessler, R. C., Pearson, E. L., & Lucia, V. C. (1999). Vulnerability to assaultive violence: Further specification of the sex difference in post-traumatic stress disorder. *Psychological Medicine, 29,* 813–21.

Breslau, N., Davis, G. C., Andreski, P., & Peterson, E. I. (1997). Sex differences in posttraumatic stress disorder. *Archives of General Psychiatry, 54,* 1044–48.

Brickman, E. (2003). *Development of a national study of victim needs and assistance.* Report submitted to the US Department of Justice. (Doc No.195625). Washington, DC: US Department of Justice.

Brownmiller, S. (1975) *Against our will: Men, women, and rape.* Toronto, ON: Bantam Books.

Brzozowski, J. (2004). Family violence against children and youth. In J. Brzozowski (Ed.), *Family Violence in Canada: A Statistical Profile 2004* (pp. 16–25). Ottawa, ON: Canadian Centre for Justice Statistics, Minister of Industry.

Brzozowski, J., Taylor-Butts, A., & Johnson, S. (2006). Victimization and offending among the Aboriginal population in Canada. *Juristat, 26*(3). Ottawa, ON: Canadian Centre for Justice Statistics, Minister of Industry.

Bunge, V. P., Johnson, H., & Balde, T. (2005). Exploring crime patterns in Canada. *Crime and Justice Research Paper Series.* Ottawa, ON: Canadian Centre for Justice Statistics and Time Series Research and Analysis Centre, Minister of Industry. Retrieved 10 June 2010, from www.statcan.gc.ca/pub/85-561-m/85-561-m2005005-eng.pdf.

Burt, M. R. (1980). Cultural myths and support for rape. *Journal of Personality and Social Psychology, 38,* 217–30.

Bush, R. A. B., & Folger, J. P. (1994). *The Promise of Mediation: Responding to Conflict through Empowerment and Recognition.* San

Francisco, CA: Jossey-Bass Publishers.

Campbell, R. C. (2005). What really happened? A validation study of rape survivors' help-seeking experiences with the legal and medical systems. *Violence and Victims, 20*(1), 55–68.

Canada. (1992). Corrections and Conditional Release Act. Ottawa, ON: Minster of Justice. Retrieved 17 June 2010, from http://laws.justice.gc.ca/PDF/Statute/C/C-44.6.pdf.

Canada. (2008). *Innovation and growth in Victims Services: Manitoba's Victims' Bill of Rights.* Ottawa, ON: Department of Justice. Retrieved 2 March 2009, from www.victimsweek.gc.ca/archive2007/resource_guide/r67.html.

Canadian Anti-Fraud Centre. (n.d.) *Statistics on fraud.* Retrieved 25 March 2009, from www.phonebusters.com/english/statistics.html.

Canadian Broadcasting Corporation (CBC) Archives. (2008). A long awaited apology. Retrieved 3 February 2009, from http://archives.cbc.ca/society/native_issues/clips/15394/.

Canadian Centre for Addiction and Mental Health (CAMH). (n.d.). *Stress.* Retrieved 3 April 2009, from www.cmha.ca/bins/content_page.asp?cid=2-28&lang=1.

Canadian Mental Health Association. (n.d.) *Post Traumatic Stress Disorder.* Retrieved 6 April 2009, from www.cmha.ca/bins/content_page.asp?cid=3-94-97&lang=1.

Canadian Press (CP). (2003, 24 April). Money for abused Mount Cashel victims offered deal. Retrieved 19 February 2009, from www.canadiancrc.com/Newspaper_Articles/Toronto_Sun_Money_for_abused_24APR03.aspx.

Canadian Resource Centre for Victims of Crime. (2006). *Victims' Rights in Canada.* Retrieved 4 January 2008, from www.crcvc.ca/docs/vicrights.pdf.

Cann, A., Calhoun, L. C., Selby, J. W., & King, H. E. (Eds.). (1981). Rape. *Journal of Social Issues, 37*(4), 1–162.

Caregiver in W-FIVE video acquitted of assault. (2004, 9 March). *CTV News.* Retrieved 30 April 2010, from www.ctv.ca/servlet/ArticleNews/story/CTVNews/20040309/elderly_abuse_video_040309?s_name=&no_ads=.

Cavaiola, A., & Lavender, N. (2000). *Toxic Coworkers.* Oakland, CA: Harbinger.

CAVEAT. (1993). Lasting Living Tribute to Nina de Villiers. Retrieved 8 April 2008, from www.caveat.org/publications/sw/cav_1993_nov.html.

CAVEAT. (2000). *Background.* Retrieved 6 April 2008, from www.caveat.org/history.

CBCnews.ca. (2000, 13 April). Former Mount Cashel victim rips down signs. Retrieved 19 February 2009, from www.cbc.ca/news/story/2000/04/13/nf_cashel000413.html.

CBC News (2006, 12 September). Ralph Klein: Alberta's populist premier. *CBC News In Depth.* Retrieved from www.cbc.ca/news/background/klein-ralph/.

Chan, J. H. F. (2009). Where is the Imbalance? *Journal of School Violence, 8*(2), 177–190.

Classmates of slain teenager share their loss. (2005, 30 December). *CBC News Online.* Retrieved from www.ctv.ca/servlet/ArticleNews/story/CTVNews/20051230/grieving_students_051230?s_name=election2006&no_ads=CTV.

Cohen, L. E., & Felson, M. (1979). Social change and crime rate trends: A routine activity approach. *American Sociological Review, 44,* 588–608.

Consumer Protection Branch of the Ministry of Justice and Attorney General. (n.d) *Tips for reducing the risk of identity theft.* Retrieved 18 January 2009, from www.safecanada.ca/identitytheft_e.asp.

Cooley, C. H. (1902). *Human Nature and the Social Order.* New York, NY: Scribner's.

Cooper, C. L. (2000). *Theories of organizational stress.* New York, NY: Oxford University Press.

Cornish, D. B., & Clarke, R. V. (1986). *The Reasoning Criminal.* New York, NY: Springer-Verlag.

Coyne, I., Craig, J., & Chong, P. (2004). Workplace bullying in a group context. *British Journal of Guidance and Counselling, 32*(3), 301–17.

Crown wants Ellard sentenced to maximum for killing Reena Virk. (2005, 7 July). *CBC News Online.* Retrieved from www.cbc.ca/canada/story/2005/07/06/virk050706.html.

Davis, R. C., Lurigio, A. J., & Skogan, W. G. (1999). Services for victims: A market research study. *International Journal of Victimology, 6,* 101–15.

de Léséleuc, S. (2007) Criminal victimization in the workplace 2004. *Canadian Centre for Justice Statistics Profile Series.* Ottawa, ON: Canadian Centre for Justice Statistics, Minister of Industry.

Department of Justice (1985). *Sexual assault legislation in Canada: An evaluation.* Ottawa, ON: Supply and Services Canada.

Department of Justice. (2001). *Family violence initiative.* Retrieved 14 March 2009, from www.justice.gc.ca/eng/pi/fv-vf/facts-info/sa-vc.html.

Deukmedjian, J. E. (2008). The rise and fall of RCMP community justice forums: Restorative justice and public safety interoperability in Canada. *Canadian Journal of Criminology and Criminal Justice, 50*(2), 117–51.

Doctor accused of infant euthanasia. (2009, 7 March). *National Post,* p. A16.

Doob, A., Grossman, M., & Auger, R. (1994). Aboriginal homicides in Ontario. *Canadian Journal of Criminology, 36,* 29–62.

Dugan, L. (2003). Domestic violence legislation: Exploring its impact on the likelihood of domestic violence police involvement and arrest. *Criminology and Public Policy, 2*(2), 283–312.

Egger, S. A. (1984). A working definition of serial murder and the reduction of linkage blindness. *Journal of Police Science and Administration, 12,* 348–57.

Egger, S. A. (1990). Serial murder: An elusive phenomenon. In *Encyclopaedia of Murder* (p. 1984). London, England: Pan Books.

Egger, S. A. (2002). *Killers among us: The Examination of serial murder and investigations.* Upper Saddle River, NJ: Prentice Hall.

Eigenberg, H. (2003). Victim Blaming. In L. Moriarty (Ed.), *Controversies in Victimology* (pp. 15–24). Cincinnati, OH: Anderson.

Ellenberger, T. (1955). Psychological Relationships between the Criminal and His Victim. *Archives of Criminal Psychology, 2,* 257–90.

Entous, A. (2009, 7 March). Gaza, West Bank offered record aid: US$14 billion, questions raised over donor pledges to help Abbas. *National Post,* p. A17.

Erez, E. (1990). Victim participation in sentencing: Rhetoric and reality. *Journal of Criminal Justice, 18,* 19–31.

Erez, E. (1994). Victim participation in sentencing: And the debate goes on. *International Review of Victimology, 3,* 17–32.

Erez, E., & Rogers, L. (1999). Victim impact statements and sentencing outcomes and processes: The perspectives of legal professionals. *British Journal of Criminology, 39*(2), 216–39.

Erez, E., Rogers, L., & O'Connell, M. (2000). *Victim impact statements in South Australia.* Paper presented at International Symposium on Victimology, Montreal, Canada.

Fahrmeir, A. (n.d.) [Review of the book *Kriminologie und Strafrecht zwischen Kaiserreich und Nationalsozialismus,* by David von Mayenburg]. Retrieved 14 April 2010, from www.sehepunkte.de/2008/05/13221.html.

Family of slain Toronto teen remembers their 'bright light' (2005, 29 December). *CBC News Online.* Retrieved from www.cbc.ca/canada/story/2005/12/29/newshootingToronto051229.html.

Fattah, E. (1976). The use of the victim as an agent of self-legitimation: Towards a dynamic explanation of criminal behavior. In E. Viano (Ed.), *Victims and Society* (pp. 105–29). Washington, DC: Visage.

Federal Trade Commission (2004). *Identity theft survey report.* McLean, VA: Synovate.

Fenwick, H. (1997). Procedural 'rights' of victims of crime: Public or private ordering of the criminal justice process? *Modern Law Review, 60,* 317–33.

Ferraro, K. F. (1996). Women's Fear of Victimization: Shadow of Sexual Assault? *Social Forces, 75*(2), 667–90.

Ferraro, K. F., & LaGrange, R. (1987). The measurement of fear of crime. *Sociological Inquiry, 57,* 70–101.

First Nations Summit. (n.d.). Text of Prime Minister Harper's apology. Retrieved 1 June 2010, from www.fns.bc.ca/pdf/TextofApology.pdf.

Fisher, B. S., & Regan, S. L. (2006). The extent and frequency of abuse in the lives of older women and their relationship with health outcomes. *The Gerontologist, 46*(2), 200–9.

Flaten, C. (1996). Victim-offender mediation: Application with serious offenses committed by juveniles. In B. Galaway & J. Hudson (Eds.), *Restorative Justice: International Perspectives* (pp. 387–401). New York, NY: Criminal Justice Press.

Former CFLer guilty of aggravated sexual assault (2007, 8 February). *CTV News*. Retrieved from www.ctv.ca/servlet/ArticleNews/story/CTVNews/20070208/smith_CFL_070208/20070208?hub=TopStories.

Foucault, M. (1977). *Discipline and punish: The birth of the prison*. London, England: Penguin Books.

Fournier, S., & Crey, E. (1998). *Stolen from our embrace: The Abduction of First Nations children and the restoration of Aboriginal communities*. Toronto, ON: Douglas and McIntyre.

Fournier, S., Fraser, K., & Jiwa, S. (2002, 26 February). Daughter phoned daily for 13 years. *The Province*. Retrieved from www.missingpeople.net/cgi-bin/2002/sereen_abotsway-2002.htm.

Fraser, N. (n.d.). Restraining orders in Canada. *The Lawyers Weekly*. Retrieved 20 February 2009, from Lexis Nexis: www.canadian-lawyers.ca/understand-your-legal-issue/general-info/1022868/.

Frazier, P. A., & Borgida, E. (1992). Rape trauma syndrome: A review of case law and psychological research. *Law and Human Behavior, 16*, 293–311.

Friedman, K., Bischoff, H., Davis, R., & Person, A. (1982). *Victims and helpers: Reactions to crime*. Washington, DC: National Institute of Justice.

Frisen, A., Jonsson, A. K., & Persson, C. (2007). Adolescents' perception of bullying: Who is the victim? Who is the bully? What can be done to stop the bullying? *Adolescence, 42*.

Frye, V., Haviland, M., & Rajah, V. (2007). Dual arrest and other unintended consequences of mandatory arrest in New York City: A brief report. *Journal of Family Violence, 22*, 397–405. Retrieved 25 February 2009, from Scholars Portal.

Furnell, S. (2007). Identity impairment: The problems facing victims of identity fraud. *Computer Fraud & Security, 2007*(12), 6–11.

Furstenberg, F. F. (1972). Fear of crime and its effects on citizen behaviour. In A. Biderman (Ed.), *Crime and justice: A symposium*. New York, NY: Nailburg.

Gabor, T. (1994). The suppression of crime statistics on race and ethnicity: The price of political correctness. *Canadian Journal of Criminology, 36*, 153–63.

Gaes, G.G., & Goldberg, A.L. (2004). *Prison rape: A critical review of the literature* (Working paper). Washington, DC: National Institute of Justice.

Gaetz, S. (2004). Safe streets for whom? Homeless youth, social exclusion, and criminal victimization. *Canadian Journal of Criminology and Criminal Justice, 3*, 423–55.

Gannon, M. (2001). Crime comparisons between Canada and the United States. *Juristat, 21*(11). Ottawa, ON: Canadian Centre for Justice Statistics, Minister of Industry.

Gannon, M. (2006). Crime statistics in Canada, 2005. *Juristat, 26*(4), 8. Ottawa, ON: Canadian Centre for Justice Statistics, Minister of Industry.

Gannon, M., & Mihorean, K. (2005). Criminal Victimization in Canada. *Juristat, 25*(7). Ottawa, ON: Canadian Centre for Justice Statistics, Minister of Industry.

Gannon, M., & Mihorean, K. (2005). Sexual offences in Canada, 2004. *Juristat, 25*(7). Ottawa, ON: Canadian Centre for Justice Statistics, Minister of Industry.

Giannelli, P. (1997). Rape trauma syndrome. *Criminal Law Bulletin, 33*, 270–9.

Giliberti, C. (1990). Victim Impact Statements in Canada. *Volume 7: A summary of the findings*. Ottawa, ON: Department of Justice Canada

Gionet, L. (2009). First Nations people: Selected findings from the 2006 census. In *Canadian Social Trends* (pp. 52–8). Ottawa, ON: Minister of Industry.

Goffman, E. (1963). *Stigma: Notes on the management of the spoiled identity*. Englewood Cliffs, NJ: Prentice Hall.

Goffman, E. (1968). *Asylums*. Harmondsworth, England: Penguin.

Government of Ontario. (2006). *What is identity theft?* Retrieved 18 January 2009, from www.gov.on.ca/MGS/en/ConsProt/STEL02_045992.html.

Graham, D. L., Rawlings, E. I., & Rigsby, R. K. (1994). *Loving to survive: Sexual terror, men's violence, and women's lives.* New York, NY: New York University Press.

Graham-Kevan, N., & Archer, J. (2003). Intimate terrorism and common couple violence a test of Johnson's predictions in four British samples. *Journal of Interpersonal Violence, 18*(11), 1247–70.

Green, R. G. (1998). *Justice in Aboriginal communities: Sentencing alternatives.* Saskatoon, SK: Purich Publishing.

Gunman massacres 14 women (1989, 6 December). Canadian Broadcasting Corporation. Retrieved from The CBC Digital Archives Website: http://archives.cbc.ca/society/crime_justice/topics/398-2236/.

Hamilton man admits to manslaughter during drunken, fatal fight, (2008, 28 March). *Hamilton Spectator.* Retrieved 17 June 2008, from ProQuest.

Hare, R. (1991). *The Hare Psychopathy Checklist-Revised.* Toronto, ON: Multi-Health Systems.

Hare, R. (1996). Psychopathy: A clinical construct whose time has come. *Criminal Justice and Behavior, 23,* 25–54.

Hickey, E. W. (2002). *Serial Murderers and Their Victims.* (3rd ed.). Belmont, CA: Wadsworth Publishing Company.

Hill, P. C., & Pargament, K. I. (2003). Advances in the conceptualization and measurement of religion and spirituality: Implications for physical and mental health research. *American Psychologist, 58,* 64–74.

Hinch, R. (1985). Canada's new sexual assault laws: A stop forward for women? *Contemporary Crises, 9*(1), 33–44.

Hindelang, M. J., Gottfredson, M. R., & Garofalo, J. (1978). *Victims of personal crime: An empirical foundation for a theory of personal victimization.* Cambridge, MA: Ballinger.

Hirschel, J., & Buzawa, E. (2002). Understanding the context of dual arrest with directions for future research. *Violence Against Women, 8*(12), 1449–73.

Holmes, T. H., & Matsuda, M. (1973). Psychosomatic syndrome: When mothers-in-law and other disasters visit, a person can develop a bad, bad, cold. *Psychology Today, 5*(11), 71–2, 106.

Holmes, T. H., & Rahe, R. H. (1967). The Social Readjustment Rating Scale. *Journal of Psychosomatic Research, II,* 213–18.

Horovitz, D. (2009, 7 March). Bats, balls and bullets. *National Post,* p. A20.

Husband arrested after Vancouver woman shot dead in India, family says. (2009, 7 March). *National Post,* p. A5.

Hutchinson, B. (2009, 7 March). B.C. RCMP crisis of confidence: Civilian oversight over police could help boost trust. *National Post,* p. A8.

Hwang, S.W., Tolomiczenko, G., Kouyoumdjian, F. G., & Garner, R. E. (2005). Interventions to improve the health of the homeless: A systematic review. *American Journal of Preventive Medicine, 29*(4), 311–19.

Janoff-Bulman, R., & Frantz, C. M. (1997). The impact of trauma on meaning: From meaningless world to meaningful life. In M. Power & C. R. Brewin (Eds.), *The transformation of meaning in psychological therapies* (pp. 91–106). New York, NY: Wiley.

Jasinski, J. L., Wesely, J., Mustaine, E., & Wright, J. D. (2005). *The experience of violence in the lives of homeless women: A research report.* Washington, DC: National Institute of Justice.

Jiwani, Y. (1997). *Reena Virk: The erasure of race.* Retrieved 19 January 2008, from the FREDA Centre for Research on Violence against Women and Children website: www.harbour.sfu.ca/freda/articles/virk.htm.

Johnson, H. (1996). *Dangerous domains: Violence against women in Canada.* Toronto, ON: Nelson.

Johnson, H. (2006). *Measuring violence against women: Statistical trends 2006.* Ottawa, ON: Canadian Centre for Justice Statistics, Minister of Industry.

Johnson, M. P. & Ferraro, K. J. (2000). Research on domestic violence in the 1990s: Making distinctions. *Journal of Marriage and the Family, 62,* 948–63.

Jones, D., & Belknap, J. (1999). Police responses to bettering in a progressive pro-arrest jurisdiction. *Justice Quarterly, 16,* 249–73.

Jowett, C. (2009, 7 March). Local businessman appears calm despite being jailed on murder charges. *National Post,* p. A14.

Kadushin, A., & Martin, J. A. (1988). *Child Welfare Services* (4th ed.). New York, NY: MacMillan.

Kahn, R., & Byosiere, P. (Eds.). (1992). *Stress in organizations.* Palo Alto, CA: Consulting Psychologist Press.

Kari, S. (2009, 7 March). 'I said I want her dead,' accused tells police: Murdered teen was spreading rumours, girl alleges. *National Post,* p. A9.

Karmen, A. (1980). Auto theft: Beyond victim blaming. *Victimology, 5,* 161–74.

Karmen, A. (2007). *Crime victims: An introduction to victimology* (6th ed.). Belmont, CA: Thomson Higher Education.

Karmen, A. (2010). *Crime victims: An introduction to crime victims.* Belmont, CA: Wadsworth.

Katz, M. (1996). *In the shadow of the poorhouse: A history of welfare in America.* New York, NY: Basic Books.

Keane, C. (1995). Evaluating the influence of fear of crime as an environmental mobility restrictor on women's routine activities. *Environment and Behavior, 30*(1), 60–74.

Keeney, B. T., & Heide, K. M. (1994). Gender differences in serial murderers: A preliminary analysis. *Journal of Interpersonal Violence, 9,* 383–398.

Kennard, K. (1989). The victim's veto: A way to increase victim impact on criminal case dispositions. *California Law Review, 77,* 417–53.

Kids Help Phone. (2010). It's Time to Stop Bullying. Teens Info Booth. Retrieved 18 May 2010, from www.kidshelpphone.ca/Teens/InfoBooth/Bullying/24-hours-of-bullying-text-version.aspx.

Kilpatrick, D., Beatty, D., & Smith Howley, S. (1998). *The rights of crime victims— Does legal protection make a difference?* Washington, DC: National Institute of Justice, US Department of Justice.

Kirmayer, L. J., Brass, G. M., Holton, T., Paul, K., Simpson, C., & Tait, C. (2007). *Suicide among Aboriginal people in Canada.* Ottawa, ON: Aboriginal Healing Foundation.

Klein, D. (1973). The etiology of female crime: A review of the literature. *Issues in Criminology, 8,* 3–30.

Kong, R., & Beattie, K. (2005). *Collecting data on Aboriginal people in the criminal justice system: Methods and challenges.* Ottawa, ON: Canadian Centre for Justice Statistics, Minister of Industry.

Kong, R., Johnson, H., Beattie, S., & Cardillo, A. (2003). Sexual offences in Canada. *Juristat, 23*(6), 1–26. Ottawa, ON: Canadian Centre for Justice Statistics, Minister of Industy.

Kraus. K. (2008). Paul Croutch: A casualty of war on the poor. *Rabble News.* Retrieved 3 June 2010, from www.rabble.ca/news/paul-croutch-casualty-war-poor.

Kuleshnyk, I. (1984). The Stockholm Syndrome: Towards an understanding. *Social Action and the Law, 10,* 37–42.

Lamborn, L. (1968). Towards a victim orientation in criminology and theory. *Rutgers Law Review, 22,* 733–68.

Lane, P., Bopp, J., & Bopp, M. (2003). *Aboriginal domestic violence in Canada.* Ottawa, ON: Aboriginal Healing Foundation.

Lang, D. (1974, 25 November). The Bank Drama. *The New Yorker,* p. 56. Retrieved from *The New Yorker* Archive.

LaPrairie, C. (1990). The role of sentencing in the over-representation of Aboriginal people in correctional institutions. *Canadian Journal of Criminology, 32,* 429–40.

LaRocque, E. (1994). *Violence in Aboriginal Communities.* Ottawa, ON: Royal Commission on Aboriginal Peoples.

Latimer, J., Dowden, C., & Muise, D. (2001) *The effectiveness of restorative justice practices: A meta-analysis.* Ottawa, ON: Justice Canada, Minister of Industry.

Lawrence, G., & Adams, F. D. (2006). For every bully there is a victim. *American Secondary Education, 35*(1), 66–71.

Lazarus, R. S. (1974). Psychological stress and coping in adaptation and illness. *International Journal of Psychiatry in Medicine 5,* 321–33.

Lazarus, R. S. (1991). *Emotion & Adaptation.* New York, NY: Oxford University Press.

Lazarus, R. S., & Folkman, S. (1984). *Stress, appraisal and coping.* New York, NY: Springer Publishing Company.

Lee, B. A., & Schreck, C. J. (2005). Danger on the streets: Marginality and victimization among homeless people. *American Behavioral Scientist, 48*(8), 1055–81.

Lee, R. B. (1979). *The Dobe !Kung.* New York, NY: Holt, Rinehart, and Winston.

Lemert, E. M. (1951). *Social pathology: Systematic approaches to the study of sociopathic behavior.* New York, NY: McGraw-Hill.

Leonard, E. (1982). *Women, crime and society: A critique of theoretical criminology.* New York, NY: Longman.

Levin, J., & Fox, J. A. (1985). *Mass murder: America's growing menace.* New York, NY: Plenum Press.

Levy, S., & Guttman, L. (1985). Worry, fear, and concern differentiated. *Issues in Mental Health Nursing, 7*(1–4), 251–64.

Leyton, E. (1986). *Hunting humans: The rise of the modern multiple murderer.* Toronto, ON: McClelland-Bantam, Inc.

Li, G. (2007). Homicide in Canada, 2006. *Juristat, 27*(8). Ottawa, ON: Canadian Centre for Justice Statistics, Minister of Industy.

Libin, K. (2009, 7 March). Father of frozen girls gets 3 years. *National Post,* pp. A1, A8.

Lombroso, C. (1899/1911). *Crime: Its causes and remedies.* Boston, MA: Little, Brown.

Luckenbill, D. F. (1977). Criminal homicide as a situated transaction. *Social Problems, 25,* 176–86.

Lunde, D. T. (1979). *Murder and madness.* New York, NY: W. W. Norton.

McCold, P. (2000, April). *Overview of Mediation, Conferencing and Circles.* Paper presented to the Tenth United Nations Congress on Crime Prevention and the Treatment of Offenders, Vienna, Austria.

McCullough, M. E., Hoyt, W. T., Larson, D. B., Koenig, H. G., & Thoresen, C. (2000). Religious involvement and mortality: A meta-analytic review. *Health Psychology, 19,* 211–22.

McIntyre, M. (2008, 6 May). Child witnessed alcohol-fuelled axe slaying on troubled reserve. *Winnipeg Free Press.* Retrieved 17 June 2008, from ProQuest.

McKiernan, M. (2009, 7 March). Police find stolen cargo of chicken breasts in Etobicoke warehouse. *National Post,* p. A15.

MacKinnon, M. (2009, 7 March). Fifty years after Chinese rule began, Tibet's leader is still in exile, and many fear chaos will erupt if the conflict with China isn't resolved within his lifetime. *The Globe and Mail,* pp. A1, A16.

Maclean's. (1995). de Villers, Priscilla: Maclean's 1995 Honour Roll. Retrieved 6 April 2008, from www.thecanadianencyclopedia.com/index.cfm?PgNm=TCE&Params=M1ARTM0010547.

Mahoney, J. (2001, 15 December). Red-faced Klein sorry for late-night hostel visit. *The Globe and Mail,* p. A1. Retrieved from Lexis Nexis.

Man charged after bloodied abduction victim found running down B.C. highway. (2009, 7 March). *National Post,* p. A9.

Man pleads guilty to fatal stabbing. (2008, 14 May). *Edmonton Journal.* Retrieved 17 June 2008, from ProQuest.

Manitoba Justice. (n.d.). Victim impact statement form. Retrieved 14 June 2010, from www.gov.mb.ca/justice/victims/pdf/victim-impactstatementform.pdf.

Marenin, O. (1992). Explaining Patterns of Crime in Native Villages in Alaska. *Canadian Journal of Criminology, 34*(3–4), 339–68.

Martin, M. (1997). Double your trouble: Dual Arrest in family violence. *Journal of Family Violence, 12,* 139–157.

Mason, G. (2009, 7 March). Decision not to charge in taser case stands on ever more shakey ground. *The Globe and Mail,* p. A10.

Maxim, P. S., White, J. P., Beavon, D., & Whitehead, P. C. (2001). Dispersion and polarization among Aboriginal and non-Aboriginal Canadians. *Canadian Review of Sociology and Anthropology, 38,* 465–76.

Mead, G. H. (1913). The social self. *The Journal of Philosophy, Psychology and Scientific Methods, 10*(14), 274–380.

Mead, G. H. (1934). *Mind, self, and society.* Chicago, IL: University of Chicago Press.

Meissner, D. (2007, 19 January). Sereena Abotsway: Life was always about hope. *Canadian Press.* Retrieved from www.ctv.ca/servlet/ArticleNews/story/CTVNews/20070117/missing_abotsway_071117/20070119.

Melnitzer, J. (2002). *Maximum, minimum, medium: A journey through Canadian prisons.* Toronto, ON: Key Porter Books.

Mendelsohn, B. (1956). The victimology. In S. Schafer (Ed.) *The victim and his criminal: A study in functional responsibility.* New York: Random House.

Mendelsohn, B. (1963). The origin of the doctrine of victimology. In I. Drapkin & E. Viano (Eds.), *Victimology.* Lexington, MA: D.C. Heath.

Men wearing white ribbons. (1991, 27 November 27). Canadian Broadcasting Corporation. Retrieved 19 June 2008, from The CBC Digital Archives Website: http://archives.cbc.ca/society/crime_justice/topics/398-2240/.

Mihorean, K. (2005). Trends in self-reported spousal violence. In *Family Violence in Canada: A Statistical Profile, 2005* (pp.13–32). Ottawa, ON: Canadian Centre for Justice Statistics, Minister of Industry.

Miller, J. (2003). An arresting experiment: Domestic violence victim experiences and perceptions. *Journal of Interpersonal Violence, 18*(7), 695–716.

Miller, S. L. (2001). The paradox of women arrested for domestic violence: Criminal justice professionals and service providers respond. *Violence Against Women, 7,* 1339–1376.

Moore, E., & Mills, M. (1990). The Neglected Victims and Unexamined Costs of White-Collar Crime. *Crime & Delinquency, 36,* 408–18.

Moore, O. (2008, 14 January). Deaths darken N.B. community: City faces grim task of organizing mass funeral, while tragedy raises questions on school-trip safety standards. *The Globe and Mail.* Retrieved from www.theglobeandmail.com/servlet/story/RTGAM.20080114.wbathurst14/BNStory/.

Moore, O. (2008, 15 January). Tears flow as students try to cope with loss: Memorials for basketball players arrive from around the province as grief counsellors help teenagers begin recovering. *The Globe and Mail.* Retrieved from http://v1.theglobeandmail.com/servlet/story/RTGAM.20080115.wschool15/front/Front/Front/.

Moore, O. (2008, 16 January). Survivor recalls van crash that killed 7 friends: A fellow student was praying, he said: 'I just called his name, reached over my hand and told him I loved him.' *The Globe and Mail.* Retrieved from www.theglobeandmail.com/servlet/story/RTGAM.20080116.wbus16/BNStory/Natio.

Moriarty, L. J. (1988). *A social learning approach to explaining fear of crime.* Unpublished doctoral dissertation. Huntsville, TX: Sam Houston State University.

Mount Cashel Orphanage. (n.d.). Mount Cashel orphanage: Newfoundland's house of horrors. Retrieved 19 February 2009, from www.mountcashelorphanage.com/.

Murder of Kenyan activists campaigning against police killings sparks protests. *National Post,* p. A16.

National Defence and Canadian Forces (NDCF) Ombudsman. (2002). *Special report: Systematic treatment of CF members with PTSD complaint: Christian McEachern.* Ottawa, ON: Nationl Defence.

Nemr, R. (2009). Fact sheet—Police-reported family violence against children and youth. *From Family Violence in Canada: A Statistical Profile 2009* (pp. 32–41). Ottawa, ON: Canadian Centre for Justice Statistics, Minister of Industry.

Nina's Place. (2008). Retrieved 6 April 2008, from www.ninasplace.ca.

O'Donnell, I., & Edgar, K. (1998). Routine victimization in prisons. *Howard Journal of Criminal Justice, 37,* 266–79.

O'Donnell, I., & Edgar, K. (1999). Fear in prison. *The Prison Journal, 79*(1), 90–99.

O'Toole, M. (2009, 7 March). Victim identified four decades after murder: Reconstruction. *National Post,* p. A14.

Office of the Privacy Commissioner of Canada. (2005). *Five key steps to reduce the risk of identity theft.* Retrieved 18 January 2009, from www.privcom.gc.ca/fs-fi/02_05_d_27_e.asp.

Ogrodnik, L. (2007). Seniors as victims of crime, 2004 and 2005. *Canadian Centre for Justice Statistics Profile Series.* Ottawa, ON: Canadian Centre for Justice Statistics, Minister of Industry.

Pantazis, C. (2000), 'Fear of crime', vulnerability and poverty: Evidence from the British Crime Survey. *British Journal of Criminology, 40,* 414–36.

Pargament, K. I. (1997). *The psychology of religion and coping.* New York, NY: Guilford.

Perreault, S. (2009). Criminal victimization and health: A profile of victimization among persons with activity limitations or other health problems. *Canadian Centre for Justice Statistics Profile Series.* Ottawa, ON: Canadian Centre for Justice Statistics, Minister of Industry.

Peterson, C., & Seligman, M. E. P. (2004). *Character strengths and virtues: A classification and handbook.* Washington, DC: American Psychological Association & Oxford University Press.

Pflanz, M., & Moore, M. (2009, 7 March). Zimbabwe's PM injured in crash. *National Post,* p. A16.

Postmus, J. (2007). Challenging the negative assumptions surrounding civil protection orders. *Affilia, 22*(4), 347–56.

Protester throws custard at minister. (2009, 7 March). *National Post,* p. A16.

Public Safety Canada. (2004). *Report on identity theft: A report to the Minister of Public Safety Canada and the Attorney General of the United States.* Bi-national Working Group on Cross-Border Mass Marketing Fraud. Retrieved 30 May 2009, from www.publicsafety.gc.ca/prg/le/bs/report-eng.aspx.

R. v. O'Connor, [1995] 4 S.C.R. 411. Retrieved 27 May 2010, from http://csc.lexum.umontreal.ca/en/1995/1995scr4-411/1995scr4-411.html.

R. v. Seaboyer; R. v. Gayme, [1991] 2 S.C.R. 577. Retrieved 8 January 2010, from http://csc.lexum.umontreal.ca/en/1991/1991scr2-577/1991scr2-577.html.

Radelet, M. L., & Borg, M. J. (2000). Comment on Umbreit and Vos: Retributive versus restorative justice. *Homicide Studies, 4*(1), 88–92.

Rafter, N. H. (1997). *Creating Born Criminals.* Chicago, IL: University of Illinois Press.

Rebovich, D., Layne, J., Jiandani, J., & Hage, S. (2000). *The national public survey on white collar crime.* Morgantown, WV: National White Collar Crime Center.

Reed, M., & Morrison, P. (1997). Adult correctional services in Canada, 1995–96. *Juristat, 17*(4). Ottawa, ON: Canadian Centre for Justice Statistics, Minister of Industry.

Renner, M. J., & Macklin, R. S. (1998). A stress life instrument for classroom life. *Teaching of Psychology, 25,* 46–48.

Rennison, C. (2001). Violent victimization and race, 1993–98. *Bureau of Justice Statistics special report.* Washington, DC: United States Department of Justice, Office of Justice Programs.

Rienick, C., Mulmat, D. H., & Pennell, S. (1997). *Meeting the needs of victims.* San Diego, CA: San Diego Association of Governments.

Riga, A. (2005). Lawyer blames victim in rape sentencing case. *CanWest News.* Retrieved 10 April 2008, from ProQuest.

Roberts, J. V. (1994). Crime and race statistics: Toward a Canadian solution. *Canadian Journal of Criminology, 36,* 175–85.

Roberts, J. V., & Gebotys, R. (1992). Reforming Rape Laws. *Law and Human Behaviour, 16*(5), 555–73.

Roberts, J. V., & Grossman, M. (1994). Changing definitions of sexual assault: An analysis of Police Statistics. In J. Roberts & R. Mohr (Eds.), *Confronting sexual assault: A decade of legal and social change* (pp. 57–83). Toronto, ON: University of Toronto Press.

Robinson, B. A. (2002, 26 March). *Sexual abuse by Catholic clergy: The Canadian situation.* Retrieved 19 February 2009, from www.religioustolerance.org/clergy_sex3.htm.

Rodkin, P., & Berger, C. (2008). Who bullies whom? Social status asymmetries by victim gender. *International Journal of Behavioral Development, 32*(6), 473–85.

Rosella, L. (2008, 26 June). Realtor Guilty of Sexual Assault. *The Mississauga News.* Retrieved from www.mississauganews.com/article/16057.

Ruback, R. B., & Ivie, D. L. (1988). Prior relationships, resistance, and injury in rapes: An analysis of crisis centre records. *Violence and Victims, 3,* 99–111.

Russell, M., & Light, L. (2006). Police and victim perspectives on empowerment of domestic violence victims. *Police Quarterly, 9*(4), 375–96.

Ryan, W. (1971). *Blaming the victim*. New York, NY: Vintage.

Sacco, V. F., & Kennedy, L. W. (2002). *The criminal event perspective: Perspectives in space and time* (2nd ed.). Scarborough, ON: Nelson Thomson Learning.

Salazar, L. F., Bake, C. K., Price, A. W., & Carlin, K. (2003). Moving beyond the individual: Examining the effects of domestic violence policies on social norms. *American Journal of Community Psychology, 32*(3–4), 253–64.

Sanders, A., Hoyle, S., Morgan, R., & Cape, E. (2001, June). Victim impact statements: Don't work, can't work. *Criminal Law Review*, 447–58.

Savoie, J. (2007). Youth self-reported delinquency, 2006. *Juristat, 27*(6), Ottawa, ON: Canadian Centre for Justice Statistics, Minster of Industry.

Schafer, S. (1968). *The victim and his criminal: A study in functional responsibility*. New York, NY: Random House.

Schafer, S. (1977). *Victimology, the victim, and his criminal*. Reston, VA: Reston Publishing Company.

Schoepfer, A., & Piquero, N. L. (2009). Study of the correlates of fraud victimization reporting. *Journal of Criminal Justice, 37*(2), 209–15.

Schwendinger, R., & Schwendinger, H. (1974). Rape myths: In legal, theoretical, and everyday practice. *Crime and Social Justice, 1,* 18–26.

Scott, H. (2003). Stranger danger: Explaining women's fear of crime. *Western Criminology Review, 4*(3), 203–14.

Scott, H. (2005). *The female serial murderer: A sociological study of homicide and the 'gentler sex'*. Lewiston, NY: Edwin Mellen Press.

Scott, H. & Beaman, R. (2003) Sexual assault among Aboriginal and non-Aboriginal peoples in a Western Canadian city: A case for including race when collecting crime data. *Online Journal of Justice Studies, 1,* Retrieved 27 January 2009, from ojjs.uoit.ca/JOURNAL/BACKISSUES%20PDF/scott-beaman.pdf.

Scott, H. & Beaman, R. (2004). Demographic and situational factors affecting injury, resistance, completion and charges brought in sexual assault cases: What's best for arrest? *Violence and Victims, 19,* 479–94.

Scully, D. (1990). *Understanding Sexual Violence: A Study of Convicted Rapists*. Cambridge, MA: Unwin Hyman, Ltd.

Sebba, L. (1996). *Third parties: Victims and the criminal justice system*. Columbus, OH: Ohio State University Press.

Seligman, M., & Csikszentmihalyi, M. (2000). Positive psychology: An introduction. *American Psychologist, 55,* 5–14.

Selye, H. (1936/1998). A syndrome produced by diverse nocuous agents. *Journal of Neuropsychiatry and Clinical Neuroscience, 10,* 230–1.

Shaw, A. (2009, 7 March). Zimbabwe PM's wife killed in crash: Tsvangirai injured as car sideswipes truck on notoriously poor road near Harare. *The Globe and Mail,* p. A18.

Shaw, C. (1930). *The Jack-Roller*. Chicago, IL: University of Chicago Press.

Sheldon, K. M., & King, L. (2001). Why positive psychology is necessary. *American Psychologist, 55,* 216–17.

Sheley, J. (1979). *Understanding Crime: Issues, Concepts, Decisions*. Belmont, CA: Wadsworth.

Sherry, P. (1991). Person-environment fit and accident prediction. *Journal of Business and Psychology, 5,* 411–16.

Shichor, D. (2002). Victimology and the Victims of White-Collar Crime. In Shichor, D., and Tibbetts, S. G. (Eds.), *Victims and Victimization* (pp.191–209). Prospect Heights, IL: Waveland Press, Inc.

Siggner, A. J. (2003). Urban Aboriginal populations: An update using the 2001 Census results. In D. Newhouse and E. Peters (Eds.), *Not strangers in these parts: Urban Aboriginal populations*. Ottawa, ON: Policy Research Initiative.

Silver, I. (1974). Introduction. In E. M. Schur and I. Silver (Eds.) *The Crime Control Establishment*, pp. 1–15. Englewood Cliffs, NJ: Prentice Hall.

Silver, W. (2007). Crime statistics in Canada, 2006. *Juristat, 27*(5). Ottawa, ON: Canadian Centre for Justice Statistics, Minister of Industry.

Silverman, R. (1973). Victim precipitation: An examination of the concept. In I. Drapkin and E. Viano (Eds.), *Victimology: A New Focus* (pp. 99–110). Lexington, MA: D.C. Heath.

Simons, R., Whitbeck, L. B., & Bales, A. (1989). Life on the streets: Victimization and psychological distress among adult homeless. *Journal of Interpersonal Violence, 4*(4), 482–501.

Skogan, W. (1986). *Fear of crime and neigbourhood change.* Chicago, IL: The University of Chicago.

Slade, D. (2008, 5 April). Killer convicted for gunning down bar owner. *Calgary Herald.* Retrieved 17 June 2008, from ProQuest.

Small, P. (2008a). Homeless man was kicked 'like a football' trial told. *The Toronto Star.* Retrieved 4 June 2009, from www.thestar.com/printArticle/347166.

Small, P. (2008b). The real Paul Croutch. *The Toronto Star.* Retrieved 5 June 2009, from www.thestar.com/News/GTA/article/416169.

Smith, B., Watkins, E., & Morgan, K. (1997). The effects of victim participation on parole decisions: Results from a southeastern state. *Criminal Justice Policy Review, 8,* 57–74.

Spencer, H. (1864/1900) *The Principles of biology* (Vol. I, Revised). New York, NY: D. Appleton & Co.

Statistics Canada. (2000). Cycle 13 Victimization: Public Use Microdata File Documentation and User's Guide: Appendix B - Victimization Questionnaire Ages 15 Years and over. In *The 1999 General Social Survey.* Ottawa, ON: Housing Family and Social Statistics Division, Minister of Industry.

Statistics Canada. (2005a). *General Social Survey: Criminal Victimization.* Retrieved 20 June 2006, from www.statcan.ca/Daily/English/051124/d051124b.htm.

Statistics Canada. (2005b). *General Social Survey, cycle 18 overview: Personal safety and perceptions of the criminal justice system, 2004.* Ottawa, ON: Minister of Industry.

Statistics Canada. (2005c). Main Survey — Questionnaire Package. In *General Social Survey, 2004, Cycle 18 — Victimization (GSS).*

Ottawa, ON: Housing, Family and Social Statistics Division, Minister of Industry.

Statistics Canada. (2006a). *A feasibility report on improving the measurement of fraud in Canada, 2005.* Ottawa, ON: Centre for Justice Statistics, Minister of Industry, 8–9.

Statistics Canada. (2006b). Aboriginal peoples as victims and offenders. *The Daily.* Ottawa, ON: Minster of Industry. Retrieved from www.statcan.gc.ca/daily-quotidien/060606/dq060606b-eng.htm.

Statistics Canada. (2006c). *The General Social Survey: An overview.* Ottawa, ON: Social and Aboriginal Statistics Division, Minister of Industry.

Statistics Canada. (2008). Table 13: Reported crime statistics. In *Canada at a glance: Justice.* Retrieved 22 April 2009, from www45.statcan.gc.ca/2008/cgco_2008_004-eng.htm.

Statistics Canada (2009). *Summary tables: Crimes by offences, by province and territory.* Retrieved 22 April 2009, from www40.statcan.gc.ca/l01/cst01/legal04d-eng.htm.

Stermac, L., & Del Bove, G. (2004). Stranger and acquaintance sexual assault of adult males. *Journal of Interpersonal Violence, 19*(8), 901–915.

Strentz, T. (1982). The Stockholm Syndrome: Law enforcement policy and hostage behavior. In D. A. Soskis & F. M. Ochberg (Eds.), *Victims of terrorism* (pp. 149–63). Boulder, CO: Westview Press.

Stuart, A. F. H., Schuck, A. M., & Lersch, K. M. (2004). Exploring the crime of identity theft: Prevalence, clearance rates, and victim/offender characteristics. *Journal of Criminal Justice, 10*(7), 19–29.

Summer, C. J. (1987). Victim participation in the criminal justice system. *Australian and New Zealand Journal of Criminology, 20,* 195–217.

Sutherland, E. (1924). *Criminology.* Philadelphia, PA: J.B. Lippincott.

Sutherland, E. (1937). *The professional thief.* Chicago, IL: University of Chicago Press.

Sutherland, E. (1949). *White collar crime.* New York, NY: Dryden Press.

Takagi, P., & Shank, G. (2004). Critique of restorative justice. *Social Justice, 31*(3), 147–63.

Tannenbaum, F. (1938). *Crime and the Community*. New York, NY, and London, England: Columbia University Press.

Taylor, S. E., Klein, L. C., Lewis, B. P., Gruenewald, T. L., Gurung, R. A., & Updegraff, J. A. (2000). Biobehavioral responses to stress in females: tend-and-befriend, not fight-or-flight. *Psychological Review, 107*(3), 411–29.

Taylor-Butts, A. (2009). Fact sheet—Police-reported spousal violence in Canada. In *Family Violence in Canada: A Statistical Profile 2009* (pp. 24–31). Ottawa, ON: Canadian Centre for Justice Statistics, Minister of Industry.

Taylor-Butts, A., & Bressan, A. (2008). Youth crime in Canada, 2006. *Juristat, 27*(6), Ottawa, ON: Canadian Centre for Justice Statistics, Minster of Industry.

Titus, R. M., Heinzelmann, F., & Boyle, J. M. (1995). Victimization of persons by fraud. *Crime & Delinquency, 41*, 54–72.

Tjaden, P., & Thoennes, N. (2000). *Full report of the prevalence, incidence, and consequences of violence against women: Findings from the national violence against women survey*. Washington, DC: National Institute of Justice and the Centers for Disease Control and Prevention.

Tobolowski, P. (1999). Victim participation in the criminal justice process. *New England Journal on Criminal and Civil Confinement, 25*, 21–105.

The murder of Reena Virk: A timeline (2005, 13 April). *CBC News Online*. Retrieved from www.cbc.ca/news/background/virk/.

Thomas, W. I., & Znaniecki, F. (1918). *The Polish Peasant in Europe and America*. Chicago, IL: University of Chicago Press.

Thrasher, F. M. (1927). *The Gang*. Chicago, IL: University of Chicago Press.

Tönnies, F. (1887). *Gemeinschaft und Gesellschaft* (2nd ed.). Leipzig: Fues's Verlag.

Turner, J. T. (1990). Preparing individuals at risk for victimization as hostages. In E. Viano (Ed.), *The victimology handbook: Research findings, treatment and public policy* (pp. 217–26). New York, NY: Garland Publishing.

Ullman, S. (1998). Does offender violence escalate when rape victims fight back?

Journal of Interpersonal Violence, 13(2), 179–192.

Umbreit, M. S. (1994). *Victim meets offender: The impact of restorative justice and mediation*. Monsey, NY: Criminal Justice Press.

Umbreit, M. S. (1995). *Mediation of criminal conflict: An assessment of programs in four Canadian Provinces*. St. Paul, MN: Center for Restorative Justice & Mediation, University of Minnesota.

Umbreit, M. S. (1998). Restorative justice through victim-offender mediation: A multi-site assessment. *Western Criminology Review, 1*(1). Retrieved from http://wcr.sonoma.edu/v1n1/umbreit.html.

Umbreit, M. S., & Niemeyer, M. (1996). Victim offender mediation: From the margins to the mainstream. *Perspectives, 20*(1), 28–30.

Umbreit, M. S., & Vos, B. (2000). Homicide survivors meeting the offender prior to execution: Restorative justice through dialogue. *Homicide Studies, 4*(1), 63–87.

United States. (n.d.). *Is Social Security a Ponzi scheme? Ponzi schemes: The real Ponzi*. Washington, DC: Social Security Administration. Retrieved 22 April 2009, from www.socialsecurity.gov/history/ponzi.html.

Vaillancourt, R. (2009). Fact sheet—Police-reported family violence against older adults. In *Family Violence in Canada: A Statistical Profile 2009* (pp. 42–7). Ottawa, ON: Canadian Centre for Justice Statistics, Minister of Industry.

Vaillancourt, R., & Taylor-Butts, A. (2007). *Transition homes in Canada: National, provincial and territorial fact sheets 2005/2006*. Ottawa, ON: Canadian Centre for Justice Statistics, Minister of Industry.

Vancouver Sun. (2008, 20 June). Con artists sell homes without owners knowing: When the annual assessment for Norman Gettel's home didn't arrive in the mail this year, he phoned the BC Assessment Authority. Retrieved 7 June 2010, from www.canada.com/story_print.html?id=929a42de-6d51-46d2-87a7-debc8924db79&sponsor=.

Verdun-Jones, S. M., & Tijerino, A. A. (2002). *Victim participation in the plea negotiation process in Canada*. Ottawa, ON: Policy Centre for Victim Issues: Department of Justice, Canada. Retrieved 23 March 2009, from www.justice.gc.ca/eng/pi/rs/rep-rap/2002/rr02_5/index.html.

Victims of Montreal school massacre remembered 15 years later (2004, 4 December). Retrieved from www.pej.org/html/modules.php?op=modload&name=News&file=article&sid=1126&mode=thread&order=0&thold=0.

Victim. (n.d.). Retrieved 3 December 2007, from http://dictionary.reference.com/browse/victim.

von Hentig, H. (1948/1967) *The criminal and his victim: Studies in the sociology of crime*. Hamden, CT: Archon Books.

Wachholz, S. (2005). Hate crimes against the homeless: Warning-out New England style. *Journal of Sociology and Social Welfare, 32,* 141–63.

Waldie, P. (2009, 7 March). White-collar workers among hardest hit as recession deepens. *The Globe and Mail,* p. A12.

Waldie, P. (2009, 7 April). Collected Woes. *The Globe and Mail*. Retrieved 2 June 2009, from www.theglobeandmail.com/report-on-business/article856533.ece.

Walton, D. (2009, 7 March). Accused reserves plea in kidnap, rape case. *The Globe and Mail,* p. A11.

Warner, T. D. (2010). Violent acts and injurious consequences: An examination of competing hypotheses about intimate partner violence using agency-based data. *Journal of Family Violence,* 25(2), 183–93.

Warr, M. (1884). Fear of victimization: Why are women and the elderly more afraid? *Social Science Quarterly,* 65(3), 681–702.

Weinrath, M. (1999). Violent victimization and fear of crime among Canadian Aboriginals. *Journal of Offender Rehabilitation, 30,* 107–20.

Weis, C., & Borges, S. (1973). Victimology and the case of the legitimate victim. In L.G. Schultz (Eds.), *Rape Victimology,* (pp. 91–141). Springfield, IL: Charles C. Thomas.

Wemmers, J. A. (1999). Victim notification and public support for the criminal justice system. *International Review of Victimology, 6,* 167–78.

Wemmers, J. A., & Canuto, M. (2002). *Victims' experiences with, expectations and perceptions of restorative justice: A critical review of the literature*. Montreal, QC: Policy Centre for Victim Issues, Research and Statistics Division, International Centre for Comparative Criminology.

Wertham, F. (1949). *The show of violence*. New York, NY: Doubleday.

White, M. (2007, 28 December). Quebec City closing in on a year without murder. *The National Post*. Retrieved from www.nationalpost.com/news/canada/story.html?id=203698.

White, P. (2009, 7 March). How the mental health system failed Vince Li: Family, friends and doctors knew he was troubled, yet he spiralled deeper into schizophrenia and murder. *The Globe and Mail,* p. A4.

Williams, F. P. & Akers, R. L. (1987) Fear of crime: A comparison of measurement approaches. Presented at the Academy of Criminal Justice Sciences.

Williamson, D. (2008, 12 April). Drifter sentenced to two years in Windsor man's death. *Windsor Star*. Retrieved 17 June 2008, from ProQuest.

Wingrove, J. (2009, 7 March). TTC shooting suspect turns self in. *The Globe and Mail,* p. A14.

Winkel, F. W., & Koppelaar, L. (1991). Rape victims' style of self-presentation and secondary victimization by the environment: An experiment. *Journal of Interpersonal Violence,* 6(1), 29–40.

Winnipeg police looking for suspect on sexual assault on man in park. (2008, 3 July). *Canadian Press*. Retrieved 15 July 2008, from ProQuest.

Winnipeg Police Service. (2008). *Crime prevention: Identity theft—Could it happen to you?* Retrieved 18 January 2009, from www.winnipeg.ca/police/TakeAction/identity_theft.stm.

Winnipegger who killed a man over stolen cigarettes should get 15 years: Crown. (2008, 18 April). *Winnipeg Sun*. Retrieved 17 June 2008, from ProQuest.

Wolff, N., Shi, J., & Bachman, R. (2008). Measuring victimization inside prisons: Questioning the questions. *Journal of Interpersonal Violence, 23*(10), 1343–1362.

Wolfgang, M. E. (1958). *Patterns of Criminal Homicide.* Philadelphia, PA: University of Pennsylvania Press.

Wright, M., & Galaway, B. (1989). *Mediation and criminal justice.* London, England: Sage.

Young, A. (2001). *The role of the victims in the criminal process: A literature review—1989 to 1999.* Ottawa, ON: Department of Justice Canada.

Zickefoose, S. (2006, 16 August). Family in 'living hell' after attack. *Calgary Herald.* Retrieved from www.canada.com/calgary-herald/news/story.html?id=63769aa2-9ccb-4ec6-8940-3d76038d51e5.

Index

Note: Page numbers in *italics* refer to tables and charts. Page numbers followed by a '*t*' refer to text boxes. Page numbers followed by a '*g*' refer to glossary terms.